Pro Vim

Mark McDonnell

Apress®

Pro Vim

ISBN-13 (pbk): 978-1-4842-0251-7

ISBN-13 (electronic): 978-1-4842-0250-0

Managing Director: Welmoed Spahr
Lead Editor: Louise Corrigan
Technical Reviewers: Jayant Varma, Jenna Pederson
Editorial Board: Steve Anglin, Mark Beckner, Ewan Buckingham, Gary Cornell, Louise Corrigan, Jim DeWolf, Jonathan Gennick, Robert Hutchinson, Michelle Lowman, James Markham, Matthew Moodie, Jeff Olson, Jeffrey Pepper, Douglas Pundick, Ben Renow-Clarke, Dominic Shakeshaft, Gwenan Spearing, Matt Wade, Steve Weiss
Coordinating Editor: Christine Ricketts
Copy Editor: Michael G. Laraque
Compositor: SPi Global
Indexer: SPi Global
Artist: SPi Global
Cover Designer: Anna Ishchenko

Distributed to the book trade worldwide by Springer Science+Business Media New York, 233 Spring Street, 6th Floor, New York, NY 10013. Phone 1-800-SPRINGER, fax (201) 348-4505, e-mail orders-ny@springer-sbm.com, or visit www.springeronline.com. Apress Media, LLC is a California LLC and the sole member (owner) is Springer Science + Business Media Finance Inc (SSBM Finance Inc). SSBM Finance Inc is a Delaware corporation.

For information on translations, please e-mail rights@apress.com, or visit www.apress.com.

Apress and friends of ED books may be purchased in bulk for academic, corporate, or promotional use. eBook versions and licenses are also available for most titles. For more information, reference our Special Bulk Sales–eBook Licensing web page at www.apress.com/bulk-sales.

Any source code or other supplementary material referenced by the author in this text is available to readers at www.apress.com. For detailed information about how to locate your book's source code, go to www.apress.com/source-code/.

This book is dedicated to my family (Catherine, Richard, Katie, Vincent, Mum & Dad). You all know how much I love what I do, but I love you all so much more.

Contents at a Glance

Contents

About the Author

Mark McDonnell is a London-based software engineer currently working for BBC News as a senior developer. Over the past 15 years, Mark has worked his way up the ranks of the agency lifestyle. Along the way, he has built software applications in Classic ASP, ASP.NET, Flash, PHP, Node, and Ruby. He has also had the pleasure of managing and mentoring teams of highly talented developers before moving on to the BBC as a responsive front-end specialist, evolving from the client side back to the server side to work on cloud-based distributed and concurrent systems. He is a lover of the Unix philosophy and the power of the command line and always relishes the opportunity to learn new technologies. You'll normally find him chattering about functional programming with Clojure or how best to solve a technical problem, using design patterns and S.O.L.I.D principles.

About the Technical Reviewers

Jayant Varma is a technophile and was introduced to computing from the days of 8-bit computers and Z80 chips. While managing IT and Telecom at the BMW Dealerships in India and Oman and at Nissan in Qatar, he worked extensively on Windows, AS/400, and Unix. His love of traveling inspired him to work in and explore several countries, and he is currently based in Australia.

His technological journey began as a Microsoft technologies developer and has diversified to currently focus on Apple and mobile technologies. He holds a master's degree in business administration and IT from James Cook University (Australia). He also lectured at James Cook University (Australia) and coordinated the onshore and offshore teaching of Linux/Unix administration. He worked closely with the ACS (Australian Computer Society) and AUC (Apple University Consortium) on workshops and projects.

He authored the book *Learn Lua for iOS Game Development* for those about to Lua and is currently working on Swift- and iOS-related titles. As a founder, consultant, and developer at OZ Apps (www.oz-apps.com), he helps organizations and individuals integrate technology into their business and strategies. He also conducts training sessions and workshops and writes blogs to share his knowledge with the community.

Jenna Pederson became fascinated with building things at an early age. By age 13, she had run a couple of lemonade stands, a tie-dye T-shirt company, and various other businesses. She transformed her entrepreneurial drive and desire to build cool things into her career. She worked as a software engineer and technical manager before stepping out on her own in 2011. Today, Jenna runs her own company, 612 Software Foundry, helping clients translate technical needs into working software. She shares her knowledge and experience with others by presenting at tech conferences, blogging, mentoring, and volunteering.

Acknowledgments

So, here you find me, dear reader, tired, weary, and yet oh so *excited* all at the same time. For here sits an author who is on the verge of his first published book. I've written many a technical article in my 15-plus years as a programmer, and there came a point when I found myself writing more and more on a particular topic, of which this book you're holding is based.

The start of this journey was nothing more than a short set of notes that I had cobbled together for what was to become my fourth article on the subject of Vim. I kept delaying its publication, simply because I couldn't stop adding bits of information that I felt were critical to *really* understanding Vim, until one day I finally realized that this "article" had evolved into something much more. The time had come to accept the fact that this "article" needed to take book form.

I have poured a lot of time and hard work into this book, but it would be wrong of me not to acknowledge the people who have helped, either directly or indirectly, to get this book (and myself!) into the state of completion that you find it now. People such as Drew Neil, author of *Practical Vim* and the entire http://vimcasts.org/ series, whose knowledge of Vim is wide, deep, and unquestionable. If you ever find yourself in the London area, be sure to check out the Vim London events (https://twitter.com/VimLondon), which Drew kindly organizes for the community.

There is also Tim Pope, a prolific Vim plug-in creator. His work has produced a vast selection of plug-ins, which have helped make the Vim environment a much saner place. Let's take a brief moment to consider the sheer number of plug-ins he has released on which I rely daily: vim-endwise, vim-fireplace, vim-dispatch, vim-fugitive, vim-haml, vim-surround, vim-sexp-mappings-for-regular-people, vim-pathogen, vim-markdown, vim-commentary, vim-classpath, vim-repeat, vim-cucumber, timl. Phew!

Arguably, one of the most important people on this list is Simon Thulbourn (@sthulb), who is possibly *the* most sarcastic person I've ever met. (Sorry @dblooman, but you were a close second.) Before my time at the BBC, I had attempted, on a couple of occasions, to understand Vim and failed, but it was Simon who convinced me to give Vim one last try, and it was that last try that finally "broke the camel's back." Not only was I starting to make some headway with seeing myself using Vim long-term, but I also had an experienced Vim user on tap to answer questions I had when I hit a problem. I would then proceed to pester Simon on a regular basis for the next few months on every minor issue I encountered, and he would eventually (I mean graciously!) concede his valuable time to help me understand where I had gone wrong (albeit usually via the most sarcastic response he could muster). If it were not for his help, I would have likely failed for a second time, and this book would not have been.

Throughout my time at the BBC, I've had the opportunity to work with some fantastically talented developers. Dan Scotton (@danscotton) is one of those rare breeds of human being who is unbearably talented, while also being unbelievably positive and friendly. Working with Dan has been one of the highlights of my career. There is also Tom Maslen (@tmaslen) and John Cleveley (@jcleveley), neither of whom are Vim users, but don't hold that against them! I get the impression they think I'm smarter than I actually am, but, ultimately, they gave me the chance to become part of their team, for which I'm very grateful, as it has helped me progress more in the past couple of years than I could ever have imagined.

Robert Kenny (@kenturamon) and Steven Jack (@stevenjack85) are two fellow colleagues who I've worked with at the BBC, and they, too, are keen Vim users. Both Kenny and Steve have given positive comments and encouraged this project from the beginning. They arrive here in the form of people who I greatly respect and admire and whose company I have enjoyed immensely. The amount I have learned from these two people in such a short span of time is incredible. Although the lessons I have learned from them were admittedly not directly related to the subject of Vim, they are some of the nicest and most intelligent people to spend your working hours solving complex problems with. I'm a better software engineer now, thanks to them.

Last and *most important* is the person who is my ultimate inspiration and support: my wife and soul mate, Catherine. Her tireless patience and encouragement of *everything* I do is the primary reason I have achieved one of my dreams in life. I could not have done this without her.

Introduction

Text. That's ultimately why you're here. One of the most fundamental aspects of using a computer comes down to dealing with text-based content. We want to write text, edit, and manipulate it. Whether we're writing a book, a blog post, an e-mail, or developing a web application written in whichever programming language happens to be your flavor of choice, it all comes down to text in the end.

How you go about writing that text is up to you, but the tools you use will determine how efficient you are at carrying out that task. The more efficient you are, the quicker you'll complete that task and have more time for other things in life, such as like leaving work behind and being with family and friends.

I'm a software engineer by trade, and so I spend an awful lot of time sitting at a desk with my laptop writing (mainly code). Although the target audience of this book is primarily technical users (such as programmers), it should not be a concern if you're not a technical user. We're going to be focusing on learning how to take advantage of the Vim text editor and, so, really, dealing with "text" is all you need to be concerned about while reading through these chapters.

Throughout the book, you'll learn about techniques and tricks that will help you to best utilize Vim, so that you can manipulate and control your text content. We look at topics that sound like they would be useful only to programmers (such as "code folding"), but in reality, the features we cover are just as useful to any long-form text-based content. There is, in fact, very little in this book that is applicable solely to programmers. We look at how to automate your workflow, using "macros," different techniques for searching and replacing content across multiple files, as well as file comparison/validation through Vim's built-in "diff" utility. These features are useful to users from all industries.

It's also worth noting that the chapters in this book were written to be focused and concise on the problem being presented. I don't deviate much from the topics being discussed, and because of this, some chapters are significantly shorter than others. This is a deliberate decision. I wanted all fundamental features to be easy to locate by skimming through the book's table of contents and not hidden inside another chapter that you wouldn't know to look inside of. (That sort of thing always bugs me when I'm looking for a quick answer or to reference some specific detail, as it usually means I've got to spend time searching through an index trying to find the feature I'm after.)

Regardless of skill level, we're all professionals. The sheer fact you've purchased this book is an indication that you're someone with a professional mindset, willing to improve your capabilities and to take your editing skills to the next level. I do not wish to waste your time covering every conceivable feature available within Vim, as we would need about three books' worth of content to do that. I provide you with as much information as is needed to solve a particular problem, allowing you to learn and get on with being productive.

What I present to you in this book are both the fundamentals of how to use Vim and real-world experience with practical topics and examples. Everything mentioned in this book I either use a lot or have been required to know and have used in the past in a professional capacity. Anywhere I discuss a topic that isn't absolutely critical to your use of Vim, I will do my best to notify you. But rest assured, I've not included anything in this book that I didn't personally feel was useful and relevant to a professional Vim user.

With all this in mind, I hope you enjoy reading *Pro Vim* and that you'll be sure to get in contact to let me know if, and how, this fantastic tool has helped you to improve your own workflow.

CHAPTER 1

Vim Primer

It seems that starting something new is always the hardest part, and the same is true of the topic of this book, Vim. But after that initial tension—once the ball starts rolling—we usually find that what we struggled with in the beginning now becomes easier, as we start flowing with the tide, rather than trying to fight against it. This common stumbling block is an important first point to remember: everything gets easier with experience and confidence.

This book is primarily focused on teaching you how to use the Vim text editor. Over the course of this introductory chapter, I'll be giving a brief explanation of Vim's history, some alternatives, and why you should be excited to learn Vim.

For the moment, it's only fair to forewarn you (if you weren't already aware) that Vim has a reputation, for both beginners and advanced technical users, of being difficult to learn and awkward to use. But fear not! I hope to alleviate those concerns and to demonstrate throughout this book how learning Vim isn't as hard as you may have been led to believe.

In the latter chapters, I'll also cover a popular terminal-based tool called tmux. These two tools (Vim and tmux) go hand-in-hand, and it's beneficial (once you've acquired a solid understanding of Vim) to also see how you can use it alongside tmux to improve your day-to-day workflow. Now, tmux isn't a requirement for using Vim—it's a supplement for more advanced technical users—so don't feel obliged to read that section, if it's not of interest or relevance to you (although I would recommend reading through it and trying to understand more about what tmux *can* offer you).

Before we get started, there are a few quick points about Vim and tmux that I want to share with you and have you memorize.

1. Neither Vim nor tmux is as hard to learn as you may have previously thought.

2. You don't have to learn everything all at once. Start small and build up your knowledge incrementally.

3. You'll become more efficient the more you use the two tools.

4. A new world of command-line tooling will open up to you as you become more comfortable working inside a terminal environment.

5. Vim and tmux *are* a lot of fun to use.

That last point is one of the most important ones! As with anything in life, to be truly good at something typically means you enjoy it as well. I'm very passionate about the tools I use, and that helps me delve deeper into what they can do and how they work.

Although being passionate about Vim isn't a prerequisite to using Vim, it will help the learning curve, if you're someone who genuinely enjoys improving his or her workflow and tooling. If you're happy with your current editor of choice (of which there are many) and you're being forced to read this book by a colleague who feels you'd be a better writer/author/programmer/whatever by using Vim, or if you're here because you think learning Vim makes you smarter than your colleagues using an alternative editor, then you're probably not going to reap the benefits as much as someone who is holding this book because he or she saw it and really *wanted* to read it.

Also, although the title of this book is *Pro Vim*, it doesn't mean you require any prior knowledge of Vim. This book is aimed at total beginners and covers all the practical sides of Vim, such as the fundamentals of how it works, and offers real-world advice and experience, in the hope that you can avoid similar pitfalls that traditionally both new and experienced users of Vim stumble across.

The reason this book is considered "pro" is simply because there isn't really a lot of middle ground when it comes to using tools such as Vim and tmux. They are inherently advanced tools that offer a lot of complex functionality. If there were such a thing as a "beginners" book to Vim, chances are it would be a lot shorter and would avoid discussing a lot of important fundamental concepts, which ultimately means you wouldn't be using the tool to its potential and, subsequently, you would become less productive using it. Even beginners have to properly understand the tool they're using. A lack of understanding the fundamentals will only introduce frustration with the tools and ultimately result in a user abandoning them for less powerful ones.

What Is Vim?

Vim (`www.vim.org/about.php`) is a free, open source text editor. It was originally released in 1991 for Unix-based computer systems and is considered to be an enhancement to the original Vi text editor (`http://en.wikipedia.org/wiki/Vi`), which was released way back in 1976 (to put this into context, I wasn't *born* until six years later).

■ **Note** Vim is an acronym for "Vi Improved." The majority of the standard editing "commands" available within Vim are actually provided by Vi.

One of the big selling points, if you like to think of software that way, is that Vim (and especially its predecessor Vi) is available almost everywhere. If you're running a Unix- or Linux-based system (e.g., the popular Macintosh operating system is Unix-based), you'll likely find that Vim is installed by default.

Vim traditionally does not have a GUI (graphical user interface) like other text/code editors you may have used in the past (e.g., Sublime Text, Chocolat, Coda, Aptana, NetBeans, Eclipse, DreamWeaver, etc.), although there is a separate install of Vim available called gVim that provides a GUI.

■ **Note** There are a few GUI-based versions of Vim, notably MacVim (`https://code.google.com/p/macvim`), which has better integration with the Macintosh operating system than the standard implementation of Vi and Vim. Most of the Vim specific features I cover in this book are still relevant to MacVim, so you shouldn't encounter any issues.

The standard installation of Vim is usually run from within a terminal/shell environment rather than as a separate application. Because the terminal is designed for power users and has the potential to do a lot of damage to your computer (if misused), it can be a scary and hostile environment. Again, fear not. Although visually, the terminal isn't the prettiest of beasts, I'll show you how you can spruce it up and get it looking a little bit more presentable and easier on the eyes. A nice-looking terminal theme can make the world of difference when you're going to be spending as much time as we are in the shell environment.

Modern Editors?

At the time of writing (2014), the hot editor of choice for a lot of developers would be GitHub's Atom editor (https://atom.io). This editor is heavily based on the Sublime Text editor (www.sublimetext.com), which, until Atom was released, was considered to be the best editor for developers. This brings me to my first concern: longevity. It seems we spend a large amount of time committing to memory key bindings and features that are specific to the editor we're using, and yet within the space of a year, maybe two years, that knowledge is made redundant by the need to move to the next great editor. Vim and its predecessor Vi have been used consistently since their inception.

Both Atom and Sublime Text mix together a graphical interface alongside a need for more straightforward coding features. This was an attempt to move away from the late-90s-era editors such as Adobe DreamWeaver (which was aimed more at web designers than programmers). This was also to move away from very heavyweight and sluggish IDEs (Integrated Development Environments) such as Eclipse, which included everything *and* the kitchen sink.

Neither Atom nor Sublime Text is as lightweight as Vim, nor are they as ubiquitous as Vim. This is another reason why Vim is so enticing. Vim is effectively available everywhere by default (even on much older operating systems that only have Vi installed—the editing commands are the same, and this allows you to get to work fixing problems immediately, not trying to figure out how you're going to get another editor installed).

The problem with using a heavyweight IDE is that you mostly have no choice in the features that are provided. They can be slow to run and difficult to use, due to the myriad of built-in options (take a look at the GUI for a typical Eclipse user—so many distracting buttons that most people don't use or don't even know how to use.) On the flip side, IDEs have the benefit of being able to target a specific platform (e.g., Java or PHP), meaning the IDE can provide more fine-grain control and tooling, compared to a lightweight text editor that is *enhanced* with additional features to improve its range of uses.

Emacs?

When talking about Vim, you'll usually also hear the word *Emacs* (http://en.wikipedia.org/wiki/Emacs) being referenced as an alternative.

Emacs is an editor, which like Vim can be run with a GUI as well as a more lightweight terminal variation. The GUI is configurable to a highly granular level (if you can see it, you can configure it—even down to the OS level components, such as the interface itself). The reason for this level of configurability is because Emacs is written in a subset of Lisp called elisp, which means you are able to customize every detail of the editor. Vim, on the other hand, is written in C, but plug-ins for Vim have to be written in a language called VimScript (or VimL), which is a built-in interface allowing developers to enhance Vim's capabilities. Because plug-ins are built against an interface, you're limited to what can be modified.

There is also a lifestyle difference between Vim and Emacs, in the sense that Emacs users will pretty much live their lives inside of Emacs. They'll use its built-in shell access and file system; they'll integrate their e-mails and web browsing. You name it, you'll do it *within* Emacs.

■ **Note** Vim allows you to add functionality through the use of plug-ins written with a built-in language called VimL (http://vimdoc.sourceforge.net/htmldoc/usr_41.html), and as of Vim version 7.3 (if compiled appropriately), you can utilize other programming languages, such as Ruby, Python, Perl, or even Lisp-based languages, to extend Vim.

The downside of Emacs is that you might not need all this functionality. It's even harder to learn (believe it or not) than Vim and even has its own in-joke for a symptom known as "Emacs pinky" (see Figure 1-1).

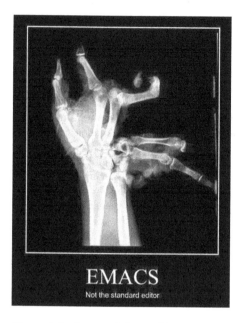

Figure 1-1. *Emacs pinky, ouch!*

All joking aside (as "Emacs pinky" equally affects Vim users and is easy to work around—as we'll see—by rebinding the default editor keys), the reason to choose Emacs or Vim comes down to what you're using it for.

You'll find that technically minded people are quite passionate about the tools they use and will defend them to the death (rightly or wrongly). In the online community, there is much heated debate as to which editor (Emacs or Vim) is best and why you should use one over the other.

I personally find arguments like that (or comparison to any other editor, for that matter) a waste of time. We all have our preferences, and choosing a text editor is very much a matter of preference. Yes, Emacs might do some things better than Vim, and vice versa, but for me, Vi/Vim's ubiquitous influence, easier learning path, powerful editing capabilities, plug-in architecture, and lightweight footprint make it the obvious choice.

How Do You Become Good at Vim?

This is a common question for new Vim users who are overwhelmed by the difference between their previous editor and this terminal-based application that now feels so alien and unwelcoming.

Typically when learning Vim, you'll find yourself being enticed with a dreamy notion of efficiency and elegance, only to be presented with (*Warning*: sarcasm ahead) comments such as:

> *Look at these amazingly cryptic ways you can manipulate a document of text. Just run 3wce to edit the fourth word in that sentence. Look at how productive we are!*

It's almost as if "editing" were the mandatory starting point for learning Vim. I know from my own personal experience that focusing on editing alone (when you know nothing about Vim) is a mistake. I know, the irony is that we're learning how to use a "text editor," so why should it be so strange to start by focusing on editing commands? For me, it's because you have no real investment in the software yet (and I'll explain what I mean by that in just a moment).

Unless you're looking to do nothing but edit plain text content, then starting to learn about Vim by studying its editing commands feels like jumping the gun somewhat.

In my experience, the decision to change text editors usually arises from frustration with an existing tool. Chances are you've searched around for an alternative tool that will, it is hoped, give you all the features you like from your current editor plus work around any past issues and annoyances.

Yes, Vim is notorious for its advanced—yet terse—editing features. It's one of the main reasons you can become really efficient while using it.

■ **Note** Vim is not just for programming. It's used by book authors, blog writers, system administrators, and, yes, programmers.

Although editing in Vim *is* important, it is equally important to realize that Vim, "out of the box," is actually very nondescript. By that, I mean it looks very plain. It does, indeed, look like something designed from the 1970s (see Figure 1-2).

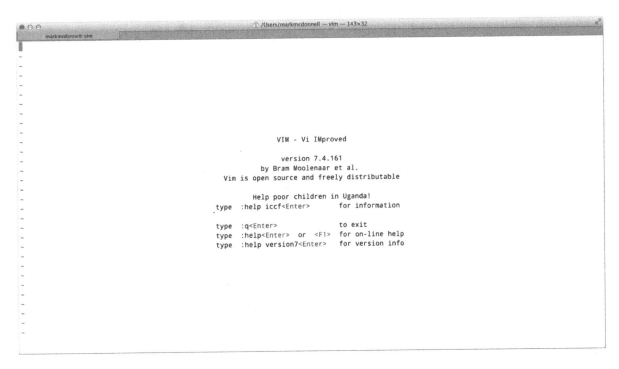

Figure 1-2. Vim in its unmodified form

That may sound strange to you. Maybe you watched some videos about using Vim (or maybe one of your colleagues uses Vim) and found it to look quite colorful! Add on top visual themes, custom status bars (showing all sorts of tweaked useful information about the document being worked on), along with features such as syntax highlighting for multiple languages, file system integration, shortcuts for running tests, shortcuts for doing advanced editing and manipulation of data, code linting, integrating REPL servers (e.g., when writing code in a language such as Clojure) . . . the list really goes on and on.

But what I personally didn't realize when I first started looking into using Vim was that a lot of these nice visual enhancements and features were users' own customizations! So when I fired up Vim (with all my knowledge of editing commands that I spent a lot of time learning and trying to commit to memory), I was very disappointed to discover that it didn't look or work much like the editor I had been led to believe it was.

Because of this misunderstanding, I stopped using Vim altogether. At the time I remember thinking the following:

What's the point of a plain (black-and-white) editor, if all it's good for are some complicated keyboard shortcuts?

I had totally missed the potential of what Vim was capable of providing me. So, with my own past experience firmly set in your mind, I would instead like to focus on getting your Vim environment set up properly first, and then we can start looking at the different features Vim provides.

To begin with, we'll use my own set of configuration files to get Vim configured, and I'll be covering exactly how it all works. Later on, when you're more comfortable with Vim (and doing things yourself), you can either remove my config completely and start again or just tweak it to fit your own needs.

Once you're all set up and configured, I'll start explaining the principles of Vim. The most important thing to keep in mind is that the installation, setting up, and configuring of Vim are arguably the hardest part. Getting it to look and work the way you really want it to is a lot more awkward than using the features of Vim. Once Vim is configured to your liking, actually learning shortcut key bindings is a trivial process in comparison.

The only final comment I would make before we move on is don't try to memorize all of the things you read about. There is no point; you won't be able to. Instead, later on (after we start reviewing some of Vim's editing features), just pick a few commands and try to memorize those. Once you use them enough to have committed them to memory, grab another bunch of commands and try to incorporate those into your day-to-day Vim'ing (yes, I just made that word up). You can always use this book as a reference point whenever you get stuck.

Some people actually like to have a Vim cheat sheet nearby (usually open inside a split window within Vim—I'll cover what this means later), so they have quick access to a selection of commands they wish to memorize. This can work quite well in the beginning, but if you do go down that route, remember not to overload your cheat sheet with too many commands (you can only take in a limited amount of information).

I personally found I had so many notes on my cheat sheet that it took me just as long to search through the cheat sheet as it would've taken me to Google for the solution. It's best to focus on a small number of commands and replace them on your cheat sheet as you become more comfortable with using them in Vim.

▦ **Note** No one attempts to learn a language (whether a spoken language or a programming one) by memorizing all the dialect up front in one hit. So, please don't try to do that with Vim; it's the same principle.

Remember: *You can learn Vim.*

Mac, Linux, Windows?

This book assumes the reader is running a Unix-based system such as Mac OS X. Although the commands for Vim and tmux will be similar across operating systems, if you're using Linux or some other Unix-based system, you may find that some things (such as Vim's runtime paths) may vary.

Most books on the subject of Vim avoid this issue by ignoring the installation process, and although installing Vim is a fairly standard process, to provide instructions for every single variation isn't really feasible. For us, I will provide *standard* installation instructions for the main three operating systems (Mac, Linux, Windows), and when discussing a feature (such as the plug-in architecture), I will provide as much information for the differing environments as possible.

It's worth remembering that Vim was specifically designed to work on the Unix operating system, and so to get it (and tmux) to work as intended on other operating systems can be tricky, as it requires a "Unix-like" environment. With Windows, there are multiple ways you can install Vim and tmux, but I've found that a lot of Windows users recommend the use of a program such as Cywin (http://cygwin.com). This can also be an issue when I discuss how to configure your shell environment. As I've mentioned, your mileage may vary if you're using Windows.

If you're using Linux, then although the majority of the terminal/shell-based configuration information will work fine, there is a section on installing color themes using a .terminal file format that is only really relevant to the Macintosh operating system.

Configuring the terminal shell isn't required to complete this book or have anything to do with Vim itself; it's merely a pleasant addition. Configuring Vim is much more important, and that's primarily what we want to focus on. Luckily, once you have Vim installed, configuring it is much more consistent across the different systems.

Visualizing the Outcome

The hardest part of using Vim is not learning to use it; *describing* how to set it up and configure it will be.

To help us keep focus on what it is we're trying to achieve (i.e., getting Vim set up correctly), I'll provide, following, an outline of the directory structure we are aiming to have by the end of the setup. This is done to help you better understand the structure of our Vim installation.

If we were in your computer's home directory, we would want to end up with the following files and folders:

```
.
├── .tmux.conf
├── .vim
│   ├── autoload
│   │   ├── *scripts loaded automatically when Vim starts up*
│   │   ├── pathogen.vim (Pathogen will be our plugin manager)
│   ├── bundle
│   │   ├── *custom folder used by Pathogen*
│   │   ├── *list of Vim plugin folders*
│   ├── colors
│   │   ├── *theme files*
│   ├── plugin
│   │   ├── *traditional plugin files*
├── .vimrc
├── .zshrc
```

■ **Note** The "home directory" refers to a directory on your computer that holds files specific to your personal operating system account. For example, I log into my computer as user "markmcdonnell." My home directory is labeled "markmcdonnell," and it holds folders such as Desktop, Documents, Downloads, Movies, Music, and Pictures (among others) that are specific to my user login.

There are a couple of items in the preceding folder structure that are worth briefly clarifying (although they will get more coverage in the upcoming chapters). The first item of interest is the .tmux.conf file, which is specifically used by tmux for its configuration. I've included it here in this top-level view, because in the next chapter, you'll download a set of files that include it, and so I want you to be aware that it's an expected file to have.

The other item of interest is the pathogen.vim file, which will be our plug-in manager for Vim. I discuss plug-ins, Pathogen, and other alternatives in more detail in Chapter 17.

The last item of interest is the use of the `.zshrc` file, which is a configuration file for our terminal application's specified shell (I cover what this all means in more detail in the next chapter). For Macintosh users, this file will work fine, as it will for any other Linux distribution in which Zsh is preinstalled or installable separately. If for some reason Zsh isn't available on your platform, I will show you how you can install it.

Don't worry too much just yet about what the preceding files are. To save time, we'll be using my own Vim/tmux folder structure, as it'll be the quickest and easiest way to get you up and running.

As you work your way through the chapters in this book, I intend to explain enough about Vim and tmux that you'll be comfortable going back to this directory and modifying it to suit your own needs.

Summary

So, here we are at the end of Chapter 1. Let's see what's been covered so far.

1. I've introduced the Vim text editor.

2. I explained how Vim will be reflected throughout the book, as well as some alternatives, such as Emacs and MacVim.

3. I offered some suggestions on how you can focus your energies to best learn Vim, while sharing some of my own past experiences.

4. I also briefly discussed the book's focus on Unix-based operating systems and potential stumbling blocks that may arise.

5. Finally, we took a top-level look at the folder structure we are aiming to produce in the coming chapter.

CHAPTER 2

Installation and Configuration

You may find this strange, but this chapter is arguably one of the most important of the entire book. It's also, ironically, one of the most daunting. The reason why is because it covers the fundamental aspects of setting up both Vim and your terminal environment to have saner configuration and key bindings/plug-in settings, as well as making the terminal and Vim look more visually pleasing than it would by default. For most readers, this time spent configuring our environment will be the key difference in how successful they are in learning and using Vim.

I appreciate that when reading through this chapter you may start to feel overwhelmed, and that this could be discouraging at such an early stage of the book. But, dear reader, fear not, and have faith, because I am about to summarize the entire contents of this long chapter into a bulleted list, so you will be able to grasp the focus of this chapter more easily. Having a "top-level" view of this chapter will make it easier to understand, even if at times it can seem like quite a daunting process.

Please also take comfort in knowing that once you make it through this chapter, you should find no other chapter in this book (in my personal opinion) as complicated or confusing for a new user.

What We'll Cover

- What the "terminal" and "shell environment" are
- What "shell commands" are (and how to read them)
- The difference between the Bash and Zsh shells
- How to switch to using the Zsh shell
- What "dotfiles" are
- Creating a dotfile for our Zsh configuration

  (Be aware that we'll be adding a large chunk of shell code that you can safely just copy/paste and skip over, if you prefer).

- Clarifying some parts of the Zsh file content
- Downloading and installing a new terminal theme
- Seeing that there is a theme for the terminal and one for Vim

- Installation of Vim

- Installation of Git (so we can download our Vim configuration)

- Moving the Vim configuration into the correct location

- Opening our Vim configuration and having a look around

  (This explanation can be skipped, if you prefer).

- How to split the configuration file into chunks

- Finally, opening Vim for the first time

So, let's get started . . .

Terminal Emulators and Shell Environments

Let's start by understanding where and how we run Vim. If you're new to working in the shell/terminal environment, then knowing the background to the software that allows us to run Vim will be essential to starting your Vim journey.

Vim is a piece of software that is run from within your computer's terminal emulator (a command-line interface). A "terminal emulator" is a historical name. It's based on users not having direct access to the underlying computer system and having to sit at a physical terminal interface that allows the user to execute commands that will be sent to the system to run.

Similarly, the terminal "emulator" on your computer is an application that gives you access to your computer's shell program. Within the shell, you enter "commands," which are sent to the underlying operating system to execute.

■ **Note**   On the Macintosh operating system, you access the terminal by opening the default "Terminal" application. For a more complete list of emulators, see the related article at
`http://en.wikipedia.org/wiki/List_of_terminal_emulators`.

If we imagine that we have Vim installed, when accessing the shell environment from your terminal application, you'll be able to execute the command `vim`, which will be sent to the underlying computer system and result in Vim being started.

In Figure 2-1, we can see what a default install of the terminal looks like.

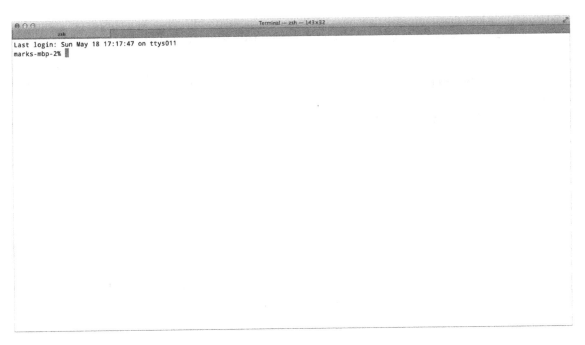

Figure 2-1. *Standard terminal interface*

Pretty, huh? Now take a look at Figure 2-2, which demonstrates how we will be tweaking the terminal.

Figure 2-2. *Enhanced terminal interface*

OK, so it might not look that impressive right now, but trust me, in a short while, when we come to configuring the terminal, you'll see we'll be making fundamental improvements that add lots of useful features to the shell.

■ **Note** in the top right corner of the terminal you'll see some text coloured red, which is the version number of the Ruby programming language available (at that moment) to the terminal. The Ruby version is acquired and inserted by our custom configuration (Listing 2-1), which we'll look at shortly.

Shell Commands

Throughout this book, I'll be using shell commands to do such things as creating files and folders, changing directories, cloning Git repositories, downloading files, etc. I do this so it limits the need to move between the terminal and your operating system's GUI.

■ **Note** Anytime I tell you to "run a command," it is implied that I mean to either type the command (or copy and paste it) into your terminal and press the carriage return/Enter key to run the command.

You should be fine to just run the commands as and when I instruct you to do so. Although I'll explain each and every command I ask you to run, if you're interested to know more about the command and the options available, you can view the relevant documentation for a command either online or within the operating system's built-in manual.

To access the shell manual, you have to run the following command from your terminal (remember to substitute {command} for the actual command):

```
man {command}
```

For example, imagine I tell you to run the following command:

```
ls -la | grep vimrc
```

In the preceding example, what we have are two commands separated by a pipe |. ls is the first command, and -la are the options. The result of the ls command is then passed over to the grep command, where we also pass in vimrc as an argument to the grep command.

Again, you should be fine just running the commands as and when I instruct. But it can be helpful to understand how to read shell commands and where to find help.

To understand the preceding command, you'll have to learn to break it down into its component parts (the individual commands and options/flags). Commands can be constructed from multiple other commands (much like connecting bits of Lego pieces together). Whenever you see the pipe character |, that is effectively telling us that we're passing the result of the command to the left of it as input for the command to the right of it.

If we consider the preceding command ls -la | grep vimrc, we can see that this command is made up of two sub-commands. The first part of the command is ls -la, and the second part of the command is the grep vimrc part.

Commands are typically made up of the command itself (in this case, the commands are ls and grep), followed by optional "flags" and then a parameter (or multiple parameters). In the preceding example, only the ls command has specified some flags to alter the behavior of the command. You can tell when a flag is provided, because it is prefixed by a hyphen (-). Here, we've passed in two flags, -l and -a, but we've used a shorthand version, -la, which combines both flags into one, to save on space. In this case, providing an argument to the ls command is optional (the command by default will list any files in the current, or specified, directory) The flags provided to the ls command determine how the results are displayed.

The grep command, on the other hand, doesn't have any flags specified, but it does have a single parameter, which indicates to the command what it should do. In this case, the grep command is used to search files for a specific phrase. We're taking the list of directory files and telling grep to filter the results by any that contain the word vimrc.

Now that we know how to roughly interpret the structure of a command, we can use another command to help us figure out what they do. I've already explained what the ls and grep commands do, but if you wanted extra information about them and to see what flags they provide, then you could ask the terminal to display the official documentation for the command.

By executing the command man ls, we're asking the terminal to display the manual/documentation for the ls command. Similarly, by executing the command man grep, we'll be shown the documentation for the grep command.

■ **Reminder**   For any shell commands that I provide throughout the book, I'll explain what they do, so don't worry too much if you're not a command-line wizard.

Configuring Your Terminal

Before we begin configuring our terminal's appearance, let's take a brief detour to change our terminal from its default shell, which will likely be Bash (see http://en.wikipedia.org/wiki/Bash_shell) to another shell called Zsh (see http://en.wikipedia.org/wiki/Z_shell).

Zsh is a drop-in replacement for Bash and can be thought of as an improvement to the features found in the Bash shell (much like Vim is an extension/improvement on top of the original Vi editor).

If you intend on using the ProVim shell configuration files (which I'll show you in just a moment), it's worth being aware that they take advantage of some of Zsh's extended features, which aren't available within Bash. A short list of Zsh features include more advanced and efficient auto-completion for typing and tabbing, command prompt color settings, and intelligent handling of ambiguous commands (among other things). The ProVim .zshrc file is heavily commented, so if you wish to see what else is preconfigured for you, I suggest taking some time to read through it (although that's not required).

■ **Note**   You can happily run Vim and tmux using the Bash shell. Nothing in our Vim configuration will rely on Zsh, but our terminal environment and configuration uses a few Zsh-specific settings.

Changing Shells

Before you can actually install Zsh, you must know if you have it available. To check what shells are installed on your system, open your terminal application and run the following command:

```
cat /etc/shells
```

■ **Note**   The preceding command displays all shell binaries available on the current system.

I hope that you'll see something similar to the following output:

```
□ cat /etc/shells
# List of acceptable shells for chpass(1).
# Ftpd will not allow users to connect who are not using
# one of these shells.

/bin/bash
/bin/csh
/bin/ksh
/bin/sh
/bin/tcsh
/bin/zsh
```

As you can see from the preceding output, we have /bin/zsh listed. This means we can indeed switch to the Zsh shell. To change to the Zsh shell, run the following command:

```
chsh -s /bin/zsh
```

Dotfiles

Dotfiles are software/system files whose file name begins with a period (dot) character. The majority of settings for your computer and installed software can be configured from specific dotfiles.

Dotfiles are also hidden by default. This is because any file that starts with a period character (e.g., .zshrc) is considered to be a system file and should be hidden to protect general users from accidentally changing or deleting those files, which could cause preinstalled software to break.

If you want to see the hidden files on your system, the easiest way to do so is to run the following command:

```
ls -a ~/
```

The preceding command lists (ls) all (-a) files (and by "all," we mean including hidden files) within your home directory (~/). Following is the output from my own home directory:

```
.                       .filezilla          .node-gyp           .viminfo            Downloads
..                      .fop                .npm                .viminfw.tmp        Dropbox
.Box Sync               .forever            .npmrc              .viminfz.tmp        Justinmind
.CFUserTextEncoding     .gem                .php_history        .vimrc              Library
.DS_Store               .gist-vim           .phpsh              .vmail              Movies
.NERDTreeBookmarks      .gitconfig          .profile            .weechat            Music
.Trash                  .gitignore_global   .pry_history        .zcompcache         Pictures
.atom                   .gitk               .psysh              .zcompdump          Public
.bash_history           .guard_history      .rnd                .zcompdump.zwc      VirtualBox VMs
.cache                  .heroku             .rubies             .zhistory           bin
.config                 .ievms              .sqlite_history     .zsh-update         db
.cups                   .irb_history        .ssh                .zsh_history        lib
.dbshell                .lein               .subversion         .zshrc              man
.distlib                .lesshst            .task               Applications        npm-debug.log
.dnc                    .local              .taskrc             Box Documents (backup) src
.docx4all               .m2                 .tmux.conf          Box Sync
.docx4j                 .mongorc.js         .vagrant            Code
.dropbox                .nave               .vagrant.d          Desktop
.dropbox-master         .netrc              .vim                Documents
```

As you can probably tell at the moment, the terminal can be a pretty bland environment—a white background and a black ominous $ prompt flashing back at you. It would be good if we could make our terminal look a bit nicer and display some more useful information.

Editing .zshrc

To configure what our terminal looks like, we have to edit a dotfile for that specific environment. In this case, as we're using the Zsh shell, we'll want to edit a .zshrc configuration file (which should be placed within your home directory).

■ **Note** If you were using the Bash shell, you would edit a .bashrc file instead. The ProVim repo is configured specifically for the Zsh environment, so if your Linux distribution doesn't have the Zsh shell installed by default, you can install it manually, using the command apt-get install zsh.

Let's start by looking inside your home directory and make sure you actually have a .zshrc file (if you don't, we'll have to create one). To do that, run the following command:

```
ls -a ~/ | grep zshrc
```

If the preceding command doesn't output anything to the terminal, then the file .zshrc doesn't exist, and if that's the case, we'll have to run the following command to create it:

```
touch ~/.zshrc
```

We now have to open up the .zshrc file and add some configuration settings that will allow us to configure our terminal shell to look like Figure 2-2. I would use Vim to edit this dotfile, but as you've not yet learned how to use Vim, I would suggest, for now, editing the file with the default text editor on your system.

If you're on a Mac, the standard text editor is the TextEdit application (see http://en.wikipedia.org/wiki/TextEdit). Running the following command will open the .zshrc file in TextEdit:

```
open -a TextEdit ~/.zshrc
```

■ **Note** If you're using a Linux-based machine, you're either already comfortable using Vi/Vim or you can use the Nano editor nano ~/.zshrc instead. If you're on Windows and are using Cygwin, you should be able to run cygstart {filename}; however, as Windows is not a naturally Unix-based environment, I don't cater for its configuration. If you wish to configure your terminal on Windows, I would suggest using a script such as "Oh-my-cygwin" instead (see https://github.com/haithembelhaj/oh-my-cygwin).

The file should now be open within your default editor, ready for you to start making some configuration changes. Add Listing 2-1 into the .zshrc file (an easier to read online version can be found at https://github.com/Integralist/ProVim/blob/master/.zshrc and will make it simpler for you to copy and paste from).

Listing 2-1. Contents of Our `.zshrc` File

```
# Exports {{{
export GITHUB_USER="your-username"
export PATH=/usr/local/bin:/usr/bin:/bin:/usr/sbin:/sbin # Reorder PATH so local bin is first
export GREP_OPTIONS='--color=auto'
export GREP_COLOR='1;32'
export MANPAGER="less -X" # Don't clear the screen after quitting a manual page
export EDITOR="vim"
export TERM="screen-256color"
export CLICOLOR=1
export LSCOLORS=Gxfxcxdxbxegedabagacad
export LS_COLORS=Gxfxcxdxbxegedabagacad
# }}}

# Ruby {{{
function get_ruby_version() {
  ruby -v | awk '{print $1 " " $2}'
}
# }}}

# Tmux {{{
# Makes creating a new tmux session (with a specific name) easier
function tmuxopen() {
  tmux attach -t $1
}

# Makes creating a new tmux session (with a specific name) easier
function tmuxnew() {
  tmux new -s $1
}

# Makes deleting a tmux session easier
function tmuxkill() {
  tmux kill-session -t $1
}
# }}}

# Alias' {{{
alias vi="vim"
alias r="source ~/.zshrc"
alias tat='tmux new-session -As $(basename "$PWD" | tr . -)' # will attach if session exists, or
create a new session
alias tmuxsrc="tmux source-file ~/.tmux.conf"
alias tmuxkillall="tmux ls | cut -d : -f 1 | xargs -I {} tmux kill-session -t {}" # tmux kill all
sessions
alias ct="ctags -R --exclude=.git --exclude=node_modules"
alias dotfiles="ls -a | grep '^\.' | grep --invert-match '\.DS_Store\|\.$'"
# }}}

# Auto Completion {{{
autoload -U compinit && compinit
zmodload -i zsh/complist
```

```
# man zshcontrib
zstyle ':vcs_info:*' actionformats '%F{5}(%f%s%F{5})%F{3}-%F{5}[%F{2}%b%F{3}|%F{1}%a%F{5}]%f '
zstyle ':vcs_info:*' formats '%F{5}(%f%s%F{5})%F{3}-%F{5}[%F{2}%b%F{5}]%f '
zstyle ':vcs_info:*' enable git #svn cvs

# Enable completion caching, use rehash to clear
zstyle ':completion::complete:*' use-cache on
zstyle ':completion::complete:*' cache-path ~/.zsh/cache/$HOST

# Fallback to built in ls colors
zstyle ':completion:*' list-colors ''

# Make the list prompt friendly
zstyle ':completion:*' list-prompt '%SAt %p: Hit TAB for more, or the character to insert%s'

# Make the selection prompt friendly when there are a lot of choices
zstyle ':completion:*' select-prompt '%SScrolling active: current selection at %p%s'

# Add simple colors to kill
zstyle ':completion:*:*:kill:*:processes' list-colors '=(#b) #([0-9]#) ([0-9a-z-]#)*=01;34=0=01'

# list of completers to use
zstyle ':completion:*::::' completer _expand _complete _ignored _approximate
zstyle ':completion:*' menu select=1 _complete _ignored _approximate

# match uppercase from lowercase
zstyle ':completion:*' matcher-list 'm:{a-z}={A-Z}'

# offer indexes before parameters in subscripts
zstyle ':completion:*:*:-subscript-:*' tag-order indexes parameters

# formatting and messages
zstyle ':completion:*' verbose yes
zstyle ':completion:*:descriptions' format '%B%d%b'
zstyle ':completion:*:messages' format '%d'
zstyle ':completion:*:warnings' format 'No matches for: %d'
zstyle ':completion:*:corrections' format '%B%d (errors: %e)%b'
zstyle ':completion:*' group-name ''

# ignore completion functions (until the _ignored completer)
zstyle ':completion:*:functions' ignored-patterns '_*'
zstyle ':completion:*:scp:*' tag-order files users 'hosts:-host hosts:-domain:domain hosts:-
ipaddr"IP\ Address *'
zstyle ':completion:*:scp:*' group-order files all-files users hosts-domain hosts-host hosts-ipaddr
zstyle ':completion:*:ssh:*' tag-order users 'hosts:-host hosts:-domain:domain hosts:-ipaddr"IP\
Address *'
zstyle ':completion:*:ssh:*' group-order hosts-domain hosts-host users hosts-ipaddr
zstyle '*' single-ignored show
# }}}
```

```
# Key Bindings {{{
# Make the delete key (or Fn + Delete on the Mac) work instead of outputting a ~
bindkey '^?' backward-delete-char
bindkey "^[[3~" delete-char
bindkey "^[3;5~" delete-char
bindkey "\e[3~" delete-char

# Make the `beginning/end` of line and `bck-i-search` commands work within tmux
bindkey '^R' history-incremental-search-backward
bindkey '^A' beginning-of-line
bindkey '^E' end-of-line
# }}}

# Colours {{{
autoload colors; colors

# The variables are wrapped in \%\{\%\}. This should be the case for every
# variable that does not contain space.
for COLOR in RED GREEN YELLOW BLUE MAGENTA CYAN BLACK WHITE; do
  eval PR_$COLOR='%{$fg_no_bold[${(L)COLOR}]%}'
  eval PR_BOLD_$COLOR='%{$fg_bold[${(L)COLOR}]%}'
done

eval RESET='$reset_color'
export PR_RED PR_GREEN PR_YELLOW PR_BLUE PR_WHITE PR_BLACK
export PR_BOLD_RED PR_BOLD_GREEN PR_BOLD_YELLOW PR_BOLD_BLUE
export PR_BOLD_WHITE PR_BOLD_BLACK

# Clear LSCOLORS
unset LSCOLORS
# }}}

# Set Options {{{
# ===== Basics
setopt no_beep # don't beep on error
setopt interactive_comments # Allow comments even in interactive shells (especially for Muness)

# ===== Changing Directories
setopt auto_cd # If you type foo, and it isn't a command, and it is a directory in your cdpath, go
there
setopt cdablevarS # if argument to cd is the name of a parameter whose value is a valid directory,
it will become the current directory
setopt pushd_ignore_dups # don't push multiple copies of the same directory onto the directory stack

# ===== Expansion and Globbing
setopt extended_glob # treat #, ~, and ^ as part of patterns for filename generation

# ===== History
setopt append_history # Allow multiple terminal sessions to all append to one zsh command history
setopt extended_history # save timestamp of command and duration
setopt inc_append_history # Add comamnds as they are typed, don't wait until shell exit
setopt hist_expire_dups_first # when trimming history, lose oldest duplicates first
```

```
setopt hist_ignore_dups # Do not write events to history that are duplicates of previous events
setopt hist_ignore_space # remove command line from history list when first character on the line is
a space
setopt hist_find_no_dups # When searching history don't display results already cycled through twice
setopt hist_reduce_blanks # Remove extra blanks from each command line being added to history
setopt hist_verify # don't execute, just expand history
setopt share_history # imports new commands and appends typed commands to history


# ===== Completion
setopt always_to_end # When completing from the middle of a word, move the cursor to the end of the
word
setopt auto_menu # show completion menu on successive tab press. needs unsetop menu_complete to work
setopt auto_name_dirs # any parameter that is set to the absolute name of a directory immediately
becomes a name for that directory
setopt complete_in_word # Allow completion from within a word/phrase

unsetopt menu_complete # do not autoselect the first completion entry


# ===== Correction
setopt correct # spelling correction for commands
setopt correctall # spelling correction for arguments


# ===== Prompt
setopt prompt_subst # Enable parameter expansion, command substitution, and arithmetic expansion in
the prompt
setopt transient_rprompt # only show the rprompt on the current prompt


# ===== Scripts and Functions
setopt multios # perform implicit tees or cats when multiple redirections are attempted
# }}}

# Prompt {{{
function virtualenv_info {
  [ $VIRTUAL_ENV ] && echo '(`basename $VIRTUAL_ENV`) '
}

function prompt_char {
  git branch >/dev/null 2>/dev/null && echo '±' && return
  hg root >/dev/null 2>/dev/null && echo '☿' && return
  echo '○'
}

function box_name {
  [ -f ~/.box-name ] && cat ~/.box-name || hostname -s
}

# http://blog.joshdick.net/2012/12/30/my_git_prompt_for_zsh.html
# copied from https://gist.github.com/4415470
# Adapted from code found at <https://gist.github.com/1712320>.
```

```
# setopt promptsubst
autoload -U colors && colors # Enable colors in prompt

# Modify the colors and symbols in these variables as desired.
GIT_PROMPT_SYMBOL="%{$fg[blue]%}±"
GIT_PROMPT_PREFIX="%{$fg[green]%} [%{$reset_color%}"
GIT_PROMPT_SUFFIX="%{$fg[green]%}]%{$reset_color%}"
GIT_PROMPT_AHEAD="%{$fg[red]%}ANUM%{$reset_color%}"
GIT_PROMPT_BEHIND="%{$fg[cyan]%}BNUM%{$reset_color%}"
GIT_PROMPT_MERGING="%{$fg_bold[magenta]%} %{$reset_color%}"
GIT_PROMPT_UNTRACKED="%{$fg_bold[red]%}u%{$reset_color%}"
GIT_PROMPT_MODIFIED="%{$fg_bold[yellow]%}m%{$reset_color%}"
GIT_PROMPT_STAGED="%{$fg_bold[green]%}s%{$reset_color%}"

# Show Git branch/tag, or name-rev if on detached head
function parse_git_branch() {
  (git symbolic-ref -q HEAD || git name-rev --name-only --no-undefined --always HEAD) 2> /dev/null
}

# Show different symbols as appropriate for various Git repository states
function parse_git_state() {
  # Compose this value via multiple conditional appends.
  local GIT_STATE=""

  local NUM_AHEAD="$(git log --oneline @{u}.. 2> /dev/null | wc -l | tr -d ' ')"
  if [ "$NUM_AHEAD" -gt 0 ]; then
    GIT_STATE=$GIT_STATE${GIT_PROMPT_AHEAD//NUM/$NUM_AHEAD}
  fi

  local NUM_BEHIND="$(git log --oneline ..@{u} 2> /dev/null | wc -l | tr -d ' ')"
  if [ "$NUM_BEHIND" -gt 0 ]; then
    GIT_STATE=$GIT_STATE${GIT_PROMPT_BEHIND//NUM/$NUM_BEHIND}
  fi

  local GIT_DIR="$(git rev-parse --git-dir 2> /dev/null)"
  if [ -n $GIT_DIR ] && test -r $GIT_DIR/MERGE_HEAD; then
    GIT_STATE=$GIT_STATE$GIT_PROMPT_MERGING
  fi

  if [[ -n $(git ls-files --other --exclude-standard 2> /dev/null) ]]; then
    GIT_STATE=$GIT_STATE$GIT_PROMPT_UNTRACKED
  fi

  if ! git diff --quiet 2> /dev/null; then
    GIT_STATE=$GIT_STATE$GIT_PROMPT_MODIFIED
  fi

  if ! git diff --cached --quiet 2> /dev/null; then
    GIT_STATE=$GIT_STATE$GIT_PROMPT_STAGED
  fi
```

```
  if [[ -n $GIT_STATE ]]; then
    echo "$GIT_PROMPT_PREFIX$GIT_STATE$GIT_PROMPT_SUFFIX"
  fi
}

# If inside a Git repository, print its branch and state
function git_prompt_string() {
  local git_where="$(parse_git_branch)"
  [ -n "$git_where" ] && echo "on %{$fg[blue]%}${git_where#(refs/heads/|tags/)}$(parse_git_state)"
}

function current_pwd {
  echo $(pwd | sed -e "s,^$HOME,~,")
}

PROMPT='
${PR_GREEN}M.%{$reset_color%} ${PR_BOLD_YELLOW}$(current_pwd)%{$reset_color%} $(git_prompt_string)
$(prompt_char) '

export SPROMPT="Correct $fg[red]%R$reset_color to $fg[green]%r$reset_color [(y)es (n)o (a)bort (e)
dit]? "

RPROMPT='${PR_GREEN}$(virtualenv_info)%{$reset_color%} ${PR_RED}$(get_ruby_version)%{$reset_color%}'
# }}}

# History {{{
HISTSIZE=10000
SAVEHIST=9000
HISTFILE=~/.zsh_history
# }}}

# Zsh Hooks {{{
function precmd {
  # vcs_info
  # Put the string "hostname::/full/directory/path" in the title bar:
  echo -ne "\e]2;$PWD\a"

  # Put the parentdir/currentdir in the tab
  echo -ne "\e]1;$PWD:h:t/$PWD:t\a"
}

function set_running_app {
  printf "\e]1; $PWD:t:$(history $HISTCMD | cut -b7- ) \a"
}

function preexec {
  set_running_app
}

function postexec {
  set_running_app
}
# }}}
```

It's likely, if you're not familiar with shell scripting languages or Vim's ability to fold long chunks of text into one line (which can later be expanded at the touch of a command), that the preceding content might seem like a large blob of unintelligible gobbledygook. If that's the case, I'll give you a brief breakdown of what we have inside this file.

Although this looks like one large chunk of shell-based code, when opened within a properly configured Vim instance, it'll look something like the following:

```
+-- 12 lines: Exports ---------

+-- 5 lines: Ruby -------------

+-- 16 lines: Tmux ------------

+--  8 lines: Alias' ----------

+-- 51 lines: Auto Completion -

+-- 12 lines: Key Bindings ----

+-- 18 lines: Colours ---------

+-- 44 lines: Set Options -----

+-- 98 lines: Prompt ----------

+--  5 lines: History ---------

+-- 22 lines: Zsh Hooks -------
```

The reason the file is compressed when opened inside of Vim is because of a feature known as "code folding." Vim can (if configured to do so) compress any lines that are wrapped in text markers, which Vim recognizes as "fold" areas.

```
# my fold title {{{
Line 1
Line 2
Line 3
This line and the preceding lines 1-3 will all be folded down into one line
# }}}
```

■ **Note** I'll cover code folding in more detail, in Chapter 7.

So what does this file do? Well, the first section, Exports, handles setting up environment variables for the shell (such as GITHUB_USER ->, which you should change to your own username!).

■ **Note** Environment variables are a `key=value` pair (e.g., `FOO=bar`) and are used by many different shell processes. We can see all environment variables that have been set, by running the command `env`. Processes can query these variables and, depending on the value returned, could affect the way the process itself runs (e.g., the process might query the `HOME` variable so that it knows where to create a directory or file).

The section Ruby contains a single function that parses out the currently installed version of Ruby on the operating system. In a later section of the configuration file, we'll use this function to create a value that is stored as part of our customized command-line prompt. If you're not interested in seeing the version of Ruby available within your terminal, then you can remove the following line of code (or you can modify it to suit your needs):

```
RPROMPT='${PR_GREEN}$(virtualenv_info)%{$reset_color%} ${PR_RED}$(get_ruby_version)%{$reset_color%}'
```

The section Tmux contains a few functions I've defined that make running certain tmux commands slightly less tedious. We'll be discussing tmux in a lot more detail in the coming Chapters 23–30.

The section `Alias'` contains some useful shell aliases. (These are similar to functions but don't offer as much granular control.) For example, I define a `vi` alias, which, when I run within my terminal, simply executes the `vim` command instead. This might seem like a strange thing to do, considering that "vim" is only one more character than "vi," so why go to all the trouble of defining an alias (especially, considering that Vi isn't as powerful as Vim, why would we want someone staring over our shoulder to think we were using Vi and not Vim)? Well, the reasoning is that as part of my job, I have to log in to many different remote servers and carry out work on them. These servers can vary in specification, and so some don't have Vim installed (or bizarrely, in some instances, they have Vim installed, but it's only accessible via the `vi` command!?). So, to save on confusion when I try to open a file in Vim on a server that only has Vi, which can be quite frustrating (as your muscle memory is used to using `vim`), I now just use `vi` all the time, safe in the knowledge that it'll either just use Vi or it'll use Vim.

The section Auto Completion contains cryptic Zsh voodoo that enables all kinds of awesome command auto-completion in your terminal. Sadly, shell scripting is outside the scope of this book, so I won't cover how it's written.

The section "Key Bindings" contains some custom key bindings (I cover this in more detail in Chapter 19) that make integrating Vim with tmux a lot easier, as well as allowing me to use my `<fn>+<Backspace>` key combination to delete characters in front of the cursor.

All the other remaining sections are very heavily shell scripting based –and commented– if you wish to review what they do; however, the titles alone (e.g., colors, history, prompt) should be enough to give you a vague idea of the category of terminal features they apply to.

Restart Your Engines!

OK, if you shut down and restart your terminal application, it should, I hope, now look a bit like Figure 2-2 (it won't entirely look the same until we install the new terminal theme; see the following section).

■ **Note** You'll notice that I've not spent any time describing the contents of the `.zshrc` file. This is because it's written purely in Zsh shell scripting language, and that is outside the scope of this book. But you should note that the file content is heavily commented, so although you might not understand the syntax (especially if you're not a programmer), you will at least have an idea of what the script is trying to achieve. All "comments" are prefixed with a hash mark (#) at the start of a line.

Choosing a New Theme for Your Terminal

The color schemes that come built-in with the default Mac OS X Terminal application aren't that great, so most terminal users will look elsewhere for colorful themes they can install. So, we'll download and install a popular terminal theme called "Solarized."

First, we'll have to run the following command, which will download the relevant terminal theme file, called SolarizedLight.terminal, to your desktop:

```
curl "https://raw.githubusercontent.com/Integralist/ProVim/master/themes/Solarized Light.terminal"
-o ~/Desktop/SolarizedLight.terminal
```

Once the terminal theme file is downloaded, we'll have to run the following command to have it automatically open the terminal's preference pane, so that you can select it and set it to be the "default" theme (this is so that every time you open the terminal, it'll use that color scheme):

```
open ~/Desktop/SolarizedLight.terminal
```

Once installed, your shell should resemble Figure 2-2. From this point, you can safely delete the SolarizedLight.terminal file currently sitting on your desktop. The following command will handle that for you:

```
rm ~/Desktop/SolarizedLight.terminal
```

Two Types of Themes

Before we move on to installing Vim, I want to clarify that there are in fact *two* themes that we will want to have installed by the time we're finished:

1. Terminal theme (we installed this a moment ago)

2. Vim theme

Later on, when we come to configuring Vim (using a .vimrc dotfile), you'll see that I specify a "Tomorrow-Night" theme in our configuration settings. At that point, we'll look at creating the relevant Vim theme file. But for now, let's move on.

Installing Vim

As I explained earlier, Vi (an earlier implementation of Vim) and Vim each hold a lion's share of operating systems they're installed on by default (this is practically all Unix-based systems and includes Linux systems as well as Mac OS X).

This ubiquitousness is useful, because in your career, you'll likely find yourself spending a fair amount of time working from someone else's machine (whether you're pair programming with someone or you've had to remotely log into a client's web server to fix a problem), and to have access to Vim (or Vi) means you can still carry out the majority of your editing tasks a lot more easily than you would by using another editor, such as Nano (www.nano-editor.org), or having to go through the hassle of installing an editor yourself on some obscure distribution of Linux or, worst yet, having to use someone else's primitive code editor and figure out how all their shortcuts work.

Mac

Although Vim is preinstalled, the default version on the Mac has a lot of really useful features disabled that I'll be demonstrating in later chapters. (I'm really not sure why they decided to lock it down so much. Luckily, updating Vim is really easy on this OS).

Run the following command to see a list of features that are both enabled and disabled for the currently installed version of Vim (commonly referred to as the "system Vim"):

```
vim --version
```

You'll know what's enabled and what's disabled, because the output from that command will include a line that says something like the following:

```
Features included (+) or not (-)
```

So, if a listed feature has a + prefixed to it, then you know it's enabled, and if a feature has a - prefixed to it, you know it's disabled. We'll see a real example of this in the next section.

Using Homebrew

For most operating systems, there exists a software application known as a "package manager," whose job is to handle the awkward and time-consuming work of installing software for you, by providing you with a simple command-line interface for downloading, installing, and uninstalling specific software packages. On a Mac, the recommended package manager is the fantastic Homebrew (http://brew.sh).

First thing you have to do is go to the Homebrew page and follow the installation instructions. At the time of writing, the installation process is to run the following command (but best to double-check the Homebrew page, just in case it has changed by the time you read this):

```
ruby -e "$(curl -fsSL https://raw.github.com/Homebrew/homebrew/go/install)"
```

Once Homebrew is installed, you can install Vim, by running the following command:

```
brew install vim --override-system-vim
```

Now when you run vim --version, you should see something similar to the following output (note that there are now a lot more "enabled" features, compared to the system Vim):

```
VIM - Vi IMproved 7.4 (2013 Aug 10, compiled Dec 29 2013 17:56:22)
MacOS X (unix) version
Included patches: 1-52
Compiled by Homebrew
Huge version without GUI.  Features included (+) or not (-):
+acl             +farsi          +mouse_netterm    +syntax
+arabic          +file_in_path   +mouse_sgr        +tag_binary
+autocmd         +find_in_path   -mouse_sysmouse   +tag_old_static
-balloon_eval    +float          +mouse_urxvt      -tag_any_white
-browse          +folding        +mouse_xterm      -tcl
++builtin_terms  -footer         +multi_byte       +terminfo
+byte_offset     +fork()         +multi_lang       +termresponse
+cindent         -gettext        -mzscheme         +textobjects
-clientserver    -hangul_input   +netbeans_intg    +title
```

```
+clipboard          +iconv              +path_extra        -toolbar
+cmdline_compl      +insert_expand      -perl              +user_commands
+cmdline_hist       +jumplist           +persistent_undo   +vertsplit
+cmdline_info       +keymap             +postscript        +virtualedit
+comments           +langmap            +printer           +visual
+conceal            +libcall            +profile           +visualextra
+cryptv             +linebreak          +python            +viminfo
+cscope             +lispindent         -python3           +vreplace
+cursorbind         +listcmds           +quickfix          +wildignore
+cursorshape        +localmap           +reltime           +wildmenu
+dialog_con         -lua                +rightleft         +windows
+diff               +menu               +ruby              +writebackup
+digraphs           +mksession          +scrollbind        -X11
-dnd                +modify_fname       +signs             -xfontset
-ebcdic             +mouse              +smartindent       -xim
+emacs_tags         -mouseshape         -sniff             -xsmp
+eval               +mouse_dec          +startuptime       -xterm_clipboard
+ex_extra           -mouse_gpm          +statusline        -xterm_save
+extra_search       -mouse_jsbterm      -sun_workshop      -xpm
    system vimrc file: "$VIM/vimrc"
      user vimrc file: "$HOME/.vimrc"
 2nd user vimrc file: "~/.vim/vimrc"
      user exrc file: "$HOME/.exrc"
  fall-back for $VIM: "/usr/local/share/vim"
Compilation: /usr/bin/clang -c -I. -Iproto -DHAVE_CONFIG_H   -DMACOS_X_UNIX   -Os -w -pipe
-march=native -mmacosx-version-min=10.9 -U_FORTIFY_SOURCE -D_FORTIFY_SOURCE=1
Linking: /usr/bin/clang   -L. -L/usr/local/lib -L/usr/local/lib -Wl,-headerpad_max_install_names -o
vim        -lm  -lncurses -liconv -framework Cocoa    -framework Python   -lruby.2.0.0 -lobjc
```

Linux

Installation on Linux requires two simple commands:

```
sudo apt-get update
sudo apt-get install vim
```

■ **Note**   Homebrew is working on a specialized Linux fork called Linuxbrew
(https://github.com/Homebrew/linuxbrew).

Windows

If you're on a Windows machine, you can install Vim as a Cygwin package.

■ **Note**   If Cygwin is already installed, you'll have to rerun setup.exe and make sure to select the Vim package.

Installing Git

Because some of the Vim plug-ins we'll be using are coming from GitHub repositories, we'll need you to have Git (http://git-scm.com), a version control system, installed.

If you're unsure of what Git and/or what GitHub (www.github.com) is, then you will be OK to just follow the commands I tell you to run. Using a version control system is not explicitly a prerequisite for using Vim, although nowadays a lot of useful plug-ins for Vim are hosted on the popular GitHub web site. I would recommend though that you at least have a read up on the subject of Git and GitHub to see how you might benefit from using it. I would suggest reading "How to use Git and GitHub" (www.integralist.co.uk/posts/how-to-use-git-and-github).

Mac

You can install Git on Mac OS X by running the following command:

```
brew install git
```

Linux

Installation on Linux requires two simple commands:

```
sudo apt-get update
sudo apt-get install git
```

Windows

The official suggestion for installing Git on Windows is to use the msysGit project exe installer, which can be downloaded from http://msysgit.github.com.

Although it's also suggested that if you already use Cygwin, then best to keep to using that as your package manager, as Window users have found issues mixing Cygwin and msysGit.

■ **Note**   If Cygwin is already installed, you'll have to rerun setup.exe and make sure to select the Git package.

Configuring Vim

As I mentioned earlier, Vim by itself is very nondescript (see Figure 2-1), so we will be configuring Vim to look much slicker and streamlined (as well as taking advantage of its more advanced features).

The quickest way to configure Vim (at this stage) is to use a preconfigured setup. If you search the GitHub web site for Vim configuration files, you'll find a wide range of different setups, such as my "ProVim" (https://github.com/Integralist/ProVim). As part of the "ProVim" repo, I include both the .zshrc we used earlier and .vimrc files. We'll use this repo as the starting point for our next main task, which will be to configure Vim.

Copying the .vim Folder

Because we have Git installed, we can download the "ProVim" repository and make a copy of the .vim folder contained inside. Running the following command will handle that for us:

```
git clone https://github.com/Integralist/ProVim.git ~/ProVim && cp -r ~/ProVim/.vim ~/.vim
```

Let's quickly recap how the preceding command works. First, the Git repository is copied (git clone) to your HOME directory into a "ProVim" folder (~/ProVim) and, finally, we copy the .vim folder (cp -r) over to the correct location within your home directory. After running the preceding command, we should end up with the following folder structure:

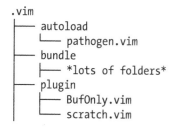

```
.vim
├── autoload
│   └── pathogen.vim
├── bundle
│   ├── *lots of folders*
├── plugin
│   ├── BufOnly.vim
│   └── scratch.vim
```

Let's briefly go over each of these folders, so that you understand what they do. You can see that we have an autoload folder, which, (as the name suggests, automatically loads all the scripts stored inside of it at the point when Vim starts up. In this instance, we have a single file, pathogen.vim, which will be loaded. (We'll cover this file in more detail in Chapter 19).

The bundle folder is a custom directory used by our plug-in manager, Pathogen. This folder will hold all the plug-ins we install via Pathogen.

The plugin folder holds (again, as the name suggests) script files that add additional functionality to Vim through its plug-in mechanism. In this example, you can see that there are two plug-in script files inside the plugin folder:

1   BufOnly.vim

2   scratch.vim

As with the pathogen.vim file, I'll come back to these scripts in Chapter 17, in which I discuss plug-ins in more detail.

Copying the .vimrc File

We now have to copy the .vimrc file out from the ProVim folder in your HOME directory into the root of your home directory. The following command will handle that for you:

```
cp ~/ProVim/.vimrc ~/.vimrc
```

Once you have the .vimrc file copied into your home directory, let's open the file and take a look through it to see what it does. (I've tried to include a reasonable amount of comments within the file itself, but there are a couple of items that should be clarified further).

As before, if you want to view the content of the file on your computer, you'll have to open the file in either the TextEdit application, if you're on a Mac (as we've yet to actually look at how to open files in Vim). The following command will open the file for you:

```
open -a TextEdit ~/.vimrc
```

Because this book doesn't have color-coded syntax highlighting (which can really help with the readability of this type of terse content), you might find it easier to view this file directly within the GitHub repository: https://github.com/Integralist/ProVim/blob/master/.vimrc.

So let's discuss what makes up this file. Although this looks like one large chunk of shell-based code (as we saw earlier with the `.zshrc` file), when opened within a properly configured Vim instance, it'll look something like the following:

```
+--119 lines: Settings -

+-- 61 lines: Plugins --

+-- 75 lines: Mappings -

+-- 66 lines: Commands -
```

So let's take a peek inside this file. We won't cover every single line (most of which is commented inside the file anyway), but there are a few items that are worthy of some extra explanation beyond just the code comments. Let's begin with our first item.

```
set nocompatible
```

This tells Vim that we do not care to use any of the old Vi-style APIs that Vim inherits from. What's confusing is that when you read the help documents, it seems like setting this property is actually a noop (i.e., no-operation/a pointless exercise). The documentation states that if Vim finds a user `.vimrc` (it'll look for it in one of four different locations; your home directory being one of them), it'll default to setting `nocompatible`.

So isn't it odd that we set `nocompatible` if the mere act of having a `.vimrc` file should mean we don't need to set it!? Well the reasoning behind why some people still include it is that it helps to overrule instances where a user might try to start Vim by using the –C flag, which itself tries to enforce `compatible`.

Also, if you're changing the system-wide `.vimrc` (yes, there is a system-wide version that Vim starts up with, and then your user-based `.vimrc` then kicks into effect after it), it'll use `compatible`, unless you specify `nocompatible`.

To find your system-wide Vim within Vim, you'll have to run the command `:echo $VIM`, and this will point you to the folder in which your Vim binary is stored. See also `:h system-vimrc` from within Vim.

```
set nobackup
set nowritebackup
set noswapfile
```

The preceding settings are all closely related in what they're doing: we're telling Vim we want no extraneous files to be produced. Vim claims that these files help you recover corrupted files, by keeping internal track of your buffers and original source files (we'll cover buffers and how they work in Chapter 3). Personally, I've never had any issue without them and feel they aren't required, as Vim is very stable already. If you're concerned about losing any of your work, then by all means remove these settings, but trust a longtime (and very intense) user of Vim: I have *never* had an issue with corrupting files that made me wish I had Vim backup and store data in a swap file.

■ **Note** Vim's swap file feature can still be useful if you're the type of user who opens the same file within different shells on the same system (or within different tmux sessions) and then forgets to close them appropriately. A swap file will display a message to alert you to the fact you're about to modify a file that is already open and prevents you from overwriting your own changes.

```
set ruler
```

I mention the "ruler" setting simply because it has nothing to do with what you would typically associate with that word. Instead, this setting (when enabled) displays the cursor's current column and line number, something I find very useful while scrolling through a very long document.

```
set ignorecase
set smartcase
```

Upon first inspection, it would seem that these two settings have cross purposes. When reading the documentation, you'll find that `ignorecase` does what you would expect and ignores the case sensitivity of a pattern when carrying out a search on your document. `smartcase`, on the other hand, only works in certain scenarios (such as when `ignorecase` is enabled and when you're doing a manual search rather than an automated one—we'll see what this means in practice when we come to Chapter 12). The reason we use both is that, together, they cover all searching scenarios available within Vim, and in each of them, we're able to avoid case-sensitivity issues when searching for a particular pattern.

```
set list listchars=tab:\ \ ,trail:·
```

The preceding setting is very useful when it comes to committing files into a version control system, because without it, you could miss the fact that you have empty space at the end of a line and commit that change. About 99% of the time, you won't care about empty whitespace at the end of a line, and so to be notified of that for every single line in your committed file is just tedious and frustrating to have to sift through (especially if you're reviewing someone else's commit). This setting allows us to select what hidden characters we want to highlight, so we can recognize them immediately.

```
set autoread
```

Setting Vim to `autoread` is really useful, because you will often find yourself in a situation in which you're editing a file in a buffer, only to have another instance of Vim open where you jump over to, and open up, the same file again and edit it there. With this setting enabled, if you jump back over to the original Vim instance and try to write the (now old) buffer back to the file (I'll cover buffers and how they work, in Chapter 3), then Vim will display an error alerting you that you're about to make a destructive write.

```
set shortmess+=I
```

Take a look at Figure 2-3. You'll see that when we run Vim (without the configurations within our custom .vimrc file) that by default, an introductory message is displayed. For me, this is a waste of time and offers no real benefit to you as a user of Vim, unless you're absolutely stone cold new to Vim and don't have ProVim (or any other article, post, or reference) to guide you in how to use Vim. So, we turn off that introductory message.

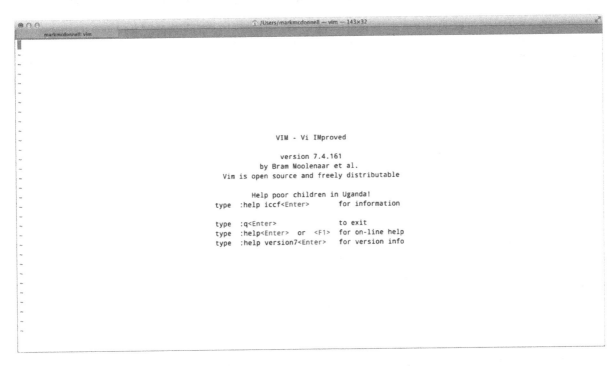

Figure 2-3. *Vim's default introductory message*

I'll skip over the Plugins, Mappings, and Commands sections of the .vimrc file, as I'll be covering these details in later chapters.

Dynamic Loading

I prefer to keep all my configuration settings within a single .vimrc file, as I find it is easier to navigate around and to maintain. It's made simple for me by utilizing Vim's "code folding" feature (which we'll take a look at later, in Chapter 7). Although my .vimrc is quite long (about 323 lines), the ability to fold groups of lines nicely condenses my configuration file.

Now, that being said, some people (including myself, at one point near the start of my Vim career) don't like folding content, so let's consider some alternative ways you might take a long configuration file and break it down into more manageable pieces.

There are primarily two options:

1. Add the files to Vim's runtime path

2. Source individual files (either manually or automatically)

Let's take a quick look at each option.

Runtime Path

When Vim starts up, it passes through a list of directories looking for Vim script files to read and execute. This is so that Vim has a baseline set of functionality built in by the time you come to open and edit some files (such as the ability to recognize the file format and apply the appropriate syntax highlighting for that specific file type, among other things).

Let's take a brief look at how you can see what directories are searched by Vim. Vim provides a global variable (only accessible inside Vim) called $VIMRUNTIME. This variable contains the directory in which Vim will start looking for scripts to bootstrap.

For example, if you run :echo $VIMRUNTIME, you should see output similar to: /usr/local/share/vim/vim74 (it'll be different, depending on your own system). Run the following command to list all the files located within the $VIMRUNTIME folder:

```
ls -la /usr/local/share/vim/vim74/
```

The output of this command should look something like the following:

```
drwxr-xr-x    33 markmcdonnell  admin    1122 28 Mar 19:11 .
drwxr-xr-x     3 markmcdonnell  admin     102 28 Mar 19:11 ..
drwxr-xr-x    32 markmcdonnell  admin    1088 28 Mar 19:11 autoload
-rw-r--r--     1 markmcdonnell  admin    1955 28 Mar 19:11 bugreport.vim
drwxr-xr-x    20 markmcdonnell  admin     680 28 Mar 19:11 colors
drwxr-xr-x    60 markmcdonnell  admin    2040 28 Mar 19:11 compiler
-rw-r--r--     1 markmcdonnell  admin     645 28 Mar 19:11 delmenu.vim
drwxr-xr-x   135 markmcdonnell  admin    4590 28 Mar 19:11 doc
-rw-r--r--     1 markmcdonnell  admin    1965 28 Mar 19:11 evim.vim
-rw-r--r--     1 markmcdonnell  admin   68506 28 Mar 19:11 filetype.vim
-rw-r--r--     1 markmcdonnell  admin     280 28 Mar 19:11 ftoff.vim
drwxr-xr-x   189 markmcdonnell  admin    6426 28 Mar 19:11 ftplugin
-rw-r--r--     1 markmcdonnell  admin     971 28 Mar 19:11 ftplugin.vim
-rw-r--r--     1 markmcdonnell  admin     337 28 Mar 19:11 ftplugof.vim
-rw-r--r--     1 markmcdonnell  admin    1698 28 Mar 19:11 gvimrc_example.vim
drwxr-xr-x   106 markmcdonnell  admin    3604 28 Mar 19:11 indent
-rw-r--r--     1 markmcdonnell  admin     767 28 Mar 19:11 indent.vim
-rw-r--r--     1 markmcdonnell  admin     282 28 Mar 19:11 indoff.vim
drwxr-xr-x    68 markmcdonnell  admin    2312 28 Mar 19:11 keymap
drwxr-xr-x   135 markmcdonnell  admin    4590 28 Mar 19:11 lang
drwxr-xr-x    17 markmcdonnell  admin     578 28 Mar 19:11 macros
-rw-r--r--     1 markmcdonnell  admin   38494 28 Mar 19:11 menu.vim
-rw-r--r--     1 markmcdonnell  admin    2650 28 Mar 19:11 mswin.vim
-rw-r--r--     1 markmcdonnell  admin   55439 28 Mar 19:11 optwin.vim
drwxr-xr-x    13 markmcdonnell  admin     442 28 Mar 19:11 plugin
drwxr-xr-x    35 markmcdonnell  admin    1190 28 Mar 19:11 print
-rw-r--r--     1 markmcdonnell  admin   10393 28 Mar 19:11 scripts.vim
drwxr-xr-x    14 markmcdonnell  admin     476 28 Mar 19:11 spell
-rw-r--r--     1 markmcdonnell  admin   36816 28 Mar 19:11 synmenu.vim
drwxr-xr-x   571 markmcdonnell  admin   19414 28 Mar 19:11 syntax
drwxr-xr-x    23 markmcdonnell  admin     782 28 Mar 19:11 tools
drwxr-xr-x    66 markmcdonnell  admin    2244 28 Mar 19:11 tutor
-rw-r--r--     1 markmcdonnell  admin    2945 28 Mar 19:11 vimrc_example.vim
```

As you can see from the preceding output, there are quite a few folders and files that Vim uses to bootstrap itself. There are a couple of additional folders and files listed, though, that aren't standard and have been added dynamically. The Vim defaults are the following:

autoload/	automatically loaded scripts
colors/	color scheme files
compiler/	compiler files
doc/	documentation
filetype.vim	filetypes by file name
ftplugin/	filetype plugins
indent/	indent scripts
keymap/	key mapping files
lang/	menu translations
menu.vim	GUI menus
plugin/	plugin scripts
print/	files for printing
scripts.vim	filetypes by file contents
spell/	spell checking files
syntax/	syntax files
tutor/	files for vimtutor

Another way to access similar information is to use `:scriptnames`, which will list all sourced files but, more important, it'll list them in the actual order they were sourced.

To understand where the other nonstandard files and folders have come from, you'll have to understand how you can add new folders and files to Vim's runtime lookup path.

■ **Note** There are many ways to get files dynamically loaded. I show the two most popular variations: updating the runtime path and sourcing them directly.

As an example, imagine you have created the following directory: `~/.vim/config`, and inside of that, you have created individual files for each type of configuration setting you have in your `.vimrc` file. So, you might have one file for basic settings, one for plug-in settings, and one for custom key bindings.

To get Vim to locate these files, add the following code inside your `.vimrc` file:

```
set runtimepath+=~/.vim/config
runtime basic.vim
runtime plugins.vim
runtime bindings.vim
```

■ **Note** You should add the preceding code to the top of your `.vimrc` file.

Effectively, what the preceding snippet of code does is set the Vim variable `runtimepath` to be whatever it was set to by default but to also include the folder `~/.vim/config`. We then execute Vim's `runtime` command, which sources (i.e., loads) each file specified (and because we have the config folder within Vim's list of runtime paths, it can safely locate the specified files).

■ **Note**   We don't have to specify each individual file, if there are lots we need to load, as we can also use a wildcard/glob * to indicate any file that ends with a `.vim` extension like so: runtime `*.vim`. But be aware that this means files are loaded in alphabetical order (if your files have to be loaded in a specific order, it's best to explicitly execute them as we've done in the original example).

Once you start understanding more about Vim and are able to confidently navigate its help files, you'll discover many other ways to implement this code (some solutions being more terse and concise than others).

Sourcing Files

You can also automatically load files using the `source` command. The following code demonstrates how you could use this feature (again, you would add this code to the top of your `.vimrc` file):

```
for f in split(glob('~/.vim/config/*.vim'), '\n')
  exe 'source' f
endfor
```

If you're new to programming and the typical constructs (expressions, statements, functions, etc.), the preceding code might seem a little confusing, but if we break it down into chunks, it will, I hope, make a bit more sense.

1. First, we find all the `.vim` files within the `~/.vim/config` folder, using the `glob` function.

2. We make a list out of the return data using the `split` function.

3. We then loop over each item in the list (an "item" being the path to each file found from the `glob`).

4. Finally, we run the exe command, which evaluates some code. In this instance, we tell Vim to `source` each file in the list (and by "source," we simply mean "we load in" the specified file).

The preceding code is an example of Vim's own built-in language: VimL. VimL is the building block behind writing plug-ins and allowing other forms of customization in Vim. I don't go into detail on this topic, as it would require a book unto itself. If you are interested in learning more, a good online resource is available at `http://learnvimscriptthehardway.stevelosh.com`.

■ **Note**   Vim's plug-ins are typically written in Vim's built-in language, "Vim script". But the name of this language causes a bit of contention with Vim users, because there doesn't appear to be an official definition. Looking at Vim's documentation (`:h usr_41.txt`), it would appear that "Vim scripts" refers to individual scripts, whereas "Vim script language" refers to the overall language, which the community has since adopted as VimL. We will be using VimL throughout this book.

Opening Vim

Now that we have everything we need set up correctly, we have finally reached the point where we can actually open Vim! It's been a long time coming, but the moment has arrived.

To start Vim (in its most basic state), all we have to do is to run the following command: vim.

Yup, that was it. All of what we've read so far has been leading up to that one command. You should now see something that looks like Figure 2-4.

Figure 2-4. *Vim in all its configured glory. Be prepared to be amazed!*

That's it. Vim is configured and open, ready for us to start working. But before we jump straight into learning some Vim commands, let's move on to the next chapter, which will cover a few of the concepts that are fundamental to properly understanding Vim and will set us up nicely for learning some editing commands.

■ **Note**   One specific item provided by the ProVim configuration is the plug-in vim-airline (https://github.com/bling/vim-airline), which provides a clean and lightweight status bar display; as can be seen in Figure 2-4. In Chapter 17, I discuss how plug-ins work and how you can install and configure them, but I don't cover vim-airline in any further detail, other than to provide the installation instructions in this chapter. So, if you're interested in configuring the status bar further than the default setup (which is what the ProVim configuration uses), then I recommend viewing the GitHub repository for more details.

Summary

So, here we are at the end of yet another chapter. Let's recap what you've learned so far. First, we started by learning about the terminal application and how it gives us access to the underlying system via the shell environment.

Next, you learned how to interpret and read shell commands (as well as where to find help via the built-in manuals). We copied and pasted quite a few commands to convert from Bash to Zsh and to get our terminal environment in a better state than we found it.

We then moved on to learning about dotfiles, what they do, and some examples. Once we figured out how dotfiles work, we were able to edit our .zshrc file and download/install a new terminal theme.

After that, we installed an updated version of Vim, in addition to the Git version control system, looked at how Vim loads files when it starts up, and demonstrated a couple of ways to add our own bootstrap scripts via the Vim runtime path.

Finally, we opened Vim! The next step is to learn about the fundamental concepts that Vim is based on.

■ ■ ■

## CHAPTER 3

Fundamentals

In this chapter, we'll be reviewing the fundamental concepts of how Vim works. This includes looking at how Vim opens files and the different editing modes available. We'll also take a quick look at features such as windows and tabs, which allow us to better manage our workspace environment.

How Vim Works

OK, let's quickly recap what we have done so far in the previous chapters.

- We have added our `.vim` folder (and all relevant sub-folders, such as our `bundle` and `plugin` folders).

- We have created our `.vimrc` configuration file (and added the relevant settings borrowed from the ProVim repo).

- Vim was installed (and opened).

So, as I mentioned a moment ago, before we look at how to edit files in Vim, we'll first have to understand a bit about how Vim actually works and the concepts that it uses. I know I must sound like a bit of an old bore, but I can't stress enough how important it is to take a moment to really understand the principles of Vim.

Vim can be broken down and analyzed in many ways; but for me, the fundamental concepts of Vim are as follows:

- Commands

- Buffers

- Windows

- Tabs

- Modes

Let's look into each of these concepts individually and see what they mean and how they'll affect our understanding of Vim.

Commands

Most of what we do within Vim is the result of executing a command. Commands take many forms, such as single-line, mapped, and editing commands (the terminology I use isn't "official," but for now, it helps simplify the varying amount of concepts we would otherwise have to know). We'll look at a couple of these variations next.

Single-Line Commands

A command can be expressed in a single-line form, using the following syntax:

```
:{my command}
```

Where {my command} is the command you want to execute (for example :echo $VIM). The preceding single-line command is known as running a command from Vim's COMMAND-LINE "mode." We'll cover Vim's different modes in more detail shortly.

Mapping Commands

A long or awkward-to-remember command (such as :'<,'>Tabularize /=) can also be associated with, and executed using, a short keystroke sequence (also known as a "key binding" or "key mapping").

I have conveniently mapped the preceding example of an awkward-to-remember command to the key sequence \e in my own .vimrc file, and I'm sure you'll agree it is both much easier to remember and quicker to type.

I utilize a lot of these types of mappings in my configuration file, as many of the plug-ins and built-in features of Vim I use have longer identifiers. Being able to associate a command with an easy-to-remember mapping makes me much more efficient when using Vim. I'll cover how to create your own mappings in Chapter 19.

Editing Commands

We've seen single-line commands (again, I'll cover these in more detail later when we review Vim's COMMAND-LINE mode), and we've seen how we can map commands to a shorter set of keystrokes. But commands can also be run from many of Vim's other modes, such as NORMAL and INSERT mode (among others).

To give you an example, the following command is something you might run from Vim's NORMAL mode. Don't worry about what it means for now, as I'll be covering Vim's commands in a lot more detail in Chapter 5. The following is merely to introduce you to the concept of what commands typically look like:

```
2wciw
```

Later on in Chapter 5, we'll also see how to control the amount of times a certain command is executed and even in what direction it is executed, using operators in Vim known as "motions."

Terminology

Wait! Pit stop! Before we go any further, I'll briefly cover some terminology. Sorry, but it's important to clarify the terminology we're going to be using throughout the rest of the book; otherwise, it might not be clear what I'm talking about at certain times.

There are two terms I want to cover: *commands* and *keystrokes*. Throughout the following sections and chapters, I'll refer to commands and keystrokes in a shorthand notation. Let me quickly demonstrate what that notation looks like.

For example, if you see <C-w>, then this cryptic-looking snippet actually expands to mean <Ctrl>+w, OK? That's a little better, but not crystal clear, so let's expand what this means again: press down the <Ctrl> key and the w key at once.

So, if while reading through this book, I say to you, Now execute the <C-w>| command, what that means is that I want you to execute a command that consists of pressing the <Ctrl> key and the w key (at once), followed by pressing the pipe (|) key.

■ **Note** Typically, when I tell you to run a command, I'll also have given you the appropriate context to go along with it, such as what mode you should be in when running the command. If I don't specify a mode, it means it doesn't matter what mode you're in when you execute the command.

You may notice that I'll usually combine the two terms ("command" and "keystroke") into just "command." This is because when we execute a command, we're really just constructing a "command" from multiple keystrokes. I'll also refer to a set of keystrokes as a "key binding." Different Vim users will use different terminology, so it's good to have a solid understanding of the concepts that underpin this different nomenclature, so that you can better interpret what another person is talking about when discussing Vim.

There are a few other keys worth clarifying. I've created a matrix in Table 3-1 that you can use as a quick reference, if you have to remember what one of these keys refers to.

Table 3-1. *Matrix of Keys and Their Associated Explanation*

Key	Meaning
<CR>	This stands for "carriage return" (also known as the <Enter> key on your keyboard).
<Esc>	This is the escape key (usually placed top left) on your keyboard.
<Leader>	This is, by default, the \ character (but it can be modified).
<Space>	This is the spacebar key (usually placed bottom) on your keyboard.

Last, just so I don't have to keep repeating myself in later chapters, if you notice the use of curly braces within a code example, such as :h {your-command}, this means you should replace the curly braces (and their content) with your own string of characters. This is a common practice, whereby a command can take in any number of different values. Rather than using a single value to demonstrate an example, I'll use this notation instead. That way, you won't get confused and think the value I've used in the example is the only value that can be used.

Buffers

Buffers are a very important concept to understand, because you will be using them a lot, and in the beginning, when you first use Vim, it's likely you won't realize that you're even using buffers, because your experience with editing files is based on more traditional software. So, let's see how buffers are used in Vim and what they do.

When you open a file in Vim and start editing it, you are, in fact, only editing a "copy" of the file. The file has actually been opened into a "buffer," and that buffer is just a chunk of memory allocated to holding a copy of the file you wanted to edit.

The original file remains unchanged until you actually "write" the buffer back to the file (that's where the :w write command comes in; it effectively "saves" the file). I'll cover this in more detail in both Chapters 4 and 5.

Another reason why buffers are important to understand is that we can utilize them in different ways. For example, because we're dealing with buffers and not the original file, we can safely split the buffer into multiple windows (see next section for more details on Windows), using the :sp command. From there, we can edit/write the buffer in either window, without any conflicts.

Buffers have multiple states: active, hidden, and inactive. If the buffer is currently visible inside the viewport, it is considered to be active. If the buffer is not visible, it's considered hidden. If you have an empty buffer (i.e., it has no file read in), and it's not visible, the buffer is considered inactive.

[No Name] Buffers

As Vim's foundations are built on buffers for handling files and their content, if you want to create a new file (as you would in a traditional text editor), you have to create a new buffer, but a buffer of a specific kind, known as a [No Name] buffer. This is because a buffer that hasn't had a file read into it is by definition empty.

When you first ran the vim command (to open Vim), we didn't specify any files for Vim to open. This means Vim will initially open with a single [No Name] buffer created for you by default. The [No Name] buffer is a buffer that is not associated with a file (i.e., empty). Its purpose is for the user to add some content and then save that content to a new file. The new file is actually created as the user writes the buffer.

Scratch Buffers

Vim also has a type of buffer known as a "Scratch" buffer. This is similar to a [No Name] buffer, in that it is not associated with any file, but this type of buffer exists primarily to be disposable.

The problem with a [No Name] buffer is if you add some content to it and then attempt to close the buffer, Vim will try to protect you from losing your work by asking you if you want to save the file or not. But with a Scratch buffer, you can add as much content as you want and then close the buffer, and Vim will not attempt to warn you. It's designed to be truly disposable.

You'll learn more about creating both [No Name] and Scratch buffers in Chapter 4.

Windows

Vim allows you to split the current viewport/screen (i.e., buffer) into smaller "windows" (see Figure 3-1).

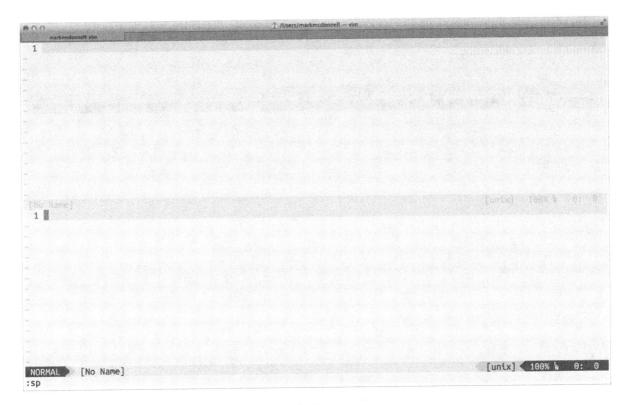

Figure 3-1. Example of a Vim split window on a single buffer

Each window is a viewport on a specific buffer. This means that if you have a buffer open and you create a new split window, then initially, that window will open the same buffer you were just in.

One benefit of viewing the same buffer from multiple windows is that if you have a very long file, you can view different parts of the same file in different windows (letting you cross-reference information).

Vim allows you to manipulate windows in multiple ways: reposition them, change their layout, move them into separate tabs (see the next section), among many other things. We'll look at windows in more detail in Chapter 12.

Tabs

Tabs work exactly how you've probably come to expect them in other applications. A tab can hold a single window, or it can hold a collection of windows (see Figure 3-2).

I personally find myself not using tabs in Vim that much (if at all), because the terminal application on the Mac already natively supports creating its own tabs, and so I find it more efficient to use the native tabs built into the terminal than Vim's.

■ **Note** There is one exception, which is that when I need a scratch pad to jot down some notes, but I don't want to open a new buffer in my current window (as I've probably got too many splits already), and I don't want to use a separate application. I'll create instead a new tab to act like a Scratch buffer.

That being said, if you're working on a remote server via an SSH connection (such as a Linux-based web server), and you're not using a tool such as tmux!, you'll have to utilize tabs to help control the working environment more efficiently.

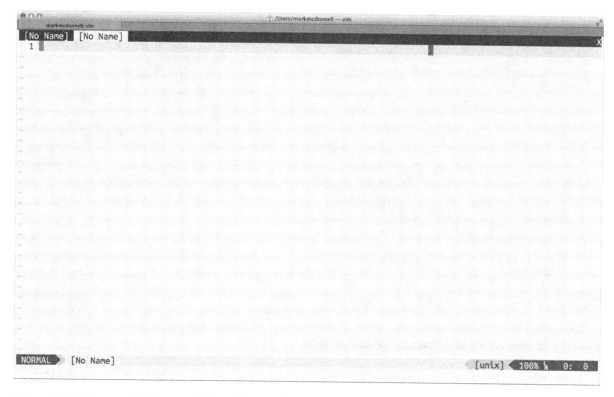

Figure 3-2. *Vim opened with two tabs (both [No Name] tabs)*

Modes

One of the most important concepts in Vim is its built-in "modes," of which there are six main ones. There are others, such as SELECT and EX, but the following are the ones I think are most useful to know:

- NORMAL
- INSERT
- VISUAL
- REPLACE
- COMMAND-LINE
- VISUAL-BLOCK

Vim starts up in NORMAL mode, and to switch between modes, you must first press the <Esc> key, followed by the relevant keystroke that triggers the mode you want to enter into. Refer to Table 3-2, which shows the associations.

Table 3-2. *Matrix of Modes and Their Triggers*

Mode	Trigger
<Esc>	NORMAL
i	INSERT
v	VISUAL
R	REPLACE
:	COMMAND-LINE (also known as the command prompt)
<C-v>	VISUAL-BLOCK

NORMAL

Vim starts in NORMAL mode. This is the primary mode for running commands.

INSERT

This mode is where you're able to directly edit the content of a buffer.

Vim beginners find it quite hard to believe that this is the mode they will spend the least amount of time in. Once you start utilizing all of the different motion and editing Vim commands, you'll find that you just dip in and out of INSERT mode; but use NORMAL mode to move around and execute commands that take care of the rest of your requirements.

VISUAL

If you need to select some content within your buffer, you'll switch to VISUAL mode (Figure 3-3). This mode's main purpose is to let you visually highlight portions of your content (either by using the mouse keys or specific Vim motion commands).

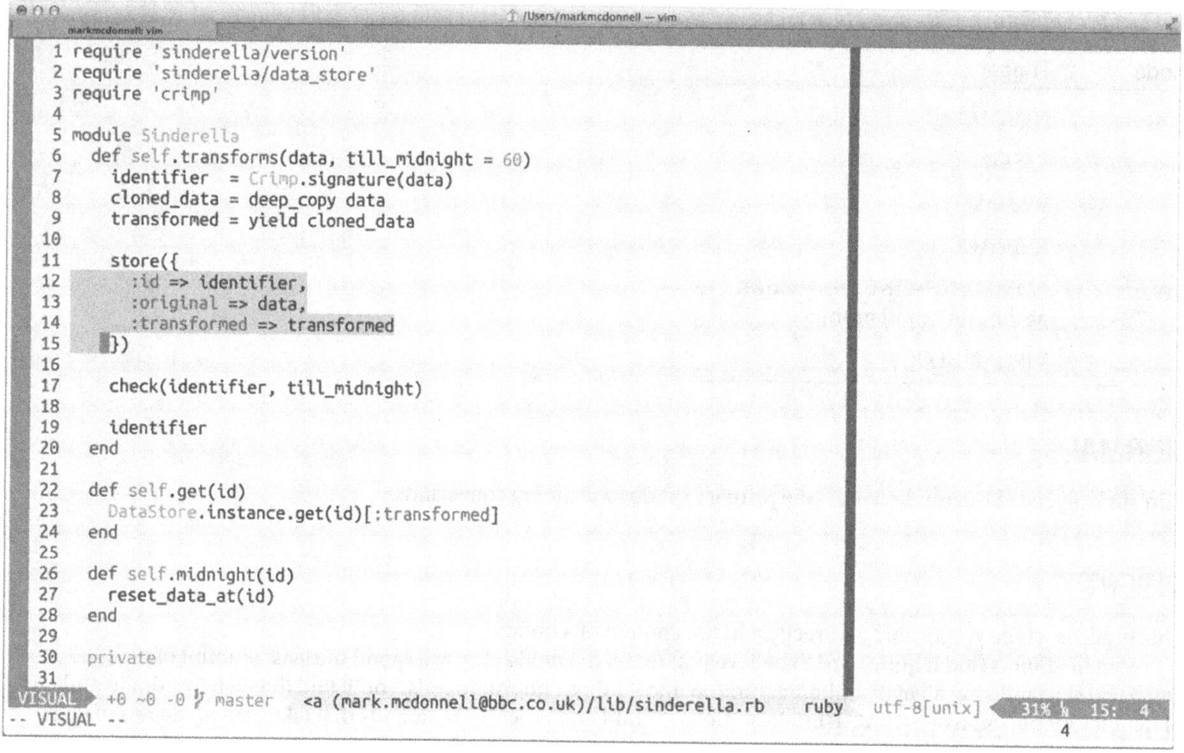

Figure 3-3. *Vim's VISUAL mode*

There is actually another visual mode, called VISUAL-BLOCK, which lets you select multiple columns of content and make the same change across all selected lines. For example, if you selected three lines, then typed in "abc," "abc" would be added to all three lines. This mode allows you to implement some useful ways of bulk-editing your content, and I'll cover it in more detail in Chapter 9.

REPLACE

I very rarely use this mode, but it effectively allows you to type over the top (thus "replacing") preexisting content.

For example, if you have a line of text, "this is my line," and with your cursor, at the start of the line, you enter REPLACE mode and begin typing the word *hello*, you'll see that the line now reads, "hellois my line."

COMMAND-LINE

Vim allows you to execute commands via its own command-line prompt. To access the COMMAND-LINE mode, simply press the : key while in any mode that is not the INSERT mode (see Figure 3-4). You can even execute command-line commands against a VISUAL mode selection. Doing so will drop you immediately into Vim's COMMAND-LINE mode. You'll see that we use the COMMAND-LINE mode a lot throughout this book.

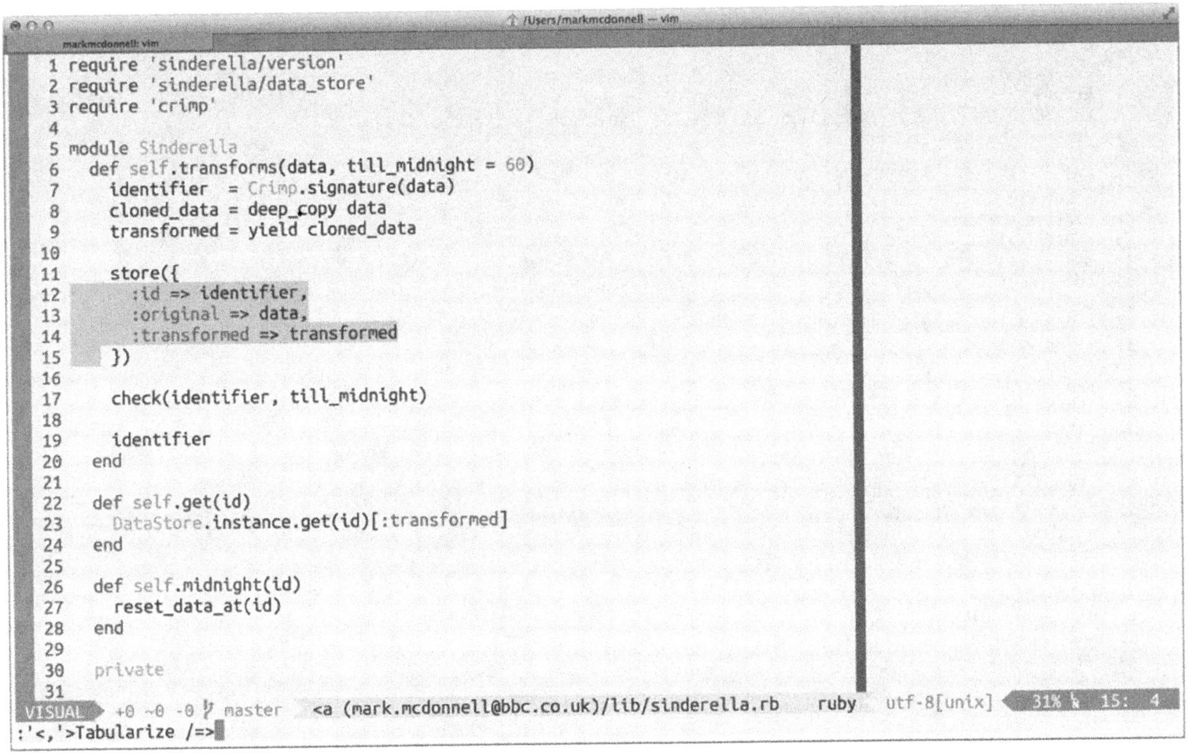

```
1 require 'sinderella/version'
2 require 'sinderella/data_store'
3 require 'crimp'
4
5 module Sinderella
6   def self.transforms(data, till_midnight = 60)
7     identifier  = Crimp.signature(data)
8     cloned_data = deep_copy data
9     transformed = yield cloned_data
10
11    store({
12      :id => identifier,
13      :original => data,
14      :transformed => transformed
15    })
16
17    check(identifier, till_midnight)
18
19    identifier
20  end
21
22  def self.get(id)
23    DataStore.instance.get(id)[:transformed]
24  end
25
26  def self.midnight(id)
27    reset_data_at(id)
28  end
29
30  private
31
```

VISUAL   +0 ~0 -0 ⑂ master   <a (mark.mcdonnell@bbc.co.uk)/lib/sinderella.rb   ruby   utf-8[unix]   31% ⊾   15:   4
:'<,'>Tabularize /=>█

Figure 3-4. *Vim's COMMAND-LINE mode (triggered after making a visual selection)*

It can be helpful to be able to recap all the commands previously executed within the command-line prompt's history. (Maybe we entered a long command and don't want to type it all out again.) To do this, Vim provides us with the following couple of options:

1. Access to a static list

2. Access to a dynamic list (i.e., the "Command Line Window")

The "static list" history can be accessed using the following command (see Figure 3-5):

```
:history
```

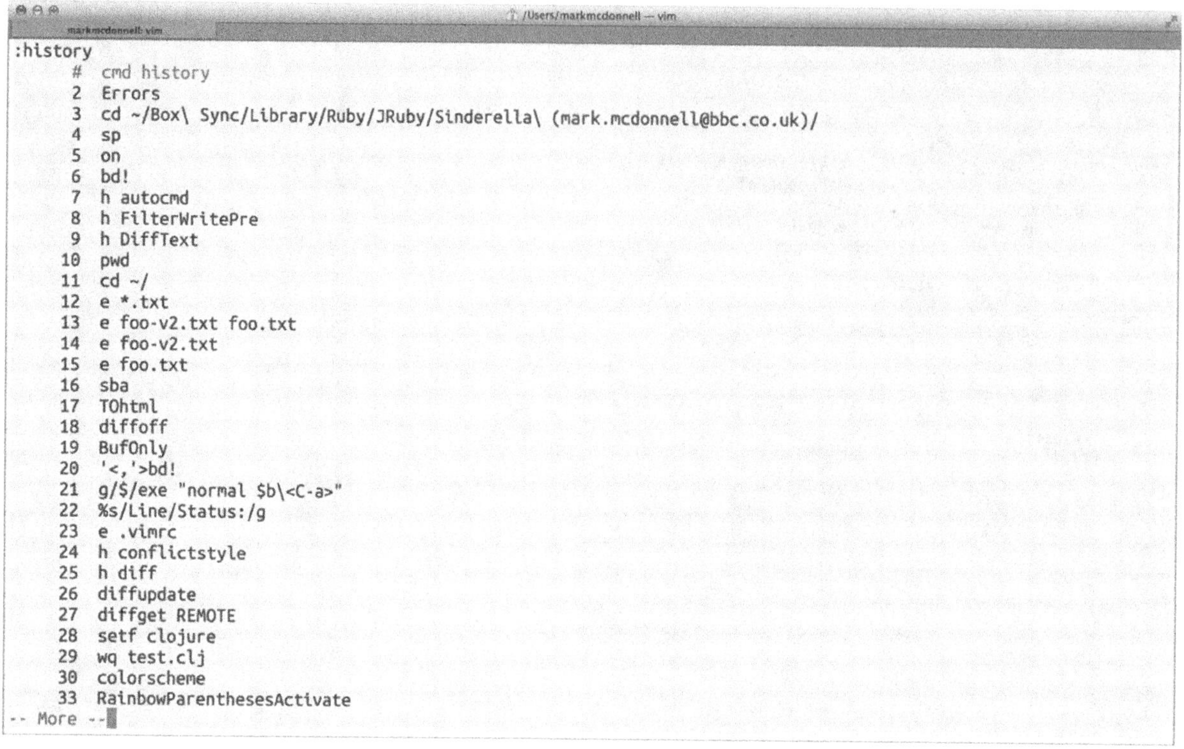

```
:history
        #  cmd history
        2  Errors
        3  cd ~/Box\ Sync/Library/Ruby/JRuby/Sinderella\ (mark.mcdonnell@bbc.co.uk)/
        4  sp
        5  on
        6  bd!
        7  h autocmd
        8  h FilterWritePre
        9  h DiffText
       10  pwd
       11  cd ~/
       12  e *.txt
       13  e foo-v2.txt foo.txt
       14  e foo-v2.txt
       15  e foo.txt
       16  sba
       17  TOhtml
       18  diffoff
       19  BufOnly
       20  '<,'>bd!
       21  g/$/exe "normal $b\<C-a>"
       22  %s/Line/Status:/g
       23  e .vimrc
       24  h conflictstyle
       25  h diff
       26  diffupdate
       27  diffget REMOTE
       28  setf clojure
       29  wq test.clj
       30  colorscheme
       33  RainbowParenthesesActivate
-- More --
```

Figure 3-5. *Example of Vim's* `:history` *command*

The result of executing this command will be a static list of previous commands. But be aware that you won't be able to select any of the commands or re-execute them. You're only able to view the commands (see Figure 3-6).

The "dynamic list" is a much more useful feature, and it can be accessed while in any mode that is not the INSERT mode, by using the following command:

```
q:
```

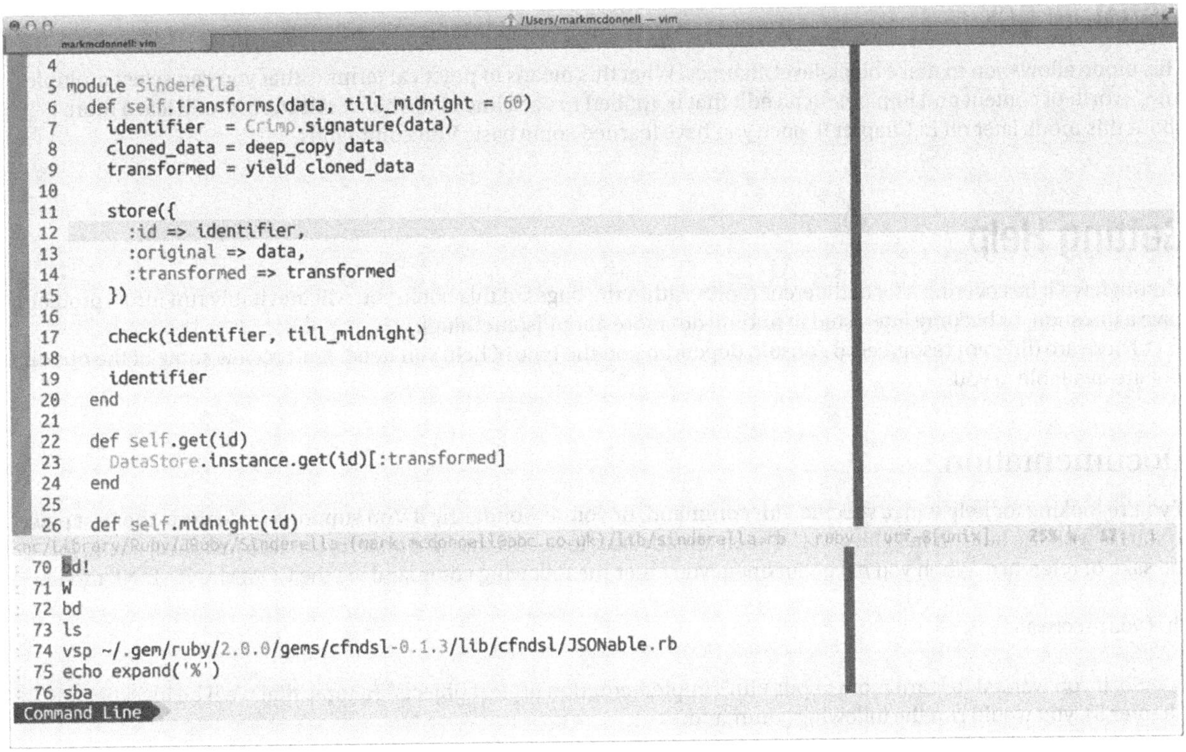

Figure 3-6. *Example of Vim's Command Line Window*

What the preceding command does is open up Vim's Command Line Window (see also `:h command-line-window`). Let's take a quick look at the differences between the static and dynamic lists.

- The dynamic list is a separate window, so you are able to visually select any of the content of the window.

- The dynamic list can re-execute any of the listed commands: press the `<CR>` key while the cursor is over one of the listed commands.

- The dynamic list allows you not only to re-execute any previous command but to edit the command first before doing so. This is useful in case you typed out a long command but made a mistake and have to correct it.

■ **Note** If you're already in COMMAND-LINE mode, pressing `<C-f>` will drop you into the Command Line Window.

VISUAL-BLOCK

This mode allows you to make block-level changes. What this means in practical terms is that you can select multiple rows' worth of content and implement an edit that is applied to each line of the block selection. You'll learn more about this mode later on in Chapter 9, once you have learned some basic Vim commands.

Getting Help

Although we'll be covering a lot of different topics within the pages of this book, you will inevitably run into a problem, have a question, or become interested in finding out more about {something}.

There are different resources to consult, depending on the type of help you need. Let's review some of the options that are available to you.

Documentation

If you're looking for help with a specific Vim command, or you're wondering if Vim supports {x} feature, the best place to start is with the built-in help files. We've seen already how to access the help system, but let's just see it again, for the sake of reference. When you have Vim open, you enter the following command via the COMMAND-LINE mode:

```
:h {your-command}
```

So, if you wanted to learn more about Vim's implementation of "text objects" (a topic that we'll be investigating in Chapter 5), you would run the following command:

```
:h text-objects
```

Within the help files themselves, you can jump to specific sections by using the <C-]> keystroke. This movement between help files is only possible when your cursor is placed on top of a "tag," which is a highlighted piece of text that Vim links to another help file. For an example of a tag, take a look at Figure 3-7, which shows the result of running the command :h text-objects. From that image, you should see a highlighted (red, in this case) piece of text that says +textobjects; this is the tag.

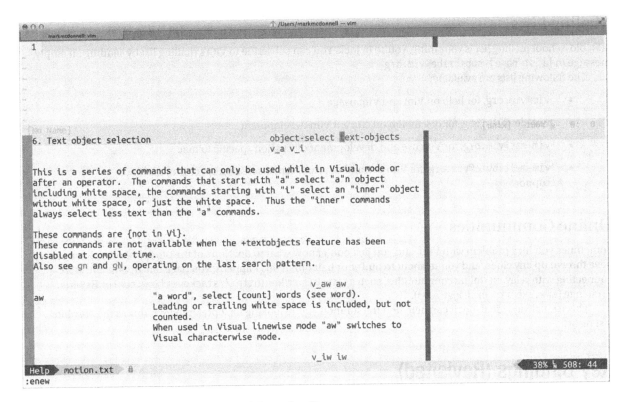

Figure 3-7. *Vim's help files (notice the +textobjects "tag")*

For a top-level summary of the available functionality the help system provides, execute the following command :h help-summary, which demonstrates how to best utilize the help system. For example, it'll highlight tips such as how to search for help on a command that is specific to INSERT mode. So, if you were to execute :h i_CTRL-R, you would see the help file for the <C-r> key (specifically explaining what the key does when executed within INSERT mode).

Vim's Wiki

If you're after tips and tricks about how to use Vim or do something specific with Vim, chances are it has a page on the Wiki: http://vim.wikia.com. There have been quite a few times I've Googled for help with some specific edge-case issue with Vim, only to end up on the Vim wiki (it usually ranks quite highly on search engines, simply because its varied content is that good).

If I had the time (and if I thought you weren't already a busy person), I would recommend sitting down and just reading through the Vim wiki, as it really does have some solid gems stored away. Well worth your time, I can assure you.

IRC

Some people prefer a quicker form of communication. If you're one of those people, then you should join the #vim channel on the freenode network: irc.freenode.net.

Mailing Lists

If an old-school mailing list is your thing, you're in luck. You can subscribe to Vim's mailing list by sending an empty message to [list-name]-subscribe@vim.org.

The following lists are available:

- vim@vim.org, for help on Vim and Vim usage

- vim-dev@vim.org, for discussion on current Vim development

- vim-mac@vim.org, for Vim use and development discussion specific to mac

- vim-multibyte@vim.org, for Vim use and development discussion specific to multibyte support

Online Communities

Sometimes you hit a problem with Vim, and you just don't know what to do. None of the other avenues of support have thrown up any clues, and you're about to pull your hair out. If this happens, you have one option left: start connecting with relevant online communities, such as Stack Overflow (http://stackoverflow.com) or Experts Exchange (www.experts-exchange.com).

This isn't always ideal, but it can help find the solution you're looking for. I prefer to treat this as the absolute last resort.

Key Bindings (Revisited)

I realized while writing this book that it can be difficult to organize content in such a way that makes a table of contents easier for the reader to navigate and to find the desired content. Some information you want to explain earlier than other information, and yet that information might rely on more advanced knowledge that you don't want to explain to the reader that early, as it could potentially cause confusion.

Key bindings is one such example. I wanted to explain the concept of commands and key mappings early, but at that point, we hadn't looked at the different Vim modes, so you wouldn't have had the right context in which to understand the following information.

Now that you've seen the different fundamental concepts that Vim is built on, we can revisit some information about key bindings that I had to leave out earlier, which is that it can be handy to use to see all the custom key bindings that have been added to your Vim configuration (either those you have set within your .vimrc file or those implemented via third-party plug-ins you've installed).

The commands in Table 3-3 will display a list of the relevant commands for the specific mode you're interested in.

Table 3-3. *Matrix of Commands That List All Key Bindings for a Specific Mode*

Command	Bindings
:nmap	Display key bindings for NORMAL mode
:vmap	Display key bindings for VISUAL mode
:imap	Display key bindings for INSERT mode
:map	Display key bindings for all modes

■ **Note** Adding the keyword verbose to the start of the command (e.g., :verbose nmap) will display the same list as before, but with the location of the file in which the key binding was defined. This can be useful for debugging either a broken or unexpected key binding.

What About All the Default Vim Bindings?

The preceding commands won't help you, however, if you're looking specifically for a default key binding (i.e., one implemented by Vim itself). To see all the default bindings Vim implements, you'll have to refer to the help files.

Running the following command will open up Vim's main index of all commands and the associated modes they're defined in. You can then navigate the help file, looking for the command type you're interested in.

```
:h index
```

As an example, after entering the preceding command, I am presented with a list of modes, as follows:

```
1. Insert mode                    insert-index
2. Normal mode                    normal-index
   2.1. Text objects              objects
   2.2. Window commands           CTRL-W
   2.3. Square bracket commands   [
   2.4. Commands starting with 'g' g
   2.5. Commands starting with 'z' z
3. Visual mode                    visual-index
4. Command-line editing           ex-edit-index
5. EX commands                    ex-cmd-index
```

I can see under Normal mode a sublist that includes 2.2. Window commands, which seems interesting. So, let's see what commands Vim defines for windows (when inside NORMAL mode), by moving to the end of that line and running <C-]>, to enter that area of the help system (in future, we know we can get there by simply running :h CTRL-W).

Once there, we can scroll down the list, and we'll see items such as CTRL-W + and its associated description: "increase current window height N lines." Continue to poke around the Vim documentation, and you'll soon discover that it's one of the most useful things you can do to truly understand the full power and potential of Vim.

Key Binding Debug Example

To give you a practical example of how you might use these commands, I want to share a quick story of how they helped me recently.

I wanted to install a plug-in. This plug-in mapped some functionality to the <C-w>o binding. I wanted to make sure that this binding wasn't already set within Vim, and if so, to make sure it didn't do anything important that I would prefer to keep.

Initially, I ran the :map command, so I could see if it had already been mapped by another plug-in (or myself, and I just forgotten about it). It hadn't, so onto the next step. I then decided to look it up in the Vim help system, so I ran the :help index command, and looking through the "table of contents," I found what I was looking for:

```
2.2. Window commands        |CTRL-W|
```

The command I was researching is `<C-w>o`, and as it starts with the `CTRL-W` keystrokes, I knew this was the section I wanted to dive into. Pressing `<C-]>` over the words `CTRL-W` (as we saw before) took me directly to the relevant help section, where I started scrolling through the list until I saw the following:

```
|CTRL-W_CTRL-O|    CTRL-W CTRL-O      same as "CTRL-W o"
```

Again, this was what I was looking for, and so I followed the `CTRL-W_CTRL-O` link by pressing `<C-]>`, and there, I was directed to the help file for the command `:only`.

■ **Note**   The `:only` command closes all split windows until there is only one window left open.

To ensure the key binding did as it was described (in case I missed something when looking through `:map` and it had actually already been reassigned to a different action), I then opened three split windows and ran the command `<C-w>o`. It did indeed do what was described, and it closed all the subsequent splits until there was only one window left open.

I don't use the `:only` command that much, and so I didn't feel like the key mapping `<C-w>o` version offered me any improvement in speed over using the COMMAND-LINE mode version. Because of this, I was happy to give up the `<C-w>o` key binding to the plug-in I was about to install.

I hope that this short story has given you an example of how you can utilize the tools Vim provides to debug and analyze how your environment works, before installing a third-party plug-in that could potentially cause some confusing problems that are hard to debug after the plug-in has been installed.

Summary

OK, you've learned a lot in this chapter. We're finally starting to get to the meat of how Vim works. We covered all the core fundamental areas of Vim, such as

- Commands
- Buffers
- Windows
- Tabs
- Modes

This means we saw the different types of commands (COMMAND-LINE, commands aliased to specific key bindings, standard editing commands). We also took some time to consider the terminology I plan to use throughout the rest of this book.

We learned the role that buffers play in comparison to traditional editors, as well as the various different types of buffers (such as the [No Name] buffer and Scratch buffers).

While looking into Vim's COMMAND-LINE mode, we saw how to look back at our prompt's history, using both a static and dynamic form of history list (the dynamic list uses Vim's Command Line Window).

We also covered some of the different sources from which you can find help, and let's face it, we all need help at one time or another, so don't be afraid to ask questions if you have to.

Finally, we revisited how Vim key bindings work and learned an important lesson on how to use some of Vim's commands to debug where certain bindings are made and whether they'll affect us when installing certain plug-ins. We also discovered a good way to see *all* the default bindings that Vim implements.

CHAPTER 4

Files

In the previous chapter, you learned a lot about the fundamentals of Vim (commands, buffers, windows, tabs, editing modes, etc.), but before moving on to learning how you can edit files and their content, let's first review the multitude of ways you can utilize Vim to open and manage multiple files.

It may seem strange to dedicate an entire chapter to a topic such as this, but there are quite a few important concepts you can learn about Vim from considering its file capabilities.

For example, Vim offers us lots of tools to handle how we may want to manage our files, including the following:

- Various options for opening

- Ability to handle the many different scenarios of modified files and multiple file format types

- Options for how we might preview files in their native applications

- Multiple options for creating new files or reading content from another file into our current buffer, as well as for utilizing templates to load for specific file types

- Ability to modify our working directory from within Vim

Opening Files

Let's begin with the basics: opening files. Vim allows us to open files both from within Vim and from outside of Vim (by this, I mean before you've actually opened Vim). This can also be a single file or multiple files. If we specify multiple files, we can either enter the file names manually or have them dynamically injected by utilizing a pattern-matching algorithm with wildcard characters (more commonly known as a "glob").

To start the Vim process with a single file (e.g., file.txt) opened, you have to pass the file name as an argument to the vim command, as follows:

```
vim file.txt
```

If we wanted to open multiple files at once, we could manually specify them like so:

```
vim file1.txt file2.txt
```

Or we could be more efficient and specify a file glob that the shell will expand as it starts the Vim process (for example, vim *.txt). What I mean by "expand" is that it'll take something like *.txt, and if you had two files with an extension of txt, the shell would pass this through to Vim as file1.txt file2.txt (as if you had manually typed them, as in the preceding example).

53

Once you're within Vim, you still have the ability to open files, using the "edit" command (:e), followed by the path to the file. To open a file within Vim, you'll have to run the following command (the path can either be absolute or relative to the current working directory):

```
:e /path/to/your/file.txt
```

> **Note**   When using the edit command :e, if you press <Space> and then <C-d>, you'll be able to list all available directories/files (just in case you forget the structure of your project). Alternatively, you can simply run :e, followed by pressing the <Tab> key multiple times, to cycle through all available items. Either way, these two tips can save you from having to memorize the entire path to a file.

File Formats

Internally, Vim handles issues such as EOL (end of line) for us automatically. We don't need to be concerned about it, but it's worth understanding what Vim is doing "under the covers" when it encounters files from different systems.

When Vim reads a file to load into a buffer, it will try to determine the file system format, based on the EOL characters used by the file. For example, if we're on a Unix machine and we open a text file that was created on that system, the EOL character is a new-line character (NL for short).

See Table 4-1, which displays each of the different systems supported and their recognized EOL characters.

Table 4-1. *EOL Characters for Different Systems Types*

System	EOL
dos	<CR><NL> or <NL>
mac	<CR>
unix	<NL>

Vim lets us change the file format while we are editing it, by running the following command (subsequently changing the EOL to the other system's format):

```
:set fileformat=dos
```

Inserting Files

Vim has a powerful feature that lets us inject content from another file directly into our current buffer. This might not seem that useful at first, but when you consider that we're able to not only manually specify a file to load but also dynamically input content based on the result of a shell script, you can start to see that this is potentially a very powerful mechanism for editing files based on dynamic conditions.

To do a basic file load, we'll have to use Vim's :read command. This command works by accepting two arguments:

1. A set of options that allow us to control the file format and encoding (most of the time this isn't a concern)

2. A file path pointing to the file to be loaded

So, imagine that we have two files in our current directory: file1.txt and file2.txt. The content of file1.txt consists of the numbers 1–10 (each number is separated by a new line), and the content of file2.txt is: "Hello from file 2!" If we had file1.txt open with our cursor on line 5 and we then ran the following command:

```
:read file2.txt
```

we would find the contents of file2.txt placed on the line directly underneath our cursor (in this case: line 6). If, on the other hand, we modified the command slightly to include a range (in this case, we want to tell Vim to read the file content into a specific section of our file1.txt content), it would look something like the following command:

```
:8read file2.txt
```

The preceding command would result in the content of file2.txt being placed on the line directly below the line we specified (which, in this example, is line 8), so the content would be placed on line 9 of file1.txt.

Finally, and most interestingly, let's see how we can load content that resulted from executing a shell script. I have a list of dotfiles in my project's current directory, and I want to load those into my file1.txt file. To do this, I first need a shell script that will parse my directory for dotfiles and then return that list (see the following code snippet).

```
ls -a | grep '^\.' | grep --invert-match '\.DS_Store\|\.$'
```

This results in the following standard output to the terminal. (The preceding shell command filters out any dotfiles that match .DS_Store. These include Mac-specific directory files as well as directories that typically are displayed as a single period [.] character):

```
.gitignore
.ruby-version
```

Once we have this working shell script, we can incorporate it into Vim by utilizing its ! command, which lets us execute arbitrary shell commands, such as the one we've defined previously. This would look like the following command:

```
:read !ls -a | grep '^\.' | grep --invert-match '\.DS_Store\|\.$'
```

Effectively, we're putting our shell command directly after the ! character, and when we execute this command, Vim is placed in a background process while the shell command is executed. Once the shell command is finished, the resulting output is placed into our buffer, directly beneath our current cursor position.

Moving Between Files

When we have multiple files open (i.e., multiple buffers created), we need a way to move easily between them. This is done using Vim's suite of buffer commands.

- `:bn`: Allows us to move to the next buffer in the list, or we can specify a numeric value and move directly to that nth buffer. (For example, b5 would move us to the fifth buffer available. If the buffer didn't exist, Vim would display an error alerting us to this fact.)

- `:bp`: Works in exactly the same way as bn but in reverse. So, it allows us to move to the previous buffer in the list, or we can specify a numeric value and move directly to that nth buffer.

- `:ls`: Lets us list out all buffers that are available. You should notice a % character next to the current visible buffer and a # next to what Vim refers to as the "alternate" buffer. (This is the buffer you were in before the current buffer.)

- `:b#`: Is a convenience to let you move more quickly to the alternative buffer (because a lot of times, you'll find yourself jumping back and forth between two primary buffers). You can also use the key mapping <C-6> (or <C-^>, depending on your system).

- `:bf`: Takes us to the first buffer in the list

- `:bl`: Takes us to the last buffer in the list

- `:bm`: Takes us to the next modified buffer (which is useful in case you're reviewing all changes before carrying out a final write command)

There are many more buffer-related commands, some of which I'll cover in more detail in Chapter 12.

Saving Files

Note that the title of this section is "Saving Files." You'll probably have noticed that I have a habit of interchanging the word *buffers* and the more traditional *files*. It's best for beginners to always be explicit and to use the word *buffer*, as it cements the idea of how Vim actually modifies buffers and not files. It's easier, and OK, to talk to other developers in normal software terminology (such as "I need to save this file" as opposed to "I need to write the buffer"), as long as *you* know what it really means to "save a file." If you don't, then I would strongly recommend going back and reading Chapter 3, which should clarify how Vim works.

Let's look at a few different options for saving a file (which, as we should now know, really means we want to write our buffer back to the source file). The following command is known as the "write" command (we saw this in the last chapter when discussing how buffers work). It's fairly straightforward, in that it does what you would expect from its name, and writes the buffer content back to the source file.

`:w`

You can also choose to "save and close," by running the following composite command (by that I simply mean that we have combined two commands, the "write" command, :w, and the "quit" command, :q):

`:wq`

If you prefer something a little more concise (well, one character less), you can use the alternative :x command, which differs only slightly, in that it will only write the buffer when a modification is actually detected.

■ **Note** When writing this book I wasn't sure where to place this note, and in the end I settled on adding it within this chapter, as we're already starting to see a lot of Vim commands (although no commands yet related to actually editing content). The point I wanted to make you aware of is that all the commands I've shown you so far have either more concise or verbose variations. For example, the `:w` command can be written more explicitly as `:write`. If you look up any command within Vim's help files, you'll see all the different variations of a command, and you can be as explicit or implicit as you like. I usually prefer the more concise syntax.

Because commands are composable in Vim (i.e., you can construct more complex commands by stringing them together), if you have made lots of changes to a buffer but only want to write a specific section of those modifications, you can do so using a range.

For example, if we had a file with 10 lines of content and in which every line was modified in some way, we could choose to write only the changes on lines 5–9, by using the following command:

`:5,9wq`

It's important to realize that if you have one viewport but multiple buffers open, it might not be clear that you have other buffers open at the same time and if some of those hidden buffers have been modified or not. If you were to try and quit Vim while some buffers had unsaved modifications, Vim would complain by throwing an error at you. If this happens, there are a few options available to you.

1. Quit Vim and ignore any modified buffers (e.g., your changes will be lost). To do this, you would run the "quit all" command, followed by an exclamation mark, `:qa!`.

2. Write all modified buffers and then quit (this will still throw an error if some buffers are read-only or can't be written for some other reason). To do this, you would run the "write and quit all" command, `:wqa`.

3. Ask Vim to write all modified buffers but to let you know of any problems before attempting to quit. To do this, you would run the "write and quit all" command but precede it with the "confirm" command, `:conf wqa`.

4. Write all modified buffers, and override even those buffers that are read-only. To do this, you would run the "write and quit all" command, followed by an exclamation mark, `:wqa!`.

Creating New Files

If we want to create a new file in Vim, we'll have to create a buffer first and then write that buffer to a file path that doesn't yet exist. (Or if it does exist, be aware that Vim will ask you to confirm if you're sure you want to overwrite the existing file.)

As we saw in the previous chapter on the fundamentals of Vim, a fresh empty buffer is called a `[No Name]` buffer. Vim provides us with a few ways to create a new empty buffer. Let's review each of them.

- `:new`

- `:enew`

- `:vnew`

- `:tabnew`

■ **Note**   Each of these commands allows you to specify a file name. For example :new myfile.txt.

---

new

The :new command will create a new empty buffer within a horizontal split window, as demonstrated in Figure 4-1. There is also a key binding for this command, <C-w>n, but I personally prefer to use the COMMAND-LINE variation, as it's easier to remember.

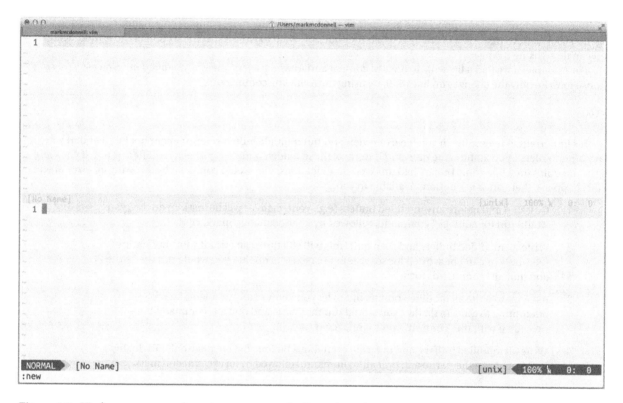

Figure 4-1. *Vim's :new command creates a new empty buffer within a horizontal split window*

enew

The :enew command also creates a new empty buffer, but within the current window/viewport. (It doesn't create a split.)

vnew

The :vnew command will create a new empty buffer within a vertical split window, as demonstrated in Figure 4-2. Oddly, there is no key binding provided by Vim for this command, although, as we'll see in Chapter 19, you can map your own custom key binding to make a shortcut for this command.

Figure 4-2. *Vim's* :vnew *command creates a new empty buffer within a vertical split window*

tabnew

The :tabnew command will create a new empty buffer within a new tab, as demonstrated in Figure 4-3. Again, there is no key mapping provided by Vim for this command, but as we've mentioned before, this doesn't prevent you from extending Vim to allow that.

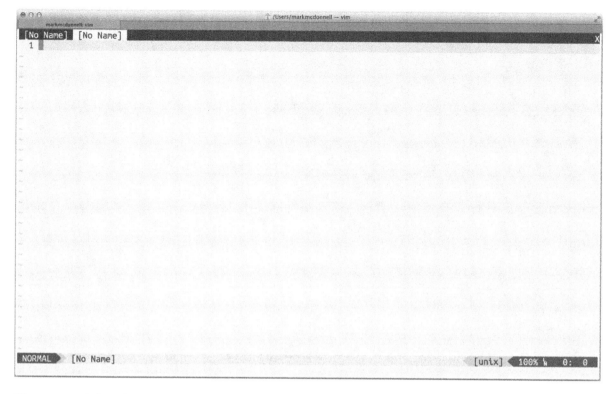

Figure 4-3. Vim's `:tabnew` command creates a new empty buffer within a new tab

Creating New Files from a Template

Vim provides the tools that let you utilize custom templates based on the type of file you happen to be working on. This can be implemented in both a static and dynamic fashion, meaning that you can just have a standard template file that Vim loads automatically, based on the file type, and you edit it from there, *or* you can utilize some VimL to implement a more dynamic template in which certain values are replaced from the results of certain expressions.

■ **Note**   I personally have found that I don't have much use for dynamic templates. That's not to say they aren't useful, but to write your own (or to adapt from an existing script), they require a fair amount of VimL knowledge. I find the standard static templates more than sufficient for my needs, and so I'll only be demonstrating this variation. If you are interested in the dynamic variation, there are many plug-ins that extend Vim to allow this, or you can review the following script that demonstrates the principles of the following technique: `http://vim.wikia.com/wiki/Use_eval_to_create_dynamic_templates`.

So, to see an example of a static template implementation, you will have to make some changes to your `.vimrc` file. The following is an example that automatically loads a `skeleton.html` file when opening a new HTML file inside Vim (e.g., if you were to run a command such as `:new test.html`):

```
autocmd BufNewFile  *.html   Or ~/skeleton.html
```

As you can imagine, this will require you to add a `skeleton.html` file within the `~/ HOME` directory (as seen in the preceding configuration code). I created the `skeleton.html` file and added the content "Hello!" inside of it. Now, when I run the command `:new test.html`, Vim opens a horizontal split window with the content of my `~/skeleton.html` file preloaded inside of it (see Figure 4-4). This is an incredibly useful feature and one that can really save me a lot of time, considering that when I work on a specific file type (such as an HTML web page), chances are I'll start from the same baseline boilerplate code and modify it from there.

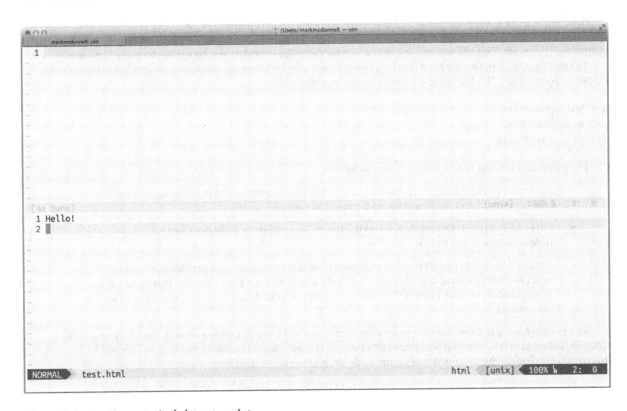

Figure 4-4. *Creating a static skeleton template*

You could also modify the preceding configuration code so that it loaded a specific template for a specific file name. For example, when I write a class in Ruby code, I might find I usually have the same boilerplate layout (a constructor, attributes for reading/writing, etc.). I wouldn't want that type of template to be loaded every time I created a new `.rb` file, but only when creating a file named `ruby_class.rb`. I could change the configuration file to allow that, like so:

```
autocmd BufNewFile ruby_class.rb   or ~/ruby_class_template.rb
```

Creating a Scratch Buffer

You've already read, in the previous chapter, what a "scratch buffer" is. It's a buffer whose sole purpose is to be disposable. By this I mean, if you wanted to create a buffer exclusively for writing some pseudo-code or brain dumping some thoughts (but you didn't want to save that buffer), you might think to create a [No Name] buffer to add your content and then, when you're finished, just quit (:q). But if you do this, Vim will ask you to confirm if you're sure you want to quit (which can be annoying more often than not).

Also, Vim will try to store the buffer in a hidden file (in case of corruption), yet you really don't care about this content you're writing, as you have no intention of keeping it. That's where a scratch buffer comes in handy. It's utterly disposable. If you quit, Vim will instantly close it and won't attempt to bother you by asking for a confirmation.

To create a scratch buffer, we have first to create a new buffer and then set some specific attributes that convert our buffer accordingly. The following are the three settings we need:

```
:set buftype=nofile
:set bufhidden=hide
:setlocal noswapfile
```

The preceding settings can be broken down as follows:

- buftype=nofile: Changes the buffer so that Vim understands that it is not related to any file (i.e., it's empty) and never will be, so it cannot be written

- bufhidden=hide: Tells Vim that, when the buffer isn't visible in a window, not to unload/delete it, just hide it

- noswapfile: Tells Vim not to use a swapfile (remember: swapfiles are provided by Vim in order to prevent corruption of content), but if we're creating a scratch buffer that is meant to be disposable, we don't care if the buffer is corrupted or lost, as we have no intention of saving the content

Rather than having to remember these settings every time you want to create a scratch buffer, there is already a plug-in, called scratch.vim, that automates this for you. (I cover plug-ins such as this one, in Chapter 17.) This particular plug-in gives you two new commands for opening scratch buffers.

- :Scratch: This creates a scratch buffer (with the name __Scratch__) in the current window.

- :Sscratch: This (and, no, that's not a typo, it's definitely a capital S followed by a lowercase s) creates a scratch buffer (with the name __Scratch__) in a horizontal split window.

File Name Modifiers

I want to show you a useful feature of Vim called *file name modifiers*. These are a bit of an advanced topic this early on in your Vim learning, so I don't want to go into too much depth about them at this stage, but as you're learning about files and how to utilize them within Vim, I think it's important that you're at least aware of these modifiers and why they're useful. (If you're eager, see :h filename-modifiers for complete details.) So, let's take a look at a couple of examples.

Previewing Files

With the help of the Mac's open command, we can utilize some small amount of VimL code to help us preview our files in their default applications. Imagine we have the following HTML file:

```
<!doctype html>
<html lang="en" dir="ltr">
    <head>
        <title>Foo</title>
    </head>
    <body>
        Bar
    </body>
</html>
```

If we wanted to view this file in our web browser, we would have first to open up our browser of choice (my personal favorite is Google's Chrome web browser: www.google.co.uk/chrome) and then, using its interface, locate the file on our computer and open the file. This might not sound like a slow process, but it can be made much quicker and easier by opening the file within our browser directly from Vim.

To do this, we have to use a VimL feature called a file name modifier. It takes the form of %{:option}, and there are a few different options available (the % gives us the name of the current file). The option we're interested in is :p. What this particular option does is convert the current file name into a fully qualified directory path (e.g., it'll turn index.html into /Users/markmcdonnell/Code/index.html).

If you have a file open in Vim (let's imagine it's the index.html file found inside a "Code" folder inside my HOME directory), then running the command :echo expand('%:p') will display back in the command prompt of Vim /Users/markmcdonnell/Code/index.html.

The way this works is that we use echo to display a message in the command prompt. The message that is displayed is the result of using VimL's expand function (see :h expand for details) and passing it the argument %:p. If we echo'ed expand('%') (notice we didn't use the :p file name modifier option), that would have displayed only the name of the file index.html and not its full path.

Note The reason we need the expand function is because we want to display content using the echo function. If we're just passing the value onto another command, we don't have to use the expand function (as you'll see in the following code example).

But as you'll see from the following command, we need the full path to the file, so that we can tell our web browser to open the file (and thus preview it appropriately):

```
:!open -a Google\ Chrome.app %:p
```

As you can see from the proceeding example, we're utilizing a ! character (which I'll discuss further in Chapter 20). This puts Vim into a background process and passes whatever commands follow it over to the shell to execute.

Note Vim evaluates any VimL expression *first*, before passing a command through to the shell. If we look at the previous code example, %:p is a VimL feature, and it would throw an error if we tried to execute that within the shell environment.

So, the command that is sent to the shell to execute is `open -a Google\ Chrome.app /Users/markmcdonnell/ Code/index.html`. This should, I hope, start to look familiar to you, as we're using the Mac's open command along with the `-a` option to tell it to look for the application Google Chrome. After that, we pass through the URL for the Chrome web browser to open. We could also have avoided specifying an application and let the operating system use whatever default application is assigned to handling HTML files, like so: `:!open %:p`.

Switching Working Directories

Now that we have a bit of an understanding of what file name modifiers are in Vim, we can look at another way to take advantage of them. In this example, we'll look at how we can change the working directory of our project while we're already inside Vim.

Let's quickly clarify what the problem is that we're trying to solve. If we are inside the folder `~/Code/ProjectA/` and we open Vim (let's also assume we have some files from `ProjectA` open as well at this point), then Vim's working directory will be `ProjectA`. Meaning, if we decide that we need to find some content that we know is inside another project directory (e.g., `~/Code/ProjectB/`), we won't be able to do that without either restarting Vim from within the `ProjectB` folder, finding the file and then jumping back to `ProjectA`, *or* opening a new shell and running Vim from the `ProjectB` folder and finding the file we're after. (A real-world example for me is that I need to find a snippet of code I know I've used in another project, and so I want to copy it over to this project.)

Ideally, we would like to temporarily change the working directory while still inside the `ProjectA` folder, so we could find the file in `ProjectB` and then change the working directory back again to `ProjectA`. Using a combination of file name modifiers and Vim's built-in `cd` command, this is not only possible but allows us to implement in a much simpler way. First, take a look at the following command:

```
:cd ~/Code/ProjectB
```

The preceding command does exactly what we need. We have now successfully changed the working directory so that Vim thinks we're inside `ProjectB`. If we were to run the command `:pwd`, we'd now see that. From here, I can now find the file I'm after, and then once I have the `ProjectB` file open, I can use the same command as before to take me back to the previous working directory (e.g., `:cd ~/Code/ProjectA`).

At the moment (unless you are a mind reader and already know what I'm about to show you), it's arguably quicker and easier just to type in `:cd ~/Code/ProjectA`. But what if the directory path we wanted to jump back to was much longer (as is the case in most real-world scenarios)?

Imagine, instead, that the directory we needed to jump back to was more like this: `/User/markmcdonnell/ Dropbox/Library/Projects/Node/FooBar/`. (With the exception of the FooBar part, that's a real directory for me.) Now that's a little bit more awkward to type, and very likely along the way, I'll type it incorrectly (especially if I'm trying to do it fast). This is where the use of file name modifiers can come in handy. If we go back to the original example, we know that we have a few `ProjectA` files already open. If I open up one of those `ProjectA` buffers, I can then run the following command instead:

```
:cd %:p:h
```

What the preceding command does is change the directory to the result of the `%:p:h`. We already know that `%` gives us the file name and that the option `:p` converts that into a full path to the file. From there, we use the `:h` option to then give us back the full path, but minus "head" (which is the file name), so that we end up with the following: `/Users/markmcdonnell/Code/ProjectA`.

■ **Note** There is also a `:lcd` command, which is the same as `:cd` but only changes the working directory for the current window.

Summary

Although I might not have delved too deeply into some of the file features available within Vim, I have covered a lot of important topics. Let's quickly recap some of them.

- We looked at how to open files from outside Vim, using globs/wildcards, and how to manipulate the :e command within Vim, using certain keyboard shortcuts.

- I discussed how Vim handles certain file formats across different operating systems and how to dynamically change those values by resetting the fileformat option.

- We saw how to inject content both manually and dynamically (by combining the read command with the ! command), which provides very powerful tools to construct data on the fly for us to manipulate within Vim.

- We looked at how to navigate Vim's open buffers. You'll use these commands a lot, and so it's crucial that you start learning about them now.

- You learned the many ways to create and write files (including splitting them into different window splits and tabs, as well as dynamically loading boilerplate skeleton templates based on the type of file you're creating).

- We saw how to create scratch buffers to quickly and efficiently create content deemed to be completely deposable and, more important, secure it from being stored accidentally by swapfiles or backup processes.

- Finally, we looked at Vim's powerful file name modifiers feature and different examples of how we might want to utilize it.

CHAPTER 5

Commands

In this chapter, we'll be looking at Vim's editing capabilities. This is where we finally get to use Vim for its primary function: editing and manipulating text-based content.

What may be surprising to some users is that the commands for editing content are probably the least of what it means to be an advanced Vim user. Although what you learn in this chapter will be fundamental to using Vim, the things you've learned before this point, and the things you will learn after, share equal importance and usefulness when we require more from Vim than just straight text-editor functionality.

Vim's strength is in the fact that it can sit between two different worlds: one in which it's an extremely lightweight editing tool, and one in which it is extensible to cater to more advanced users. My own opinion is that Vim would become too diluted to be useful if it became just about editing. My workflow requires more features than just a text editor, but not so much that I feel like I need something extremely granular, like Emacs.

Note The question of Vim being too simple or too complex is actually a really tough discussion point for those users who aren't sure whether they should be using Vim or something like Emacs. Emacs focuses on being an entire suite of tools, whereas Vim was designed around the very lightweight Vi text editor, and extra features were added on top to allow users to better integrate more advanced workflows. As we'll see later (in Chapter 17), the extensibility of Vim has meant that it straddles that confused line of lightweight and full-fat IDE. Most Emacs users started as Vim users and decided their usage was so extreme that Emacs was the next logical choice.

Editing Commands

Commands for editing content are used primarily within NORMAL mode. These commands are made up of counts, operators, and motions. As Vim doesn't distinguish between different command types (by that, I mean the documentation simply refers to operators and motions, and a generic term of "commands" to encapsulate them), I typically refer to these types of commands as "editing commands."

Let's now analyze the structure of an editing command, to see how we would construct our own command to be run. In the following code snippet, we'll see a square bracket. These brackets denote an optional value (meaning you don't have to provide one), and the pipe character (|) denotes that you can use either one of the options listed.

```
[count] {operator} {[count] motion|text object}
```

Hmm, OK, there's a lot going on here, so I'll clarify further.

- An editing command can be considered a "container" of counts, operators, and motions or text objects.

- In the preceding command structure, we can see that a command can start with a "count" (which is an optional numerical value) and is used to indicate how many times the following operator is executed.

- Either a "motion" or a "text object" can follow the operator, and if it is a motion, it can also accept a preceding optional count, which informs Vim how many times the motion should be applied.

■ **Note**   Later on in this chapter, when we look at how text objects work, we'll see that they also accept a motion, but one I've given the name "special motion," as they aren't quite the same.

Table 5-1 tries to again break down the different terminology of what constitutes a command. One of the best ways to learn how commands really work is to memorize the command structure (as we've seen already in the preceding code snippet).

Table 5-1. *List of Parts That Make Up an Editing Command*

Title	Explanation
Command	A generic term used to group/contain the following items
Count	An optional numerical value to indicate number of executions
Operator	The command to be executed
Motion	The direction the operator should be applied
Text Object	The area the operator should be applied to

If we look at the command structure again, we can see that an editing command has many different permutations. As an example we could

- Execute an operator with or without a motion (some operators are useless without a motion, but we'll come back to that).

- Execute an operator with or without a text object.

- Execute an operator with or without a count.

- Execute an operator with a count and a motion with a count.

- Execute an operator without a count but a motion with a count.

On and on it goes. But it's important to realize that there are many types of operators and motions, and although most of them work fine by themselves, some of them do need each other to work. In the next couple of sections, we'll be looking at some useful operators and motions and also see which ones need to work together.

■ **Note** Anytime you find yourself confused about how an editing command should work, I recommend sticking the preceding code structure into a Vim cheat sheet and to use that structure as a reference.

Operators

At this point, we've reviewed a bit about the structure and component parts of an editing command. Let's now take a look at the different operators that Vim implements and see which ones work with editing (and so allow us to manipulate the content of the buffer in different ways) and which ones work in different areas (such as searching the buffer content or repeating previous edits).

As we now know, operators can be used by themselves or alongside motions (we'll look at motions in the next section). Let's see a quick example of an operator that works by itself. One such example would be the x operator. This particular operator is assigned the action of "cutting" the content underneath the cursor (effectively removing it from the buffer). Let's now see this operator in action. Imagine you have the following content:

```
This is some example text
in a plain text document.
```

If your cursor were at the start of the document, it would effectively be sitting on top of the *T* from the word *This*. If at that point (I'm going to assume—unless I say otherwise—that we're in NORMAL mode when executing these commands) I pressed the x key, triggering the associated "cut" action, then the contents of my buffer would change to look like the following content (notice the first capital *T* is now gone):

```
his is some example text
in a plain text document.
```

Table 5-2 provides a short list of useful operators. This is by no means an exhaustive list, but I do find myself using a lot of them in my daily workflow.

Table 5-2. *List of Operators*

Operator	Explanation
yy	Yanks (i.e., copies) the entire line
p	Pastes content after the current cursor position
P	Pastes content before the current cursor position
i	Puts you into INSERT mode before the current cursor position
a	Puts you into INSERT mode after the current cursor position
f	Finds specified character to the right of current cursor position
t	Same as f but searches *until* the specified character
o	Moves cursor to the next line and enters INSERT mode
O	Moves cursor to the previous line and enters INSERT mode
x	Cuts the character (or the selection of characters)
s	Substitutes the character (or the selection of characters)
S	Substitutes the entire line
u	Undoes the last edit
~	Swaps character casing (e.g., converts a to A)
.	Repeats the last INSERT edit
dd	Deletes the current line
D	Deletes from the cursor until the end of the line (same as d$)
gx	Opens the URL under your cursor in a web browser

Examples: Operators

We're going to demonstrate examples from the list of operators in Table 5-2 above. The following content is what we'll be using to run our commands against (our cursor will be placed at the start of the first line for each example):

```
This is some example text
in a plain text document.
```

I only specify the content once (above), because I assume that if you're playing along at home (and I would highly recommend that you do), at the end of each example, you'll put any edited content back to its unedited form, so you can start the next example afresh.

- yy: This operator will copy the entire first line into multiple "registers" such as the unnamed, numbered, and selection registers (we'll cover this in more detail in Chapter 6), but effectively, we have the ability to now paste this copied content.

- p: If we had the content "abc" inside our clipboard ready to be pasted, this operator would result in the first word *This* becoming *Tabchis*.

- P: If we had the content "abc" inside our clipboard ready to be pasted, then this operator would result in the first word *This* becoming *abcThis*.

- i: This operator will drop us into INSERT mode, so that we can start adding content (new content is added behind the current cursor position). If I press this command and type "abc," then the first line will now start *abcThis* . . .

- a: This operator will drop us into INSERT mode, so that we can start adding content (new content is added after the current cursor position). If I press this command and type "abc," then the first line will now start *Tabchis* . . .

- f: This operator requires an additional character (not a motion). If we ran fe, the cursor would be placed at the letter *e* on the word *some*.

- t: This operator requires an additional character (not a motion). If we ran te, the cursor would be placed at the letter *m* on the word *some* (as it moves the cursor *until* the specified character).

- o: This operator creates a new line under the current line and enters into INSERT mode automatically.

- O: This operator creates a new line above the current line and enters into INSERT mode automatically.

- x: This operator cuts the current letter under the cursor (or selection), so that it's removed from the buffer. This would result in the first word *This* becoming *his* (you stay in NORMAL mode after the command has been completed).

- s: This operator is the same as x but enters you into INSERT mode after the letter (or selection) has been removed. This is so you can begin to type and "substitute" the removed content with some new content.

- S: This operator is similar to the s operator but is closer in result to executing a command such as c$, which deletes the entire line and places the cursor into INSERT mode, ready to add new content.

- u: This operator executes an undo request on the last edit/change made to the buffer. So, if I pressed x to cut the letter *T* from the first word *This* (subsequently changing it to be *his*), I could press u to undo that change, and the word would change back to *This*.

- ~: This operator swaps the casing of the letter under the cursor (or selection). So, if I pressed ~, the letter *T* from the first word, *This* would be transformed to lowercase, and the word subsequently would change to *this*.

- .: This operator repeats the last editing command. So, if I ran the command d2w (to delete two words), the first line would read *some example text*. If I were to press the . key, the same d2w command would be repeated, and so the first line would then read *text*.

- dd: This operator deletes the entire line, meaning that if we have a three-line file and we execute dd on line 2, line 3 will become the new line 2.

- D: This operator deletes from the current cursor position until the end of the line.

Motions

Motions allow you to dictate the direction of an operation. Some motions can be run without any operator (for example, w is a motion that moves the cursor forward word-by-word, and so it works fine on its own), and some motions explicitly require an operator before they will work (for example, d is a delete command, but it won't delete anything until it has been provided a motion to tell it which direction it should start deleting).

Following are some different motions that you can use (this is by no means an exhaustive list, but you should find these are the typical motions you'll end up using). If you want a full list of motions, I would suggest searching through the help documentation starting with :h motions.

Table 5-3. *List of Motions*

Motion	Explanation
0	Moves cursor to the start of the line
$	Moves cursor to the end of the line (inclusive of newline)
g_	Moves cursor to the end of the line (exclusive of newline)
b	Moves cursor backward through each word
e	Moves cursor to the end of the word
w	Moves cursor to the start of the next word
gg	Moves cursor to the start of the buffer
G	Moves cursor to the end of the buffer
%	Moves cursor to the next bracket (or parenthesis)
(	Moves cursor to the previous sentence
)	Moves cursor to the next sentence
{	Moves cursor to the start of a paragraph
}	Moves cursor to the end of a paragraph
[(	Moves cursor to previous available parenthesis
])	Moves cursor to next available parenthesis
[{	Moves cursor to previous available bracket
]}	Moves cursor to next available bracket

■ **Note**   Some operators and motions have different meanings when run within the COMMAND-LINE mode. For example, % refers to the entire file. So when used alongside an operator such as d (delete), we can use it as a shortcut to delete the entire contents of the buffer, like so: :%d. Also, the dot/period character refers to the current line number when used in COMMAND-LINE mode. So you can use it (for example) to delete from the current line to the start of the file, by passing it as part of a range :.,0d.

Examples: Motions

We're going to demonstrate examples from the list of motions in Table 5-3. The following content is what we'll be using to run our commands against (our cursor will be placed at the start of the first line for each example):

```
// This is a programming file
// I use it because it's the best way
// to run motions against punctionation
// such as (), [], {}, <>
function thisIsAnExample(collection) {
    return collection.map(function(item) { return item * 2 })
}
var hash = { foo: 1, baz: { qux: 2 }}
console.log(thisIsAnExample([1, 2, 3])) // => [2, 4, 6]
```

I only specify the content once (preceding), because I assume that if you're playing along at home (and I would highly recommend that you do), at the end of each example, you'll put any edited content back to its unedited form, so that you can start the next example afresh.

- 0: This motion moves our cursor to the start of the current line. So, if we move down to line 5 and run f(, this will move our cursor to the first opening parenthesis. From here, we can then press 0 to take our cursor back to the first column (which would be the *f* of *function*).

- $: This motion moves our cursor to the end of the current line. So, if we run that operator, it'll move our cursor so that it sits on the *e* of *file*.

- g_: This motion is very similar to $ but can be more useful if you're trying to copy from the current cursor position to the end of the line. This is because $ includes the newline, whereas g_ doesn't. So, if we run fp, this will move our cursor to the first *p* of *programming*. If we were to then run vg_x, this would select (v) to the end of the line (g_) and then cut (x) the selected content. But compare that to v$x, and you'll notice that because $ includes the newline character at the end of the line, we end up with the second line moving up to the first, which isn't what we want. Hence, using g_ is more useful in instances in which you need to yank or edit to the end of a line.

- b: This motion moves the cursor back by one word boundary. If I move the cursor to the end of the line, using the motion $ and then press b, the cursor will be placed on the letter *t* of the word *text*.

- e: This motion moves the cursor to the end of a word boundary. If we run 5e, the cursor will be placed at the last *g* of the word programming. The first e moved the cursor to the end of the //; the second moved to the *s* of *this*; the third moved to the *s* of *is*; the fourth moved to the *a*; and the fifth moved to the last *g* of *programming*.

- w: This motion is similar to e but moves to the start of the next word. So, 5w would move the cursor to the *f* of *file* (we're already on the first character of the sentence, so // isn't counted as part of this command).

- gg: This motion will move the cursor to the first line of the buffer. We can also specify a count before this motion, and that will mean we move the cursor to that specific line. For example, 5gg will move the cursor to line 5.

- G: This motion will move the cursor to the last line of the buffer. We can also specify a count before this motion, and that will mean we move the cursor to that specific line. For example, 5G will move the cursor to line 5 (same as the gg motion).

- %: This motion moves to the next block syntax available (these being ( ), { }, and [ ]). If we move to line 5 using 5gg and then press %, the cursor will move to the opening parenthesis (character. If we press % again, it'll move to the closing parenthesis character). Repeated pressing of % at this point will jump back and forth between the parentheses. If we move the cursor past the closing parenthesis and press %, it'll look for the next block syntax, which, in this instance, is the { character (% searches forward if there is more than one block syntax on the line). If we now press % again, we'll see we jump down to line 7, where the closing } character sits.

- (: This motion moves the cursor to the previous sentence boundary. (This could be the end of the sentence or the start of a sentence.)

-): This motion moves the cursor to the next sentence boundary. (This could be the end of the sentence or the start of a sentence.)

- {: this motion moves the cursor to the previous paragraph boundary. (This could be the end of the paragraph or the start of a paragraph.)

- }: This motion moves the cursor to the previous paragraph boundary. (This could be the end of the paragraph or the start of a paragraph.)

- [(: This motion moves the cursor to the previous opening parenthesis. If we move to line 9 using 9gg and inside the Array [1, 2, 3] using f2, from here, we can test this motion. Running [(will move the cursor to the previous ((i.e., ([1, 2, 3])). Running [(again will now move the cursor to the (of the outer pair of brackets (i.e., console.log()).

-]): This motion moves the cursor to the next closing parenthesis. If we move to line 9 using 9gg and inside the Array [1, 2, 3] using f2, from here, we can test this motion. Running [) will move the cursor to the next) (i.e., ([1, 2, 3])). Running [) again will now move the cursor to the) of the outer pair of brackets (i.e., console.log()).

- [{: This motion moves the cursor to the previous opening curly bracket. If we move to line 8 using 8gg and inside the inner set of brackets using f2, from here, we can test this motion. Running [{ will move the cursor to the previous { (which is the inner set of brackets { qux: 2 }). Running [{ again will now move the cursor to the { of the outer pair of brackets.

-]}: This motion moves the cursor to the next closing curly bracket. If we move to line 8 using 8gg and inside the inner set of brackets using f2, from here, we can test this motion. Running]} will move the cursor to the next } (which is the closing bracket for the inner set of brackets { qux: 2 }). Running]} again will now move the cursor to the } of the outer pair of brackets.

■ **Note** Another motion that is related to the COMMAND-LINE mode is :{n}, which allows you to specify a line number to jump to (similar to {n}gg).

Examples: Operators That Require Motions or Other Commands

Table 5-4 provides some examples of different operators that require either motions or other commands to work.

Table 5-4. *List of Operators That Require a Motion*

Operator	Explanation
v	Puts you into VISUAL mode, so that you can start a selection
V	Selects the entire line
y	Yanks (i.e., copies) the selected text
d	Deletes the character (or the selection of characters)
c	Changes the character (or the selection of characters)
gu	Lowercases the character (or the selection of characters)
gU	Uppercases the character (or the selection of characters)

We're going to demonstrate examples from the list of operators (that require a motion to work) in Table 5-4 (preceding). The following content is what we'll be using to run our commands against (our cursor will be placed at the start of the first line for each example):

```
This is some example text
in a plain text document.
```

I only specify the content once (preceding), because I assume that if you're playing along at home (and I would highly recommend that you do), at the end of each example, you'll put any edited content back to its unedited form, so that you can start the next example afresh.

- v: This operator allows us to select content. If we press v and then press e, we will have visually selected the first word of the first sentence: *This*.

- V: This operator selects the entire line (including the newline at the end of the line, which means that using 0vg_ is sometimes preferred).

- y: This operator yanks (i.e., copies) the selection into multiple "registers," such as the unnamed and numbered registers (I'll cover this in more detail in Chapter 6). If you press v to select the current character under the cursor (which would be the *T* from *This*) and then press y, you'll be able to check the registers (by running :reg).

- d: This operator deletes the specified range of content. If we press d2w, then we're telling Vim to delete (d) two (2) words (w), which would change the first line to be *some example text*.

- c: This operator changes the specified range of content. If we press c2w and type "abc," then we're telling Vim to change (c) two (2) words (w) (and by change, we mean "remove so we can replace them with something else"), which would change the first line to *abc some example text*.

- gu: This operator converts the selection into lowercase. If we press gue, the word *This* will be transformed to *this*.

- gU: This operator converts the selection into uppercase. If we press gUe, the word *This* will be transformed to *THIS*.

Examples: Operators Combined with Motions

Table 5-5 provides a few examples of different operators and motions used together.

Table 5-5. *Examples of Operators That Are Combined with Motions*

Command	Explanation
3e	Moves cursor to the end of the third word
3w	Moves cursor to the start of the fourth word
2G	Moves cursor to the second line of the buffer (could also use 2gg)

We're going to demonstrate examples from the list of operators (that are optionally combined with motions) in Table 5-5 (preceding). The following content is what we'll be using to run our commands against (our cursor will be placed at the start of the first line for each example):

```
This is some example text
in a plain text document.
```

I only specify the content once (preceding), because I assume that if you're playing along at home (and I would highly recommend that you do), at the end of each example, you'll put any edited content back to its unedited form, so you can start the next example afresh.

- 3e: This command moves the cursor to the end of the third word boundary, which would be the *e* of *some*.

- 3w: This command moves the cursor to the start of the fourth word boundary, which would be the *e* of *example*. (This doesn't take into account the word boundary the cursor is already on; hence, we move three times after the first word *This*.)

- 2G: This command moves us to the second line of the buffer.

I've not covered many (or even complex) variations of combining different operators and motions, because I want to leave that as an exercise for the reader. I could give a thousand examples, but it wouldn't help you as much as playing around with the different permutations yourself. The best thing to do is to memorize the syntax structure (see following), as that is your primary reference for constructing complex editing commands.

```
[count] {operator} {[count] motion|text object}
```

There's More Than One Way to Skin a Cat

What makes editing commands so confusing for a lot of Vim users is that they forget the "editing command" structure. This structure allows us to achieve the same result but in different ways. This is because there are two sets of "counts" that you can provide as part of the overall command (one for the operator, and one for the motion).

I know we've only just finished looking at some example operators and motions, but "there is no time like the present," and I would like to provide just one quick example of how you can achieve a result in two different ways, thanks to the multiple counts we have available to construct a command with. (It's also a good chance to recap the command syntax structure we looked at near the start of this chapter and to ensure you've not forgotten it already!)

Imagine you have the following content (it's a file with two lines of text):

```
This is some example text
in a plain text document.
```

If your cursor was at the start of the document, it would effectively be sitting on top of the *T* from the word *This*. If you wanted to delete the first two words of the document (that being *This is*), then you could achieve that in two different ways:

1. 2dw

2. d2w

In the first example, we have constructed our command using the following structure:

```
[count] {operator} {motion}
```

In the second example, we have constructed our command using a similar but different structure (we've not supplied a count to the operator, but we have supplied a count to the motion).

```
{operator} [count] {motion}
```

I guess the point I would like to get across to you now (and if it wasn't clear before, then I hope after this chapter it will be) is that commands in Vim are composite, meaning we can create different side effects (i.e., changes), based on how we construct the parts of a command.

If I were to reuse the second example but now add a count of 4 to the operator, like so: 4d2w, this would give us the following command structure:

```
[count] {operator} [count] {motion}
```

Executing that command would leave us with a buffer whose content was *text document.* To clarify how this works, I'll break down the command executed by Vim into chunks, so that it's easier to understand the flow.

- Our command 4d2w, if said in English, would equate to: "I want you to delete two words and then repeat that action four times." It's as if Vim wrapped the action following the count (the action in this case being d2w) inside parentheses, so that it was grouped (much like in mathematics, wherein you group symbols together so that they are evaluated first).

- So, the first time d2w was executed, we deleted the words *This is* (remember that the w motion includes whitespace after each word).

- The second time d2w was executed, we then deleted the words *some example* .

- The third time d2w was executed, we then deleted the words *text in* .(Note that Vim was able to move to the next line to find the second word, as *text* was the only word left on the first line by that point.)

- Finally, the fourth time d2w was executed, we deleted the words *a plain* , leaving us with a one-line file consisting of the words *text document.*

■ **Note**　You can follow the preceding step-by-step process by executing the command d2w and then using the . operator to repeat that edit again and again, until you reach the final step.

Command Inversion

Some commands and motions have an exact opposite. We've actually seen this already when we looked at the p and P operators. The p operator pastes content *after* the cursor, whereas the P operator pastes content *before* the cursor.

Consider the f operator, which is used to search for a character on the current line (ahead of where the cursor currently sits). Again, let's imagine we have a text file with the following content:

```
This is my text. This is quite nice.
```

If my cursor was currently on the period character ., and I was to run the command ft, the cursor would move forward from its current position to the next lowercase *t* it could find (which would be inside the word *quite*). As you can see, the f operator is case sensitive, so it ignored the capital *T* from the word *This*.

If, on the other hand, I ran the command Ft (note that I'm now using a capital F for the operator, rather than a lowercase one), this would inverse the operator, so that it searched *backward* from the current cursor position (rather than searching forward). This would mean the first *t* found would be the character directly behind the period. In this case, the last *t* in the word *text*.

Nearly all operators have an inverse version. Another (but not as obvious) example is the r operator, which replaces a single character. If you used the capital R instead, you would be placed inside REPLACE mode; but the side effect of this mode is that you would end up replacing multiple characters (rather than just a single character).

It's worth experimenting with different operators, to see how they react. If you're unsure whether an operator has an inverse, the simplest thing to do is to search for the inverse character in the Vim help files.

Two other operators (with inverses) that I use a lot are a and i. You may remember that a allows us to start appending new content after the current cursor position, whereas A moves the cursor to the end of the line, where you can start appending more content. Similarly, you may remember that the i operator is used to insert content before the current cursor position; whereas I places the cursor at the start of the line, ready for content to be inserted.

Cursor Movement

Vim provides a primary set of motions for Vim called "home row keys" (Table 5-6). The reason it does this is because not all environments in which you will run Vi/Vim will have access to arrow keys.

Table 5-6. *List of Cursor Motions*

Command	Explanation
h	Moves the cursor one column to the left
j	Moves the cursor one row down
k	Moves the cursor one row up
l	Moves the cursor one column to the right

Another reason why it can be beneficial to practice using the home row keys (instead of the standard arrow keys) is that they are designed to allow for minimum hand and wrist movement, while still providing a wide range of access to the rest of the keyboard (reducing what's commonly known as "repetitive strain injury").

We can see the four keys defined in Table 5-6 (preceding). The use of these keys is considered the best-practice way to move your cursor around when you are using Vim. Although, I prefer just to use the arrow keys, I'm sure there are Vim purists who'll protest loudly about this opinion. Remember, however, that you're free to make your own decisions about what works best for you.

You may also hear Vim purists say (usually after telling you that you should be strict on yourself and only use the home row keys to navigate Vim) that after a few days, you should be accustomed to using the home row keys. My issue with this "advice" is twofold.

1. The home row keys don't work in tmux (not without extra configuration, and you're not going to want to do that every time you jump on a new remote server), and they also don't work at all within the terminal, which is where I work almost exclusively. Because of this, I've become very efficient at using the arrow keys, and that means while I'm not in Vim, my efficiency stays at a peak.

2. It's just advice, not a rule. Yet most purists believe there is some actual laws about how you use Vim, and if you don't follow those laws, you are somehow a less advanced user. Again, just to nail this idea home, you're completely free to use Vim in whatever way suits you.

It's very annoying having the power of the home keys within Vim, only to have to stop using them the moment you leave Vim. My workflow requires me to drop in and out of Vim on a very regular basis, so being super strict on myself to use the home row keys is a bit pointless, and you may find yourself in a similar situation. I recommend having an open mind and using whatever works best for you.

■ **Note** The naming of these keys originally stems from what touch typists traditionally refer to as the "home row" of the keyboard.

Page Movement

Rather than moving up and down a file line by line, we have much more granular movements available to us. Table 5-7 lists these options.

Table 5-7. *List of Page Movement Commands*

Command	Explanation
<C-u>	Move half page up
<C-d>	Move half page down
<C-b>	Move one page up
<C-f>	Move one page down
zt	Shifts page content so current line sits at the top of the viewport
zb	Shifts page content so current line sits at the bottom of the viewport
zz	Shifts page content so current line sits at the middle of the viewport
H	Moves cursor to the top of the viewport
M	Moves cursor to the middle of the viewport
L	Moves cursor to the bottom of the viewport

One recommendation I would make at this stage is for you to avoid having the following configuration option set within your .vimrc file:

```
set scrolloff = {n}
```

The scrolloff setting allows us to assign a numerical value (its default value being 0), which results in that number of lines being placed around the top and bottom of the current line as spacing. Its purpose is to make sure that whatever line your cursor is on, you have sufficient lines of space around it, so visually, it feels less constrained.

I don't have much use for this feature, but I did notice one negative side effect of having it (if you do decide to set it). The side effect being that it will affect the commands zt, zb, and zz. If I run the zt command, the viewport will no longer move so that the current line is at the top of the viewport but actually 10 lines from the top of the viewport (if I had set the value of scrolloff to 10, that is).

Text Objects

When editing your content, Vim provides not only granular commands (like w or e) but also a higher-level concept called "text objects."

These text objects allow you to work more easily with words, sentences, paragraphs, and tags (e.g., HTML tags), and their true value becomes even more apparent when working with a programming syntax (which we'll see an example of later).

The syntax structure of a text object looks like the following:

```
{special motion} {object}
```

As you can see from the preceding structure, text objects are commands that require you to first specify one of two special motions (I call these special motions, because they are only available to text objects), followed by the object itself.

The motions are "inside" (i) and "around" (a), followed by the object itself, which will be either a "word" (w), "sentence" (s), "paragraph" (p), "tag" (t), "quote" ("|'|`), or "block" ({}|[]|<>|()). Table 5-8 lists and clarifies these options.

Table 5-8. *Text Object Motions and Operators (sp Is Short for Special)*

Type	Name	Explanation
sp motion	Inside (i)	Selects inside the object (excludes whitespace)
sp motion	Around (a)	Selects around the object (includes whitespace)
object	Word (w)	Selects a single word
object	Sentence (s)	Selects a single sentence
object	Paragraph (p)	Selects a single paragraph
object	Tag (t)	Selects a single XML/HTML mark-up tag
object	Quote ("|'|`)	Selects content inside/around quotation marks
object	Block ({}|[]|<>|())	Selects content inside/around blocks (excludes whitespace)

> ■ **Note** The a motion is actually called "a" in the Vim documentation and not "around" (as I've labeled it). Personally, however, I find the word *around* better describes the difference between (for example) "a word" and "inside word," the former meaning that it selects the word and the whitespace after it, whereas the latter selects only the word itself and excludes the whitespace.

Examples: Text Objects

Let's look at a sample piece of text content that we can use to test on some of these text objects.

```
This is my test content. It'll have lots of strange syntaxes to help demonstrate text-objects.
It'll have object maps such as `{ foo: 123 }` (that come from programming syntax)
It'll have Array/vectors such as [a, b, c, d] (again from programming syntax)

We'll have another paragraph to separate the content up a bit.
It'll also have HTML tags such as <example>foobar</example>
Lastly it'll have a single tag such as <br /> and a broken set of tags <b>don't match</i>
```

Let's recap the different object types we're going to test.

- Words
- Sentences
- Paragraphs
- Tags
- Quotes
- Blocks

Words

Imagine your cursor is at the start of the first line of our test file, and you decide you want to select the word *demonstrate*. How would you think to do this, based on your knowledge and understanding of operators and motions?

Well, there are many ways to solve this problem, but let's assume you're reasonably clued-in, and you decide to use the f operator to move the cursor to the first letter of the word we're after (e.g., fd), and then you select the word using the e motion (e.g., ve). That's great, but what happens if your cursor is actually on the word *demonstrate* already? Let's assume your cursor is sitting on top of the letter *t* of the word *demonstrate*. How are you going to select the word now?

Well, you might try moving back to the start of the word, using the b motion, and then again using the ve command to select the whole word. That would work. But you could also use the iw (inside word) text object, like so: viw (which equates to: "select inside the word"). This might not seem like much of an improvement, because it's still the same number of key presses, right? So what's the big deal? The benefit of text objects comes from their semantics.

When I want to select the word, I say exactly that in my head: "select *that* word." But for me to action that thought, I have to first stop and think "Oh, OK, how am I going to do that from where I am?" This is the issue lots of new Vim users suffer with: the agony of choice. I have to think more (although only for a moment) about what to do. New users get caught up in the choices and feel like they've become less efficient than they would have been with their previous text editor when, really, it's about knowing that text objects can help speed up that process. Now the command I execute (viw) more closely matches my own thought pattern: "select (v) inside word (iw)."

Sentences

Imagine that your cursor is placed in the middle of the first line of our test file (let's say that the cursor is in the middle of the word *syntaxes*), and you decide that you want to select the word *It'll* from the second sentence, *It'll have lots of*. . . . How would you think to do this?

You could keep using the b motion to jump back to the start of the sentence. Or maybe you prefer to manually count the number of words back that you need to jump and use a count with the motion, like so: 6b. (Whoops! Did you get tripped up by the apostrophe in *It'll*? I did! That's two extra boundaries we must jump back through, so the count is actually 8b.) But even then, you have to select the rest of the line from there, so it's more like 8bvg_, and that's just a headache to think about.

I prefer to use the much simpler to remember vis, which equates to more or less how I thought about the problem in my head: "select inside sentence." Also, using the is (inside sentence) text object, it doesn't matter where inside that sentence my cursor is already (i.e., I don't have to count how many words to jump around before I can start selecting stuff, although some of you may have thought to work around that by using an inversed find, like so: FIvg_, which equates to searches backwards [F] for the first *I* [I], and then you can continue selecting the rest of the sentence [vg_], but this still isn't nearly as intuitive or easy to remember).

Paragraphs

Imagine that your cursor is at the start of the second line of our test file, and you decide you want to select the entire first paragraph. How would you think to do this?

Maybe you thought to try ggV2j, which equates to "go to the first line (gg) and then select the entire line (V); finally, select the following two lines down (2j)." That's not only long-winded but confusing to think about and to remember—not intuitive at all.

With text objects such as ip (inside paragraph), the solution of vip reads as you would likely think it in your head: select (v) inside paragraph (ip). This is much simpler.

Tags

Imagine that your cursor is at the start of the sixth line and on the letter *b* of the word *foobar*. You decide you want to select the entire HTML element (so, <example>foobar</example>). How would you think to do this?

You might try using the back motion (b) multiple times, but that's tedious, as both left and right angle brackets (< >) are considered word boundaries, so you would have to use it four times. Or maybe you think to use an inversed search (F) for the opening angled bracket like so: F<, which would work. Next, you might think to try selecting to the closing angled bracket, so that the whole command becomes F<v>. But that doesn't work, as the > operator is also used to shift content. So, you'll have to select to the end of the line instead: F<vg_. Wow, that took longer than expected.

Instead, the simple solution is to use the at (around tag) text object, like so: vat. This equates to "select (v) around tag (at)." This is much easier and results in less time spent realizing that trying to select to the closing angled bracket doesn't work.

It's important to note that the tag text object only works with true tags (i.e., tags that have a pair). So, if our cursor were on line 7 of our test file, the inside/around tag text object would not work with either of the angled bracket objects (i.e., <br /> or <b>don't match</i>). In those instances, you would have to use one of the block-type text objects (specifically, the angled bracket block).

Quotes

Imagine that your cursor is at the start of the second line of our test file, and you decide you want to select the contents of the backtick (`) quotes. How would you think to do this?

Well you might try f{vt`, which equates to "find (f) the first { and then select (v) until (t) the first backtick (`)," as you remember that the until (t) motion will move to the character before the specified character to be matched.

But yet again, the beauty of text objects is that you don't always have to be inside of the object to use the corresponding text object command. In this instance, we don't have to move anywhere. We can leave our cursor at the start of the line and simply run `vi\``, which (as you probably know by now) equates to "select (v) inside backtick (i\`)."

Blocks

Imagine that your cursor is at the start of the second line of our test file, and you decide you want to select the object `map { foo: 123 }`. How would you think to do this?

Well, this is actually the same problem as before but only rephrased! Which again goes to show that Vim provides us many ways to solve a problem. This time, I'm just going to give you the answer straightaway, as I think you probably get the idea by now.

The solution is to simply execute `va{`, which equates to "select (v) around the curly braces (a{)."

Programming Constructs

We've already covered text objects in their entirety, but let's just take a quick look at a different kind of example, one that uses a programming syntax. Imagine that we're working with the following JavaScript file:

```
function test() {
    var foo = "bar";
    var baz = "qux";
    return false;
}
```

Ignoring the fact that this is utterly nonsense code, if our cursor was inside the `test` function block (let's say, specifically, on the line `return false;`) and we wanted to select all the code within the curly brackets (including the curly brackets themselves), without text objects to help us, this would require a tedious amount of standard Vim commands.

Here is a sample sequence of commands you could try: `ggF{v%`, which equates to "move to the first line (gg) and then find (F) the first curly bracket ({), then select down to the closing curly bracket (%)."

How about instead we just use `va{`, which equates to "select(v) around the curly brackets (a{)." I hope you're seeing why text objects are such a powerful tool to make you more proficient at using Vim for editing.

Plug-ins

In addition to the standard built-in text objects, there are many Vim plug-ins that extend these objects to include functionality that works for more languages and file types. The following are a few different plug-ins you might find useful:

- `https://github.com/vim-scripts/camelcasemotion`
- `https://github.com/vim-scripts/argtextobj.vim`
- `https://github.com/michaeljsmith/vim-indent-object`
- `https://github.com/nelstrom/vim-textobj-rubyblock`

■ **Note**   For readers who are new to Vim, we'll be covering plug-ins (including the first plug-in the preceding list) in Chapter 17.

Executing Commands Within INSERT Mode

Although editing commands are primarily used within NORMAL mode, you are technically able to use them even inside INSERT mode (see `:h ins-special-special` for the full gory details). There is only one instance that I believe justifies using this feature, and that's to dynamically evaluate content to inject into the buffer. (We'll see how dynamic evaluation works in the next chapter, which covers Vim's Register feature.)

But regardless of whether this feature should be used or not, let's consider an example. Imagine that we have a file that consists of the content `I told him "no!"`. If you were currently in INSERT mode but wanted to transform the content inside the quotes so that it was uppercase, by using some editing commands (i.e., without leaving INSERT mode), you could use `<C-o>`, to enter a special mode in which you're placed back in NORMAL mode. When you'd executed a command, however, Vim would automatically drop you back into INSERT mode.

So, the solution to the sample problem would be to run (from INSERT mode) `<C-o>vi"~`, which equates to "enter our special mode (`<C-o>`) and then select (`v`) inside our quotes (`i"`) and then transform the content casing (`~`)." After this command had completed, you would find yourself dropped back into INSERT mode.

Summary

This was a detailed chapter, with lots of fine-grain commands to learn, understand, and, more important, practice using. I've said it a few times now, but if there is one thing you should take away from this chapter, it is to memorize the syntax structure of an editing command.

Keep it on a cheat sheet, if you have to, but learn it, because anytime you find yourself scratching your head, unsure of why a command worked (or more likely, why it didn't work), the syntax structure will help you figure out the solution. Let's have a quick recap of what we learned in this chapter . . .

- I discussed what editing commands are, and, most important, we covered the underlying syntax structure for an editing command.

- You understood that this syntax structure provides us with the capability to construct complex editing commands that can have multiple permutations.

- We saw the constructs of editing commands, such as operators and motions and how to use them in some basic example scenarios.

- You learned about how some operators and motions have an inverse variation.

- You learned about Vim's home row keys and how best practices and advanced users shouldn't influence whether you use these keys or not.

- Most important, you learned a lot about Vim's text object models and how they offer us powerful means to manipulate content at a higher level than just individual characters and letters.

- Finally, we had a quick look at how to execute editing commands from within the INSERT mode.

CHAPTER 6

Registers

Vim provides a mechanism for allowing you to store arbitrary pieces of content in a list called a "register." There are nine different registers; each one handles different content that has been placed into it, via a specific user action. We will see what these different registers are in just a moment.

The register feature itself is both interesting and confusing. It offers some uniquely powerful tools, and yet these tools don't completely work as intuitively as we would like them to. But if you're to understand how to automate your workflow (something we'll look at in more detail in Chapter 13), it's essential for you to understand at least the basic concept of how registers work.

So what are these different registers and how do they work? Well, registers work by storing information, based on specific actions you take. So, as an example, anytime you yank, cut, delete, or edit some content within Vim, it is placed inside the "unnamed" register. If you were to yank some content, it actually ends up in three different registers: the unnamed register, the "numbered" register, and the "selection" register.

Here is a breakdown of each register type:

1. The unnamed register ""
2. 10 numbered registers "0 to "9
3. The small delete register "-
4. 26 named registers "a to "z or "A to "Z
5. 4 read-only registers ":, "., "%, and "#
6. The expression register "=
7. The selection and drop registers "*, "+, and "~
8. The black hole register "_
9. Last search pattern register "/

■ **Note** You may have noticed that each type of register (e.g., the named registers "a, "b, "c, etc.) is prefixed with a double quote. This is an indicator required by Vim to access the specified register.

You can always view the contents of each register by running the command :reg. This will open up a temporary window inside Vim, listing each register. (See Figure 6-1 following. But don't hold your breath expecting to see anything exciting in my registers; it's thoroughly boring stuff, I'm afraid.) You can also filter the list down to a single register (or a specific set of registers), by passing the required registers as parameters to the :reg command, like so: :reg a and :reg 0 * a (which displays the 0, *, and a registers).

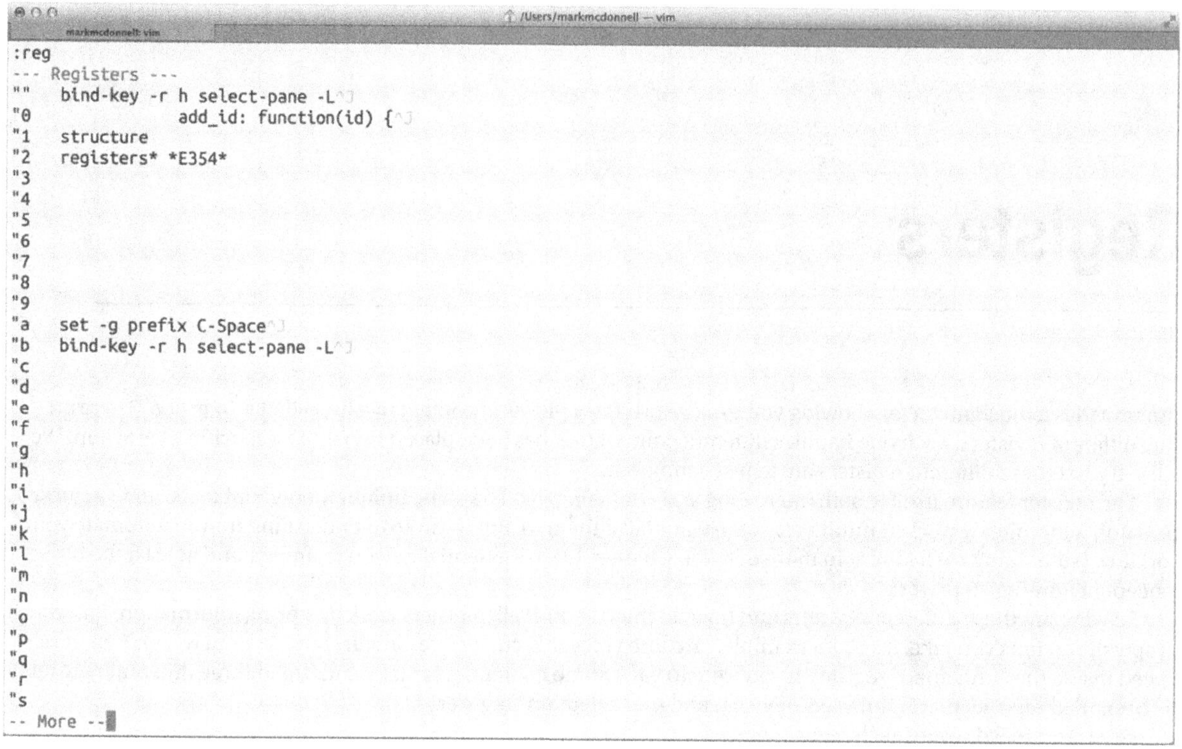
/Users/markmcdonnell — vim
markmcdonnell: vim
:reg
--- Registers ---
""   bind-key -r h select-pane -L^J
"0   add_id: function(id) {^J
"1   structure
"2   registers* *E354*
"3
"4
"5
"6
"7
"8
"9
"a   set -g prefix C-Space^J
"b   bind-key -r h select-pane -L^J
"c
"d
"e
"f
"g
"h
"i
"j
"k
"l
"m
"n
"o
"p
"q
"r
"s
-- More --

Figure 6-1. *List of Vim's registers*

Accessing a Specific Register

Chances are, since working your way through this book, you've acquired some content that is now sitting in a few of these registers. If you wanted to insert some of this content back into your buffer, all you'd need to do is tell Vim where to look and then execute the paste (`p`) command.

So how do we tell Vim where to look when pasting? Vim actually already uses one of the registers when you paste, by default. If you don't specify a register, Vim will assume that you want to paste the content from the unnamed register.

To specify a register, simply enter a double quote character `"`, followed by the register identifier you want to access. For example, if we wanted to paste the content of the named register `b` into our buffer, we would run (from NORMAL mode) `"bp`, and that would paste the content of the `b` register just after our current cursor position.

■ **Note** Interestingly, the contents of the registers are also stored in a local file, `~/.viminfo`, that is loaded when Vim starts up. (This is how Vim remembers the content of your registers even after you restart Vim).

Let's now take a brief look at each of these registers, so that we can understand where they pull their content from and why this might be useful to us.

Unnamed Register

We've already heard of this particular register now, but let's recap. If we were to delete (d), change (c), substitute (s), cut (x), or yank (y) content, that content would end up in the unnamed register. Vim uses this register effectively as a "last used register."

We also now know that up until this point, we've only pasted content that had been yanked (y or yy) and just assumed that there was a single clipboard area where Vim yanked this content to. We now know that when we yank content, it ends up in multiple different registers, meaning that we can paste content blindly, using the p command (I say "blindly," because unless you keep a close eye on what you're doing, it's easy to forget what's in the unnamed register, unless you cheat and check :reg first before pasting), or we can choose to take control of where Vim pastes from, by specifying a specific register we know to hold the content we're interested in.

You can actually be explicit with the unnamed register as well. You can access it using ""p, which equates to "access (") explicitly the unnamed register (") and paste (p) its content."

Numbered Register

Text that is yanked (y) or deleted (d) is automatically placed inside the numbered registers 0–9. Each subsequent piece of content that is stored will shift the previous stored content down into the next numbered register.

If you have all ten numbered registers filled with content and you then yank or delete some more content, the content inside the "9 register will then be lost, as there are no more spaces in that register to hold it.

To access the content inside a numbered register, you again run ", followed by the number of the register you want to pull content from. If we want to pull out the content from the fifth register, we'd run "4p (remember that the numbered register is zero-indexed, so the fifth register is actually number four).

You can also be explicit and store content in a specific numbered register, by specifying the register identifier before you yank or delete your content. For example, if I wanted to place the current word underneath my cursor inside the numbered register 2, I would run the following command: viw"2y. This equates to "select the current word (viw), specify the register ("2), and yank the word into the register (y)."

■ **Note** Not all content that is yanked or deleted will automatically end up in the numbered register. That content will only go into a numbered register if the content itself is a full line (or more). Otherwise, if you delete a single word, for example, that will be stored in the "Small delete" register.

Small Delete Register

If you delete content that is less than one line in length, it'll be placed inside the "Small delete" buffer ("-). One important caveat to that rule is if the yank/deleted content is explicitly placed inside another register, such as a numbered or named register.

Named Register

Named registers are based on the alphabet, so there are 26 named registers. . .

"a
"b
"c
"d

. . . etc., but Vim only stores content in the named register when you explicitly tell it to do so. There is no other way for content to end up in the named register unless you tell it to go there.

There are actually two ways to store information in the named register: the first is the standard way that you will already know by now (e.g., to yank the current word into the " named register, you would use viw"ay); the other is to use a capitalized version of the identifier. The point of the capitalized name isn't that there is a whole other set of 26 spaces (there isn't). What happens when you call "A instead of "a is that the capitalized version appends content to whatever already exists, and the lowercase variation wipes the space before storing content.

■ **Note**　You can also place content into a register by using a range; for example, the following command, :5,10 d x, will delete the lines five to ten and place them into the x register. You can also use the VimL function setreg, as shown in the following example: :echo setreg('a', 'foo').

Read-Only Register

The "read-only" register holds content that you can't overwrite by trying to store explicitly in the register. It has four different spaces that you can access; these are %, #, :, and ..

Let's look at each of them and see what they hold.

- ".: This space holds the last edit made via INSERT mode.

- "%: This space holds the name of the current file. (This value will change the moment you move to another buffer).

- "#: This space holds the name of the alternative file. (Again, this value will change the moment you move to another buffer).

- ":: This space holds the most recently executed COMMAND-LINE command. (So, as you can imagine, this value will change regularly).

■ **Note**　An interesting feature of the ": register is that you can re-execute the last command by using the @ command (for example, running @:). We'll see this command in Chapter 13, where we utilize Vim's macro system to automate some processes.

Expression Register

The "expression" register is a powerful tool that lets us tap into the power of VimL, if we have to dynamically create content by evaluating expressions. This section will be much longer than the other registers, simply because the other registers are generally quite dumb, in that they accept content and allow you to access content. The expression register is seriously powerful and unique, compared to the rest (as we'll soon see).

If you were to look at your registers now (:reg), chances are there isn't an expression register "= set yet. So, let's take a look at a few examples of how to use it and why it's a very powerful register. I'm going to start with a basic example and then a more advanced example.

Basic Example

Imagine you have a buffer with the following content:

```
9 * 16 =
```

We want to calculate 9 * 16 and put the result after the = sign. Now, I don't know about you, but that's not a calculation I happen to know off the top of my head. So, for me, I'd have to use a calculator. But rather than open up a calculator application and manually copy/paste the result back into Vim, we can instead get Vim to handle this for us, by using the expression register.

So, if we imagine our cursor is at the beginning of that line of content, let's press A to enter INSERT mode, and this will place our cursor at the end of the line, ready for us to enter some content. At that point, we'll enter the expression register by running <C-r>=.

■ **Note** Entering the expression register only works when you're inside INSERT mode.

When you enter the expression register, you'll see that we stay in INSERT mode, but our cursor is now focused inside the command-line bar, ready for us to enter some code to evaluate.

If we type in 9 * 16 and press <CR>, Vim will calculate the result and insert it into the buffer for us at the point where our cursor was last placed.

If you check the register :reg now, you'll see that the expression register appears and has the value 9 * 16, so we know what the last expression was that we tried to evaluate (and we can reuse it if we wish to).

Advanced Example

OK, so now that you have a basic idea of how the expression register works, let's take a look at a more advanced example. (This would become even more advanced if we were to utilize Vim's macro feature, which I will cover in Chapter 13.) So, let's start by imagining you have a buffer with the following content:

```
Mark was born in 1982. Catherine was born in 1987.
```

Let's say we wanted to put Mark's and Catherine's ages in parentheses after their respective birth years, so that the content became

```
Mark was born in 1982 (x). Catherine was born in 1987 (x).
```

Where x is would be their age based on the current year you happen to be reading this book. We could figure this out in our heads, that's not a problem for most of us, but for the sake of demonstration, let's pretend that calculating how old Mark and Catherine are would be too taxing on our tired brains right now.

To do this, we have to use our knowledge of how registers work, in addition to a tiny bit of help from VimL. (Don't worry if you don't know any VimL; most of the time, if you search Google for what you're trying to do, you'll find an answer. The Internet is a wonderful place).

Let's break down the steps we're going to need to take to complete this challenge.

- Get the year stored in the register.

- Insert parenthesis.

- Calculate the age.

- Insert the result inside the parenthesis.

OK, so the solution for doing this (shield your eyes) for Mark would look something like the following:
`0f1viwyea<Space>()<Esc>i<C-r>=strftime("%Y")-<C-r>"<CR>`.

BOOM! If that's the sound of your brain melting, then fear not. We're going to break this down step-by-step, so you can understand completely what just happened.

- `0`: Move the cursor to the start of the line.

- `f1`: Find the start of Mark's year by searching for "1."

- `viw`: Select the year.

- `y`: Yank the year, so that it'll be stored in the unnamed register (and in the numbered register as well, if you were paying attention).

- `e`: Move to the end of the year.

- `a`: Enter INSERT mode, so the cursor is placed after the year.

- `<Space>()`: Type in a space and then the set of parentheses.

- `<Esc>i`: Move into NORMAL mode and then back into INSERT mode.

- `<C-r>=`: Enter the expression register.

- `strftime("%y")`: Get the current year (this is VimL syntax that Vim will evaluate).

- `-`: We enter the minus symbol (as we want to minus Mark's year from the current year) . . .

- `<C-r>"`: followed by the contents of the unnamed register.

- `<CR>`: Finally, press the `<Enter>` key to pass the result of the expression (e.g., `2014-1982`) back to INSERT mode, in which it'll be inserted into the content inside the parentheses.

So, that wasn't really a lot of steps, but it probably was enough to confuse you. I definitely recommend that you play along at home, test these commands, and make sure they work for you and that you understand how each one works, before moving on.

■ **Note** You can also insert content from other registers while still inside the expression register, by using `<C-r>{register}`.

Selection/Drop Register

The "selection/drop" register holds content that is typically related to the GUI versions of Vim. Much like the read-only register, you will be unable to overwrite the content of this register by trying to store explicitly in the spaces available. It has three different spaces that you can retrieve content from. These are *, +, and ~.

Let's look at each of them and see what they hold.

- "*: This space holds content that was yanked into the system clipboard.

- "+: This space holds content similar to "* but is specific to X11 systems (see :h x11-selection for more details).

- "~: This space holds content that was "drag and dropped" into Vim (again, only really relevant to the GUI versions of Vim).

■ **Note**   When we yank content, it ends up in the "* and "+ registers, because inside our .vimrc file, we have the setting set clipboard+=unnamed, which tells Vim to take any content from the unnamed register and stick it in the system clipboard register. This trick allows us to copy content from one Vim instance and paste it into a totally separate Vim instance.

Blackhole Register

The "blackhole" register is a little bit like /dev/null in that you can use it to read or write yanked/deleted content, and yet nothing will be written to it or read back from it.

It is for all intents and purposes a "black hole." You may wonder why this is useful. The example given by most users is that it helps to avoid side effects when you're using the register to hold other content that you wish to reuse.

For example, you might yank some content with the intention of reusing it, by pasting it elsewhere within your buffer, but you might also first have to delete some other content. By deleting the content directly into the blackhole register, you won't cause your other register content to be replaced by the deleted content.

Personally, I've never found a need to use this register.

■ **Note**   If the term /dev/null is unfamiliar to you, all you have to really know is that it's a fundamental part of the Unix operating system and that any data passed to it is discarded by the OS, but at the same time, the OS confirms that everything worked fine. This may seem like a pointless feature, but it's used to avoid side effects when executing certain commands. It's also used as a form of joke in technical communities, such as: "please send all complaints to /dev/null."

Last Search Register

Anytime you carry out an inline search (e.g., /foobar), the search term used is recorded into the "last search" register.

■ **Note**   We'll see the use of the inline search in Chapter 11.

Clearing Your Registers

Interestingly, there isn't a simple way to clear your Vim registers. I assume the reason why Vim doesn't provide a function to handle this is because it considers the use case to be so rare as to not warrant the extra code required.

But a quick Google search will result in some clever hacks to work around this, if you do need to clear your recorded set of registers. Following is one such example:

```
:let regs='abcdefghijklmnopqrstuvwxyzABCDEFGHIJKLMNOPQRSTUVWXYZ0123456789/-"' | let i=0 | while
(i<strlen(regs)) | exec 'let @'.regs[i].'=""' | let i=i+1 | endwhile | unlet regs
```

If that command looks terrifying; then that's because it is! It is using VimL to loop through our registers and manually clear their contents one by one. After you run the command, if you execute :reg, you should see something like Figure 6-2.

Figure 6-2. *Vim's registers cleared of all content*

Note   Theoretically, you could also open the ~/.viminfo file and manually edit that, but I personally find copy-and-pasting the preceding command is a lot quicker and easier (and once you see, following, the explanation of how it works, I hope you will too).

The breakdown of the preceding command looks something like the following (note that I'm going to try to explain this in such a way that you don't have to know programming terminology—such as *array, variables,* etc.—to understand what the command is doing, which, however, results in the explanation becoming a little bit long-winded):

- :let regs='...': The ... is a list of the identifiers for each register. (I removed them for brevity). The identifiers are stored in a container called regs in a data format that allows us to easily loop over each identifier and do something with each one.

- |: The pipe character takes the result of the previous chunk of code and passes it over to the next. (We see it used a few times in this command, to help keep Vim executing the command sequentially).

- let i=0: We create another container called i, and inside of that, we store the value zero. This will be used as a counter (as we loop through each identifier in the regs container).

- while (i<strlen(regs)): The while(some_condition) construct is our loop. As long as the code inside the parentheses results in something that's considered "true," the loop will continue to run. In this case, we're saying "while the value of i is less than the total length of regs, run whatever command comes next." So, we loop over the regs container (one loop iteration for each item in the regs container).

- exec 'let @'.regs[i].'=""': This piece of code is what gets executed on every successful loop iteration. It effectively tells Vim to access the register identifier that matches what we currently have pulled out of the reg container and to assign it a new value of "" (which is empty content).

- let i=i+1: This is the other piece of code that is executed on every successful loop iteration. This one updates the value of i, so that it acts like a counter (e.g., after the first loop, change i from zero to one, after the second loop change i from one to two; and so on).

- endwhile: This piece of code is the end of our loop construct (e.g., we don't want any more code to be executed while our loop is running).

- unlet regs: This piece of code will execute once our loop has completed, and all it does is delete the regs container, as we no longer need it now that our code has finished.

Summary

So, this wasn't a particularly long chapter; but that's because, although we were focusing on a core feature of Vim (that still confuses even long-term Vim users), there isn't really that much to it, when you start digging around. Let's, however, just quickly recap what we have learned, before we move on.

- We took a quick top-level look at the different types of registers and what their identifiers are.

- You learned that we can always access the register's content, either by running :reg or by checking the content of a local ~/.viminfo file.

- You learned how to access specific registers, so we can do something with their content (mostly paste that content somewhere else).

- We went through and studied each of the nine registers and what their purposes are.

- Finally, we looked at a way we could clear all the content from our registers, using a bit of VimL.

CHAPTER 7

■ ■ ■

Folding

Folding is the process of compressing multiple lines of content into a single line. Once folded, the content can then be expanded by executing a specific key binding. This type of feature is typically prevalent in programming environments, but it can be useful for any type of content you happen to be working with. The decision to utilize folding comes down to whether you consider a particular threshold of complexity for your content to have been reached.

You don't have to look too far before you encounter a real-world example of folding. If you took my advice from Chapter 2, you are already using my configuration files from the ProVim repository, specifically the .vimrc file. In ;that file, we're using folding to help manage the different configuration sections that otherwise would be long and dense (see Figure 7-1).

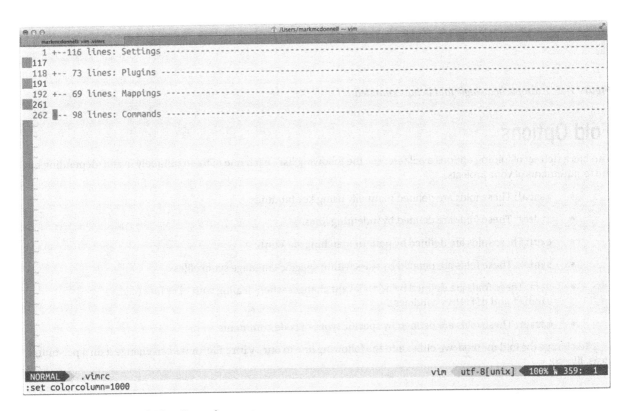

Figure 7-1. *Example of folding lines of content*

Folded areas of content can either be expanded en masse or singularly (see Figure 7-2).

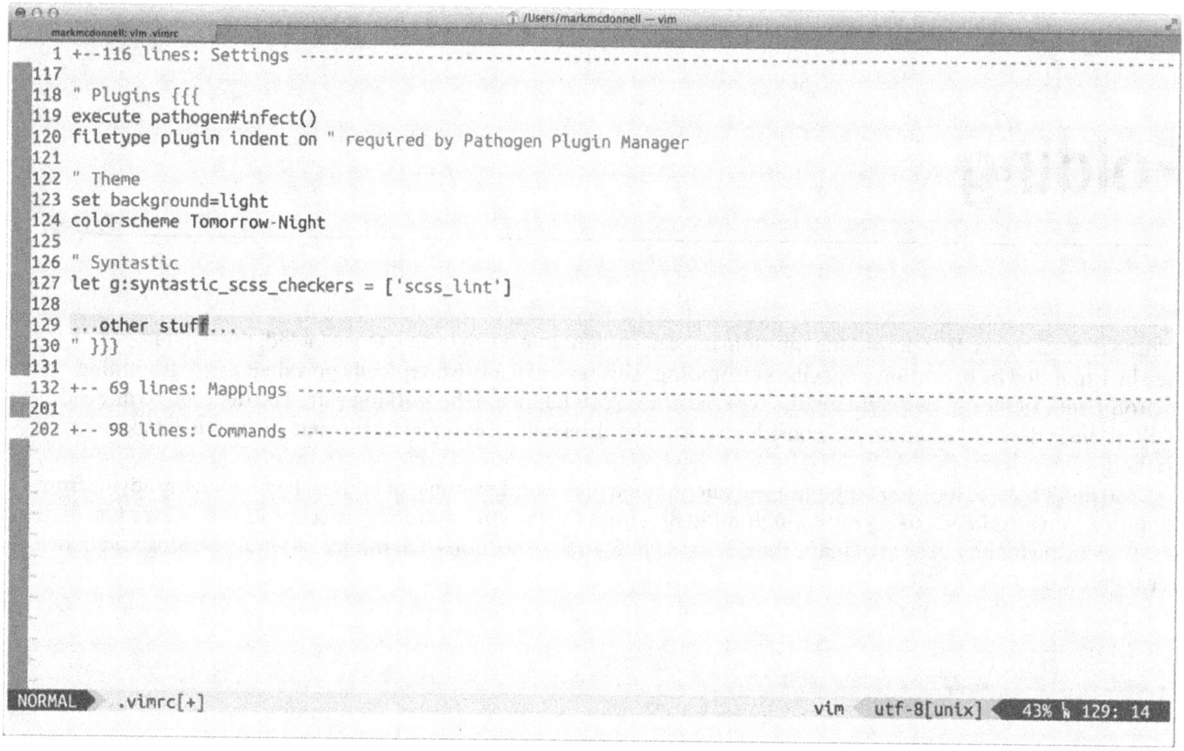

Figure 7-2. *Example of a single fold being expanded*

Fold Options

Vim has a rich set of folding options available (see the following list), each one of them uniquely useful, depending on the requirements of your projects.

- `manual`: These folds are defined manually using key bindings.

- `indent`: These folds are defined by indenting lines.

- `expr`: These folds are defined by pattern matching via VimL.

- `syntax`: These folds are defined by rules within specific language syntax files.

- `diff`: These folds are defined by nonrelevant changes when dealing with `diff` files (e.g., `vimdiff` and `diffthis` windows).

- `marker`: These folds are defined by specific types of code comments.

To change the fold method, we either add the following line to our `.vimrc` file, or we can change it on a per-buffer basis, like so:

```
:set foldmethod=manual
```

Manual

The default fold setting is manual. The biggest problem with a manual fold is that it isn't remembered after the file has been closed. But if you're only interested in temporarily folding content, this default setting is what you need.

Manual folds not being remembered after the file is closed shouldn't be a surprise, because how is Vim supposed to keep that state, unless it stores it in a file or database? But surely that would be hideously inefficient? Just imagine the large amount of files you work with over the period of a single day. Later on, we'll see how the "marker" fold method can give the *illusion* of remembering folds.

Creating Folds

To manually create a new fold, we must apply the zf command, to compress our selected content. Imagine we have the following content (admittedly it's not that long and probably isn't justified for folding; but let's give it a go anyway):

```
Here is some content.
It's a fascinating read.
If only we could fold this amazing content.
```

If we wanted to fold this content down (and the foldmethod is set to manual), we could do so by first selecting the content we want to fold and then triggering the zf command. The full command is

```
VGzf
```

This breaks down to "select the entire file (VG) and apply a fold (zf)." The following code example demonstrates the result of this action:

```
+--  3 lines: Here is some content.--
```

When used with different motions, zf can take the following multiple forms:

- v{motion|text object}zf: Fold a selection
- zf{motion|text object}: Fold around a motion or text object (e.g., zf3j)
- zf'a: Fold from current position up to the a mark (you'll read about marks in Chapter 15)
- {count}zF: Fold counted number of lines from current position

---

■ **Note**   The last variation isn't quite the same, as we have to capitalize the *f*, so that it is no longer zf but zF.

Opening/Closing/Toggling Folds

So, now we know how to create a fold manually, we should really look at how we can open a fold (otherwise, we'll never get to see our wonderful content in its full glory). The following commands can be triggered from any line of folded content:

- zc: Close the fold.

- zo: Open the fold.

- za: Alternate (i.e., toggle) the fold.

Open/Close All Folds

Rather than manually closing (or opening) each individual fold, you can run one of the following commands to toggle them en masse (i.e., all at once):

- zM: Closes all folds

- zR: Opens all folds

Marker

Manual folds have one big issue: they are not remembered after a file is closed. So, if we don't want to have to keep setting folds every time we come back to a file, we'll need to use a marker fold instead.

A marker fold gives the *illusion* of remembering the folds set in a file, when really it does this by searching the buffer as it's being read for specific tags, wrapping content we want to fold and then processing those tags. Note that marker folds are only really useful when used with programming files. (You couldn't use marker folds in nonprogramming files, because they have no concept of "code comments.") Imagine if you opened the file in an editor that didn't support folding like Vim does. You would have markers showing up around your content, and that wouldn't look very good.

Let's see an example of how the marker fold works. Imagine you're working on a long .vimrc file (such as the one we used from the ProVim repository). Because the .vimrc file is processed by the Vim editor, it means we are able to utilize VimL. The syntax in VimL to indicate a code comment is the " character.

If I wanted to write a code comment in VimL, I would do something such as the following:

```
" this is my code comment
```

Now that we know how to write a code comment in VimL, let's see how we can use this knowledge to make a marker style fold. We must first construct a specific type of code comment, which looks like the following:

```
" Name of my marker {{{
Here is my content to be hidden away
The following line indicates the end of the marker
" }}}
```

Notice that they have a triple {{{ at the start and }}} at the end. This addition to the code comment is what Vim looks for when processing a buffer. If you look at my .zshrc and .vimrc files, you'll see lots of these marker folds being used.

Automatically Closing Folds

When I initially started using folds, I noticed when I opened (for example) my `.vimrc` file, all the marker folds were open by default. That was really annoying, as it meant I had to run a command to manually close all the folds in the file (e.g., zM).

What I wanted was all the folds to be closed by default when I first opened a file. Also, I didn't want the folds to be all closed when I went back to the file, if it hadn't been closed (e.g., if I open a file, all the folds should be closed; if I open a fold and then switch buffers and then back again, I don't want Vim to think it should close all the folds again).

To achieve the preceding requirements meant that I needed to add the following configuration to my `.vimrc` file:

```
autocmd BufRead * setlocal foldmethod=marker
autocmd BufRead * normal zM
```

The preceding snippet works by applying the setting `foldmethod=marker` and zM only when the buffer is first read. This means once the buffer has been read (even if I switch back and forth between buffers), it won't reapply these settings each time.

Folding by Indentation

If you want to use folds that are remembered, but use them in a file that doesn't support the concept of "comments" (as all programming language files do), you can still fold your content, but you'll have to use an indentation in your content that Vim can hook into to recognize that a fold is applicable.

To do this, you first must add the following lines into your `.vimrc` file to enable Vim to use the indentation method (you can execute these commands individually via COMMAND-LINE mode, if you just want to experiment):

```
set foldmethod=indent
set foldlevel=5
```

■ **Note** If you're using the ProVim `.vimrc` file, then the preceding change of `foldmethod` value will cause a conflict. See the previous section, "Automatically Closing Folds," and make sure you replace the relevant lines set in the `.vimrc` file. If you still want all folds (doesn't matter what "method" is used) to be closed by default when opening a buffer, you can just remove the `autocmd BufRead * setlocal foldmethod=marker` setting and leave the other (`autocmd BufRead * normal zM`) as it is.

In the preceding code snippet, we can see that we've changed the fold method used to be indent, and we've also defined a fold level of 5, which means that for our content to be folded, we should have 5 spaces at the start of the line. Let's see an example of this:

```
This is a sentence.
This is a sentence.
     This is a sentence.
     This is a sentence.
     This is a sentence.
This is a sentence.
This is a sentence.
     This is a sentence.
     This is a sentence.
     This is a sentence.
     This is a sentence.
     This is a sentence.
     This is a sentence.
     This is a sentence.
     This is a sentence.
     This is a sentence.
     This is a sentence.
     This is a sentence.
     This is a sentence.
     This is a sentence.
This is a sentence.
```

From the preceding example, we can visually see that we have two levels of indentation. We have lines 3–5, which are indented with 5 spaces, and after that, we have lines 8–20, also indented with 5 spaces. If we were to run the command zM (which closes all folds in the current buffer), the buffer content would look like the following:

```
This is a sentence.
This is a sentence.
+--   3 lines: This is a sentence.
This is a sentence.
This is a sentence.
+-- 13 lines: This is a sentence.
This is a sentence.
```

Nested Folds

Vim also allows us to nest our folds. (This applies to all types of fold methods.) Let's see this with a slightly modified example buffer.

```
This is a sentence.
    This is a sentence.
    This is a sentence.
    This is a sentence.
    This is a sentence.
        This is a sentence.
        This is a sentence.
        This is a sentence.
        This is a sentence.
    This is a sentence.
    This is a sentence.
    This is a sentence.
    This is a sentence.
This is a sentence.
```

As you can now see, there are two levels of indentation: the first is from lines 2–13, and the second is inside that range, lines 6–9. If we were to run the command zM, then the buffer content would look like the following:

```
This is a sentence.
+-- 12 lines: This is a sentence.
This is a sentence.
```

If we ran the command za (which toggles the fold on/off) when our cursor was on the middle line of that buffer (i.e., the one starting +-- 12 lines), the first level fold would expand open, and we'd see the content it had folded; and this would include the second level fold, like so:

```
This is a sentence.
    This is a sentence.
    This is a sentence.
    This is a sentence.
    This is a sentence.
+---  4 lines: This is a sentence.
    This is a sentence.
    This is a sentence.
    This is a sentence.
    This is a sentence.
This is a sentence.
```

From here, we could keep expanding any other sublevel folds we find. Vim doesn't impose any restriction or limit on the number of sublevel folds you create.

Folding by Syntax

Vim allows us to fold content based on pre-existing syntax rules. Vim has built-in syntax rules for most programming languages, and so the simple act of switching the foldmethod value should be all you have to do. For example, running the following command will change to syntax folding mode:

```
:set foldmethod=syntax
```

Let's see an example of how this particular fold method works with a real-world code example. Following is a script taken from an open source Ruby gem called Sinderella (https://github.com/Integralist/Sinderella), written by yours truly:

```ruby
require 'sinderella/version'
require 'sinderella/data_store'
require 'crimp'

module Sinderella
  def self.transforms(data, till_midnight = 60)
    identifier  = Crimp.signature(data)
    cloned_data = deep_copy data
    transformed = yield cloned_data

    store({
      :id => identifier,
      :original => data,
      :transformed => transformed
    })

    check(identifier, till_midnight)

    identifier
  end

  def self.get(id)
    DataStore.instance.get(id)[:transformed]
  end

  def self.midnight(id)
    reset_data_at(id)
  end

  private

  def self.store(data)
    DataStore.instance.set(data)
  end
```

```
  def self.deep_copy(object)
    Marshal.load(Marshal.dump(object))
  end

  def self.check(id, seconds)
    Thread.new { sleep seconds; reset_data_at id }
  end

  def self.reset_data_at(id)
    DataStore.instance.reset(id)
  end
end
```

It's not important what this gem does, but without any configuration at all (just changing the foldmethod value), we find that Vim will compress all areas of the buffer that corresponds with syntax rules predefined by its own Ruby syntax files, as follows:

```
require 'sinderella/version'
require 'sinderella/data_store'
require 'crimp'

+-- 43 lines: module Sinderella--
```

Hmm, so this looks a little heavy-handed. It seems like it has compressed the entire file into one line. Let's expand this fold and see what we find inside:

```
require 'sinderella/version'
require 'sinderella/data_store'
require 'crimp'

module Sinderella
+--- 15 lines: def self.transforms(data, till_midnight = 60)---

+---  3 lines: def self.get(id)---

+---  3 lines: def self.midnight(id)---


  private

+---  3 lines: def self.store(data)---

+---  3 lines: def self.deep_copy(object)---

+---  3 lines: def self.check(id, seconds)---

+---  3 lines: def self.reset_data_at(id)---
end
```

This looks a bit better. We can see that the default syntax rules have defined that anything that looks like a method in the Ruby language should be folded. I can also see that inside the method self.transforms, where we make a call to the store method, Vim has also decided to fold that call, because of a syntax rule defined around the use of curly brackets.

```
def self.transforms(data, till_midnight = 60)
  identifier  = Crimp.signature(data)
  cloned_data = deep_copy data
  transformed = yield cloned_data

---   5 lines: store({---

  check(identifier, till_midnight)

  identifier
end
```

■ **Note**   If on the rare occasion your programming language of choice isn't supported, or it doesn't have the granular control you want, you can define your own set of custom syntax rules. For more information, see the help documentation :h syn-fold.

Folding Content Dynamically

Vim allows you to use VimL to dynamically fold your content. If there is a pattern in your files that you believe you can consistently match up to where a fold should appear, this is the option for you. Unfortunately, it does require you to have knowledge of VimL.

Although VimL is outside the scope of this book, we'll take a look at a short example that's slightly modified from the Vim documentation. Consider the following content:

```
> a single level fold
> a single level fold
> > a double level fold
> > a double level fold
> > > > a quadruple level fold
> > > this isn't another sub level fold
> > > because the numer of > characters are less than the containing fold
> > > > a quadruple level fold
```

If we wanted to fold all lines that begin with the > character (and any lines that have multiple > characters should become nested folds), we can do so by defining a pattern using a VimL expression and assigning the expression to the foldexpr property, like so :set foldexpr={our expression}.

Let's first see what the content looks like when properly folded.

```
+--   8 lines: > a single level fold--
```

If we were to expand this fold, we would see the following:

```
> a single level fold
> a single level fold
+---  6 lines: > > a double level fold---
```

Again, if we were to expand the nested fold, we would see the following:

```
> a single level fold
> a single level fold
> > a double level fold
> > a double level fold
+----  4 lines: > > > > a quadruple level fold----
```

Finally, if we were to expand that last nested fold, we would see the full content of our buffer. So now, let's look at the expression that provides the solution to this particular problem.

```
strlen(substitute(substitute(getline(v:lnum),'\\s','',\"g\"),'[^>].*','',''))
```

This might look like some pretty intense code, but when we break it down into its component parts, we realize that it's pretty straightforward. So, let's do exactly that and see what's going on. (Because we're composing this expression from multiple function calls, it'll make more sense—much as with a Lisp-based dialect—if we start from the inside and work our way out).

- getline(v:lnum): The getline function returns the content of a specific line in our buffer. For example, if I were to call getline(1), the contents of line 1 would be returned. In this instance, we pass v:lnum to the getline function. The argument we're passing evaluates to the current line of the file (Vim will end up running foldexpr on every line of the current buffer).

- substitute(..., '\\s','','g'): Here we take the content of the current line (remember, each line of the buffer will eventually be processed) and remove any whitespace.

- substitute(..., '[^>].*','',''): Here we take the content of the current line (that now has no whitespace) and then remove any content, leaving just the > characters (of which there could be 1 or more).

- strlen(...): This function returns the number of characters in the string that has been passed to it as an argument. In this instance, we're passing in a string which consists of a number of > characters for the current line being processed.

At this point, for each line of the buffer we process, we get an indentation count. The reason this value is important is because a fold that's based off an expression is really using the same mechanism as the indent fold method. But rather than manually specifying a value, we're able to dynamically specify that value by finding a specific pattern in our code.

Vim is intelligent enough to allow us to now define multiple indentation values within a single file, thanks to the power of using VimL expressions to fold our content.

Folding Unchanged Lines

Interestingly, Vim also provides a folding option called `diff` (see Figure 7-3). I'll cover Vim's diffing capabilities in more detail later, in Chapter 18, but for now, let's just see how it relates to code folding.

Anytime you have a different version of the same file (open in multiple windows), you can run a command in Vim that causes Vim to highlight the differences between the two files. Any lines of the files that are the same (i.e., haven't changed between versions) will be folded, so that you can focus more clearly on what *has* changed. This happens because when you run the relevant command to trigger a diff (behind the scenes), Vim will actually execute the following code for you:

```
:setlocal diff foldmethod=diff scrollbind nowrap foldlevel=1
```

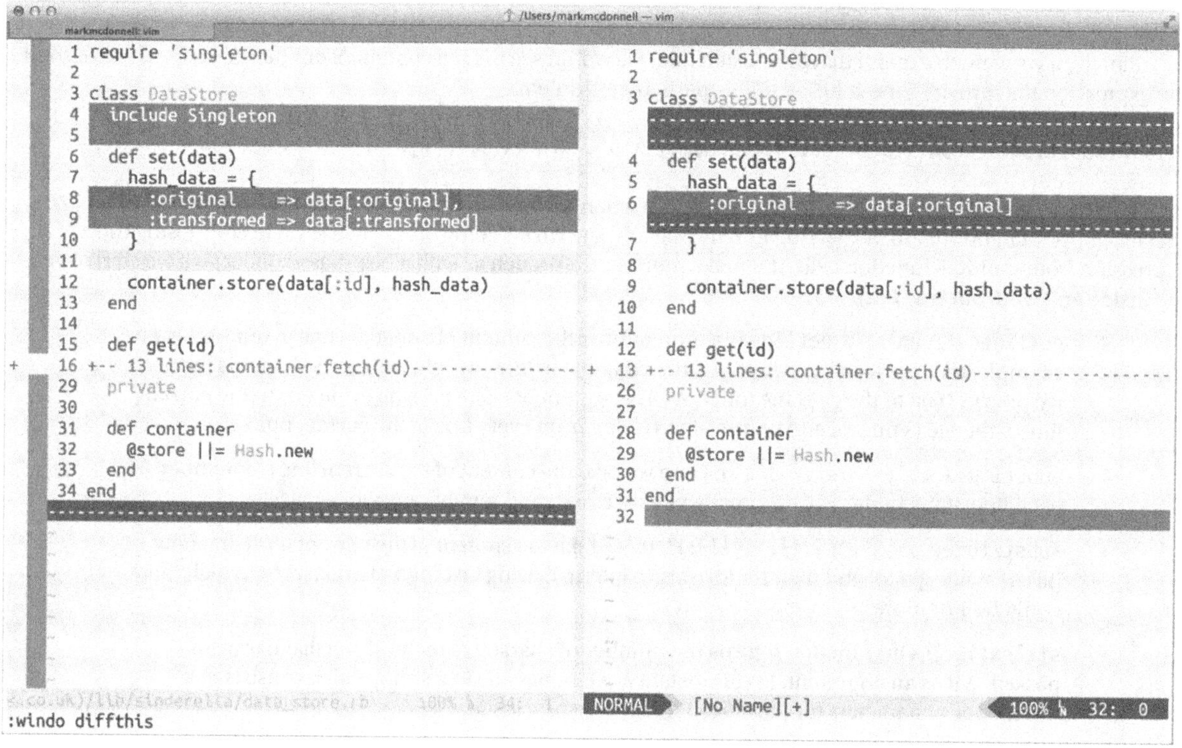

Figure 7-3. *Example of Vim diff. Note that the unchanged code is automatically folded*

Summary

I hope that you'll now have a better idea not only of when it is appropriate to use Vim's folding features but of which method best fits your project requirements. I've covered a lot of important details, so let's have a quick recap.

- We saw a real-world example of using folding content, as seen in our own `.vimrc` and `.zshrc` files.

- We looked at the six different folding methods available and then discussed each of them individually, taking into account what scenarios they work best in.

- We also saw another real-world example of using the syntax method of code folding on the Sinderella Ruby gem and how Vim provides automatic granular control over the content, without any additional configuration required by us (other than turning the feature on).

## CHAPTER 8

VISUAL-BLOCK Mode

We've already seen how Vim allows us to visually select content and manipulate the selection, using a wide range of commands. But Vim also provides a variation of the selection feature known as VISUAL-BLOCK mode.

As the name suggests, this mode allows us to select and manipulate content in a block form (meaning we can select content within a specific rectangular area and make changes that are applied to each line of the selection). This feature gives us yet another dimension for modifying and extending the granular control we have over our content.

Simple Example

The best way to understand this feature is by way of an example. Imagine you have the following content (also imagine, if you will, that this list is much longer, maybe a hundred lines or more in length):

```
_List Item 1
_List Item 2
_List Item 3
_List Item 4
_List Item 5
```

If you wanted to remove the _ (underscore) character that begins every line, you could fix this using VISUAL-BLOCK mode. (You could also use a substitution command, but that option has a more complex syntax, and so I'll cover it in another chapter.)

To begin with, we have to enter VISUAL-BLOCK mode. To do this, you will have to run <C-v> from NORMAL mode.

To implement the change we've described above (i.e., removing the underscores), we have to run the following sequence of commands:

```
gg<C-v>Gd
```

By now, you should be comfortable analyzing the construction of complex commands, but let's take a look at what this command does when we break it down into its component parts.

- gg: We move to the top of the buffer (just in case our cursor isn't already at the start of the first line).

- <C-v>: We enter into VISUAL-BLOCK mode (which selects the current character under the cursor).

- G: We move our cursor to the bottom line (which subsequently selects the first column in each line).

- d: We delete the selection.

> ░ **Note** A nice side effect of using a visual mode (whether it be a VISUAL-BLOCK or standard visual selection) is that you can filter content through an external terminal program, using the ! operator. We'll see more examples of this in Chapter 20.

Entering VISUAL-BLOCK Mode

We covered this ever so briefly in the preceding example, so let's recap it here. Entering VISUAL-BLOCK mode is achieved by running the command <C-v> from NORMAL mode. We'll know when we're in this mode, as Vim will display a message of -- VISUAL BLOCK -- near the command-line bar (see Figure 8-1).

Figure 8-1. *VISUAL-BLOCK mode*

> ░ **Note** If you're a Windows user, you may find that <C-v> doesn't work for you, as it's mapped to the operating system's paste command. If this is the case, then you can use the alternative key binding <C-Q>.

Canceling

To escape from VISUAL-BLOCK mode, you will have to run the command `<Esc>`, which will take you back into NORMAL mode. But realize that if you have started to insert or append content across a selection, pressing `<Esc>` will still apply the changes you have started to make.

If you would prefer to not have the changes applied across all selected lines, you would instead have to run the command `<C-c>`, which will keep the changes you've made to the current line but not apply them automatically to any other selected lines.

Adding Additional Content in Block Format

As well as being able to select a rectangular area and execute operators upon that selection, you can also add additional content, which gets automatically applied across the multiple lines you have selected within VISUAL-BLOCK mode. To demonstrate this, let's look at the modified version of the previous "simple example" content we had (notice the underscore character has been removed from each line).

```
List Item 1
List Item 2
List Item 3
List Item 4
List Item 5
```

If we wanted to add an asterisk character (*) to the start of each line, we could do so very easily with VISUAL-BLOCK mode. First, we would have to enter VISUAL-BLOCK mode, make our selection, and then insert the content we wanted to be applied around that selection. The specific command would be as follows:

```
gg<C-v>4jI*<Esc>
```

Running that command would result in the content being changed to the following:

```
*List Item 1
*List Item 2
*List Item 3
*List Item 4
*List Item 5
```

Let's break down the command, so that we can see what we did and, in the process, learn how to inject new content that is automatically applied to a selection.

- gg: We move to the top of the buffer (just in case our cursor isn't already at the start of the first line).

- `<C-v>`: We enter into VISUAL-BLOCK mode (which selects the current character under the cursor).

- 4j: We move down four lines (subsequently selecting the first character on each line).

- I: We tell Vim we want to "block insert." This will allow us to enter new text that is inserted into each selected line (similar to the standard i and I operators when editing content, but specifically aimed at applying the edit to multiple lines inside VISUAL-BLOCK mode).

- ***:** This is the content we want to add. You'll notice that the content is only added to the current line. (You might have expected to see it added to all other selected lines at the same time as you were typing, but Vim doesn't do this, for performance reasons.)

- **<Esc>:** By pressing the escape key, we move back into NORMAL mode, and Vim will take the new content we added and apply it to the selection we had made within VISUAL-BLOCK mode. (Subsequently, our asterisk character is added to the start of each line.)

■ **Note**   You can also use other commands, such as c, to change multiple lines, or s, to substitute the content across multiple lines, but remember that your change will only appear once you escape VISUAL-BLOCK mode.

Complex Example

Now that we know how to use VISUAL-BLOCK mode, let's see a more complex example that takes advantage of manipulating multiple lines of content. Imagine you have some tabular data. In the following code snippet, I provide some sample data of books released by Apress Publishing. It includes the name of the book, its ISBN, and its release date:

```
| Book Title                   | ISBN              | Release Date |
| ---------------------------- | ----------------- | ------------ |
| Pro JavaScript Design Patterns | 978-1-59059-908-2 | 12.16.07     |
| Practical Clojure            | 978-1-4302-7231-1 | 06.06.10     |
| Beginning Ruby               | 978-1-4302-2363-4 | 07.19.09     |
| Regular Expression Recipes   | 978-1-59059-441-4 | 12.07.04     |
| Practical Common Lisp        | 978-1-59059-239-7 | 04.06.05     |
```

I now want to modify the "Release Date" column in a couple of ways. First, I don't want to use dots to separate each section of the date; I actually want to use a / character instead. This means changing the format from month.date.year to month/date/year.

I also want to change the format of the year from being a two-digit representation and turn it into a four-digit representation, so we can see the full year displayed. This means changing the format from 07 to 2007.

Each of these requirements can be implemented using Vim's substitution command, along with a few regular expression patterns, but that comes at a price and with some caveats to consider.

1. You have to know how to write a regex pattern in the first place! If you're not a programmer, this isn't likely to be an option for you, because regexes aren't the most user-friendly tool ever designed.

2. You have to be careful that your regex pattern doesn't cause any side effects on other dates or dot characters you may have in your content already. (Luckily, in our example, we don't, so admittedly, the regex pattern would be easier to write.)

3. Time. I'm *very good* at writing regex patterns. I love them, and I'm a total geek when it comes to finding clever ways to write the most concise and efficient patterns. But even I know (and you'll see this in a moment, when I demonstrate the solution) that using VISUAL-BLOCK mode for this type of problem is the simplest and quickest way to get the change I want made done.

So, what would the solution involve if we were to utilize VISUAL-BLOCK mode instead? If we assume our cursor was at the start of the first line, we would have to execute the following command (remember that this command is both easier to implement and visualize when you actually run it in Vim, rather than reading it from a book):

`3Gf.<C-v>4jr/f..<C-v>4jA20<Esc>`

Whoa! OK, that looks a little scary, and you're probably thinking that learning how to write a regex pattern might be easier than trying to learn or even just execute that long command. But hold on for one more moment while I break down this solution into separate parts, so that you can see the reasoning behind what it does.

■ **Note** The majority of that command is us moving the cursor into the correct position. The use of VISUAL-BLOCK mode itself is very simple in comparison.

It's also important to realize that no one executes a long stream of characters in one go, as we've shown previously. What typically happens (and what did when I wrote the example) is they figure out what the first step they have to take is and execute a command that achieves that. Then they look at the next step of what they want to achieve and again execute the relevant commands that do that, and so forth, until all the requirements have been met.

So let's see the breakdown of the preceding command and what it means. Remember: Doing makes learning much easier, so don't just *read* the breakdown but actually play along in Vim to see how it works, and you'll understand it a lot quicker.

- `3G`: We move to line 3.
- `f.`: We find the first dot character (which on line 3 is the dot after 12 in `12.16.07`).
- `<C-v>`: We enter VISUAL-BLOCK mode (I'll cover this in more detail later).
- `4j`: We move four lines down, which will visually select all the dots in this column down to the last line. (See Figure 8-2 for an example of what this looks like.)
- `r/`: We replace with a forward slash character (using the `r` operator) the dots we selected. This is now the first part of the problem solved; we just have to repeat it on the next set of dots (so let's see that now . . .).
- `f.`: We move to the next dot on the line (which on line 3 is the dot after 16 in `12.16.07`).
- `.`: We use the repeat operator to apply the last edit we made (which, in this case, was selecting all the dots in the current column and replacing them with a forward slash). We can now see the power of that single operator (`.`), when used in the right situations (such as this), in helping to reduce our repeating ourselves.
- `<C-v>`: We now have to insert the characters 20 before the year, so we enter VISUAL-BLOCK mode again.
- `4j`: We again select the same column in each line down to the bottom line (similar to before, when we selected the first column of dots).
- `A`: We tell Vim we want to "block append." This will allow us to enter new text, which is appended to each selected line (similar to the standard `a` and `A` operators when editing content, but specifically aimed at applying the edit to multiple lines inside VISUAL-BLOCK mode).
- `20`: We add the text we want (in this case, 20 will be placed before the current year, so 07 will become 2007.)
- `<Esc>`: The changes we make in VISUAL-BLOCK mode are only seen in the current line *until* we escape back into NORMAL mode, where they are then automatically applied to each line that was selected via VISUAL-BLOCK mode.

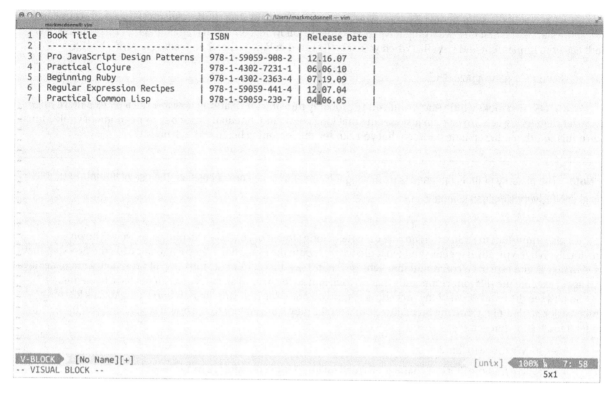

Figure 8-2. *Example of a selection in VISUAL-BLOCK mode*

As you can see, the solution actually breaks down into many small commands that I've combined to make a much more complex change to my content. If you played along and executed those commands in Vim, you would have noticed (as long as you have read the previous chapters and know how commands work) that the long command I showed you was actually quite easy to compose and to string together.

But more important, edits via VISUAL-BLOCK mode are *fast*, especially when compared to having to enter COMMAND-LINE mode and type in the syntax for a substitution (maybe you need to add a range as well) and then having to write and execute multiple regex patterns to implement a similar solution.

End-of-Line Concerns

Interestingly, Vim's VISUAL-BLOCK mode is intelligent enough to know that when we want to insert some content (or apply a change) at the end of a line, that the end of the line will be different each time.

Imagine our content looks like the following:

```
pro javascript design patterns
practical clojure
beginning ruby
regular expression recipes
practical common lisp
```

If we wanted to add an exclamation point to the end of each line, using VISUAL-BLOCK mode, we would have to use the $ operator at some point during our command, to tell Vim to move to the end of the line. But as you can see, the end of the line is different for each line, as some book titles are longer than others.

Let's run the command that implements the solution: gg<C-v>$4jA!<Esc>. (Don't worry, we'll come back and explain this command in a moment.) Once we run this command, we'll see that the result has the following content (note that the exclamation marks [!] on each line aren't placed at the same point as the longest line but are placed perfectly at the relevant position for each line):

```
pro javascript design patterns!
practical clojure!
beginning ruby!
regular expression recipes!
practical common lisp!
```

So let's take a moment to quickly explain the command we ran. (You should have been able to analyze and figure it out yourself by now; if not, then I'd suggest going back and reading Chapter 5 on how to read and run commands in Vim.)

- gg: We move to the top of the buffer (just in case our cursor isn't already at the start of the first line).

- <C-v>: We enter into VISUAL-BLOCK mode (which selects the current character under the cursor).

- $: We move the selection to the end of the line (subsequently selecting the entire line).

- 4j: We move down four lines (subsequently selecting the entire file).

- A: We tell Vim we want to "block append." (Because we used the $ operator to move to the end of the line, the append will occur at the end of the line.)

- !: We type in the exclamation point.

- <Esc>: We escape VISUAL-BLOCK mode, so the change is then applied to all selected lines.

Better Selection Capabilities

Selecting content so far has pretty much been handled in one direction. But you may have to change the selection area after you've started. This might seem unlikely, or you may have just resigned yourself to the fact that you would have to escape VISUAL-BLOCK mode and try again.

Either way, it's not true, and you have an option available to help you tweak your visual selection after you've already started. This can actually be quite a complicated feature to describe, so I'll have to rely on images to help me explain what I'm talking about.

Take a look at Figure 8-3. What this shows is a VISUAL-BLOCK selection on some content. You will note that the position of the cursor is currently placed at the bottom right (within the selection area).

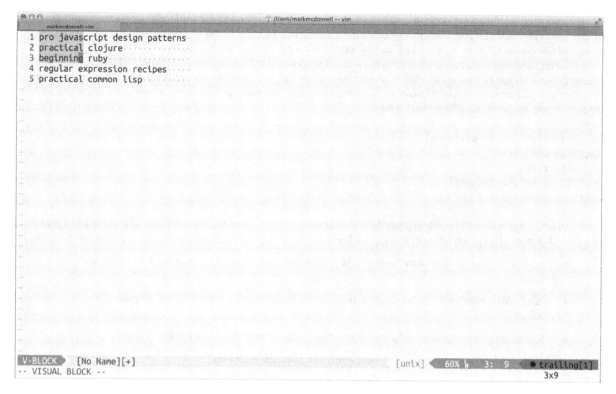

Figure 8-3. Default cursor position for VISUAL-BLOCK selection area

If we were to run the command o at this point (see also :h visual-change), this would change the cursor position so it no longer was placed at the bottom right of the selection area but would now be on the opposite side (i.e., the top left of the selection area). See Figure 8-4 for an example.

Similarly, the O command would again move the cursor position, but this time, it would move the cursor to the opposite side on the same line. This can be useful, because once the cursor position has changed, we're able to change the visual selection from the perspective of the new cursor position.

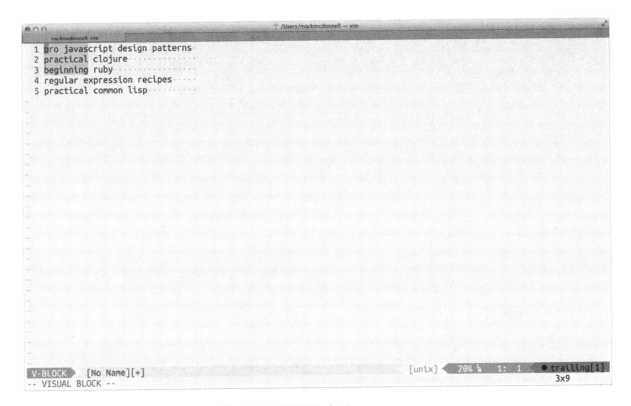

Figure 8-4. *Cursor position flipped inside VISUAL-BLOCK selection area*

Summary

VISUAL-BLOCK mode is one of those features of Vim that you might not necessarily use that much, but there will always be a day when the ability to apply familiar changes across multiple lines will be required. (This day is usually every day, if you're a programmer.) Let's look back and recap some of things you learned in this chapter.

- We looked at a simple example that demonstrates the basics of VISUAL-BLOCK mode to delete the opening character of a line across multiple lines.

- Through this example, you learned how to enter into VISUAL-BLOCK mode (and I also made mention of an alternative method for Windows users).

- We saw how to exit from VISUAL-BLOCK mode, without applying the change to all of our selection (which is useful when one has made a mistake).

- We looked at an example that demonstrates how to carry out a "block insert," which is where we insert new content before the cursor on each line of the selection area.

- We then saw a more complex example that used both a selection area and a "block append." I explained that using alternatives such as macros and substitutions are possible but fall short when compared to ease of use (especially if you're unfamiliar with writing regular expression patterns).

- You discovered that Vim is quite intelligent in how it handles implementing new content when specifying the end-of-line operator $.

- Finally, you learned how to further manipulate our visual selection, by moving the cursor position while within the selection area.

117

■ ■ ■

## CHAPTER 9

Bulk Command Processing

Vim provides an incredibly powerful (and flexible) set of commands, which allow a set of arbitrary commands to be executed against an entire list. In Vim parlance a "list" could be one of the following: a group of open buffers, tabs, windows, and even Vim's argument list (which I'll explain near the end of this chapter).

For each list type (buffer list, tab list, window list, argument list) Vim provides a command which enables us to carry out actions in bulk (i.e., across multiple items). Let's take a look at each of these commands in turn.

- `bufdo`

- `windo`

- `tabdo`

- `argdo`

bufdo

As we already know, when you open a file in Vim, you're, in fact, actually opening a buffer that holds a copy of the file you requested. (If you're unsure, I suggest going back and reading Chapter 3).

Every buffer we create in Vim is added into an internal buffer list. This internal list is what allows Vim to keep track of the current buffer and facilitates commands such as bn and bp, among others, for navigating back and forth among all open buffers.

If we wanted to execute the same command for each buffer that exists in our buffer list, we would have to use the `:bufdo` command. The flow of how this looks internally is something like the following:

- `:bf`: Vim moves to the first buffer.

- `:{command}`: Vim executes the command specified.

- `:bn`: Vim moves to the next buffer in the list.

- `:{command}`: Vim executes the command specified.

- . . . etc. . . .

At this point, if an error occurs, Vim will stop processing the buffers and return the error. If, on the other hand, Vim manages to process all the buffers, the last one becomes the current buffer within the viewport.

Simple Example

Now that we have an understanding of what a buffer list is, we can look at how the `bufdo` command works. Let's consider a simple example, in which we have a set of buffers already open within Vim and we've made changes to each of the buffers already.

We want to exit Vim, but as we do, we have to make sure that each buffer is written back to the relevant file it corresponds to, so we don't lose any of our changes. The following command demonstrates how to do this:

```
:bufdo wq
```

Effectively, we've told Vim to process each buffer (using the `bufdo` command), and within each buffer, we want Vim to execute the command `wq` (meaning we want it to first write the buffer, then close the buffer).

■ **Note**   In the preceding example, you can also achieve the same result with `:wa` (`:h :wa`), which effectively allows you to write only the buffers that have been changed in some way.

Complex Example

Imagine you have multiple buffers open, and you want to add a timestamp to the bottom of each file. We can use a combination of the `:bufdo` command, along with some basic VimL, to achieve this.

```
:bufdo exe ":normal i" . strftime("%c") | update
```

The `:bufdo` command expects an additional command to follow it, so that it can execute that additional command within each buffer it encounters. To execute multiple commands, use a pipe character (`|`) to separate the commands. In the preceding example, we have what looks like quite a complex set of commands, so let's break it down into separate parts, to help us understand what it is doing.

- exe: We use the "execute" command, which will execute the result of the code inbetween the quoted strings. The benefit of using execute instead of just trying to specify a bunch of commands by themselves is that using exe actually makes running our other commands easier (see the note below for further clarification of why).

- `":normal i"`: As per the previous point, inside our quotes is the command we want to run, which, for this example, equates to "use NORMAL mode and then trigger i (which places us into INSERT mode)."

- `. strftime("%c")`: We use the `.` character to concatenate the previous commands with the result of the VimL expression `strftime("%c")`. The `strftime` function is what returns the current date and time.

- `| update`: When the previous command (which updates the buffer with a timestamp) is completed, we pipe through to the `update` command, which causes the buffer to be written, if there have been any changes (which there obviously have been, as we've just inserted a new timestamp into the buffer).

■ **Note** The reason why the exe command makes running our own commands easier is that we are able to specify control keys (such as entering a carriage return), as long as they're properly escaped, like so: \<CR>, which isn't something we could easily do otherwise. It also allows us to construct complex commands that are built from other filters, such as VimL expressions (as our example demonstrates).

windo

The :windo command works in a similar fashion to :bufdo but with one very important difference, which is that it only works on visible buffers. Remember that Vim can have many buffers open, but if there is only one window, then only one buffer is visible at a time.

The :windo command will only execute a specified command against the visible buffers. So, if there are multiple windows, then they will each contain a visible buffer, which will be affected by the :windo command.

Let's take a look at a simple example of this. Imagine we have a file for each letter of the alphabet (that's 26, if you weren't sure). If we open all those files within Vim, we'll have 26 open buffers. Each of these files contains a timestamp (e.g., Sun 8 Jun 11:20:25 2014). Now imagine we only have four windows. This means there aren't enough viewports available to display all the buffers we have open (see Figure 9-1).

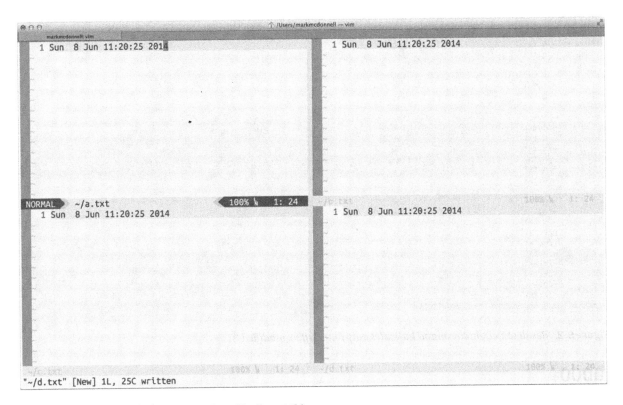

Figure 9-1. *Four windows with our selected buffers visible*

The last detail in this example to consider is that the buffer that is visible within each of the four windows has been specifically selected. By that, I mean they are the four buffers we're interested in editing (the rest of the buffers we don't want to change).

So, what is the change we want to make? Well, for each of these buffers, we want to substitute the year (which is currently set to 2014), so that it reads 1914 instead.

The following command demonstrates how we can achieve the change, using the `:windo` command:

```
:windo %s/2014/1914/ge
```

I haven't covered the substitution command yet (I'll be covering it in depth when we reach Chapter 11), but effectively, in the preceding command, we're telling Vim that in each window, we want to execute a command that searches the entire visible buffer and replaces any occurrence of 2014 to 1914.

If we take a look at Figure 9-2, we can see that when we list our buffers (by running `:ls`), the first four buffers are indicated as being modified, which is exactly the result we wanted: to change only the buffers that are visible within our available windows.

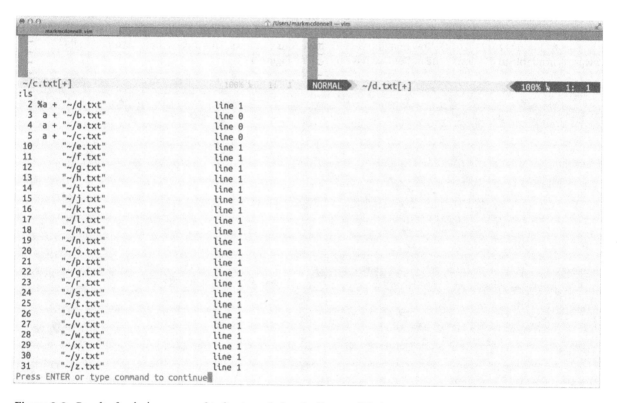

Figure 9-2. *Result of* `:windo` *command indicates only four buffers modified*

tabdo

The `:tabdo` command works in a similar manner to what we've already seen thus far in `:bufdo`/`:windo`. We pass it a command to execute, and it runs that command inside every tab we have open. But there is one slight difference: the types of commands you run will not be the same, because the tab interface is a fundamentally different environment from a window (viewport) or file buffer.

If you're unsure of what I mean by that, just take a moment to consider what types of actions you would expect to be able to carry out on a list of tabs. What does a tab contain? Well, a tab contains windows (either one window or many split windows, but essentially, a tab's main content is a window). So it would stand to reason that the commands you run would likely be focused on manipulating any windows found within a specific tab.

Let's now imagine we have three open tabs, and in each tab is a horizontally split set of windows (so, two windows, one above another, in a linear layout). See Figure 9-3 for an example.

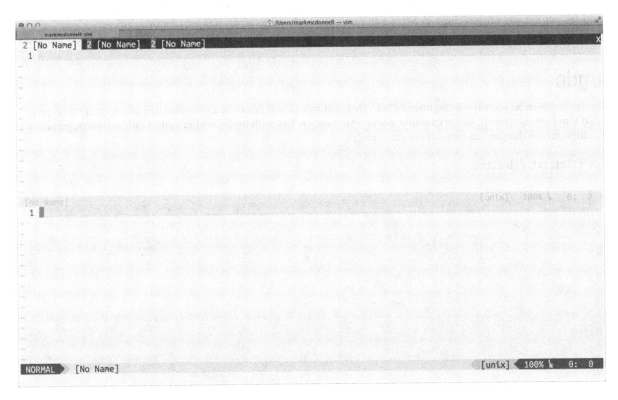

Figure 9-3. *Example of horizontal splits in a set of tabs*

In each tab, the cursor is placed in the top window, and we want the cursor to actually be in the bottom window instead. To achieve this, we have to find a command that will let us manipulate the window within the tab, so that the bottom one has focus. The following command will do exactly that:

```
:tabdo wincmd j
```

After running the preceding command, we'll see that we're now placed inside the last tab (which is expected, as Vim has successfully processed the :tabdo command for each item in the tab list), and if we cycle through each tab (using the gt command), we'll see that the cursor has indeed been placed inside the bottom window inside each tab.

So, the :tabdo part of the command should be self-explanatory by now (it executes the command that follows it inside each available tab), but what about the wincmd j part? Well, this particular command is a shortcut for any of the window-related cursor movement key bindings (see :h window-move-cursor for the full list of key bindings available).

Any of those window/cursor key bindings can be executed via the COMMAND-LINE mode. Subsequently, we took the "down" key binding (the one which allows moving the cursor to the window below the current window: <C-w>j) and used the command-line variation instead, which equates to wincmd j. (Remember: j is one of the primary cursor movement commands found on your keyboard's home row).

■ **Note** If you were to run that command when you had only one window per tab, rather than the expected two windows per tab, you wouldn't have to worry. Vim won't throw you an error; it'll just fail silently.

---

argdo

The last list item we have is the "arguments list." This particular list is populated with files that you specify when you open Vim (see Figure 9-4), as, for example, if you were to open Vim with the following command (assuming you have two files named the same as those in our example):

```
vim file1.txt file2.txt
```

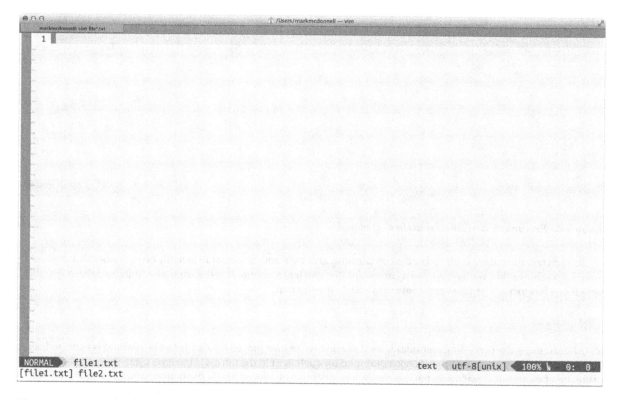

Figure 9-4. Example of the argument list content being displayed

The result of this command is that the arguments list will be populated with two items (file1.txt and file2.txt). Once you're within Vim, you can view the argument list at any time, by running the command :args.

You can then execute commands against all the items within the argument list, much as you have seen so far with the :bufdo/:window/:tabdo commands. For example, imagine you have opened Vim as described above and, so, you have two buffers open (file1.txt and file2.txt). If you were to open another file now from within Vim (e.g., :e ~/Desktop/foobar.txt), you would find that you have three buffers open: file1.txt, file2.txt, and foobar.txt, and yet checking the arguments list will still only display the buffers file1.txt and file2.txt.

This is the fundamental difference between the commands :budfo and :argdo. The argument list will only affect the buffers that have been opened via the arguments list (e.g., when specifying files at the point of opening Vim). It's a subtle but sometimes important difference, because what typically happens is that you'll open a set of important files, and then, during the course of working on those files, you'll open more files inside of Vim (so that they create new buffers but aren't part of the core argument list buffers). If you then decide to make a bulk change to the initial files you opened Vim with, that's where the granular control of the :argdo command comes in.

Modifying the Arguments List

You can also change the argument list after you've opened Vim. For example, you can use the same :args command to both display and set the list. The following is an example of changing the list to a different set of files:

```
:args ~/Desktop/{foo,bar,baz}.txt
```

If we were to look at the argument list now (:args), we would see that it no longer contains the files file1.txt, file2.txt, and foobar.txt but foo.txt, bar.txt, and baz.txt instead; so it hasn't appended these files but instead wiped the list completed and re-created it from the new files specified.

Simple Example

Let's take a look at a simple example now, in which we want to close all buffers that were opened as part of the arguments lists.

```
:argdo echo expand('%:p') | bd!
```

The preceding command first displays the full path to the current argument list buffer and then forcibly closes the buffer, without saving any potential changes. Vim then moves to the next argument list buffer to "rinse and repeat" the process, leaving behind other buffers (that had been opened after Vim had already started) untouched.

Summary

This was a short chapter, but as I mentioned in the preface to this book, the decision to have short and focused chapters was made purposely to aid new users to Vim and to help them more easily find the type of features they wanted to learn about.

With that in mind, let's first recap some of the things you learned in this chapter and then move onward!

- I explained that Vim has multiple concepts of "lists" (such as the buffer list, window list, tab list, and arguments list).

- These lists can be manipulated by using specific commands (such as :bufdo, :windo, :tabdo, and :argdo).

- You learned how Vim internally processes these commands by starting at the first item in the respective list, executing the command, and then moving to the next item in the list, until all list items have been processed and we find ourselves inside the last list item.

- We looked at both a simple and complex example using the `:bufdo` command, the latter demonstrating the use of the exe command to let us construct complex expressions from external filters (such as VimL).

- We saw how the `:windo` command only affects visible buffers, and our example included a command (substitution) that we'll see in much more detail in a later chapter.

- You learned about how `:tabdo`, although similar in principle, requires a different perspective when trying to solve problems using it, because the interface for tabs are fundamentally different from buffers and windows.

- Finally, we saw how the arguments list and the `:argdo` command work, as well as how the latter is subtlety different from the `:bufdo` command, because of the types of files it affects. We also saw how to dynamically update the arguments list from within Vim, and that it's a destructive action (i.e., it doesn't append files but completely re-creates the list).

CHAPTER 10

Editing Workflow

Editing in Vim is a combination of mode swapping and command execution. What this ultimately means is that to be comfortable editing in Vim requires practice—and lots of it. There are many resources available to help you practice (I cover some popular options at the end of the chapter). We'll also be looking at some of the commands, operators, and editing tricks I personally use in my day-to-day workflow.

In this chapter, we'll be seeing some examples of how to edit content in real documents. This isn't just about learning commands (as you've already done in previous chapters) but about seeing how you can apply the knowledge of Vim so far.

I personally find the best way to practice (and practice safely) is to find yourself a long document, or create a new file, and paste in lots of content from www.lipsum.com, and, from there, start playing with the different operators, mixing them up with the different motions and trying to get a *feel* for editing. If you can, I would suggest finding a document that best represents your work environment as possible.

For example, if you're a programmer, use a copy of a big, complex project file, rather than a plain text document, because you'll more likely want to get used to moving around code syntax, which is a bit trickier than just navigating standard punctuation. Set yourself a typical programming task and keep track of the things you find you would like to do but are having trouble with, and then make sure to focus on learning/researching Vim commands that facilitate that way of working in the most efficient form possible.

What you typically find is that you'll stumble over a problem (such as: "How do I get halfway down this document and over 10 columns, to the start of that function call, so I can edit the parameter list?"), which you're not sure how to solve. You might try out a few commands, and owing to time constraints (and just wanting to get your work done), you'll cheat by only using the cursor movement keys to get to the relevant place you're looking for. That's fine for that moment in time, but do make a note of the scenario and then, when you get a chance to practice, try to find better ways of solving it. (If you hit that issue once, it'll likely become an issue you keep hitting.)

Over time, you should find that you don't have to *think* too much about how to edit something, but just instinctively run the command, confident that it'll do what you want.

Editing in Vim really comes down to individual preference. I know a lot of hard-core Vim users (both programmers and nonprogrammers) who don't use anywhere near the number of Vim commands I do, because they're happy and comfortable with the set of Vim commands they do know and use a lot. They find that they work more quickly that way, using a specific subset of commands, rather than trying to commit to memory lots of other useful Vim commands (something I personally disagree with, believing they would become more proficient using Vim, if they tried to utilize more of its toolkit), whereas I'm more efficient using a wider range of commands.

Probably most important, however, is not to feel like you have to conform to "best practices" because some self-proclaimed Vim guru (you can substitute that word for *zealot,* if you prefer) tells you that's how it *has* to be done. Find what style and process work best for you, but if you find time to explore additional features, I would highly recommend doing so.

Practical Examples

In the following examples, I hope to demonstrate some of the types of commands and operators I find useful while navigating around and editing within Vim, so you can get a feel for a real-world practical use of the commands we've looked at so far. This is by no means an exhaustive list, as I have built up a large repertoire of commands for all sorts of scenarios, not to mention that my way of working also changes every few months, as I tweak my workflow to fit the needs I have at the time.

Because the following subsections are quite long and take us on a bit of a journey, it'll be good, before we start, to take a top-level look at what will be covered.

- First, we'll be using the gg operator to help us move around more efficiently within a single file.

- We'll then look at the f and F operators and how they can help us navigate to specific points on a single line.

- We'll move on to the / search command, which, again, can help with navigating around a single (but long) file.

- After that, we'll look at the %, va, and vt operators, as they can help us to navigate very complex syntax (as found in programming code).

- Finally, we'll take an early peek at the COMMAND-LINE substitution command s/{pattern}/{replacement}/, which (as we'll see in the next chapter) is an incredibly powerful feature for finding patterns and carrying out dynamic replacements on those matched patterns.

- To wrap up the chapter, we take a tour through Vim's state management process and also look at how to resolve issues with pasting content, which can be especially problematic for programming files, if not handled properly.

Moving Around a Single File

Let's start with [count]gg (go to line). I probably use this operator the most, as it's a convenient way to jump around to different parts of a buffer, without having additional help from a feature such as Vim marks. (This is Vim's built-in bookmarks. I'll cover how marks work in Chapter 15).

While I'm looking around a document, I might notice that farther down the page, there is a line I'm interested in. From there, I can just quickly glance at the line number (e.g., line number 105) and jump straight there, with 105gg (or 105G). I prefer using gg over G, as it's quicker for me to type.

Moving Around on a Single Line

The f/F commands are essential for searching backward and forward for a specific character on the current line (which is something I do a lot of within Vim). In this section, I'll demonstrate some examples of how to use the f/F operators to help you more easily navigate around a single line. For our first example, let's imagine we are working with the following Ruby programming file:

```ruby
class Foo
  def initialize
    puts { :foo => :bar } # TODO: implement more code
  end
end
```

You can see from the example that there is a code comment at the end of line 3 (Ruby code comments start with a hash character [#]), and I've decided to edit the code comment. There are a few ways we can do this, but I'll demonstrate one that incorporates the "find character" operator. Take a look at the following command:

```
3ggf#lc$
```

So, the preceding command is a combination of operators. Let's break this down to understand what's happening.

- `3gg` moves us to the third line.

- `f#` moves the cursor to the # character.

- `lc$` deletes the content after the #, ready for us to insert new content in its place.

Let's imagine that the third line of our Ruby code file now has the following updated code comment "implement some tests":

```
puts { :foo => :bar } # TODO: implement some tests
```

I've just realized that the property in the object I've created (e.g., `:foo`) is also incorrect, and I have to fix that as well. My cursor is currently sitting at the end of the third line. (This is where we left off at the previous change, whereby we replaced the old comment with the one we have now.) The simplest solution to get my cursor back to the `:foo` property is to search backward through the line, using the F operator. There are no other f characters in this line, so the most unique hook we can use to move our cursor is the *f* from `:foo`. The Ff command is what we must run, and it effectively moves the cursor *back* to the first f character it finds.

Admittedly, I could have searched backward for the `:` character, as that is also a fairly unique character, but as there are three of those on the line already, I would have had to count them to be sure, and once I did that, I could have then used `3F:`, but I didn't want to use that particular solution, because it results in one more character having to be typed, and it also requires more thinking power to implement the solution. I prefer not to have to think so much, when all I'm doing is moving my cursor to another place on the current line.

Another good reason to use the f/F operators is that you are able to utilize two motions that are indirectly associated with them. These motions, `;` and `,`, allow you to move your cursor onto the next occurence of the character you tried to match with f/F. So if you want to scan a line for a specific character, you can easily iterate your way through the line, finding each match.

Some inexperienced users get frustrated when they can't think of a good movement option to use (or, as often is the case with Vim, there are *too many* options), so they'll resort to using either the e or w motions multiple times (which is just plain slow). The trick is to look for a unique character and use f or F to take you there. It's not always possible to find a unique character to hook into, but that's where other ways of solving the problem come in.

Another example of thinking laterally when you don't have a unique hook in the direction you wish to move is to consider moving your cursor to the opposite end of the line (e.g., using either the motions 0 or $). Once your cursor is at the start/end of a line, you have more options available to you. Or just make an intermediate step to a unique character, thereby closing the gap just enough to try again.

Moving Around Long Files

If you find yourself working through a long document (for me, it's usually a programming file, but it could be a blog post or a chapter from a book you're writing), I usually have to find a way to navigate around the document, rather than scrolling line-by-line through dozens of pages.

The easiest way to do this is to find a unique hook that you can successfully search and step through. For example, we're going to use the search operator / to help us navigate through an open source JavaScript library I wrote a while ago called "DOM Builder" (see Listing 10-1).

Listing 10-1. Contents of our DOM Builder JavaScript file

```javascript
(function (define) {
    'use strict';

  define(function() {
      var DOM = {
          structure: '',
          storage: { tags:[] },

          add_id: function(id) {
              return id ? ' id="' + id + '"' : '';
          },

          add_class: function(classes) {
              return classes.length ? ' class="' + classes.join(' ') + '"' : '';
          },

          add_attribute: function(attributes) {
              if (!attributes) {
                  return '';
              }

              var len   = attributes.length,
                  attrs = [],
                  data, key, prop;

              while (len--) {
                  data = attributes[len].split('=');
                  key  = data[0].substring(1);
                  prop = data[1].substring(0, data[1].length-1);

                  attrs.push(' ' + key + '="' + prop + '"');
              }

              return attrs.join(' ');
          },

          content: function() {
              var counter = 0,
                  limit = arguments.length;

              while (counter < limit) {
                  if (typeof arguments[counter] == 'string') {
                      this.structure += arguments[counter];
                  }
                  counter++;
              }

              this.structure += '</' + this.storage.tags.pop() + '>'; // remove the last tag from
              the storage list and use it here
          },
```

```
el: function(tag) {
    return this.create(tag);
},

create: function(tag) {
    var tag, id, classes, attributes;

    id = /#([^.]+)/.exec(tag);
    id = (id) ? id[1] : ''; // `exec` returns `null` if there is no match

    classes = tag.split('.').splice(1); // remove the first index which should be the tag

    attributes = tag.match(/\[[^\]]+\]/g); // e.g. ["[width=100]", "[blah=abc]"]

    tag = tag.match(/[^#.\[\]]+/)[0];

    this.structure += '<' + tag + '' + this.add_class(classes) + '' + this.add_id(id) +
    '' + this.add_attribute(attributes) + '>';
    this.storage.tags.push(tag); // store the current tag so we can close off the
    element after all sub content is added.

    return this; // we return `this` so we can chain method calls
},

convert_to_node: function() {
    var doc  = document,
        frag = doc.createDocumentFragment(),
        node = doc.createElement('div'),
        counter = 0,
        limit;

    node.innerHTML = this.structure;
    this.structure = ''; // reset

    // We now need to remove the 'wrapping' <div> which was only necessary so we could
        `innerHTML` the content into it...

    limit = node.children.length;

    while (counter < limit) {
        frag.appendChild(node.children[counter].cloneNode(true));
        counter++;
    }

    node = null; // clean-up

    return frag;
},
```

```
        init: function() {
            if (!arguments.length) {
                throw new Error('Please ensure you pass in at least one argument to DOM.init()
                which is a call to either the DOM.create() or DOM.el() methods');
            }
            return this.convert_to_node();
        }
    }

    return DOM;
});
}(typeof define == 'function' && define.amd ? define : function(factory) { this.DOM = factory() } ));
```

If you're interested in what the script does and how it works, I would direct you to the relevant GitHub repository (http://github.com/integralist/DOMBuilder), but it doesn't matter, for the purposes of this exercise. What we're interested in is how to navigate through this particular file structure.

So, the first thing we need to do is scan the visible content, looking for a hook of some sort. It also helps to understand the document you're working with, as that will give you an indication of the important parts of the file.

If you were working in a Markdown (http://daringfireball.net/projects/markdown/) file, then chances are the most important items would be headers that lead into a new section of the document (headers in Markdown take the format of #Header 1, ##Header 2, ###Header 3, and so forth), so you would likely want to do a search using a regular expression pattern, such as the following:

```
/#\+\w
```

The preceding pattern is composed of the / search command, followed by the pattern we want to match, which is either single or multiple hash characters, #\+, followed by a word character, \w.

■ **Note** The search command is most useful when using regular expressions (sometimes shortened to regex, for a singular pattern, and regexes, for multiple patterns). To find out more about how to write them in Vim (there are many different variations of regex engines), I would suggest reading through www.regular-expressions.info/ first, to get an understanding of how to write regexes, and then through www.vimregex.com, to learn how to adapt them to Vim's particular implementation.

For our purposes, we're working through a JavaScript file, and so the most important syntax hook for this type of file is the function keyword. This also means that our search pattern will be much easier to write, compared to the Markdown search pattern we looked at a moment ago. (This is because we don't have to use any complex pattern-matching syntax.)

Our solution will be /function, and once we run that particular search command, we'll see that Vim highlights all the matches it has found (see Figure 10-1).

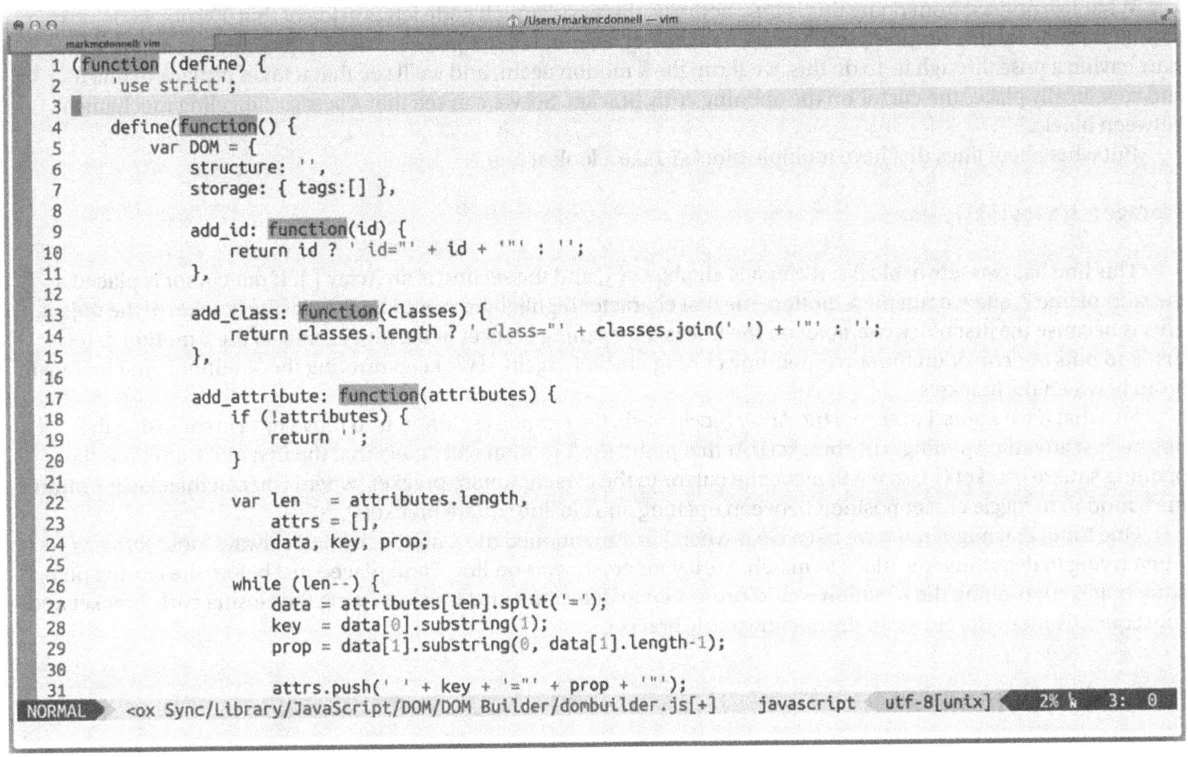

```
  1 (function (define) {
  2     'use strict';
  3
  4     define(function() {
  5         var DOM = {
  6             structure: '',
  7             storage: { tags:[] },
  8
  9             add_id: function(id) {
 10                 return id ? ' id="' + id + '"' : '';
 11             },
 12
 13             add_class: function(classes) {
 14                 return classes.length ? ' class="' + classes.join(' ') + '"' : '';
 15             },
 16
 17             add_attribute: function(attributes) {
 18                 if (!attributes) {
 19                     return '';
 20                 }
 21
 22                 var len  = attributes.length,
 23                     attrs = [],
 24                     data, key, prop;
 25
 26                 while (len--) {
 27                     data = attributes[len].split('=');
 28                     key  = data[0].substring(1);
 29                     prop = data[1].substring(0, data[1].length-1);
 30
 31                     attrs.push(' ' + key + '="' + prop + '"');
```

`NORMAL`   `<ox Sync/Library/JavaScript/DOM/DOM Builder/dombuilder.js[+]`   `javascript` `utf-8[unix]`   `2% `   `3:   0`

Figure 10-1. *Vim has highlighted our matched search pattern*

From this point, we can now execute either the n or N operators to navigate through each match one-by-one, moving either forward (n) or backward (N). This particular hook has allowed us to work our way through the file much more easily, stopping at each important section along the way.

Moving Between Blocks

Let's continue to use the "DOM Builder" script from before and see how we can use Vim's % motion to navigate easily through complex syntax, such as blocks (punctuation characters, such as {}()[]).

Imagine our cursor is currently placed at the start of line 5. The line's content looks like the following:

```
var DOM = {
```

We can see that we define an object called DOM (in JavaScript, you can create an object using the curly brackets syntax: { /* object code here */ }), and because it's a long object, its content scrolls off outside the window viewport. I'm not actually interested in this particular object, so I would rather not have to scroll through all its content (which is made up of lots of functions and would make our previous solution of using /function less useful in this scenario).

So, my requirement is to jump to the bottom of this object. But how do I do that when I don't know how long it is? Well, I can use the % motion, which, when pressed, will detect a block (in this case, the opening curly bracket) on the line and take me to the corresponding closing bracket, which is on line 103.

What I've noticed from doing this is that, actually, there isn't much code left outside of that DOM object. It looks like all the code for this script is placed inside that object. Damn, I better go back to the top of this DOM object and start having a nose through it. To do this, we'll run the % motion again, and we'll see that it takes us back to line 5 and specifically places the cursor on the opening curly bracket. So, we can see that % acts as a toggling mechanism between blocks.

But what about lines that have multiple blocks? Take a look at line 7.

```
storage: { tags:[] },
```

This line has two sets of blocks: the first is an object {}, and the second is an Array []. If our cursor is placed at the start of line 7, and we run the % motion, the first character highlighted would be the closing bracket of the object. This is because the first block character on the line is the opening bracket of the object, and so the % motion detects that and puts our cursor on the corresponding closing bracket. Again, if we keep running the % motion, our cursor will jump between the brackets.

So, what if we wanted to access the Array block? Well, the simplest solution is to move our cursor inside the object (just after the opening curly bracket). At that point, the % motion will detect that the first block after it is the opening square bracket ([), so it will move the cursor to the closing square bracket (where you can then keep running the % motion to toggle cursor position between opening and closing square brackets).

One thing that might not have been clear when I first mentioned the % motion is that it always looks *forward* when trying to determine the block to match. So, if your cursor was on line 7 and placed just before the closing object curly bracket }, running the % motion would cause Vim to detect the next block as being the closing curly bracket and subsequently move the cursor to the opening curly bracket.

Complex Syntax

If you're dealing with particularly complex content (usually this happens if you're a programmer, as code files come in many forms and syntaxes), it can be confusing to navigate through efficiently. This is where the vt{x} and va{x} commands (select until and select around) are particularly useful, as being a programmer, I usually have to take a slice of some text that doesn't fit inside the definition of a standard Vim text object.

The type of content you interact with in a real-world document/application doesn't always make selecting the content you want easy. You'll usually have to think a bit more laterally when approaching a problem such as trying to select a specific chunk of code from a nested construct.

As an example, take a look at the following line of code (this is part of a Clojure programming file; Clojure is a Lisp-based language, so you'll find that these types of files contain a *lot* of parenthesis and brackets):

```
(map
 (fn [item]
   (prn item))
 (map vector [:a :b :c] [1 2 3]))
```

Looking at this code, imagine that your cursor is inside the first set of square brackets on the last line, [:a :b :c]. If we wanted to select the entire expression (that is, all the code, including the outer parentheses), then the result we're after would be the following content to be selected:

```
(map vector [:a :b :c] [1 2 3])
```

You'll notice that we can't just yank the line with yy, because we'll get the whitespace at the start of the line as well as the closing parenthesis from the outer form. So, the solution to this problem is to utilize Vim's text object syntax and select the nearest parentheses block, using va(.

You'll remember that we saw the va(command back in Chapter 5, and effectively, we're telling Vim to select the parentheses block around our current cursor position (including the parentheses).

But what if I wanted to select both sets of vectors (the square brackets)? Well, in that instance, I would just combine two sets of commands, so that the solution became va[t).

That command breaks down into two parts: the first is va[, which selects the first vector, [:a :b :c]. The second part is t), which expands the selection until it reaches just before the first closing set of parentheses. This results in both vectors, [:a :b :c] [1 2 3], being selected.

Efficient selecting of content within Vim usually comes down to adapting to the environment you're working within. If you're working on a code file, people usually assume you'll have a harder time because of the complex syntax, but that's not true. In my opinion, there are more unique hooks to play with and to anchor your selections from.

Text Objects

I use text objects a lot in Vim, and regardless of whether you're working with a programming file or a plain text file, your understanding and handling of them is critical to becoming an efficient Vim user. I covered what text objects were in Chapter 5, so I won't repeat that information here, but it's important to realize the power of text objects and that becoming proficient with them will really move your editing skills to the professional level.

Find and Replace

A feature I may use less frequently but that is a remarkably powerful tool when used in the right situation is Vim's substitution command (when run from COMMAND-LINE mode). I'll cover it in greater detail in Chapter 11, but for now, let's take a look at its syntax structure and a quick example.

```
[range]s/{pattern}/{replacement}/[flags]
```

So, we can see from this syntax structure that we can specify an optional range, which means we determine what part of the file the substitution affects. (If we don't specify a range, it'll default to the current line.) Next, we tell Vim we're running the substitution command using the s character. After that, we pass in a pattern we want Vim to match within our range. After that, we specify what we want to replace the matched content with. Finally, we have a set of flags (which is just a fancy word for "options") that we can specify to change the default behavior of the command.

So let's see a quick example that'll whet your appetite for the next chapter, when I cover this command in much more granular detail. Imagine that your cursor is again placed at the start of line 7 of our "DOM Builder" JavaScript file, as follows:

```
storage: { tags:[] },
```

If we decided that we wanted to change the Array into an object, we could do so, using the following variation of the substitution command:

```
:s/\[\]/{}/
```

We'll break this down into its component parts, to help explain how it works. First, we use the s/{pattern}/{replacement}/ structure to inform Vim that we're going to be running a substitution command.

Next, we apply the pattern that will help us match the Array block. This pattern might look a bit cryptic, but that's because it's a regular expression pattern. (See my earlier note in this chapter about learning resources.) This effectively says that Vim should match []. If you're curious about the backslashes, this is to tell Vim's regex engine to escape the characters [and], so that the engine doesn't try to interpret them as a character class. (In a regex pattern, a character class is a set of square brackets that hold a set of characters you want to either whitelist or blacklist.)

The final part is the replacement, which is the part of the substitution in which we replace whatever was matched by the regex pattern. In this instance, we tell Vim that the matched content should be replaced with {}.

■ **Note**   There are many other ways to achieve the same result in Vim, but for the purpose of demonstration, I went with using the substitution command.

Workflow Management

Creating, moving through, and generally managing windows, buffers, and panes within both Vim and tmux is a large part of my day-to-day workflow. I'll cover workflow management of Vim and tmux in more detail near the end of the book, as it's an important topic that requires closer inspection and understanding, if you're to get the best out of these tools.

I'm mentioning this now, just so you know to keep an eye out for it when you get there. The reason for not discussing workflow management at this point is because you first must learn about tmux. Once you've done that, you will be better equipped to combine knowledge of both Vim and tmux, to improve how we can integrate these two tools into our workflow.

Vim's Multiverse

Vim has an incredibly powerful system for handling state. What you might not be aware of is that Vim creates multiple branches for certain changes you have made to your content. This feature sounds strange, but ultimately, it lets you re-track very old state much like a version control system (VCS) does, and when dealing with large files and projects, being able to more intelligently handle old state changes is an important and useful editing feature.

If you already use a VCS, this feature might seem redundant, but if you don't, and you find the idea of learning how to use a VCS very confusing (e.g., you're not a programmer), then this feature of Vim can be a nice alternative (or way of introducing you to the concept).

The best way to understand this feature is to see an example. Let's look at an open source project called Squirrel (https://github.com/Integralist/Squirrel).

```
{
  "name": "squirrel-js",
  "version": "0.1.4",
  "description": "Node based cli tool using PhantomJS to automate generation of an Application
                  Cache manifest file for a specified URL",
  "main": "lib/squirrel",
  "scripts": {
    "test": "echo \"Error: no test specified\" && exit 1"
  },
  "engines": {
    "node": ">=0.10"
  },
  "repository": {
    "type": "git",
    "url": "git://github.com/Integralist/Squirrel.git"
  },
```

```
  "preferGlobal": "true",
  "bin": {
    "squirrel": "lib/squirrel.js"
  },
  "dependencies": {
    "phantomjs": "~1.9.2-6",
    "lodash.uniq": "~2.4.1"
  },
  "keywords": [
    "appcache",
    "phantomjs",
    "cli"
  ],
  "author": "Mark McDonnell <mark.mcdx@gmail.com> (http://www.integralist.co.uk/)",
  "license": "MIT",
  "bugs": {
    "url": "https://github.com/Integralist/Squirrel/issues"
  },
  "homepage": "https://github.com/Integralist/Squirrel"
}
```

What the code from this project does isn't important (although you can get a taste for what it's about from the "description" property in the preceding file), but do feel free to peruse the README on GitHub, if you want to learn more.

■ **Note**   You may wonder why most of my code snippets are based on my own open source projects. The reason is that they're real-world projects, and one of the main tenets of this book is to demonstrate real-world solutions. It also saves me from having to make up examples!

Let's start by imagining we have the preceding file (package.json) open, and we want to see what changes have been made to the file, by running the :undolist command. What we'll see returned is the message "Nothing to undo." This is expected behavior, because we've made no changes to the file since we opened it. (There is a way to have Vim remember the changes after the file has been closed, but we'll come back to that later.)

So, to better understand what the :undolist command is for, we have to start making some changes to our file. We'll update the Node engine version on line 10 to be one version up from what it is currently. To do this, we have to execute the following command:

```
10ggf1<C-a>
```

The preceding command will first move us onto line 10 (10gg) and place our cursor at the number 10 (f1).Finally, we increase the number by one (<C-a>), so that it reads 0.11. At this point, even if we didn't write the buffer, running the command :undolist will return a table of data back that shows us that a change had indeed been made. The following is an example of this:

```
number changes  when              saved
     1        1  4 seconds ago
```

So, what this table tells us is that, so far, in this file, we have in total one change made and one change for this specific branch on our tree of changes, and that change was made approximately four seconds prior to the :undolist command being run. There is also a saved column, but it's empty. We'll come back to the saved column later in this section.

■ **Note** A change is considered anything done while inside INSERT mode, a single editing command run via standard key bindings, or via COMMAND-LINE mode. Once you leave INSERT mode, all the changes you made while inside INSERT mode are recorded as one change.

In our example, the <C-a> command is what effected a "change," as far as Vim is concerned. If we now run <C-x> (which decrements/reduces the number by one), then run :undolist again, we should see something such as the following:

```
number changes  when            saved
     2       2  17:52:43
```

What this indicates is that so far, in this file, we have in total two changes made and two changes for this specific branch on our tree of changes, and that change was made at 17:52:43 today.

Now, the difference between the number and changes columns won't make much sense until we force Vim to create a new branch on our tree of changes. So let's do that now by first undoing the last change we made, by executing the u command. (This will mean that the number moves back to being 0.11, and if we were to run :undolist, we would see the same output as before. This, then, indicates that even when we undo a change, the undo list will remember that there *were* two changes made.

Now, as far as we're concerned, we've only made one change to this file (we increased the number from 0.10 to 0.11), but as far as Vim is concerned, we're at a pivotal point to create a new branch on our tree of changes. If we now run <C-a> to again increase the number to 0.12, then run the :undolist command, we'll see some new output, as follows:

```
number changes  when            saved
     2       2  17:52:43
     3       2  3 seconds ago
```

Hmm, OK, so the difference between the number and changes columns should start becoming a little clearer. What the table is telling us is that we now have two "branches." The first branch has two changes made to it (this would be moving the number up to 0.11 and then moving it back down to 0.10), and the second branch also has two changes made to it (moving the number up to 0.11 and then moving it up again to 0.12). But we can see that the number column for the second branch says three changes have been made. This is calculated like so: in the first branch we moved the number up to 0.11 and then moved it back down to 0.10. We then forced Vim to create a new branch (by moving to a previous state using the undo command) and then moved the number from 0.11 (which was where we branched from) up to 0.12.

We can make the difference even clearer by yet another change to the second branch (in which we are currently residing). Let's run the <C-a> command, to increase the number to 0.13, and run the :undolist command once again.

```
number changes  when            saved
     2       2  17:52:43
     4       3  3 seconds ago
```

What the table is telling us is that the second branch now has three changes that we can revert back through, using the undo command (u), but that technically there have been four changes in total (as it counts the one change from when the branch was forked).

It's important to understand that a new branch is created whenever we move back a state. For example, if I run the undo command, the number will be 0.12, and if I make a new change, such as manually changing the number from 12 to 14, Vim will be forced to create a new branch at that point. If we were to then run the :undolist one more time, we would see the following output:

```
number changes  when              saved
     2       2  18:14:33
     4       3  18:20:12
     5       3  2 seconds ago
```

Once more, we can see that a new branch has been created, and it recognizes that there are only three states we can revert back through, although there have been five changes in the entire history.

Moving Through Branches

Imagine that the history of changes we have was actually a much bigger and richer set of changes, with many different branches, and that at this point, we might decide that we want to investigate one of our earlier branch's set of changes. Vim gives us a set of commands that will let us do exactly that (see Table 10-1).

Table 10-1. *Commands for moving back and forth through our change history*

Title	Explanation
g-	Move backward through history, including previous branches
g+	Move forward through history, including previous branches

The g- and g+ commands are like the undo and redo commands but are able to travel through branches! So, if we were to run g-, we would move to the previous branch and undo the last change that was made on that branch.

This is a surprisingly complicated concept to understand, so let's see a simplified example borrowed from the Vim help documentation. Imagine we have a file with the following content:

```
one two three
```

Let's start by deleting the first word, *one*, using the cut command (x), and then undo each cut, so that the file content is still one two three. Vim will think three changes have occurred, but as we're back to a previous state, any change we make now will be made on a new branch. So let's delete the word *two* again, using the cut command, and undo each cut until the file content is one two three.

So, we're currently in the second branch, but if I were to run the undo command, nothing would happen, as I'm already at the oldest change for this second branch. If, on the other hand, we were to run g-, we would jump back a single change, but, this time, from the previous branch, because there are no more changes to revert within branch two. In this example, the last change we made on the first branch was cutting the *e* from the word *one*, so we undo that cut, and the state of the document becomes: e two three.

The g+ command lets us step through all changes from all branches, but moving forward. For example, at this point in time, we're in the first branch, and we've just undone the last edit. If we were to run the redo command (<C-r>), then we would redo the last change in branch one, so the content becomes: two three, but we can't move any farther forward on this branch, because the change by which we deleted the word *two* was actually made on the second branch, not the first. If we run g+ now, we'll jump into the second branch and start stepping through to the changes made in the second branch.

As you can see, the g- and g+ commands are powerful tools, once you understand how they differ from the standard undo and redo commands. I find that they actually make more sense than the default undo and redo commands, as they work more like you would expect them to work.

Saving State

The last item to cover in this section is the "saved" column (we skipped over this earlier). Now, the ability to create branches within Vim is a great feature, but it would be better if the state could be remembered after the file has been closed. That's where the :wundo and :rundo commands come in.

To save any state that has been stored in temporary Vim memory, we must have it stored in a physical file that Vim can load. To write the history of our current buffer into a file, we would have to run the following command:

```
:wundo {name_of_file}
```

Now, when we load up the same file and want to access old state changes, we can load the history into Vim, using the :rundo command, like so:

```
:rundo {name_of_file}
```

Sorting Out How to Paste

One of the last editing tips I want to share with you is with regard to how pasting text in Vim works. You would think pasting text is something that should be a pretty standard affair, but, sadly, that appears not to be the case with Vim (that is, as long as you're not using Vim from the terminal—e.g., you're not using a GUI version of Vim and/or you're not pasting content from another application).

When pasting text from a separate application, Vim doesn't understand what to do with it, so it inserts the text into the buffer, as if the user manually typed it. This is where the problem arises: Vim may change the indentation of the next line to match the previous line. This doesn't seem like much of an issue, but when dealing with code (some programming languages have what is called "significant whitespace," meaning the whitespace affects how the program runs), you'll see how this can cause problems.

To prevent Vim from messing with content being pasted from other applications, it provides you with the following two settings:

1. :set paste

2. :set nopaste

Anytime you're about to paste content from another application, just run :set paste, and when you're finished, run the :set nopaste command.

■ **Note** There is a slightly quicker way to toggle settings, by using the ! character, like so :set paste!. If the setting is enabled, it'll be disabled, and if it was disabled, it will be re-enabled.

Alternative Options for Vim Self-Improvement

There are also some good online (and offline) resources that you can use to help improve your Vim skills. I've listed some popular choices.

- Vim Adventures (http://vim-adventures.com)
- VimGolf (www.vimgolf.com)
- Vim Tutor (run vimtutor from the terminal)

Vim Adventures

Vim Adventures is a web site that tries to make learning Vim a more enjoyable experience, by offering the beginner Vim user a colorful and graphical gaming interface to practice different types of Vim commands, operators, and motions (see Figure 10-2).

Figure 10-2. *Vim Adventures web site*

Although the web site is aimed more at beginners, it can be fun to go through each level and practice your preexisting skills. Sometimes, we get so focused on using a certain subset of Vim's capabilities that we forget the basics or other features that Vim offers. I personally like the idea of having the opportunity to practice a more full set of Vim commands in a relaxed gaming environment.

It's worth being aware (although you would find this out pretty quickly once you started the game) that you're not allowed to utilize the arrow keys to help you navigate through the game and its obstacles. This is to make sure you learn to be as efficient as possible when working in the Vim environment. You may also remember me mentioning in a previous chapter that I find myself being more efficient using just the arrow keys. As I explained then, this was because my time is evenly split across using both Vim and the terminal (where the hjkl home row keys aren't supported), so I've learned to become more efficient at using the arrow keys, as I have them available to me in both Vim and the terminal environment. That doesn't mean that it's not good to practice using just the home row keys as well. You'll be surprised how quickly you get into the swing of using the home row keys.

VimGolf

The VimGolf web site helps you to be more concise and efficient with your Vim skills, by providing you with a set of problems for which you are rewarded by aiming for the lowest number of keystrokes possible, while you look to implement a solution to the particular problems presented (see Figure 10-3).

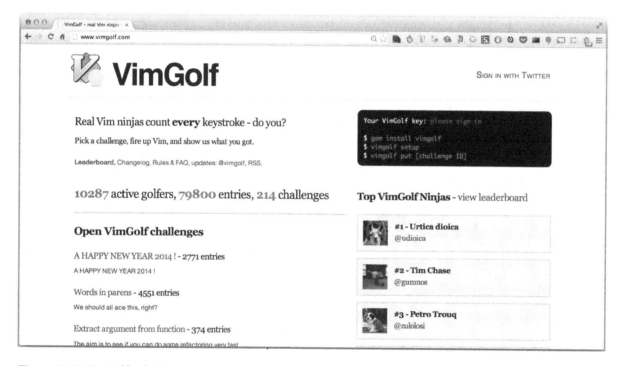

Figure 10-3. *VimGolf web site*

This site is also a perfect example of why "Code Katas" are a programmer's friend. If you've never heard of the term before, it simply means an exercise in which every time you work on the problem presented, you must provide an alternative solution.

Through the principle of practice and repetition, you gain greater insight into both the problem space and the tools you use to solve them. Katas force you to change the way you implement your solution, so that you'll become better at laterally thinking and adapting to complex problems in your real work.

Vim Tutor

Vim provides its own tutorial, which is aimed at complete beginners. It covers a wide range of topics, from basic commands using operators and motions to writing and editing files, reading in content from other files and filters, as well as searching for content and writing your own startup script (see Figure 10-4).

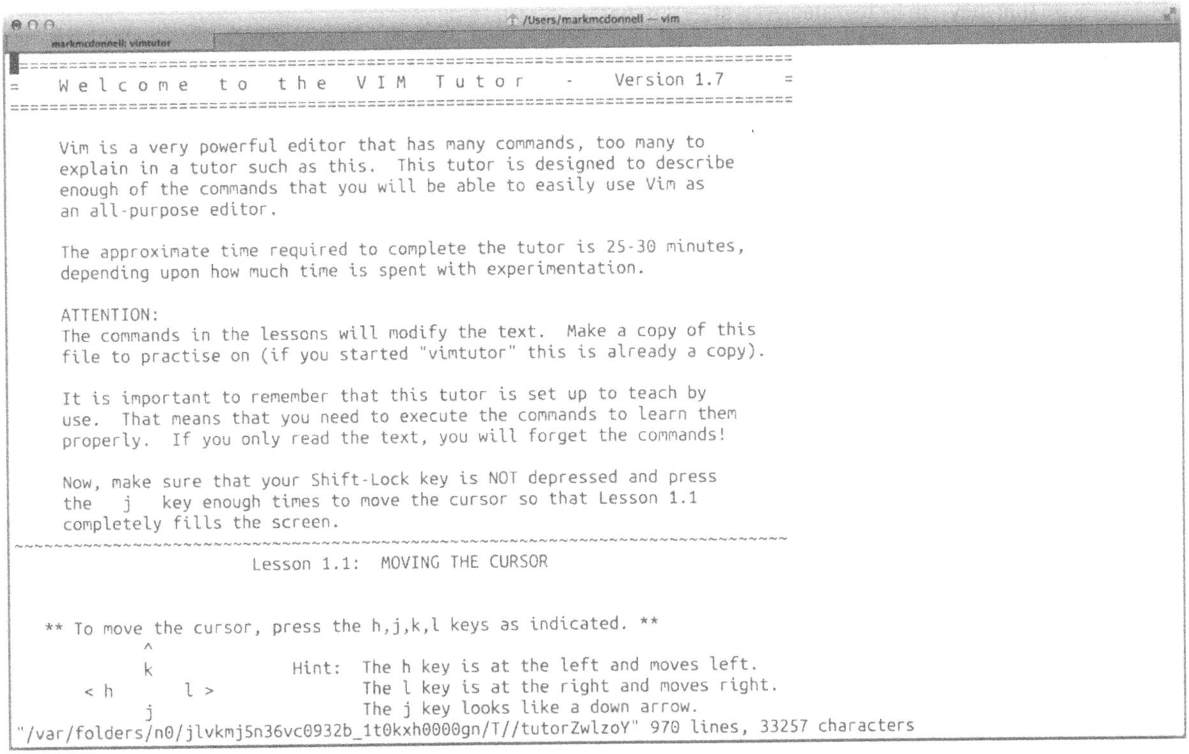

Figure 10-4. *Vim Tutor, run from the terminal application*

Although by this point in the book you'll not need to read through Vim Tutor, it can be interesting to have a look and become acquainted with what the authors of Vim felt was important for new users to know to get up to speed with how to start editing with Vim.

Summary

We covered a lot of topics in this chapter that should put us on the road to editing enlightenment. Let's have a quick recap of some of the items we've seen so far.

- The first thing I discussed was the importance of practicing your editing skills and why not to follow false idols.

- We reviewed real-world practical use of the gg operator, f/F commands, and / search command (in addition to the n and N operators) to navigate long, complex syntax files.

- We also looked at how to jump between multiple block syntaxes, using the % motion, and how to find and replace content, using the substitute command and some simple regular expressions.

- I briefly mentioned both text objects and workflow management, along with their importance with regard to editing.

- We dove into Vim's ability to remember multiple different branches of state changes, using the `:undolist` feature with the g- and g+ commands.

- We looked into how we can save those state changes, using the `:wundo` and `:rundo` commands, so that they can be revisited even after Vim has been restarted.

- We then looked at how to resolve issues with pasting content from external applications.

- Finally, we took a quick look at some alternative methods for improving your editing skills.

## CHAPTER 11

Search and Replace

One of the cornerstones of a solid text editor is the ability to find files and content and to replace the latter with new content. Many editors provide a GUI abstraction on top of underlying code that implements the search criteria for you. Vim doesn't try to hide it and, instead, exposes it to you via the COMMAND-LINE mode.

Throughout this chapter, we will look at the multitude of ways you can search for content and replace it, once you find it. As we'll see, there are many ways to "skin a cat," and when it comes to "Search and Replace," Vim is no exception.

Typically, I find myself (no pun intended) having to correct a typo throughout a text file (or a misspelled variable in a programming file), and Vim makes handling these types of occurences very quick and easy to handle. Even making changes across multiple files, which is a very powerful ability to have at your disposal, is straightforward in Vim (although, as we'll see later on in this chapter, depending on your requirements, maybe Vim isn't the best tool for very large numbers of files).

But let's start at the beginning and work our way up . . .

Finding Files

Although it is not directly related to finding *content,* I wanted to start by introducing you to the `:find` command, which allows you to search for a specific file by entering only the name of the file (including the file extension).

An example of its potential use would be if you're working in a large project folder, and you know there is a file called `foo.txt`, but you're not sure where it is. You could, in this case, use the `find` command, like so:

```
:find foo.txt
```

The preceding command should open the file (if found) in the current window viewport. If not found, Vim would display a message informing you that it was unable to find the file you specified within its "path."

Note If you prefer, there is also the ability to open the file within a split window, using the `sfind` command in COMMAND-LINE mode.

Paths

Most systems have the concept of a "load path," and Vim is no different. The fundamental principle is that when Vim starts up, it has a path variable that holds a list of folders. These folders are where Vim looks to find the file the user specified as part of the `find` command.

To see the default folders within Vim's path setting, first open Vim afresh and run the following command:

```
:set path
```

What you should see returned is something similar to the following:

```
path=.,/usr/include,
```

The preceding response shows that the path variable is set with three items (each is separated by a comma). The first is the dot/period character (`.`), and this tells you that you can search relative to the current directory. The second item is `/usr/include`, so that Vim will try inside that folder too. The last item is actually quite strange, in that it looks to be empty, but in fact, this simply means that Vim will search inside the current directory (which is subtly different to the `.`, which searches *relative* to the current directory).

These default settings probably aren't enough to help you locate that tricky file, if you don't know where it resides, so Vim lets us add additional folders into the path, to check. In the following example, I add my Desktop folder onto the list as well:

```
:set path+=~/Desktop
```

But ultimately, the `:find` command is limited in its usefulness. This is where third-party plug-ins (which we'll see in Chapter 17) help us make situations such as finding a file when we're not sure of its location much, much easier (specifically through techniques such as "fuzzy searching").

■ **Note** If you prefer a more traditional file system explorer, you have the built-in feature `:Explore` and its split-screen cousin `:Sexplore`, which allow you to navigate through the file system using a tree display of your content.

Searching for Content

OK, let's now look into the features Vim gives us for actually finding a piece of content (whether it be a word, sentence, or chunk of code). There are two options, and both are useful under different circumstances.

1. Within the current buffer
2. Within multiple buffers

Searching Within the Current Buffer

When you have a large buffer open in Vim, it can be useful to narrow down your search, using the search command `/`. This command moves you into the command prompt area, and from there, you are able to enter a search phrase you want Vim to try and match within your buffer.

Following is an example in which we're searching the current buffer (in this case, I have my Sinderella Ruby application open in Vim; we saw this in Chapter 7) for the phrase `sinderella`:

```
/sinderella
```

If you've followed along and used my .vimrc setup, you'll see that the search results are highlighted to make it easier to visualize where the results are in the buffer (see Figure 11-1). If you've not used my configuration files, to see the search results highlighted, you'll have to add the following configuration to your .vimrc:

```
set hlsearch
```

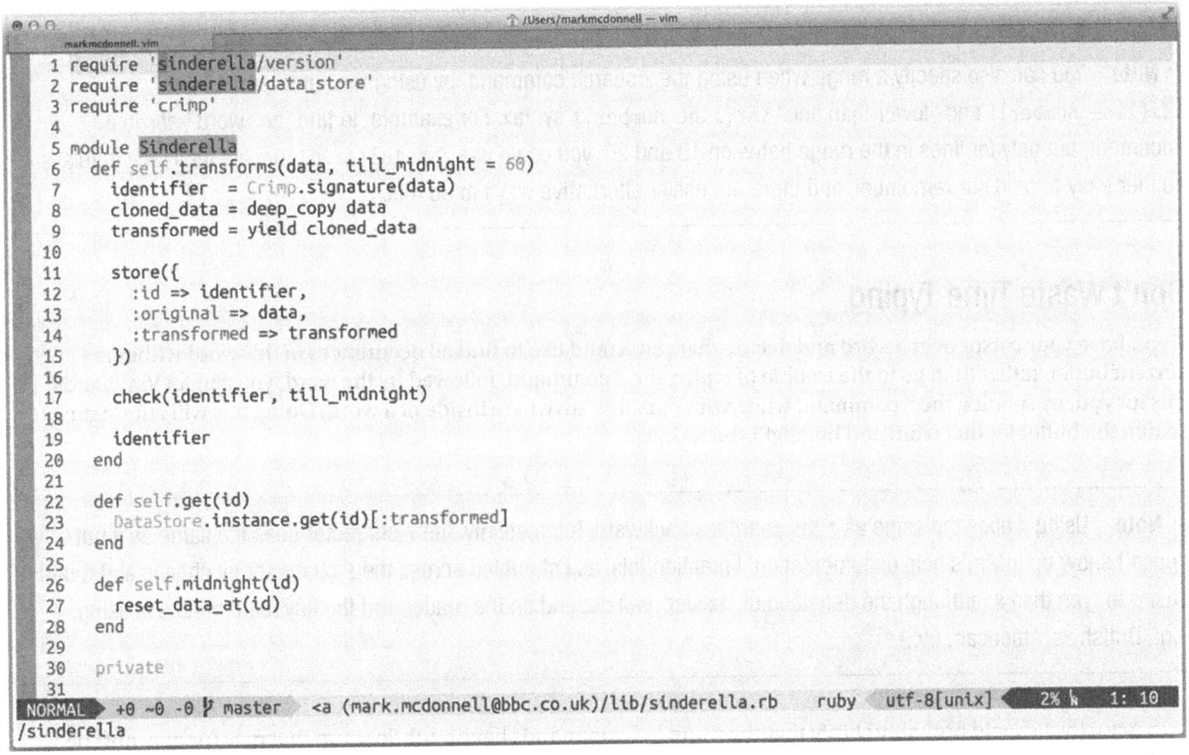

Figure 11-1. *Result of running search command* /sinderella

You may also notice that searches are case-sensitive. You can fix this in one of the following two ways:

1. Add \c to the end of your search term, like so: /sinderella\c.

2. Or use my configuration setup, which adds set ignorecase to the .vimrc, so there is no need to use \c.

Once you have successfully matched a phrase within your buffer, it would be good to be able to navigate through the buffer by just the matches. Highlighting helps, obviously, but if it's a particularly long document, you don't want to be scrolling endlessly, scanning for a highlighted word or words. To make this task easier, Vim provides commands that let you navigate through the search results (see Table 11-1).

Table 11-1. *Commands for navigating search results*

Command	Explanation
n	Steps forward through each match
N	Steps backward through each match

■ **Note** You can also specify a range when using the / search command, by using the "greater than line" `\%>{line_number}l` and "lower than line" `\%<{line_number}l` syntax. For example, to find the "word" *abc* in a document, but only for lines in the range between 10 and 20, you could use `/\%>10l\%<20labc`, but let's face it, this is neither easy to read nor remember, and there are easier alternative ways to do this.

Don't Waste Time Typing

If you have your cursor over a word and decide that you would like to find all occurences of this word within the current buffer, rather than go to the trouble of typing the / command, followed by the word, you can let Vim handle this for you, by running the * command while your cursor is anywhere inside of a word. Doing this will automatically search the buffer for that word and highlight the results.

■ **Note** Using # does the same as * but searches backward. Interestingly, the £ character does the same as # but doesn't show up in Vim's help documentation. I mention this, as I stumbled across the £ character by chance and found it easier to type than # (although the definition of "easier" will depend on the reader and the keyboard he/she is using, e.g., British vs. American, etc.).

Actually, I should probably clarify that the * and #/£ commands have a subtle setup that may (or may not) be useful to know: they search forward for the nearest word to the cursor. So, as an example, in my Sinderella document, there is the following content (line 9):

```
transformed = yield cloned_data
```

If my cursor was on the = character, and I pressed *, Vim would highlight the word `yield`, as that was the nearest "word."

Moving Backward

Vim also offers a reverse of the / command: the ? command. When using this command, not only are the matches made so that a match *above* the cursor is made first, but the direction of the navigation commands (n and N) also are reversed, so that n will move backward through the list of matches, while N will move forward through them.

Change Pattern Matches More Quickly

In more recent versions of Vim (7.4+), there is an alternative way of carrying out a change to a match. To demonstrate why this alternative solution is worth considering, let's review the previous examples in which we searched our content for a pattern using the / command.

In those examples, we searched for a pattern and were able to navigate to them, but to make a change to a specific match, we either have to have a valid text object that we can use (if that's possible with the pattern we are searching for) or we enter VISUAL mode to select the match manually and finally apply a command to make our edit.

In these situations, you'll find the gn and gN commands can save you a few keystrokes, by automatically entering VISUAL mode and selecting the match for you, ready to receive an editing command.

Let's see what this looks like in practice. Imagine you have the following content and your cursor is on the first line when you run a search for the pattern a:

```
foo
bar
baz
foo
bar
baz
```

Following, I've placed square brackets around the matches that should help indicate those that would result from the pattern searched for:

```
foo
b[a]r
b[a]z
foo
b[a]r
b[a]z
```

The examples that follow demonstrate how you would typically use the gn and gN commands to add a small increase in speed to your editing workflow. I'm aware that this may seem like a *subtle* improvement, but when you get used to using this command syntax, it will consistently help to improve how quickly you can get things done.

- cgn: If we ran this command, we would remove the a character from the first bar (matched on line 2) and place you into INSERT mode, ready to enter your change. Let's say we entered the value A!. This would result in the bar on line 2 becoming bA!r.

- .: You already know the dot command (it repeats a previous edit), and it works exactly the same in this context. So, this would re-execute the cgn command we just looked at. If we ran the . command now, it would move to the next match (baz on line 3) and replace a with A! (that was the sample change I gave previously).

- cgN: This is the same as the cgn command but moves backward through the list of matches.

Searching Within Multiple Buffers

Vim provides multiple ways to search for content within multiple buffers, including the following:

- vimgrep
- lvimgrep
- grep
- lgrep

Each of these commands let you use a basic search phrase or a more complex form of pattern, by utilizing regular expressions.

■ **Note** I won't go into the details of regular expressions, as that's outside the scope of this book, but if you're interested in learning more, I highly recommend `www.regular-expressions.info`.

The difference between each of these commands is that the Vim prefixed versions (the ones with `vim` at the start) are run from within Vim, and the latter two are piped out to the terminal that uses the shell's own `grep` program, which could potentially be much faster than Vim's own built-in engine.

Luckily, if you prefer to use an external program, as opposed to Vim's built-in commands, but you don't want to use the system grep (maybe you use something like Ack or Silver Searcher), Vim allows you to invoke a different program of your choosing to grep with. To do so, you must reset the `grepprg` options value to another command. For example, if you run `:set grepprg`, you'll see the following returned:

```
grepprg=grep -n $* /dev/null
```

As this indicates, it's using the built-in system grep programming. If you wanted to change this to another grep program, such as Ack (`http://beyondgrep.com`), you would set the value to the following:

```
set grepprg=ack
```

Another example is slightly more complicated and is modified from the Vim help files and demonstrates how you could use this option to change the `grep` command to use the GNU id-utils:

```
:set grepprg=lid\ -Rgrep\ -s
:set grepformat=%f:%l:%m
:grep (regexp)
```

But regardless of this interesting ability to change the external program when running either `grep` or `lgrep` from within Vim, we'll actually only be focusing on the first two items: `vimgrep` and `lvimgrep` (simply, because this book is about Vim, it feels more appropriate to focus on features directly related to that subject).

■ **Note** Later on, when we review some Vim plug-ins, I'll show you a plug-in that will replace all of the preceding grep'ing commands. But don't skip ahead, as there is plenty of useful stuff still to learn here!

Lists

There are subtle but important differences between `vimgrep` and `lvimgrep`:

- `vimgrep` uses Vim's quickfix list
- `lvimgrep` uses Vim's location list

I've not covered lists yet, so here's the lowdown: there is only one "quickfix" window, and it holds a list of your current search results (although other plug-ins can also access the quickfix window and place their own list items in there), whereas the "location" window is something that exists multiple times (specifically one for each window).

What this means is that as an lvimgrep search is executed within a location window, you can have a unique search within each window you have open. The quickfix window is more limited, in that it's a single window that appears below all your other windows.

So, for example, if I have two buffers split into two separate windows, and I run lvimgrep once within each window (using different search criteria for each), the location list in each window will hold its own unique search results. If I tried that with vimgrep, the results inside the quickfix window would be replaced with the latest search results.

vimgrep vs. lvimgrep

The most important question at this point time is why would you use vimgrep over lvimgrep (and vice versa)? And to be honest, I'm not sure. I generally find myself only really searching for one thing at a time, so I rarely use lvimgrep; but it is useful to know that functionality exists for those scenarios in which I *am* capable of multitasking and running multiple searches.

Following is an example of how you can use both vimgrep and lvimgrep:

```
:vimgrep /{searchTerm}/[gj] {/path/to/project/**/*.rb}
```

```
:lvimgrep /{searchTerm}/[gj] {/path/to/project/*}
```

The syntax for both types is effectively the same, so I need only explain one set of syntax rules. Let's break the commands down into segments and analyze what it's doing.

- First, we're searching for the phrase searchTerm within the specified directory of /path/to/project/.

- Next, we're using a wildcard glob (http://en.wikipedia.org/wiki/Glob_(programming)) to expand any directories and files within /path/to/project/`. So, in the vimgrep example, we're trying to find a match within any folder for an item that is a Ruby file (we tell that by the .rb extension), and in the lvimgrep example, we're using a glob to find a match against any file within only the /path/to/project/ directory.

- One item of the search criteria we skipped over was the optional flags g and j used after the pattern. If you're familiar with regular expressions, you'll already know that the g flag means "global" (so it'll return multiple matches per line), but the j flag is unique to Vim. The purpose of the j flag is to prevent Vim from trying to open the first file it finds a match in (which can be quite annoying, so it's a good flag to get used to using).

Regardless of whether you use the j flag or not, you'll have to manually open the quickfix/location list after the search has been run, as neither window type is opened automatically.

Again, the commands for the quickfix and location list windows are very similar (differing only by their prefix character c or l). See Table 11-2 for a short list of commands that demonstrate some common tasks you'll want to carry out while focused on a quickfix/location list window.

Table 11-2. *Short List of Commands for Quickfix and Location List Windows*

Command	Explanation
copen	Opens the quickfix list
cclose	Closes the quickfix list
lopen	Opens the location list
lclose	Closes the location list
cnext	Moves cursor to next quickfix result
cprev	Moves cursor to previous quickfix result
lnext	Moves cursor to next location result
lprev	Moves cursor to previous location result
<CR>	Opens file and places cursor on the match
cnfile	Opens the next file with a match
cpfile	Opens the previous file with a match

■ **Note**   You can also open a file in a horizontal split by selecting the item and then running `<C-w><CR>`. Once the file is open in a horizontal split, you can convert it into a vertical split by running the following command: `<C-w>L`.

Multiple Search History

Vim keeps track of each search you execute, and this is useful when you want to return to an earlier set of search results, rather than attempting to remember the exact pattern you entered (especially as some patterns can be quite complex).

Imagine you run a search (using `vimgrep`) for the pattern foo and then run another search, but this time for the pattern bar. If you open the quickfix window, you'll see the results for the latter search of bar. But Vim will let you navigate up and down the quickfix window stack, using the following command:

`:colder`

The preceding command would display the search results for foo. Vim doesn't rerun the search; it simply stores the results for you during this session. If you want to move to the latter search result again, use the following command:

`:cnewer`

Vim's search stack can remember the last ten search lists (which should be more than enough!). If you try and move back or forward beyond the current stack size, Vim will display an error to inform you, for example, that you're "At the bottom of quickfix stack."

■ **Note**   There's an equivalent set of commands for the location list as well: `lolder` and `lnewer`. Again, note the convention of replacing c with l.

Search and Replace

The previous sections were focused on *finding* content. But what do you do with it once you've found it? A typical scenario is to search for something, so that you can replace it (fix a typo, update a reference, etc.). Doing the replacement manually would be a bit tedious, if it was fundamentally the same change being made, except in lots of different places.

To help with this situation, Vim provides a few different solutions to finding content and then replacing it automatically. The following sections are quite long, and so for ease of future reference, I'll group them under the following two separate headings:

1.   Search and replace within the current buffer

2.   Search and replace within multiple buffers

Search and Replace Within the Current Buffer

If you have a single buffer that you want to carry out a search and replace on, Vim provides you with the substitution command, and if it looks familiar to you, it's because it's modeled around the same syntax as the Unix sed command.

```
:[range]s/{pattern}/{replacement}/[flags]
```

So, we can see from this syntax structure that we are able to specify an optional range, which means we determine what part of the file the substitution affects. (If we don't specify a range, it'll default to the current line.)

Next, we tell Vim we want to run the substitution command, using the s character. The s command alone won't do much, as we need the full command to be entered, which is effectively s/{pattern}/{replacement}/.

After that, we pass in a pattern we want Vim to match within our range. This pattern is typically a regular expression pattern, followed by the replacement pattern. Because we can use a regex for our search pattern, this means we can capture parts of a match and place it back inside the replacement area. We'll see examples of how this works and why it's useful, shortly.

Finally, we have a set of flags (which is just a fancy word for "options") that lets us specify changes to the default behaviors of the command. Again, we'll see some examples of this in just a moment.

Simple Example

Start by opening a file with some content that you want to search. I'm going to use the Sinderella (www.github.com/Integralist/Sinderella) Ruby application we've seen in a few earlier chapters (shown next, so you can follow along).

```
require 'sinderella/version'
require 'sinderella/data_store'
require 'crimp'

module Sinderella
  def self.transforms(data, till_midnight = 60)
    identifier  = Crimp.signature(data)
    cloned_data = deep_copy data
    transformed = yield cloned_data
```

```ruby
    store({
      :id => identifier,
      :original => data,
      :transformed => transformed
    })

    check(identifier, till_midnight)

    identifier
  end

  def self.get(id)
    DataStore.instance.get(id)[:transformed]
  end

  def self.midnight(id)
    reset_data_at(id)
  end

  private

  def self.store(data)
    DataStore.instance.set(data)
  end

  def self.deep_copy(object)
    Marshal.load(Marshal.dump(object))
  end

  def self.check(id, seconds)
    Thread.new { sleep seconds; reset_data_at id }
  end

  def self.reset_data_at(id)
    DataStore.instance.reset(id)
  end
end
```

In this file, I want to change all occurences of the phrase DataStore into VimStore. To do this, we'll use the following substitution command:

`:%s/DataStore/VimStore/g`

This is a pretty standard syntax and should be self-explanatory, based on the syntax structure we defined earlier. The only part you won't recognize is the flag we've used. The g stands for *global*, meaning it'll make the substitution multiple times (if needed) across all lines of the current file.

■ **Note**   We could also have used a range, such as `:1,25s/DataStore/VimStore/g`, to restrict the substitution to lines 1 through 25.

Complex Example

In this file, I want to change all occurences of the phrase "data store" (whether that be DataStore or data_store) into VimStore. To do this, we'll use the following substitution command:

```
:%s/data_\?store/VimStore/gci
```

Let's break down this command into its individual parts, so that we can better understand what it's doing and how.

- :%: We start with :, which drops us into COMMAND-LINE mode, and then we specify %, which indicates that the command we run should affect the whole file.

- s/{pattern}/{replacement}/[flags]: This is the basic syntax structure of the substitution command (we saw this earlier, but I'm repeating it here for clarity). It makes it easier to understand the command when you can pick out the structure from the patterns and replacements.

- data_\?store: This is the pattern we're searching for, and if it wasn't for the \?, this would be a standard text-based pattern. The ? character in regular expressions (which we'll see in greater detail in the next section) means the character before it is optional. For our pattern, the _ was optional. But, unfortunately, the regex engine in Vim requires ? to be escaped with a \.

- VimStore: Any matches found, we'll replace with this content.

- gci: These are the flags (options) we're passing to the command. The g, you've already seen, and it allows us to make the substitution multiple times across all lines. The c stands for *confirm*, meaning it'll ask us to confirm the replacement for each match found, and it can be omitted if you're confident your pattern won't match any unintentional targets. The i stands for *ignore*, meaning case-sensitivity is ignored when finding a match.

Regular Expressions

As I've mentioned previously, the search-and-replacement patterns can be a single phrase or a regular expression. You saw in the previous section a small example of a regex pattern (the ? character made the character preceding it "optional").

Even if you're comfortable with the standard regex syntax, you'll still have to be aware that the Vim regex engine doesn't work the same as other engines. To get a better idea of what options are available, read http://vimregex.com/.

So let's reconsider our previous example. What if we wanted the replacement value to be closer to the original, in the sense that on line 2 we had data_store, and after the substitution command, it changed to VimStore (like all other occurences of DataStore). But what if we wanted it to have become vim_store instead (so it kept the underscore between words and was also lowercase), while also changing all instances of DataStore to VimStore still?

Well, unfortunately, that isn't 100% possible within the realm of a *single* substitution command (although, as you'll see, we get pretty close). In a situation like this, we have to use two substitutions. Here's the first:

```
%s/data\(_\?\)\(store\)/Vim\1\2/gci
```

What this gives us is all instances of DataStore replaced with VimStore, while our other match of data_store is replaced with Vim_store. As you can see, we almost managed to get the perfect solution in one substitution, but we still need Vim_store to be all lowercase, so that it reads vim_store.

To do that, we'll need to run another substitution that will handle the second requirement. This substitution looks like the following:

```
:%s/V\(im_store\)/v\1/g
```

So now that we have both substitution solutions in place, let's break down each one and see how it works. We'll start with the first substitution command, followed by the second. (I won't detail the range, syntax structure, or flags, as I've already described those in the previous sample breakdowns.)

- data: We try to match the exact word *data*.

- \(_\?\): We capture the optional _ underscore. (Parentheses are used in regexes to remember a part of your match, so that you can use it again, either in the latter part of your regex or, more commonly, as part of the replacement, as we'll do ourselves.)

- \(store\): We capture the exact word *store* (or *Store*, with a capital *S*, as we've applied the case-insensitive flag).

- Vim\1\2: This is our replacement for any matches returned. We explicitly replace a match with the word *Vim*, followed by the first captured group (this was the underscore character), then the second captured group (this was the word store).

Following is the breakdown for the second substitution:

- V\(im_store\): We match the character V, followed by im_store, which we also capture, so that we can use it as part of the replacement.

- v\1: We replace the match with a lowercase *v*, followed by the content of the captured content from the pattern that was matched (in this example, \1 is the content im_store).

■ **Note**   You can also change the content of a Vim register, based on a regex pattern matched, for example, :%s/regex/\=setreg('A', submatch(0))/, but be warned that this is a fairly academic trick, as it will replace the matched content (in the buffer) with a zero.

Differences in Regex Flavors

Although I highly recommend reading through the Vim regex web site, it's worth detailing a couple of interesting items. The first is that the majority of standard syntax characters for regexes have to be escaped inside Vim. If a pattern that you know works in another engine appears not to work in Vim, double-check that your quantifiers or capturing groups don't have to be escaped! Also, word boundaries with Vim's implementation aren't the common \b syntax but \< and \>. These are the main items that trip up regex users new to Vim.

Avoiding Escaping Characters

Having to escape the regex syntax characters can make your patterns much harder to read and interpret (not to mention quite tedious as well). But by adding the \v flag (which stands for "Very Magic" mode) before the search pattern, we can avoid the need to escape characters. If we were to look at our previous regex pattern %s/data\(_\?\)\(store\)/Vim\1\2/gci, it would appear slightly easier on the eyes after using Very Magic mode.

```
%s/\vdata(_?)(store)/Vim\1\2/gci
```

Tricks Specific to Vim's Regex Flavor

Vim's own regular expression engine has some interesting features that are worth being aware of, if you want to take advantage of more powerful pattern matching. I would highly recommend reading through :h regexp.

One feature I enjoy using is \zs, which will reset the start position for your match. An example of how you might use this is to match the last instance of the word foo in the line foo foo foo foo (that's four foos, and we want the fourth to be matched). To achieve this, we could execute the following search: /.*\zsfoo.

Vim also has regex features that large-scale programming languages have failed to implement (the "programming language of the Web": JavaScript being the biggest example I could give). Let's consider one such powerful feature not found in many languages, which is the "lookbehind assertion." This feature allows you to find a match, as long as it is preceded by another pattern.

If we wanted to find the word bar, but only if bar were preceded by the word foo, we could try to use the search /foobar, but that would incorrectly match the entire word foobar, rather than just the bar part. To fix this, we can use a lookbehind assertion, like so: /\v(foo)@<=bar.

In the preceding example, I've used the "Very Magic" mode (\v), which has meant that I don't have to escape any contentious characters. If I hadn't used that, the search command would look like the following: /\(foo\)\@<=bar (note that the parentheses and the @ character have to be escaped). If we ran this search command, it would successfully match and highlight only the word *bar*. Try it out yourself on the following content:

```
foobar
bazbar
foobar
quxbar
```

■ **Note**   One thing that isn't immediately clear when reading the Vim documentation is that the parentheses around the lookbehind pattern are required. So, /\vfoo@<=bar wouldn't work. The pattern foo has to be enclosed in parentheses, like so: /\v(foo)@<=bar.

Validating Substitution Patterns

Sometimes, you'll want to carry out a search *first*, before actually actioning your substitution. This is useful in scenarios in which you're unsure of the implications your search pattern might have, and, so, you're concerned you'll end up changing something you didn't expect to.

To avoid this concern, when you can execute your substitution command, make sure to add the n flag, which reports the number of matches your pattern will affect. The following is an example of this command:

```
:%s/^#/!!/n
```

What the preceding command looks for is a hash character (#) at the start of a line. If it finds a match, it'll want to replace it with a double exclamation mark (!!). But instead of applying the substitution, we'll see that Vim returns the number of mentions:

```
8 matches on 8 lines
```

The reason this feature can be useful is that it'll let you know whether your pattern actually matches anything at all! I can't even begin to tell you the amount of times I've had silly typos or not escaped a character within my specified pattern, causing it to fail a match.

Reusing a Previous Search Pattern

Vim allows you to reuse the last successful search pattern, as part of your substitution command. To do this, you just have to make sure you have executed a search for the substitution command to utilize. If that's the case, when you construct your substitution command, you will be able to leave the search phrase part of the command empty.

This can be especially useful if your search pattern criteria requires writing out a complicated regular expression, simply because writing regexes can be time-consuming and error-prone, so doing this can help save you time typing it out again. Following is a basic example, in which we first carry out a search for the phrase *some thing* and then replace it with *more things*:

```
/some thing
:%s//more things/g
```

As described previously, we searched for "some thing," to make sure the pattern was correct. Next we carry out a substitution but leave the search section blank (as we rely on Vim remembering our previous search pattern) and replace any matches with "more things."

You can also use the tilde character (~) as your search pattern, and when running your substitution, Vim will interpret the tilde as the value of your last replacement. So, if you already executed a substitution in which you replaced the pattern matched with the characters +++ but realized you made a mistake and the +++ should have been !!!, you can quickly rectify the problem by executing another substitution, like so: `:%s/~/!!!/g`.

■ **Note** When you run a search, you can repeat it, using another forward slash. For example, /foo will highlight matches for "foo." If you execute nohl, the highlighting will be turned off. Now, if you run //, this will again highlight matches for "foo."

Search and Replace Within VISUAL-BLOCK Selection

The substitution command has a unique feature built in that lets you search vertically through a VISUAL-BLOCK selection. The reason that this is really interesting is because, typically, when you use the substitution command on a visual selection, the replacement will find matches across the entire line (i.e., it'll search horizontally).

To see an example of how this is an issue, take a look at the VISUAL-BLOCK selection in Figure 11-2, following. If we were to execute the substitution command `:'<,'>s/foo/bar/g`, the four selected references to foo would be changed to read bar (as expected), but so would the rest of the references to foo on lines two and three (not expected).

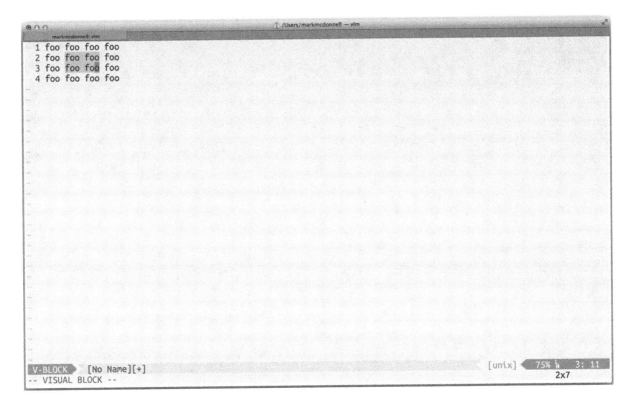

Figure 11-2. *Example of a VISUAL-BLOCK selection*

So, to get the result we want (only the four selected references to foo changed to bar), we would use the regex pattern \%V, which will match only inside the visual selection area. A working example of the command would look like the following: :'<,'>s/\%Vfoo\%V/bar/g.

Be aware, however, that this can trip people up. I discovered that this feature would only work when your visual selection contains not only the area you want to affect but also one additional column around the required area, as shown in Figure 11-3. (Note, as part of the visual selection, the empty space column before and after the words foo.)

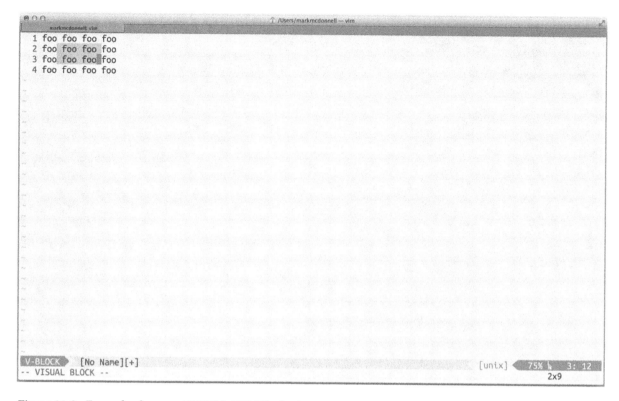

Figure 11-3. *Example of a correct VISUAL-BLOCK selection*

Search and Replace Within Multiple Buffers

A useful feature in modern text editors is the ability to search for a pattern across an entire code base and to apply a specific change to any matches. All good GUI-based text editors have this feature built in, and Vim is no exception.

The only issue with Vim's implementation is that it requires all the files to be opened first, before the replacement can be applied. If you know roughly what area of your code base the change happens to be within, you can open all files from a specific directory, using a wildcard glob *, but failing that, you'll have to open ALL files in the project, which, depending on your code base, could be an expensive operation.

So, to begin with, we'll look at Vim's standard way of making changes across multiple files, and then we'll consider an alternative solution that doesn't directly use Vim but instead works from the terminal command line.

The following are the options we'll be looking at within this section:

- The Vim way (`argdo`)
- The Unix way (`sed`)

The Vim Way

To make a change to multiple files, we must first have files open for us to search through. The easiest way to do this is to use a wildcard glob, as explained earlier. The following is an example of what this would look like if you wanted to open *all* text files within your project:

```
vim **/*.txt
```

The preceding command not only opens all text files specified by our glob pattern but also populates the `argdo` list with these files (we saw `argdo` back in Chapter 9). Once we have our files open, we can run the following command to search for a pattern and then replace it:

```
:argdo %s/{search}/{replace}/ge | update
```

You should already be familiar with most of the preceding command, such as the use of `argdo`, the substitution command syntax, and the g flag. But the last part of the command might not be familiar, so let's look at what those parts do.

- e: This flag tells Vim to ignore any errors that may occur.

- | update: If you're not used to writing shell scripts, you might not understand what this does. The pipe character (|) allows us to take the output of one command and pass it into another command. In this case, we're passing control over to the `update` command, which effectively works the same as the `:w` write command.

■ **Note**   We use the update command, as it's more performant for this type of action. This is because, rather than write to every file (regardless of whether the files have actually changed), we only write to the file if a change has occurred within the buffer.

The Unix Way

As discussed earlier, we'll now take a look at some solutions that don't utilize Vim but instead use only the terminal and shell commands. In this solution, we'll rely on the `sed` Unix command, like so:

```
sed -i -- 's/search/replace/' *.txt && rm *.txt--
```

Let's break this command down into segments, to understand what's happening at each point.

- -i: This is sed's "edit in place" command (meaning, open the file and apply the change).

- --: When using "edit in place," we have to provide a "backup" file (if an error occurs we don't want to corrupt the original file), so here, we're creating a backup file that has an extension of -- (e.g., foo.txt--). We could have specified something like .bak, and that would've created a foo.txt.bak file instead.

- 's/search/replace/': This is the standard substitution command you already know.

- *.txt && rm *.txt--: We use a glob to apply the substitution to all txt files and then when the command completes successfully, we'll remove all the backup files created.

As before, this isn't an ideal solution, because it has issues similar to the Vim way, in that you'll probably want to try and filter down files searched (due to the fact we have to create temporary backup files). But this will still be much more performant that using Vim. (See also the following note, which clarifies backup file performance concerns.)

> ■ **Note** In fact, you don't *have* to use the sed command to create a backup! If you look at the manual (man sed), you'll see that the –i option allows a "zero-length extension," meaning that if you use an empty string instead, no backup file will be created (also meaning that there's no need to remove the backup files afterward). This would look something like the following: sed –i ''s/search/replace/' *.txt.

Global Command

An alternative way to search for content using a pattern, and to make a replacement based on the returned matches, is to use the :global command. There are a couple of differences between :global and the substitution command, which are as follows:

1. Instead of applying a replacement, you instead execute commands from different modes (e.g., COMMAND-LINE or NORMAL).

2. The command affects the entire line and not necessarily a subset of content within the line.

> ■ **Note** Although the :global command can affect the entire line, it's down to the specific command you want to execute that will determine what portion of the line is modified. We'll see an example of this later, when we only delete a certain portion of the line, but reiterate that the part of the line modified is in no way related to the pattern that we matched in that line.

To better understand how the :global command works, we'll take a look at a few different examples. The first example will demonstrate how the commands affect the whole line that a match is made upon and not just the match itself.

To begin with, let's imagine we have the following content:

```
------
abbcbb
------
deefee
------
ghhihh
------
```

> ■ **Note** As with most Vim commands, there is a shortcut notation. In the following examples, I simply use :g instead of :global. Feel free to use whichever feels more natural to you.

Now imagine we want to delete the lines abbcbb and ghhihh. By using the :global command, we're able to dynamically determine lines we want to have affected, by utilizing regular expressions for our pattern-matching algorithm. In the following command, I'm deleting any lines that begin with the characters a or g. (Remember: This is different from the substitution command, in that we're affecting the entire line on which a match is found, whereas the substitution command only affects the actual match and leaves the rest of the line unmodified.)

```
:g/\v^(a|g)/:d
```

The preceding command results in the content being modified, so that it now looks like the following:

```
------
------
deefee
------
------
```

Let's now break down this command into sections, to better understand how it works.

- :g/{pattern}/{command}: This is the syntax structure of the command. We begin by specifying :g and then follow that with the pattern we're hoping to match.

- \v: We specify that we want to use "Very Magic" mode, meaning we don't have to escape lots of characters within our pattern.

- ^: The carrot symbol is an "anchor," and it tells the regex pattern that we have to find our match from the beginning of the line.

- (a|g): We use a capturing group (), not because we want to reference the match later in our pattern, but just as a way to indicate that this part of the pattern is grouped (which can make evaluating a complex pattern in your head a bit easier). Within that grouping, we use an alternation | character to, say, match either the character a *or* g.

- :d: This is the command we want to execute. You can see that we have to specify the :, to indicate that it is a COMMAND-LINE command we're going to execute.

■ **Note** To specify a NORMAL mode command to execute, add the word norm or normal instead of :, like so: :g/{pattern}/normal dd (note how that command just does the same thing as :d in our earlier example).

The full command syntax looks like the following (note that the use of the ! character will invert the functionality, so that the command is executed against lines that **DON'T** match the pattern):

```
:[range]g[lobal][!]/{pattern}/[cmd]
```

Let's now see a slightly more complex example. Imagine we're using the same (unmodified) content from our earlier :global example and that we want to delete the last three characters of each line that ends with a word character (specifically, we **DON'T** want to modify the ------ lines). The following command will do exactly that for us:

```
:g/\w$/normal $3X
```

The preceding command results in the content being modified, so that it now looks like the following:

```
------
abb
------
dee
------
ghh
------
```

Let's now break down this command into sections, to better understand how it works.

- `:g/{pattern}/{command}`: This is the syntax structure of the command. We begin by specifying `:g` and then follow that with the pattern we're hoping to match.

- `\w$`: This is the pattern we want to match, so match any line that has a word character `\w` just before the end of the line `$`.

- `normal $3X`: This is the command we want to execute. We specify that it's a NORMAL mode command by using the `normal` statement, move the cursor to the end of matched line `$`, and then do a count of 3 cuts before the current cursor position, using `X`.

Expression Replacements

What makes Vim's substitution command so powerful is that you don't just have the power of regular expressions to construct complex patterns for searching and replacing; the replacement pattern can also utilize VimL via the expression register!

Let's see an example of this. Imagine we have the following content (yes, I know, I'm a literary genius):

```
It was today that we discovered the rain wasn't going to last.
Who knew today would be the time for a new summer.
```

Let's be a bit more specific with this piece of text and replace the word *today* with an actual timestamp. We're going to use the substitute pattern you're already familiar with. The only difference will be that we'll delegate the replacement section off to the expression register.

```
:%s/today/\=strftime("%c")/
```

As you can see, we searched for the pattern `today`, and in the replacement, we escaped the equals character (`=`), so the appropriate register would assume control, and after the equation, we placed a small line of VimL code, `strftime("%c")`, which generates a timestamp for us. Executing this command will result in the content being changed to the following:

```
It was Tue 24 Jun 07:16:36 2014 that we discovered the rain wasn't going to last.
Who knew Tue 24 Jun 07:16:36 2014 would be the time for a new summer.
```

Using the expression register also allows you to also drop in content that comes from other registers. The syntax is `\=@`, followed by the register name you want to pull content from. For example, if we wanted to pull content from the x register, we would modify the command, like so:

```
:%s/\v(today)/\=@x/
```

Summary

This has been quite a packed chapter, and I've covered a lot of important topics that will be a cornerstone of your newly acquired editing capabilities. Let's take a "whistle-stop" tour of the functionality you learned in this chapter.

- We used `:find` to help us locate files, specifically within directories that Vim has access to via its runtime path. (We also looked at modifying this path to include additional directories of our choosing, using `:set path+=~/SomeOtherDirectory`.)

- We started to investigate the different ways to search for content, beginning with searching within the current buffer. Here, we revisited the / and ? search commands along with using the n/N commands for navigating matches. We also looked at the `\c` flag and `hlsearch/ignorecase` settings, to see how they affect the sensitivity and highlighting of matches.

- You learned about shorthand commands that allow us to automatically search for the word under our cursor, using the # and * commands.

- In Vim 7.4+, we discovered that we are able to make a slight increase in speed in our ability to search and edit, by utilizing the gn and gN commands.

- We then started to investigate options for searching for content within multiple buffers. This led us to vimgrep/lvimgrep, where we looked at the subtle differences and why you would use one over the other. We also saw how to modify Vim, so that we can use a different external grep'ing application.

- You learned about Vim's lesser known ability to backtrack through multiple search histories, using :colder and :cnewer (as well as the location list variations :lolder/:lnewer).

- From there, we started to investigate options for not only searching for content (either within a single file or multiple files) but to apply a replacement pattern onto matches as well. This revolved fundamentally around the substitution command and the different techniques and tips for utilizing it alongside regular expressions and the expression register.

- You learned that trying to apply replacements across multiple files can be a performance concern in Vim, and so we looked at an alternative solution within the terminal, using the sed command.

- We took a look at another (and equally powerful) way to search content and apply changes to those matches, this time using the :global command, which allowed us to execute NORMAL mode and COMMAND-LINE mode commands to matches.

CHAPTER 12

■ ■ ■

Buffer/Window/Tab Management

Once you start becoming comfortable with how Vim works and its fundamentals (such as editing commands, registers, handling files, etc.), your next area of concern may well be your workflow. In this chapter, we'll take a look at how best to manage our environment when working from buffers, windows, and tabs.

If you're already an experienced Vim user (or, at least, you consider yourself not to be strictly a Vim beginner), then a lot of the commands and suggestions in this chapter may appear simplistic. But that's the point, and in my opinion, one of the most interesting parts to becoming an advanced Vim user is utilizing the fundamentals of the Vim ecosystem.

Far too often, I see longtime Vim users who struggle to be efficient navigating around. It could be something as simple as having a single window viewport open alongside multiple buffers. They'll decide they want to have multiple windows (one for each buffer), so they'll split their current window X number of times and manually change the visible buffer within each of the windows. That's painfully slow, especially considering that they could have simply run :sba instead! (By the way, I'll cover that command later on.)

Also, and I've mentioned this before, but I'll say it again: when you're stuck in an environment in which you don't have your personal Vim configuration in place (such as on a remote server or pair programming with a colleague), knowing the real commands that are being used under your own custom mappings (which I'll cover in detail in Chapter 19) is invaluable knowledge.

If you're a new user, you'll learn quite a bit about how to be more efficient when working within Vim, and if you're a longtime Vim user, then I hope you'll discover some new gems.

Buffer Management

One of the things you'll find yourself doing most during your time using Vim is creating and opening buffers. (This is the cornerstone of Vim after all.) So, it's important to be able to understand the different ways of navigating through, creating, and manipulating buffers, so you don't find yourself having to do things manually when perhaps a built-in command would be better suited. The following sections may seem basic in nature, but you'd be surprised how many longtime Vim users still don't utilize the management features described and are pleasantly surprised when I use them as part of my Vim toolbox.

Viewing All Buffers

OK, this is *essential*: the following command will list all your currently open buffers, along with their names and buffer identifier numbers (see Figure 12-1):

```
:ls
```

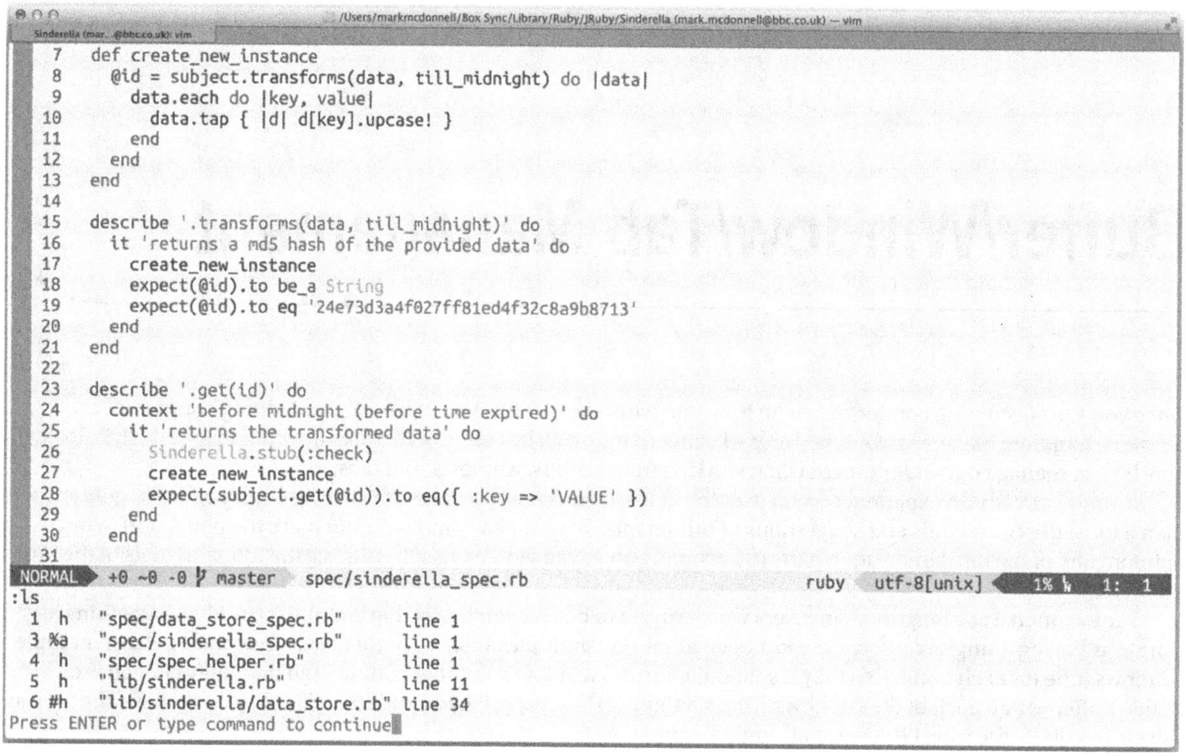

Figure 12-1. *Listing buffers using* `:ls`

You'll notice in Figure 12-1 that five buffers are open and that the current buffer is marked with a % that indicates it is the currently visible buffer for this window.

If you're also wondering what the hash character (#) below it means, this indicates that the buffer number 6 is the alternate buffer. That is, if you were to execute the command `:b #`, the current buffer would be hidden, and the alternative buffer displayed instead. If you were to now run `:ls` again, you would notice that the # and % indicators have swapped places.

■ **Note** There are other indicators available, although they are rarely useful in my humble opinion, but it's good to be aware of them. I recommend running `:h ls`, which will give you the complete details.

Splitting Buffers into Windows

Imagine that you have a single window viewport, but with lots of buffers open. This means only one of the buffers can be visible while the rest are marked as hidden. If you now wanted all your buffers to be opened within their own window, then you would have two options, as follows:

1.   `:sba`

2.   `:vert sba`

The first option will split all your buffers into horizontal windows, while the second option does the same, but into vertical windows.

Different Ways to Close Buffers

As before, imagine that you have a single window viewport, but with lots of buffers open. This means only one of the buffers can be visible, while the rest are marked as hidden. But from this perspective, there are still many different scenarios that make it difficult to close certain buffers. The following subsections will cover a few of those scenarios.

To Close a Buffer Based on Its File Type

I typically find that while working on a project, I'll mainly work on certain types of files. As an example, when working on an open-source project I'll typically choose Ruby as my go to language. But in a work environment I might be required to deal with other languages such as PHP, JavaScript, Clojure, Go etc.

Imagine that I have multiple PHP (.php) and JavaScript (.js) files open, and I've just finished working on some server-side PHP code. For the rest of the day, I intend to continue working on client-side JavaScript code. In this scenario, I don't want to see lots of PHP files in my buffer list as I jump around different JavaScript files. So, to fix this, I can run the following command:

```
:bd *.php
```

What this command will attempt to do is close any files that end with .php, as it uses a wildcard glob (*) that Vim expands to match any file name, as long as the file has .php as its extension.

But this command won't run by itself. If you enter the preceding command and then press the <CR> key, you'll notice that Vim will fail to execute the command, because it matches more than one file.

To execute the preceding command successfully, you have to run <C-a> after you've typed the command, which will tell Vim to expand any matches it can find and will subsequently display a list of open buffers it will then attempt to close. If you *now* press <CR>, the command will execute successfully.

To Close a Specific Numbered Buffer

When a buffer is created, it is given a unique identifier number. If you run the :ls (list buffers) command, you'll see this identifier in the left-most column of each buffer listed. Imagine we have a buffer whose identifier is the number 1. To close this buffer, we would again use the :bd (buffer delete) command, but now we'll pass through the identifier alongside it, like so:

```
:bd 1
```

The preceding command will now successfully remove the buffer you indicated, but confusingly, Vim will act as if nothing has happened. For example, Vim won't display a message of any kind to say a buffer has been deleted, and even the command itself will stay visible in the command-line bar (although your cursor will now be focused back on the main window). But if you now execute the :ls command, you'll notice that the buffer we specified has now been deleted.

■ **Note** If you had multiple split windows and the buffer you closed was visible in one of the windows, Vim would automatically close the window that the deleted buffer previously occupied.

To Close Multiple Buffers (Not Necessarily in Sequence)

Sometimes, it can be useful to delete a set of buffers that aren't related in any way other than by the fact that you have finished working with them. To do this, we again use the :bd (buffer delete) command, but now we'll pass through multiple identifiers alongside it, like so:

```
:bd 3 5
```

The preceding command closes the buffers 3 and 5. But unlike before, when deleting a single buffer, Vim displays the message 2 buffers deleted, once the command has been successfully executed.

To Close Multiple Buffers Using a Range

As in the preceding section, in which we used the :bd (buffer delete) command to remove a set of buffers that aren't related in any way, if we were lucky enough to have the buffers we wanted to delete next to each other by way of their identifier numbers (e.g., by coincidence, they had numbers that went from low to high), we could take advantage of not having to manually specify all the individual identifier numbers and just use a range instead, like so:

```
:4,7 bd
```

The preceding command closes the buffers 4, 5, 6, and 7. It doesn't matter if, for example, there is no buffer identifier of 6. Vim will happily ignore it, if it doesn't exist, and go ahead and close the other buffers within the specified range.

To Close All Buffers at Once

There is no Vim command to close all buffers at once, but remember that Vim's commands are about composability, and so to achieve the result we want (i.e., to close all open buffers), we simply have to compose two commands together:

```
:bufdo bd
```

The preceding command is made up of two separate commands: the first is the bufdo command, which we saw back in Chapter 9 and which allows us to execute the command that follows it against every open buffer. So the command we pass to it is the bd command.

Within my own configuration files, I've aliased the preceding command to the following keyboard shortcut: <Leader>yd (i.e. \yd). I've since realized that because I use this command so infrequently, I actually prefer to be explicit and enter the full command, rather than use a keyboard shortcut.

Closing a Buffer but Keeping the Parent Window Open

Imagine that you have two windows open with a different buffer in each. If you close one of the buffers, the window that contained the buffer will be closed as well (I mentioned this behavior in an early section of this chapter). This side effect could be quite annoying, if you still wanted to retain a split-window layout.

There is no built-in solution to this particular problem, but it annoyed me enough to seek a way to resolve it. As I mentioned at the beginning of this book, finding help for Vim problems is actually quite easy, considering the wealth of knowledge available from the online community. In this case, I found a plug-in solution on the Vim wiki: http://vim.wikia.com/wiki/Deleting_a_buffer_without_closing_the_window#Alternative_Script.

The way the plug-in works is that before it closes the buffer, it will attempt to load another buffer inside of the window. If there isn't an alternative buffer to display, it'll create a scratch buffer, thus allowing the window to stay open.

Window Management

Much the same as with buffers, window management is an essential part of being able to use Vim in a controlled and efficient manner. If you're not familiar with the different ways of manipulating windows, you'll likely find yourself more frustrated as your workflow, layouts, and buffers become more and more complex.

The following sections cover a variety of different window-based problems and will help demonstrate how much flexibility and control Vim provides us.

Opening Split Windows

Having a single window that holds multiple buffers can work fine in most scenarios. But there comes a time when you'll either want to have two (or more) files open next to each other, so that you can compare them or copy content from one to the other.

In these situations, you can utilize two specific Vim commands that let you split your current window into one or more windows:

- `:sp [file]`: Creates horizontal window split (Figure 12-2)

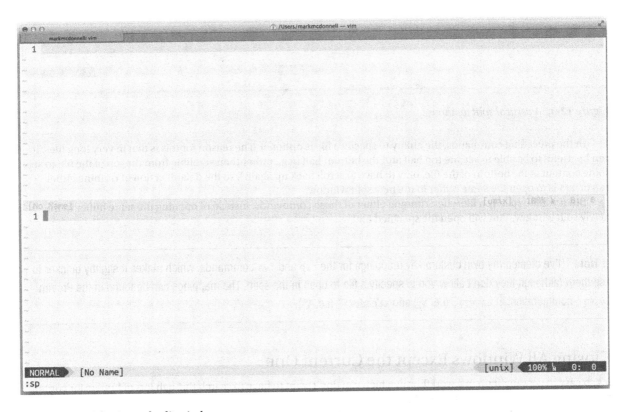

Figure 12-2. *A horizontal split window*

- `:vs [file]`: Creates vertical window split (Figure 12-3)

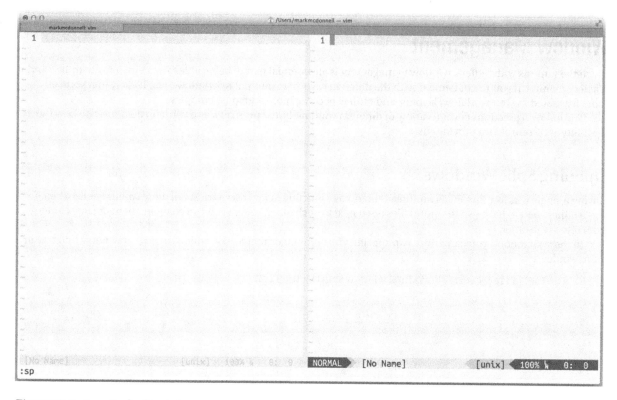

Figure 12-3. *A vertical split window*

In the preceding commands, the ability to specify a file is optional. The reason for this is that in very long files, it can be useful to be able to see the top half and the bottom half (e.g., rather than scrolling from the top of the file to see some content at the bottom of the file, only to have to scroll back up again), so the default action of running either `:sp` or `:vs` is to open the same buffer in the new split window.

But if you do specify a file when running either of those commands, instead of opening the same buffer in the newly split window, Vim will open the specified file.

■ **Note** I've created my own custom key mappings for the `:sp` and `:vs` commands, which makes it slightly quicker to use them (although they don't allow you to specify a file to open in the split). The mappings can be found in the ProVim `.vimrc` configuration: `<Leader>;` (i.e. \;) and `<Leader>` (i.e. \`).

Closing All Windows Except the Current One

It's so easy to get caught up in a workflow in which you don't want to have to search through lots of buffers for content but just have a permanent window available instead.

But I find that after a while my screen seems to become overtaken by multiple split windows, and I'll want to reset my layout, so that I can start again and either stick with a single window and multiple buffers or begin to re-create more window splits, but, this time, only for the really important files I happen to be interested in right at that moment.

To help us restart our window layout, Vim provides us with a command called :on (meaning "only") that will close all the split windows except for the window that we ran the command from.

Changing Window Layout

Imagine that you have three vertical split windows, each containing a letter of the alphabet, such as A, B, and C (see Figure 12-4 for an example). You realize that the contents of the files aren't that long, and so it would be easier to view the content if the windows were horizontal splits and not vertical ones.

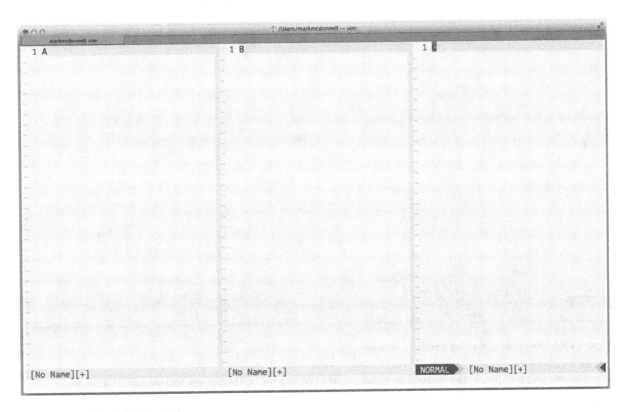

Figure 12-4. *Vertical split windows*

Because of this, you must convert the current vertical split windows into three horizontal split windows (see Figure 12-6). You *could* close all the windows, so that you're left only with one (using the :on command), and then use the :sba command to create three horizontal split windows. But this wouldn't work if you had other buffers open other than the three you want to see (as that would require manually changing the buffer within each split window you create).

Another way to solve this problem is to take advantage of Vim's window movement commands. There is one for each direction (up, down, left, right), allowing you to have fine-grained control over the layout of your windows.

- <C-w>H: left

- <C-w>J: down

- <C-w>K: up

- <C-w>L: right

Let's see how we would solve the preceding problem, using these window movement commands. I'll assume you're following along and have three separate buffers open in three vertically split windows (see Figure 12-4).

First, you should place your cursor inside the middle window, the one that currently holds the buffer "B." You should move that buffer down, using the <C-w>J command. This will create a layout that looks like that in Figure 12-5.

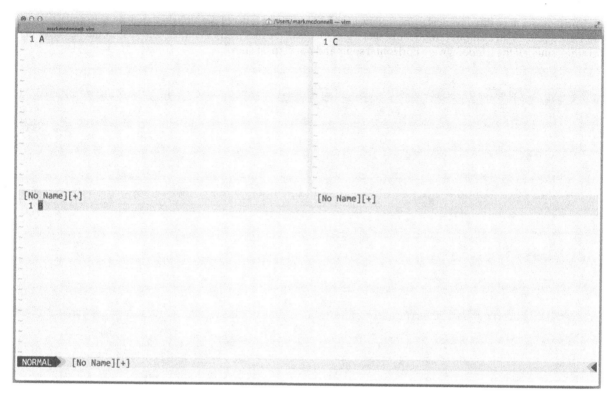

Figure 12-5. *Example of moving windows around*

The last step is to place your cursor inside the window holding the "C" buffer and run the same command, <C-w>J, to move that window down, resulting in the layout that you now require and that looks like Figure 12-6, following.

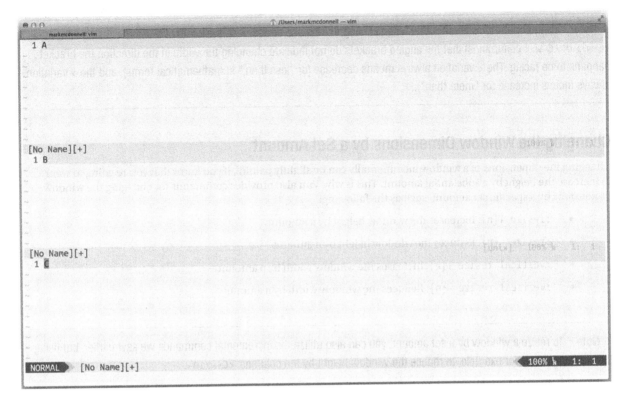

Figure 12-6. *Horizontal split windows*

Resizing Windows

In a complicated project for which you must reference lots of different files and documents, you'll find yourself creating windows all over the place. This is fine, but there comes a point when you realize your screen has become a jumble of tiny square boxes, and none of them is large enough to really be useful to work within and start editing.

This is where having an understanding of the many different ways to control the size of your windows is very useful knowledge to have.

Changing the Window Dimensions Incrementally

To help certain windows to become a little bit easier to work within, you might only have to increase the size of the window's current size by a small amount. The following commands give you the most fine-grained control over the window size, by letting you either increase or decrease the dimensions of the window by one row or one column at a time:

- <C-w>+: Increases the window height by one row

- <C-w>-: Reduces the window height by one row

- <C-w>>: Increases the window width by one column

- <C-w><: Reduces the window width by one column

■ **Note**   It's important to remember that when looking to increase or decrease the width of a window (using either the <C-w>> or <C-w>< commands) that the angled brackets do not indicate changing the width in the direction the bracket happens to be facing. The < variation always means decrease (or "less than," in mathematical terms), and the > variation always means increase (or "more than").

Changing the Window Dimensions by a Set Amount

Changing the dimensions of a window incrementally can be slightly painful, if you know that you're going to want to increase the height by a substantial amount. This is why Vim also provides commands for changing the window dimensions by a specific set amount, such as the following:

- `:resize +{n}`: Increases the window height by n amount
- `:resize -{n}`: Reduces the window height by n amount
- `:vertical resize +{n}`: Increases the window width by n amount
- `:vertical resize -{n}`: Reduces the window width by n amount

■ **Note**   To resize a window by a set amount, you can also utilize the incremental commands we saw earlier, but using them with motions; for example, to reduce the window height by ten columns: `<C-w>10-`.

Maximizing Windows

Sometimes, you want a window to temporarily take up as much screen real estate as possible. This is useful in situations in which you don't want to close other windows or change the layout permanently but only long enough so that you can focus on a specific window, to fix a problem, and then revert back to your original layout.

Vim provides the following commands, which allow you to do exactly this:

- `<C-w>_`: Enlarges current window height to full capacity
- `<C-w>|`: Enlarges current window width to full capacity
- `<C-w>=`: Resizes all windows to balanced dimension (equal space)

In my configuration files, I've also aliased two of the preceding commands. Enlarging the height to full capacity is aliased to `<Leader>w]` (i.e. `\w]`). Resizing all windows back to an equal size is aliased to `<Leader>w[` (i.e. `\w[`).

■ **Note**   You'll notice in my `.vimrc` file that I have quite a few custom mappings for the window commands we've seen so far, but after living with these mappings for many months, I've since found the default built-in commands (see preceding, e.g., `<C-w>=` and others) to be clearer and easier to remember. The built-in commands are also more useful when you're pairing with another Vim user who won't have your configuration.

Moving a Window to a Tab

You may find while working within Vim that you end up splitting the screen too much, so you end up with many split windows. The windows you have created are still important to you, however, and so you also don't want to have to use :on to reset your windows back to one, only to start splitting windows all over again.

The reason too many split windows can become a problem is that when using a feature such as maximizing the current window (e.g., <C-w>_ or <C-w>|), you'll find it doesn't really work as well as it used to. This is because even though the commands are there to maximize the current window, Vim still has to make room for the status bar of the *other* windows. (See Figure 12-7 for an example of this problem.)

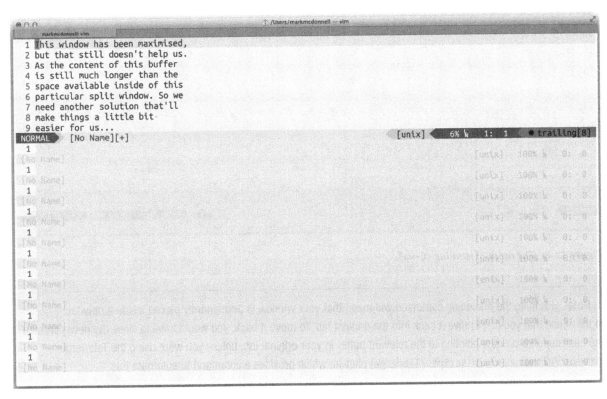

Figure 12-7. *Too many split windows means maximizing no longer works very well.*

The best thing to do in this particular situation is to move the window we're working on into its own tab, and luckily enough, Vim has exactly a command to help us to do this (see Figure 12-8 for the result):

<C-w>T

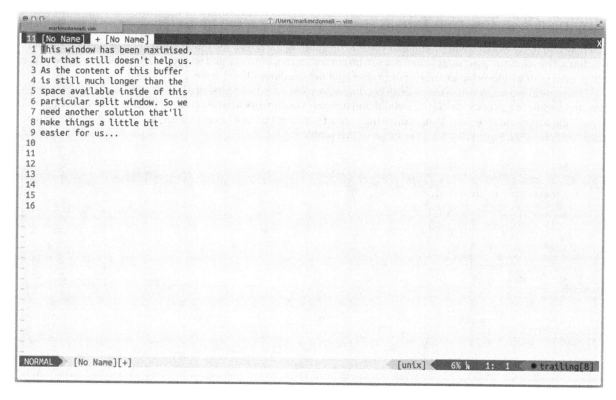

Figure 12-8. *The result of running `<C-w>T`*

■ **Note** Running the preceding command will mean that your window is permanently placed inside a new tab, in the sense that you can't move it back into the original tab. To move it back, you would have to close the newly created tab and reopen a window pointing to the relevant buffer in your original tab, unless you were using the Tabmerge (https://github.com/vim-scripts/Tabmerge) plug-in, which provides a command to automate this.

Tab Management

The feature of Vim that I use the least is tabs. You'll understand why, once we reach the latter chapters of this book, in which we explore the tmux tool and see what powerful features it provides. But if tmux isn't something you're interested in, or you are working in an environment in which you're unable to take advantage of it, then understanding how Vim's tab feature works is the next best thing.

Creating and Navigating Tabs

We saw in the previous section a scenario in which we had opened too many split windows and needed to move a specific window into a new tab. We can create any number of new tabs very easily, using the following command:

```
:tabnew
```

Once you execute this command, Vim will create a new tab and move the focus to this tab automatically. Once there, you can navigate between tabs, by utilizing one of the following commands:

- gt: Moves forward to next tab

- gT: Moves backward to previous tab

You can jump directly to a specific tab by running the command {n}gt, where n is the actual number of the tab you're interested in. For example, if you have four tabs open, the following command will switch you to the fourth tab:

```
4gt
```

Closing Tabs

Closing a tab is as simple as closing the windows it contains. Once all windows within a tab have been closed, the containing tab itself will have nothing to keep it open, and so it'll automatically close.

If, on the other hand, you have multiple tabs, and you want to quickly close them all so that you can return to a single window, you can run the following command:

```
:tabonly
```

■ **Note**   Be careful using this command, because if you make changes to a file and don't write them before running :tabonly, you'll find that the tab holding those changes will be closed, and the changes lost.

Rearranging Tabs

Vim also allows you to rearrange an existing set of tabs. If you had four tabs open, and the current tab was the fourth one, you could move the tab into a new position, by using the :tabmove command and specifying the position you wanted the tab to now occupy.

Be aware that the tab list is zero-indexed, so the command for moving the current tab to the first space would be :tabmove 0. For example, if you wanted the tab to occupy the second tab position, you would run the following command (all other tabs will shift over to the right side of this tab):

```
:tabmove 1
```

■ **Note**   If you don't specify a number when using the :tabmove command, the current tab will be moved to the end of the tab list.

Tabs As a Scratch Pad

There is only ever one instance in which I'll purposely reach for a tab in my daily workflow, and that is to use a tab as a scratch pad (which is simply a place where we put content that is disposable and which we have no intention of saving). Sometimes, we need a place to stick some content, and rather than opening up another program, I'll usually just open a new tab in Vim and place the content there instead.

Summary

Although I covered a few simpler commands and topics than in some of the earlier chapters, I want you, the faithful reader, to realize the importance of what I've discussed here. These concepts and techniques are fundamental to your use of Vim and are extremely useful, once committed to memory. Following is a quick recap of what we've covered:

- I started by explaining why it's important to learn the raw commands, such as making you much more comfortable within an environment in which your own configurations are not available, as well as ensuring that you're more efficient at controlling complex layouts that evolve over time.

- We looked at the different ways of managing lots of buffers and you learned some interesting commands, such as how to split multiple buffers into individual windows (using :sba), and a wide range of options for closing multiple buffers at once, using ranges and wildcard globbing patterns and the :bufdo command.

- We moved on to how best to manage the problem of an evolving working environment that resulted in many different windows of varying dimensions being opened and how you could take back control, by manipulating the window sizes, closing multiple windows at once, creating new split windows, and changing the layout of existing windows.

- Finally, we looked at how tabs work—how to create and close them and move separate windows into new tabs. You also learned how to rearrange an existing set of tabs, so that they are more appropriately ordered.

CHAPTER 13

Automation

Vim provides a myriad of solutions to the problem of automation. But what do we mean exactly by the phrase "automation"? Well, automation could be considered the act of preventing yourself from having to repeat any particular action.

For example, the following features are provided to help you to automate a particular action and subsequently not have to repeat yourself:

- `.`: The dot character is known as the "repeat" command, and it allows you to repeat the last edit/change. This helps you to automate your workflow, by saving you from repeating the steps involved with that last edit you made. (It may be a small saving, but this is technically an automation of sorts.)

- `s/{pattern}/{replacement}`: The substitution command is probably the most well-known and recognized feature of Vim to help you automate a particular task. This is also the most *obvious* feature for automation, because you find a pattern in your content and apply the same replacement for each match made, rather than making those replacements manually.

- `g/{pattern}/{command}`: The global command is, sadly, not as well-known as the substitution command (although *you* will know all about it, because I covered this command back in Chapter 11), but it's also a great example of a Vim feature that allows us to automate a particular task and is the closest feature to the one I'll be covering within this chapter.

- Ex mode: This is one of the modes available in Vim (which I mentioned back in Chapter 3 but did not discuss). Ex mode is a variation of Vim's COMMAND-LINE mode, meaning it has the same syntax `:{command}`, but instead of only being able to execute one command at a time like COMMAND-LINE mode, you can execute multiple commands, one after the other.

All of these features lead us to the focus of this chapter: macros.

Automation Through Ex Mode

Before we get stuck into our primary focus of Vim macros, I'd like to spend a brief moment introducing you to Vim's Ex mode, so that you can get a feel for when it might be appropriate to use it. As mentioned a moment ago, Ex mode is like COMMAND-LINE mode, with the biggest exception being that you can execute commands continuously. To get started, let's review the following items, which list the various ways to enter Ex mode:

- Typing ex in your terminal. This will start Vim in Ex mode.

- Starting Vim using the -E flag (e.g. `vim -E`)

- Executing Q from within Vim's NORMAL mode

> ■ **Note**   To exit Ex mode, you can either execute the quit command :q or move back into NORMAL mode, by executing the :visual command.

A quick example of how you might use Ex mode to carry out automative tasks is if you were provisioning files on a server. Typically, server administrators will write shell scripts that install software and configure the server as it is booting up. If you wanted to edit the contents of a configuration file, chances are you'd be using the Unix sed command to find a pattern in the file and then interactively update it.

But if using Vim is more your thing, then the problem of automating the modification of content (as part of a server bootstrap shell script) can be achieved using Vim's Ex mode, as the following code snippet demonstrates:

```
vim -E -s config.txt <<-EOF
  :%s/foo/bar/
  :update
  :quit
EOF
```

What we're doing is starting Vim in Ex mode by passing it the -E flag (we also pass the -s flag, which instructs Vim to not start but to carry out the specified commands and to then stop). We then pass the name of the file we want to edit (in this case, we pass config.txt), and then we use a HEREDOC format (http://en.wikipedia.org/wiki/ Here_document; e.g., <<-EOF {content} EOF), to construct the list of commands we wish to execute (in this example, we're replacing the word *foo* with *bar*).

> ■ **Note**   Vim also provides the -c flag, which can be specified multiple times and lets you specify a command to execute: vim -E -c "echo 123".

Vim's Ex mode is an interesting feature that isn't utilized a lot, even by hard-core Vim users, but as with everything, when the right situation arises, it can help solve some complex problems.

Also, if you want to see all the commands that are available to Vim's command prompt (this means both COMMAND-LINE mode and Ex mode), I strongly urge you to review :h holy-grail.

Automation Through Macros

Macros are seen as a complex topic, but, in fact, they are a very simple concept that translates to "take a sequence of commands; store them in a box; and then anytime you want to apply that sequence of commands, simply execute a command that will replay them."

Although this is such a simple concept, it doesn't make it any less powerful a tool for automation. Anything you can do in Vim effectively can be recorded into a macro and replayed.

To demonstrate the basics of recording macros, let's first go back to the Sinderella Ruby project that I've been using on and off in the last few chapters as my example project to work from (https://github.com/integralist/ sinderella). There is a section of the main file that looks like the following:

```
identifier  = Crimp.signature(data)
cloned_data = deep_copy data
transformed = yield cloned_data
```

I've realized that for each piece of data that is currently assigned to a variable, I want to wrap it in a function called "log." Although we won't write this function (as this isn't a book about writing Ruby code), the idea is that it'll write information to a log file but still return the required data, so that it can be stored in the relevant variable. The result of this change should mean our code looks like the following:

```
identifier   = log(Crimp.signature(data))
cloned_data  = log(deep_copy data)
transformed  = log(yield cloned_data)
```

So, let's think about this problem for moment. We have to dynamically locate the assignment of some data to a variable; we have to select the data that is to be assigned to the variable; we have to cut it, add in our new log function, and, finally, paste the cut data back inside the log function's executing parentheses.

Now, arguably, this particular problem we're trying to automate could be done manually by hand, without much overhead, as we're only applying this change to three lines of code. But imagine that we want to apply this change to *any* place we find a variable assignment, either throughout this file or even across multiple files within our entire code base. That would take quite a lot of manual work, and this is where the idea of macros comes in.

Recording Macros

When you record a macro, you start on a line that matches the criteria you want to be affected by your change. So, in this case, out of the entire file I'm working on, I wouldn't start recording my macro just anywhere. I would move to one of those three lines that had a variable assignment on it and start recording there. For the specific problem we're trying to solve, the variable assignment is my main *criteria*.

Let's see what the syntax structure looks like for recording a macro.

```
q{register}{commands}q
```

As you can see, the syntax structure lives up to the simplicity of the concept. Here, we press q to start recording; we specify a register (this can be either 0-9 or a-z); we execute the commands we want to record; and, finally, we press q again, to stop recording.

■ **Note** We'll see later on that we can record into the A–Z registers, but that is for a specific reason (i.e., appending).

So, now that we know the purpose of a macro and how to structure one, let's take a look at the entire solution required to implement the automated change discussed earlier that we want to make. (Remember: We're executing the following command on one of the lines that has a variable assignment.)

```
qa0f=wvg_xalog()<Esc>""Pjq
```

I'm going to assume that you, the faithful reader, are probably starting to understand why macros are sometimes seen as being *complex*, but let's break this long string of characters down, so that we can more easily digest it.

- q: Start recording our macro.

- a: Specify a as the register to record into.

- 0: Ensure that the cursor starts at the beginning of the line.

- f=: Search for the = character.

- w: Move the cursor to the start of the first word.

- vg_: Select until the end of the line.

- x: Cut the selection (which also moves it into our registers).

- a: Append our new content.

- log()<Esc>: Add our new content then press <Esc> to move to NORMAL mode.

- ""P: Paste the content of the " register *before* the cursor.

- j: Move down one line.

- q: Stop recording.

If we now look inside of our registers list (using :reg a), we'll see that the a register indeed has our macro stored ready to be applied.

One item in our macro recording process worth highlighting is the use of the j command to move down one line just before we stopped recording. The purpose of this action is to allow the macro to start from the next line, if we decided we wanted to execute the macro multiple times.

Macros do not automatically run through an entire file line-by-line, but instead have to be told how many times to execute. So, if we executed the macro five times but didn't have part of the macro move down a line at the end, the macro would execute five times on the same line every time (which could result in some odd changes). Moving down (or up) a line at the end of a macro is what usually confuses new users, as they don't realize that macros aren't executed line-by-line automatically; you have to tell the macro how.

Executing Macros

This finally leads us to the question of "How do I actually execute a macro?" To do that, we use the @ command and specify the relevant register we want to execute. For our preceding example, we would execute our macro, which was recording into the a register, by running the command @a.

In our example, we had three lines of code that each had a variable assignment. Imagine that we ran @a on the first of those lines, so that our content looked like the following:

```
identifier  = log(Crimp.signature(data))
cloned_data = deep_copy data)
transformed = yield cloned_data
```

At this point in time, the first line is changed successfully, but the remaining two lines must still have the macro applied to them. From here, we have a few options, and which one you pick depends purely on your own personal preference. We could

- Manually run @a two more times

- Specify a count: 2@a

- Manually run @@ twice (the only difference between this and the first bulleted item is that I don't have to explicitly provide the name of the register; it executes the last executed register)

- Specify a count with the last executed register: 2@@

■ **Note** Being able to use the @ symbol to execute the contents of a register is extremely powerful. If your last command-line command was :vs (which will create a vertical split), you can repeat that command five times (i.e., create five more splits) using 5@:.

Real-World Example

Only the other day, I had a problem that was made much easier to resolve, thanks to the use of macros. I was presented with a CSV list of users. The structure of the CSV was `"First Name"|"Last Name"|"email@email.com"`, and I was required to present the list as the full name, but not the e-mail (or any of the other syntax around them).

The macro I recorded and ran against my content was the following:

```
qa0xf"d3li<Space><Esc>eldg_jq
```

To make it easier to digest, I'll break this macro down into sections.

- `qa`: Start recording into the a register.

- `0x`: Move the cursor to the start of the line and cut the opening `"`.

- `f"`: Find the next `"`.

- `d3l`: Delete the next three characters `"|"`.

- `i<Space><Esc>`: Enter INSERT mode and add a space, then exit mode.

- `el`: Move the cursor to the character after the end of the next word.

- `dg_`: Delete from the cursor position to the end of the line.

- `jq`: Move the cursor down to the next line and stop recording.

This ended up changing the content from

```
"Bob"|"Smith"|bob@smith.com
"Jane"|"Doe"|jane@doe.com
"Bridget"|"Jones"|jane@doe.com
```

and transforming it into

```
Bob Smith
Jane Doe
Bridget Jones
```

Applying Macros Across Multiple Files

You learned back in Chapter 9 about the different techniques for executing commands across multiple buffers, using `:bufdo`. We can utilize that same technique, to allow us to apply a macro across multiple files.

In case you need a reminder, `:bufdo` works by taking the command you specify in the command-line bar and applying it to every open buffer. So, for us to apply our macro to all our open buffers, we could try running the following command:

```
:bufdo normal @a
```

The preceding command may or may not work, depending on your Vim configuration (as changing buffers when a modification has been detected can cause errors if not quieted with `:set hidden`, as in our `.vimrc` file).

If you do have issues with the preceding command, the following variation will work, because we write the modifications before moving to the next buffer (but be aware that we have to use the exe command to prevent the pipe character from being interpreted as a NORMAL mode character):

```
:bufdo exe "normal @a" | write
```

■ **Note** If you didn't want to use the set hidden option, you could work around the issue of errors being triggered by changing buffers after a modification by adding the :w command to your macro.

More Dynamic Macros Using the Expression Register

To make your macros even more powerful, you can utilize the expression register, not only to dynamically generate content based on VimL code, but also to use the expression register to access other registers.

As an example, let's consider that we have a buffer that consists of a set of numbers from zero to nine (see following), and we want to double each of the other numbers.

```
1
2
3
4
5
6
7
8
9
```

Here is the macro we'll be using:

```
qaxi<C-r>=2*<C-r>"<Enter><Esc>jq
```

When run, this macro will convert our content into the following:

```
2
4
6
8
10
12
14
16
18
```

Before we move on, let's break down this macro and understand what it is doing and how we're dynamically calculating the values.

- qa: Start recording into the a register.

- xi: Cut the current number and then enter INSERT mode.

- <C-r>=: Access the expression register.

- `2*<C-r>"`: Enter our calculation (using the unnamed register).

- `<Enter><Esc>`: Insert the result of our expression.

- `jq`: Move down a line and then stop recording.

■ **Note**   We saw in Chapter 11 the `:global` command, which allows us to execute NORMAL mode commands against specific matched patterns. We can also advance this technique by running a macro against a matched pattern: `:%g/{pattern}/norm @a`.

Editing Macros

Now that we know how to create macros, let's consider how we can edit them when we make a mistake. This seems to be a problem that confuses a lot of users. For example, I know experienced Vim users who rerecord their entire macro whenever they realize they've made a mistake or forgotten to include some specific operator at the last minute.

Effectively, there are two main ways to change a macro:

1. Append changes to the end of an existing macro.

2. Edit any part of the macro, using some "jiggery pokery." (Yes, that's a technical term.)

Appending

If all you have to do is append some additional commands to the end of your macro, the solution is very straightforward. You can use the capitalized variation for recording the macro.

qA

In the preceding example, we're telling Vim that we want to append onto the a register by using the capitalized version of the register. If we were to execute qa instead, we would erase the a register and start adding fresh commands. The capitalized variation avoids that.

Editing

Being able to append content to an existing macro is fine, but what if the change you have to make isn't just adding some new commands to the end of your macro but something more fundamental (maybe the middle of the macro needs correcting)? The trick to doing this type of granular editing is to write the macro into the buffer, edit the commands, and then yank the edit back into the relevant register.

In the previous section, we recorded a macro into the a register, and it looked like this: `qaxi<C-r>=2*<C-r>"` `<Enter><Esc>jq`. If we wanted to change the amount, we multiply by two to four, then the following steps are what we would have to take to edit the macro:

- `:put a`: Write the relevant macro to the buffer.

- `f2`: Find the number two.

- `r4`: Replace it with the number four.

- 0V: Select the macro again.

- "ay: Yank the selection into the a register.

- :put a: Display the updated register.

Summary

Macros are a powerful feature for automation. Once properly understood, they can be composed with existing commands and Vim features to extend their usefulness (such as utilizing the expression register and the :global command). Let's take a moment to review some of the topics covered in this chapter.

- First, we looked back at the many different ways we're able to automate our workflow within Vim (e.g., the repeat command, the substitution command, and the global command).

- Next, we considered an example in which a solution such as a macro would be useful, considering the dynamic nature of the problem we were trying to automate.

- I covered how to record macros, using the syntax structure q{register}{commands}q and discussed and clarified what registers could be recorded into.

- We jumped straight into an example that provided a solution to the problem presented (i.e., wrapping our expressions in a call to a log function).

- I highlighted an important point about recording macros, which was the need to make sure the macro can move up or down when being executed multiple times (otherwise, the macro will simply re-execute against the same line every time).

- You learned the many different ways to execute a macro, both singularly and with a count. You also realized that you could execute the last macro again, without specifying the register, by using the double @@ command.

- To help solidify your understanding of macros, I included a simple but practical real-world example that demonstrated how to parse a CSV file to return the specific data needed.

- We looked at how to execute macros across multiple files, again reducing our workflow by expanding the automation range across more than just a single file, while also solidifying our understanding of the exe and normal command-line commands you learned about in earlier chapters.

- You learned how to enhance the capabilities of our macros, by utilizing the expression register to dynamically generate content automatically by taking a list of numbers and doubling them. A silly example maybe, but one that I hope demonstrated the power of composing different features of Vim together, to help solve specific problems.

- Finally, you learned an often misunderstood requirement, which is how to actually edit a macro once it has been recorded. You now know that by using the uppercase range of registers A–Z, you're able to append to the lowercase range (a–z) of macros. You now also know that to have the most granular control over editing, macros require us to simply put the content into a buffer, edit, and then yank them back into the relevant buffer again, to be replayed when needed.

CHAPTER 14

Lists

There are two types of lists in Vim: a "change list" and a "jump list." They both work in fundamentally similar ways but offer subtly different solutions. The former allows us to move our cursor back and forth between a set of edits we've made to a buffer, whereas the latter allows us to move our cursor back and forth between a set of cursor jump points across multiple buffers.

What I'm about to confess might seem strange, but I'm going to say it anyway: I personally don't find the change list to be a very useful feature in my day-to-day workflow, and I've actually never seen anyone else present a good example of its use case either. The jump list, on the other hand, I *do* find very useful, and I use that particular feature on a regular basis. (Later in this chapter, I'll demonstrate a practical example of its use.)

With that confession out the way, you might now be wondering, if I don't like the change list feature, why bother covering how it works? Doesn't its lack of usefulness to me mean it's a feature without a cause? I'm not entirely sure that's the case. It merely means that I have not found a reasonable use for it, but others (maybe you) will have a perfect use case for this particular feature. I believe that both Vim's change list and jump list go hand-in-hand and that you can't learn one without the other. To me, they're like siblings and should not be separated.

So, with this in mind, let's begin by showing you how Vim's change list feature works, and then we can delve into the jump list and start to explore why I believe it to be much more useful.

Change Lists

Every time you make an edit within INSERT mode, Vim will store that change in a change list file. To view the change list for the *active* buffer/window, run the following command:

```
:changes
```

The changes command will display a table matrix of edits you have made. To understand what this table represents, let's run a test. Imagine that we have a file called A.txt open in Vim (the file should be empty). If I were to run the :changes command at this moment, we would see the following table matrix:

```
change line  col text
>
```

Notice that there is nothing but a chevron character shown (>). The chevron character indicates the current change position, and we'll see shortly how it reacts to changes we make to this document.

Now let's add the content, A, to the file and run the :changes command:

```
change line  col text
    1    1    0 A
>
```

189

Again, we see that the chevron character hasn't moved, but now we can see that the table matrix has a single change indicated. Under the "change" column, we see the number 1. This column is actually a little confusing, but I'll come back to that in a moment. First, let's continue looking at the values in the other columns. So, we have the second column "line," which indicates what line the change occurred on (in this case, line 1). The third column, "col," indicates in what column the change occurred (in this case, we added a single character to a blank document, so it's column 0). Finally, the fourth column, "text," shows us what the change was (in this case, the letter A was added).

If we add a new character, B, to the end of the first line and run the :changes command, what shall we see? Well, in this case, probably not what you were expecting for a feature that pertains to listing all changes.

```
change line  col text
    1     1    1 AB
>
```

I don't know about you, but I expected to see two rows in that table matrix. The first being the A change and the second row indicating the B change. Remember that things are never as they first appear. It would seem at this point in time that the change list doesn't work the way we expect. It would seem that, instead, the change list records the last change on a line-by-line basis (which you can see, as it indicates in the third column that the change happened in column 1 of the buffer—which is true; we added B).

But, as I said, things are never as they first appear, and if we add a few more changes, we'll see that the change list does indeed record multiple changes for a single line. The next example will help us understand how this works; so let's go ahead and add C onto line 2, then <Esc> back into NORMAL mode and add D onto line 3. If we run :changes now, we should see the following matrix:

```
change line  col text
    3     1    1 AB
    2     2    0 C
    1     3    0 D
>
```

OK, so now would be a good time to take a moment to go back and clarify what the change column displays and why. We can see that the changes are made in ascending order (which means the oldest changes are at the top, while the latest changes are at the bottom).

You may have expected the change column to be in the reverse order: the first change, AB, marked as 1 inside the change column; and the C change marked as 2 (the second change), and D marked as 3 (the third change). Well, sadly, no. The reason the numbers appear as they do is because they represent the *count* required to get back to that change. So, for example, if we wanted to move our cursor back to the position of the B change, we would have to execute the relevant command three times (or specify a count of 3).

Let's now make a change to line 2 and add an exclamation point (!) after the C character. Running :changes now will display the following matrix:

```
change line  col text
    4     1    1 AB
    3     2    0 C!
    2     3    0 D
    1     2    1 C!
>
```

OK, this helps us to make more sense of the text column. It, in fact, doesn't show the change, but the entire contents of the line affected. In this case, we can see that both the second and last change show the same value: C!

Move Back Through Our Change Positions

To access a specific change position (remember that moving through the change list is only moving the cursor *position* to where the change happened and not undoing the change itself), you'll run the following command, in which n is the number of the change position you're interested in:

`:changes {n}`

The following commands are shortcuts for moving back and forth between individual change positions:

- g;: previous position
- g,: next position

Given the previous example file that we've been modifying, if we ran the command 4g and then the :changes command, we would see that the chevron inside the table matrix has moved up to the relevant line that indicates we've moved to the specified change position, as follows:

```
change line  col text
>    4     1    1 AB
     3     2    0 C!
     2     3    0 D
     1     2    1 C!
```

To demonstrate what happens to the chevron once another change has been made to your file, edit the file line to include a question mark (?), so that the line reads AB?. Running :changes now would display the following matrix:

```
change line  col text
     5     1    1 AB?
     4     2    0 C!
     3     3    0 D
     2     2    1 C!
     1     1    1 AB?
>
```

Notice that the additional change is recorded, and the chevron has now moved outside of any of the specified lines, indicating that a new change has been made, and our cursor isn't explicitly set to sit at an earlier change.

Jump Lists

Every time you "jump" to another part of a buffer (i.e., you move your cursor to a new position), Vim records that jump into a "jump list." This is a similar concept to Vim's change list, which we looked at in the previous section.

Let's take a look at an example that will demonstrate how a motion can create a jump that Vim will store into the jump list. Imagine that we have a file that contains the letters of the alphabet (one letter per line). If we run the command 10gg, our cursor will be placed onto line 10 (the letter *J*).

■ **Note** There are a set number of commands that will trigger a jump. These include ', `, gg, G, /, ?, n, N, %, (,), [[,]], {, }, :s, :tag, L, M, H, and any commands that begin editing a file, such as a, i, A, I, o. See :h jump-motions for more information.

Now that we've moved our cursor (using the preceding motion), let's take a look at our jump list, to see what information we get back. To view the jump list, run the following command (the result of this command can be seen in Figure 14-1):

```
:jumps
```

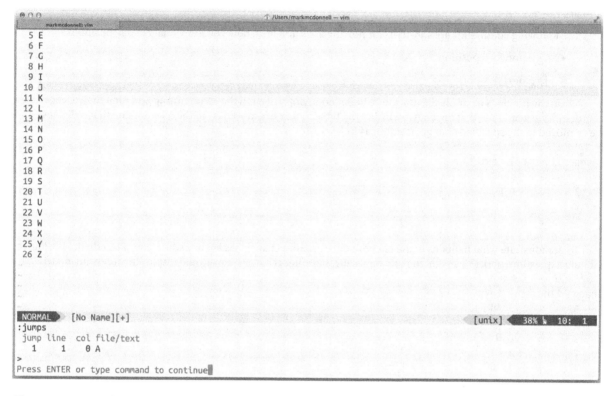

Figure 14-1. *Sample jump list*

Execute the :jumps command and see what Vim returns.

```
jump line  col file/text
   2    1    0 A
>
```

What we can see from the preceding display is that although we've jumped to line 10, the :jumps command has not displayed it. That's because it only shows jumps that have occurred previously. So, if we were to execute 20gg (to move to line 20), then executed the command :jumps again, we'd see the following output:

```
:jumps
 jump line  col file/text
   2    1    0 A
   1   10    0 J
>
```

What we can see from the preceding output is that Vim is now reporting back that the previous cursor position was line 10 (the letter *J*). We can also see that the jump column works the same as Vim's change list, which means the number displayed is the count we would use to jump back to that position. (I'll demonstrate how to do this in just a moment.)

To navigate back and forth between jumps requires the following commands, and chances are you're already well acquainted with them, as that's how you navigate through the built-in Vim help system/documentation:

- `<C-o>`: Move to previous jump position

- `<C-i>`: Move to next jump position

If you want to jump back multiple positions, you'll first have to provide a count before executing one of the preceding commands. So, if we wanted to move back to the first cursor position (which we can see was the letter *A* and was two positions back), we'd have to run the following command:

```
2<C-o>
```

It's worth noting another difference between the change list and jump list, and that is that the jump list holds positions across multiple files. So, if you jump forward or backward enough, don't be surprised if you suddenly end up in a separate file.

■ **Note**   There is a maximum of 100 jumps that can be recorded, so you don't have an unlimited supply (not that you should need that many).

Practical Example: Generating a Table of Contents

I use jump lists a lot, as they help to easily navigate between sections of my code. But let's look at a more practical example of using this feature: creating a table of contents (TOC) list for a blog post.

When writing articles for my web site http://www.integralist.co.uk/ (the source code can be found here: `https://github.com/Integralist/Website`), I'll use Markdown syntax to format the content. If you're unfamiliar with Markdown, the important thing to know for the purposes of this section is to indicate a header in your post that you'll prefix the title for with a single hash character (#) or multiple hashes, to signify sublevel titles. The following examples demonstrate this specific syntax:

```
# Level 1 Header
## Level 2 Header
### Level 3 Header
#### Level 4 Header
```

To create a TOC from each header in the document, I use the jump list to help navigate through. (This is especially useful when dealing with a very long document.) My workflow takes the following steps:

- Identify the pattern.

- Copy the required content.

- Move to the top of the buffer (where our TOC is).

- Use the jump list to navigate back to the first match.

- Move to the next match.

- Rinse and repeat from the second point.

■ **Note** Admittedly there is also an alternative where by you create a split window on your buffer (i.e. so you have the same buffer in both windows) and use one window to view the top of your file and the other to scroll down to the relevant content. But at least with the example I'm giving you'll have a better understanding of how to utilize the jump list feature.

Let's consider an example document (and the first line consisting of a dash [–] character is intentional):

```
-

## Title 1

Content 1

## Title 2

Content 2

## Title 3

Content 3
```

If we use the steps defined previously, the solution will look something like the following (be aware that this will demonstrate our first run):

- /#: Identify the pattern (in this case, we look for #).

- wg_y: Copy the required content (e.g., Title 1).

- gga<Space><Esc>p: Move back to TOC and create a new item, using the copied content.

- <C-o>: Use the jump list to navigate to the previous match (e.g., Title 1).

- nwg_y: Move to the next match (e.g., Title 2).

- ggo-<Space><Esc>p: Move back to TOC and create a new item, using the copied content (e.g., Title 2).

- <C-o>: Use the jump list to navigate to the previous match (e.g., Title 2) and rinse and repeat the process until we have a complete TOC.

```
- Title 1
- Title 2
- Title 3
- Title 4

## Title 1

Content 1
```

```
## Title 2

Content 2

## Title 3

Content 3
```

Even if you automated the preceding process using a macro, doing this type of work would be a lot more awkward without the ability to navigate with Vim's jump list feature.

▨ **Note**   Vim doesn't provide a facility with which to clear the jump list, as, in all honesty, there aren't many reasons why you would want to, but if this is something you need to do, the following VimL code is one solution: `:let i = 0 | while i < 100 | mark ' | let i = i + 1 | endwhile`. This sets the next 100 positions to the same value.

Ignoring Jumps

Imagine that you're writing a VimL plug-in and you need it to modify your buffers so that they contain a timestamp at the bottom of the document (at the moment the user wrote the buffer) and then move the cursor back to its previous position.

Not concerning ourselves with the relevant VimL code to achieve this requirement, let's consider a potential problem we'll encounter by trying to write such a plug-in: by moving the cursor to the bottom of the buffer, we have created the side effect of adding a new jump inside Vim's jump list. This would mean we'd have to move back two jump positions, rather than one, and also that we'd muddied the jump list with an additional jump that may or may not be desirable.

To avoid this issue, Vim provides us with the `:keepjumps` command. I personally find this command to be badly named, because it effectively does the opposite of what it describes: it *doesn't* keep any jump that would be created by the command specified to be run after the `:keepjumps` command.

Let's consider a quick example. Imagine that we have a buffer that contains ten lines of content open, and our cursor is currently placed on line 1. Now, enter Ex mode (Q) and run the following commands:

```
keepjumps normal G
keepjumps normal 3G
keepjumps normal 5G
keepjumps normal 10G
```

▨ **Note**   To exit Ex mode, you have to type `visual` into the command line.

If you exit Ex mode after running the preceding commands and then run `:jumps` again, you should notice that no new jumps have been added into the jump list.

Summary

This was a short chapter to cover two fundamental features of Vim that provide very granular control over how we can navigate through our content, using either a list of positions recorded by editing our content or by triggering the appropriate commands that create jump positions. Let's take a moment to recap what you learned before moving on.

- We saw how to list any edits that were made to a specific file by viewing a list of "changes," using the :changes command. You also learned how to interpret the table matrix presented back as a result of running the command.

- I demonstrated how to move the cursor back to a specific change position, by specifying a count, like so :changes 2.

- You then learned the shorthand key mappings for navigating back and forth between the change list items one-by-one, using g; to move backward through the list and g, to move forward through the list. (We again saw that specifying a count allows us to navigate multiple items, like so: 2g;.)

- After that, we moved on to learning about Vim's jump list feature and saw that there are multiple ways a changed cursor position is recorded as a jump (see :h jump-motions for the full list) and how to view the list of jumps by running the command :jumps.

- We saw how to navigate through each jump list item, using the <C-o> (move backward) and <C-i> (move forward) key mappings, and that a count could be provided to allow us to jump multiple items, like so: 2<C-o>.

- We took a moment to review a practical real-world example of how to use the jump list to help generate a Table of Contents for a blog post.

- You learned that there is currently no built-in mechanism for clearing the jump list but that we can use some VimL code to achieve this effect for us, by looping through all 100 available positions and setting them to have the same value, thus reducing the jump list down to one item.

- Finally, we took a look at the confusingly named :keepjumps command, which actually tells Vim to *not* record a jump when running a relevant command within COMMAND-LINE or Ex modes, which would normally cause the side effect of creating a jump.

CHAPTER 15

Marks

When you start dealing with large project code bases, you'll likely find that being able to navigate through all your files (and even within individual files that are quite lengthy) can become quite difficult. Vim provides multiple ways to solve this problem (for example, `vimgrep` and specific plug-ins such as CtrlP—which we'll see in Chapter 17—for fuzzy searching), but what if you already know the type of contents certain files contain, but you want an easy way to get back to specific sections more easily than carrying out the same search over and over?

Browsers solved this particular problem a long time ago; the solution is called bookmarks. Imagine you need to find some information on cars. You open up your web browser and go to a search engine and type in the word *cars*. The search engine returns thousands of results for this search term, and you find a site youarch engine returns thousands of results for this search term, and you find go to a search have to refer to on a daily basis. You could go through the whole process again (go to a search engine in your browser; run a search, which may or may not use the same search term as last time; and sift through the results until you find the same site) *or* you could bookmark the site instead, which would allow you simply to open your web browser and click a single link, to be taken directly to the page of interest.

Vim marks offer the exact same benefits. They allow for very granular control over adding multiple bookmarks to different areas of a file, being able even to set the mark position to a specific column inside a line. Vim also allows us to create two different kinds of marks:

1. *Temporary marks*: These are marks that only last as long as the buffer is open.

2. *Long-term marks*: These are marks that last until you delete them.

Creating Marks

Let's start by understanding the basics of how we can actually create a mark. In the following code snippet, we'll see the syntax structure of a mark:

```
m{a-zA-Z}
```

As the syntax structure indicates, to set a bookmark, you have to first press m, followed by a character from the alphabet (either lower- or uppercase; both behave in slightly different ways, which I'e slightly further later).

If we wanted to record a mark into the a index, we would run the following command: ma, which would save my current cursor position (down to the specific column in the line) for the current buffer.

Viewing Marks

To see all your recorded marks (along with the line and column number they correlate to), run the following command:

```
:marks
```

If you run that command with a fresh install of Vim (i.e., youou run that command with a fresh install of Vi, youn u run that command with a

```
mark line  col file/text
 '     1    0
 "     1    0
```

We can see from the result of running this command that we get a table matrix that highlights a specific mark and the line number associated with that mark. Wenum also shown the specific column for the mark. The file/text column in the preceding example is empty, as this is the result of running the :marks command on a fresh install of Vim that has no prior history. But this would typically show the path to the file where the mark was recorded, if it was a global mark, or, alternatively, the content of the line the mark points to, if it was a local mark. (Donf it was, I'ef it was a local marke the mark points toe f in the next section).

■ **Note**   If you check the :marks recorded, you'll notice there are marks 0-9 in the list. You're not able to record directly to these numbered marks; they are created dynamically by Vim and stored in its .viminfo file. For example, the 0 mark is the last location of your cursor at the point of you quitting Vim. The 1 mark is the last location before 0, and so forth.

I mentioned earlier that only a-z and A-Z marks were available for you to record into and that Vim automatically records into numbered marks, so you might be wondering what the marks ' and ", that you can see in the preceding sample output are for? Well, we already know that Vim automatically creates numbered marks 0-9, based on the position of the cursor when exiting the last file, but there are a few more marks that Vim automatically creates for us, so letat Vim automatically cre Table 15-1, following, to see what they are.

Table 15-1. *List of Marks Vim Automatically Generates*

Mark	Explanation
'	Marks the line where the cursor jumped from (in current buffer)
`	Marks the position where the cursor jumped from (in current buffer)
.	Marks the position where the last change occurred (in current buffer)
"	Marks the position where the user last exited the current buffer
[	Marks the beginning of the previously changed or yanked text
]	Marks the end of the previously changed or yanked text
<	Marks the beginning of the last visual selection
>	Marks the end of the last visual selection

Before we wrap up this section, be aware that you can also view specific marks, if you know the identifier you want to look up. In the following example, we tell Vim to display the marks a and B:

```
:marks aB
```

Local and Global Marks

It's important to realize that recording into a lowercase mark does something slightly different from recording into an uppercase mark. The difference is that lowercase marks are local to the file, whereas uppercase marks are global. This means that if you try to access a local mark from within a file where it wasn't recorded, the command will fail.

If, on the other hand, you have recorded a global mark, you will be able to access it from anywhere. What this means is that you don behave to be in the same file you recorded the global mark from. You can run the command to access the mark, and youcommand to access the markile you recorded thspecified mark inside the relevant file it was recorded.

Global marks are useful if you have specific parts of a file you know you refer back to a lot. Leta have a brief demonstration of how global marks differ from local marks. Imagine that you have a file on your desktop called `foo.txt` and that it has the following content inside of it:

```
This is my foo text file
It has a few different lines on it.
But that's about it
```

If I moved my cursor to the *t* of the word But in the last line, my cursor position would be line 3, and the column position would also be 3 (as *t* is the third letter). From here, I'll record a global mark using `mD`, and then Ia global mark using also be 3 marks differ from local mark.

If I now restart Vim (so I have no buffers open) and run the command `'D`, my `foo.txt` file will still open up, and my cursor will be on line 3, column 1 (if, instead, I were to have run `` `D ``, my cursor would have been placed on not only line 3 but into column 3 as well, the exact spot the mark was recorded into). Effectively, this demonstrates that global marks are remembered even after you have closed and restarted Vim.

■ **Note** Vim records mark information inside a `.viminfo` file (along with other session-based information, such as your command-line history, search history, registers, and jump list) located in your home directory.

Navigating Marks

There are a few other commands available that allow us to navigate through our marks (see Table 15-2). Be aware that these commands will only allow you to navigate through the marks within the *current* buffer. If you want to navigate to a mark recorded in another file, you'll have to skip ahead to the next section.

Table 15-2. *List of Commands for Navigating Vim Marks*

Operator	Explanation
]'	Next mark line position
['	Previous mark line position
]`	Next mark line and column position
[`	Previous mark line and column position

For both operators listed in Table 15-2, the syntax structure of the command looks something like [count] {operator}, meaning that an optional count can be provided. For example, imagine that we run the command 5]'. This would move our cursor to the fifth mark ahead of our current position.

■ **Note**   Both forms ' (single quote) and ` (backtick) are valid, but each has its own subtle differences (see :h mark-motions). The main thing to remember is that the ' form moves to the first non-blank character on the line, while the ` form will move to the exact column.

Moving to Specific Marks

Although being able to navigate one by one through all the marks within the current buffer can be useful, it would be even more useful (and efficient) if we could jump straight to a specific mark. Luckily for us, Vim makes that possible by using one of the following command variations:

- '{identifier}: e.g. 'a
- `{identifier}: e.g. `a

The first variation uses a single quote before the mark identifier, and this indicates that when we execute that command, our cursor will move to the start of the line for the mark we specified (the identifier being a-z, A-Z, or 0-9).

Alternatively, you can use the second variation, which is a backtick, to move the cursor to not only the relevant line but also the specific column of the line for the mark we specified (again, the identifier being a-z, A-Z, or 0-9).

As discussed earlier, if you would like to jump to a mark within another file, you would have to ensure that the mark you specify was recorded as a global mark (using the identifier range A–Z).

How to Avoid Modifying the Jump List

Typically, when moving between marks, you'll find that Vim's jump list (:jumps) will also automatically update to reflect the change of cursor position. If you want to avoid changing the jump list, then instead of directly accessing the mark, like so: '{mark} or `{mark}, you should use the g prefix: g'{mark} or g`{mark}.

Deleting Marks

Although we're able to reassign the pointer for a mark at any time, there are instances when we will want to completely remove a global mark but not necessarily have anything to replace it with. This is where deleting a global mark can come in handy.

You could open up your `.viminfo` file and manually edit it to remove any global marks, but I would recommend against doing that, as it can cause corruptions in the file, and youan cause cohaving to delete the file altogether; otherwise, Vim might not start up properly. (It's always best not to mess with the `.viminfo` file, as it is dynamically generated by Vim.)

Instead, I would suggest using the `:delmarks {marks}` command to handle this duty. As you can see from the syntax structure, we have to specify a mark (or multiple marks) to be removed. As an example, the following command will delete the global marks A and B along with the local mark c and the numbered mark 1:

```
:delmarks A B c 1
```

The following command demonstrates how to specify a range of marks to be deleted from the current buffer (e.g., deletes marks a, b, c, and d):

```
:delmarks a-d
```

■ **Note**   If you want to delete all the marks for the current buffer, rather than deleting marks manually, use the `:delmarks!` command instead.

Manipulating Content with Marks

There is a handy side effect to using marks, which is that it allows you to make multiline edits to your content. Consider the previous `foo.txt` file, in which I had recorded the position `3,3` (that being line 3, column 3) into mark D. In that sample file, imagine that we moved our cursor to the top of the buffer (gg) and then ran the following command:

```
d`D
```

WeDve composed a new command, made up of the delete command (d) and the precision f the delete command (idcommand (`` `{mark} ``). What the preceding command will do is delete from the current cursor position `1,1` (line 1, column 1) up to the position of my mark (which was `3,3`), leaving the content of the `foo.txt` buffer looking like the following:

```
t that's about it
```

Example: Moving a Visual Selection

Earlier in this chapter, I listed a group of marks that Vim automatically records on your behalf (see Table 15-1 for the full list). I want to take a moment to look at an example that creates a custom key binding that will let you move a visual selection up and down individual lines, by utilizing the < and > marks.

Although I won't cover custom key bindings until a later chapter, I wanted to demonstrate this special usage of the mark commands here, as it is a great example of the power of marks when used in the right situations.

■ **Note**   Thanks to Felippe Nardi (`https://medium.com/a-tiny-piece-of-vim`), for making me aware of this particular trick.

To begin with, letrickiny-piece-of-vimpieile with the following content and you have lines 4–6 visually selected (that being the lines J, K, and L through to P, Q, and R, which Ih to lected (that being the lines ile with the foll - - -):

```
A B C
D E F
G H I
- - -
J K L
M N O
P Q R
- - -
S T U
V W X
Y Z
```

To move our visual selection up or down the buffer, we have to use the < > marks, because they track the start and end positions of the last visual selection, so that we can combine them with the move command :m, to act like a multiline move. This trick is effectively a fancier way of executing the command :4,6m2.

With the following command, youh the fothat we bind it to the <C-k> key combination, to make it easier (read: slicker) to move a visual selection up and down the buffer. Letls see what the command looks like, and then we can break it down to understand how exactly it works:

```
xmap <C-k> :m '< -- <CR> gv
xmap <C-k> :m '> + <CR> gv
```

OK, so let :m '> + <CR> gvown er) to.

- xmap <C-k>: The xmap part allows us to map <C-k> for both VISUAL and SELECT modes. (If we were to release this particular command as part of a Vim plug-in, SELECT mode would ensure GUI-based Vim commands worked as well).

- :m: We've seen this command already. This is the "move" command, and it will move the specified line(s) to the line below a specific target line. The syntax structure for this command is [range]m[target]. Ranges take the form of {start},{end}. In this case, the range for a visual selection is always '<,'> (you've probably used the < > marks already in your short Vim experience and not even realized it!).

- '< --: In the first example, this equates to evaluating the result of finding the start position of our visual selection ('<), reducing its value by two, and subsequently moving the selection up the buffer, so that the first line of the selection is placed on line 3. (See the following note for further clarification).

- '> +: In the second example, this equates to evaluating the result of finding the end position of our visual selection ('>) and increasing its value by one. (This is so that when we execute the move command, the selection will move down the buffer, so that the first line of the selection is the line after the end of the selection).

- <CR>: This will trigger the preceding move command to be applied.

- gv: This highlights the last line of the selected content that was moved, so that your cursor is at an appropriate position to start editing again.

▪ **Note** The move command will always move the content to the line *below* the target, which means we must not target the line before the start of the selection (in this example, line 3), as we'd only end up moving the selected content back to where it started. We have to move two lines back, so that the content is effectively moved to the line above the start of the visual selection.

Plug-ins

Although marks are a very simple concept and equally simple to create, there is no shortage of Vim plug-ins that hope to extend and improve the default marks behavior and key bindings.

I personally don't extend and improve the default plug-ins for this particular feature, as I use it quite infrequently, but for a heavy user of marks, the following plug-ins might offer some additional benefits and niceties not currently implemented in the native Vim implementation:

- **ShowMarks** (https://github.com/vim-scripts/ShowMarks) A simple enhancement that adds a visual cue next to each line that has a native Vim mark recorded on it.

- **Markology** (https://github.com/jeetsukumaran/vim-markology/) This plug-in is an amalgamation of two separate plug-ins. The first is the ShowMarks plug-in, which also includes a patch of an edge case bug, and the second is the Mark_Tools plug-in, which incorporates the ability to list and navigate marks in a more user-friendly fashion.

- **Vim-Bookmarks** (https://github.com/MattesGroeger/vim-bookmarks) I'll cover this plug-in in Chapter 17. Some of its features include being able to toggle bookmarks per line, add annotations to marks, navigate marks via a quick-fix window, allow full customization (including of icons), and remain independent of native marks.

Summary

This chapter started off by covering the basics of what must have seemed like a relatively simple and straightforward Vim feature, and then near the end, I demonstrated a much more advanced and practical real-world example of the use of marks. Let's now take a moment to recap some of the things you learned.

- You saw how to create marks using the syntax structure m{a-zA-Z} (for example, to record a mark into the a identifier you would use the command ma).

- You saw how to view marks with the :marks command and how to identify global and local marks based on the file/text column's value (i.e., a file path indicates a global, and the contents of the line indicates a local).

- We looked at the different types of marks that Vim records automatically for us, such as the numbered marks, which hold the last known cursor position before the buffer was closed, and the [,], <, > marks, which are useful for creating advanced functionality, such as dynamically moving multiple lines of content.

- You now understand the difference between global and local marks (the former being available even after Vim has restarted, whereas the latter are only available for the time the buffer is open).

- You learned how to navigate marks one by one, using iteration commands such as [and] (e.g.,]` to move to the next mark position), as well as moving to a specific mark, using the syntax `{mark} (e.g., `A to move to global mark A).

- I quickly covered how to avoid modifying the jump list when navigating through our marks, by using the g`{mark} and g'{mark} commands. (This can be useful when writing dynamic scripts using VimL).

- You learned how to delete marks, using the :delmarks and :delmarks! commands (as well as the various options for passing arguments to these commands, such as specifying multiple marks either as a range or disparate list).

- You realized we could delete large chunks of content by taking advantage of the fact that we can utilize Vim's editing commands alongside the mark commands (e.g., d`{mark} to delete from the current cursor position to the specified mark).

- We ran through a practical real-world example that allowed us to make a custom key binding to move a visual selection up and down the current buffer.

- Last, we took a quick run through of some popular mark plug-ins, and one in particular that we'll come back and look at in detail in Chapter 17.

CHAPTER 16

■ ■ ■

Sessions

In this chapter, I'm going to cover a topic that it would seem most other books on the subject of Vim ignore: sessions. The principal idea behind sessions is that we're creatures of habit, and we typically find ourselves repeating things that we know and understand. Imagine a recurring project in which you end up having the same layout open (and maybe even the same files open). Why not record that setup into a session? It'll make getting up and running much quicker.

I'll give you an example: I'm a software engineer by trade, and so I work on many different style projects. One day, I might be writing PHP code, the next I might be developing an open source JRuby application, the next I'm bouncing between writing an API end point in Clojure and client-side interactions with JavaScript. If you're not a programmer, this will have no meaning and seem merely a blur of words, but the point I'm trying to make is that each project I work on potentially uses a different programming language, which itself introduces a different set of requirements, tools, and ways of designing and writing code.

It all depends on the project you're working on, but you may find, with a Ruby-based project, that you like to have two vertical split windows—one containing a Ruby file and the other containing the tests for that file—while you also have a smaller horizontal split window underneath that you use as a generic window to load up other files that you have to dip into temporarily. Figure 16-1 gives a demonstration of this layout, using my open source Sinderella Ruby gem.

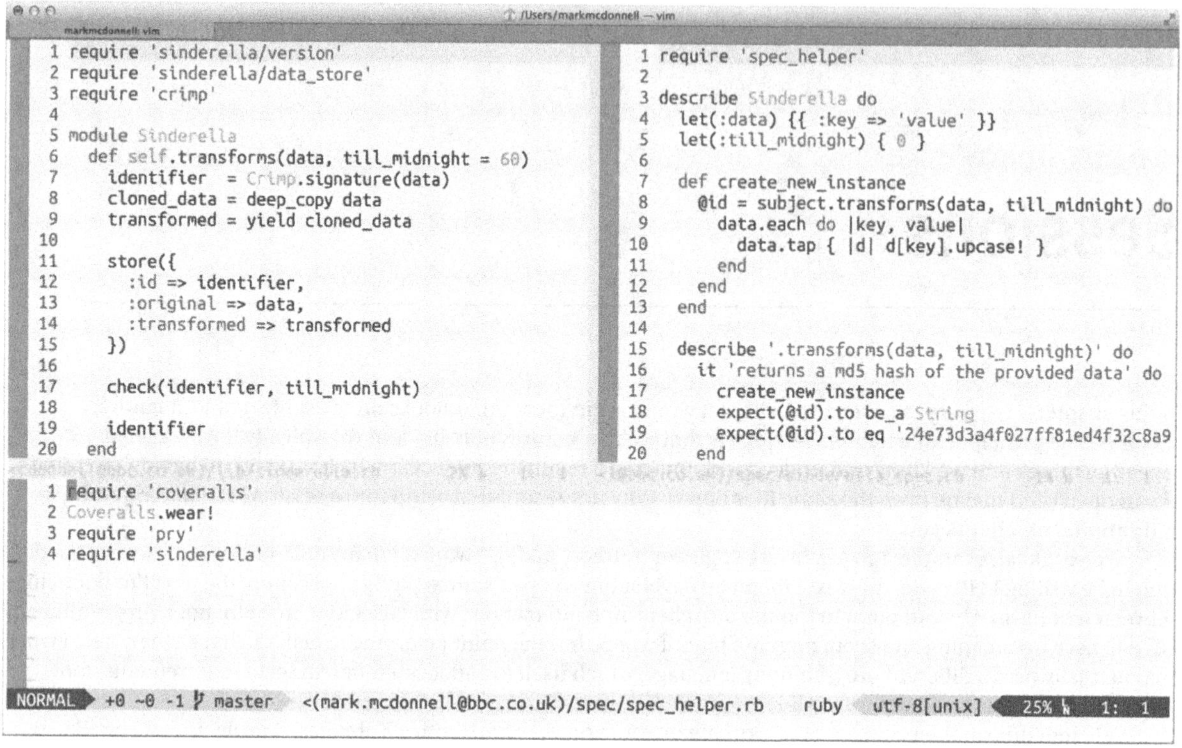

Figure 16-1. *Sample session layout for a Ruby project*

In that image, you can see that I have a left split window that holds my main `sinderella.rb` file. In the right split window, I have the associated test file open. I realized that I needed to double-check what helper files were being loaded when the tests were being run, so it was useful to have a slightly smaller bottom split window available for me to quickly view other files, without having to mess around with my main focus: the two vertical split windows.

But if I'm working only on a few miscellaneous files or a short project, I'm OK with just firing up Vim and adapting my workflow to fit my current needs. When you become comfortable with Vim, having a session is nice, but it can be easier just to "go with the flow." You become much more flexible, so recording into a session feels like it isn't worth the time.

That being said, I'm not suggesting that you completely forgo the use of sessions. If I'm working on a new feature for a web site, it's likely to take a few days. I have to write tests first and then do the "red, green, refactor" dance. I might also have to refactor some other preexisting code, to help the new features fit more easily, and chances are I'll end up having the same set of files open while I work on all of this. So, having a predefined layout that I can store at the end of the day and load up in the exact same state the next morning is something that's really useful to me.

Sessions are an interesting feature, and although it might not be as fancy a feature as, perhaps, registers or buffers, when used in the right context, they can make an incredible difference to the efficiency of your workflow.

Views and Sessions

It's important to understand that there are two concepts I'll be covering: the first is the idea of a "view," which holds information related to a single window. The other is a "session," which holds information related to the complete state of Vim at the time of creating the session.

It's recommended that you use a view instead of a session, if all you need is to remember the properties for a single window (e.g., syntax highlighting on/off, numbered lines enabled, indentation set to four spaces, etc.). If you need anything more than that, you should use a session.

Also, make sure that you understand what constitutes a *window* setting. For example, when I first started looking into creating views, I was trying out certain settings, such as disabling the status bar. I was then getting confused when I tried loading my view again (after restarting Vim), only to find that the status bar would stay visible. That's because the status bar is *outside* of a window, and so I quickly realized that I wasn't paying attention to the types of settings I was expecting to have remembered. If I wanted the status bar to be remembered as being turned off, I would have to use a session instead.

■ **Note**   None of the following items is stored within a Vim session: mark positions, registers, or your command-line history. These are all remembered/handled by your `.viminfo` file.

Creating a View

To create a view for the current file, you can use the `:mkview` command. When creating the view, you can choose to let Vim handle the naming of the view (so, effectively, it'll be an "unnamed" view), or you can specify a number between 1 and 9 or—the last option—specify the path to a file in which you want to store the settings. The syntax structure for the command to create a view is

```
:mkview [1-9|path]
```

It's important to understand that Vim associates the current file to the view you create. A view isn't like a template that you can reuse across multiple files. If I record a view with line numbers turned off and then try and load that view onto a different file, nothing would happen. Loading a view only works for the file it's associated with.

File-Based Views

Let's take a quick look at the latter variation of the `:mkview` command (i.e., specifying a file path). Specifically, I want to show you the contents of the file that Vim generates. As with the other variations (i.e., numbered and unnamed views), we don't get to see what Vim sticks in them.

Let's start by creating a file called `foo.txt` and populating it with few lines of content (it doesn't matter what the content is, as long as there are more than a couple of lines of it) for the purpose of checking to see what Vim generates. When we write a view to a file, we ideally want to make the least number of changes to the current view settings, so let's do that next.

The default setting (if you're using the ProVim configuration) is to have line numbers enabled, so to demonstrate whether the view (which we've not created yet) is loaded properly, I'll test it by saving a view that turns *off* line numbers. To do this, I'll execute the command `:set nonumber`.

If you're not using the ProVim configuration files and you don't have line numbers enabled by default, you can test this by doing the opposite and saving the view after running `:set number` instead (which will enable line numbers).

Once we change the view setting for line numbers, we can save our view to a file, like so (the file extension must be .vim); :mkview ~/Desktop/foo.vim. The contents of that file will look something like the following:

```
let s:so_save = &so | let s:siso_save = &siso | set so=0 siso=0
argglobal
edit ~/Desktop/foo.txt
setlocal keymap=
setlocal noarabic
setlocal noautoindent
setlocal nobinary
setlocal bufhidden=
setlocal buflisted
setlocal buftype=
setlocal nocindent
setlocal cinkeys=0{,0},0),:,0#,!^F,o,O,e
setlocal cinoptions=
setlocal cinwords=if,else,while,do,for,switch
setlocal colorcolumn=80
setlocal comments=s1:/*,mb:*,ex:*/,://,b:#,:%,:XCOMM,n:>,fb:-
setlocal commentstring=/*%s*/
setlocal complete=.,w,b,u,t,i
setlocal concealcursor=
setlocal conceallevel=0
setlocal completefunc=
setlocal nocopyindent
setlocal cryptmethod=
setlocal nocursorbind
setlocal nocursorcolumn
setlocal cursorline
setlocal define=
setlocal dictionary=
setlocal nodiff
setlocal equalprg=
setlocal errorformat=
setlocal expandtab
if &filetype != 'text'
setlocal filetype=text
endif
setlocal foldcolumn=0
setlocal foldenable
setlocal foldexpr=0
setlocal foldignore=#
setlocal foldlevel=0
setlocal foldmarker={{{,}}}
setlocal foldmethod=marker
setlocal foldminlines=1
setlocal foldnestmax=20
setlocal foldtext=foldtext()
setlocal formatexpr=
setlocal formatoptions=tcq
setlocal formatlistpat=^\\s*\\d\\+[\\]:.)}\\t\ ]\\s*
```

```
setlocal grepprg=
setlocal iminsert=0
setlocal imsearch=0
setlocal include=
setlocal includeexpr=
setlocal indentexpr=
setlocal indentkeys=0{,0},:,0#,!^F,o,O,e
setlocal noinfercase
setlocal iskeyword=@,48-57,_,192-255
setlocal keywordprg=
setlocal nolinebreak
setlocal nolisp
setlocal list
setlocal makeprg=
setlocal matchpairs=(:),{:},[:]
setlocal modeline
setlocal modifiable
setlocal nrformats=octal,hex
setlocal nonumber
setlocal numberwidth=4
setlocal omnifunc=
setlocal path=
setlocal nopreserveindent
setlocal nopreviewwindow
setlocal quoteescape=\\
setlocal noreadonly
setlocal norelativenumber
setlocal norightleft
setlocal rightleftcmd=search
setlocal noscrollbind
setlocal shiftwidth=4
setlocal noshortname
setlocal nosmartindent
setlocal softtabstop=0
setlocal nospell
setlocal spellcapcheck=[.?!]\\_[\\])'\"\\ ]\\+
setlocal spellfile=
setlocal spelllang=en
setlocal statusline=%!airline#statusline(1)
setlocal suffixesadd=
setlocal noswapfile
setlocal synmaxcol=3000
if &syntax != 'text'
setlocal syntax=text
endif
setlocal tabstop=4
setlocal tags=
setlocal textwidth=0
setlocal thesaurus=
setlocal noundofile
setlocal undolevels=-123456
```

```
setlocal nowinfixheight
setlocal nowinfixwidth
setlocal nowrap
setlocal wrapmargin=0
let s:l = 3 - ((2 * winheight(0) + 15) / 31)
if s:l < 1 | let s:l = 1 | endif
exe s:l
normal! zt
3
normal! 0
let &so = s:so_save | let &siso = s:siso_save
doautoall SessionLoadPost
" vim: set ft=vim :
```

There are a couple of minor points of interest to make note of regarding the content of this view file. First, we can see at the top of the file the line edit ~/Desktop/foo.txt, which is how Vim knows to associate these settings with a particular file (and why you can't load this view into a different file).

■ **Note** If you want to reuse a particular view file for another file that it's not associated with, then, depending on the number of view specific settings you have modified, it might be quicker to duplicate this view file and to simply modify the "edit" line to point to the new file to which you would like to have the view settings applied.

The other point of interest is that we can see that Vim has taken all the default settings and custom settings from our global .vimrc configuration file, added them to this view file, but set them to be local (using setlocal), so that they don't affect other windows or buffers currently open.

Loading a View

Depending on how you created your view (i.e., unnamed, numbered, or saved to a file), you'll have to load the view, using either the :loadview or :source commands. The syntax structures for these commands are as follows:

```
:loadview [1-9]
:source {path}
```

So, in the first instance, you would either leave the argument list blank and just execute :loadview, which would attempt to load the unnamed view, or specify a numeric identifier. In the second instance, we would have to call :source, using the same file path as when we recorded the view.

■ **Note** If you try to :source a view file without having the associated file for that view already open, Vim will automatically load the relevant file and make it the visible buffer.

Creating a Session

Now that we have an idea of what it means to create and save a view to be loaded again after Vim has been restarted, let's take a look at the more advanced session feature, which is effectively an enhanced view, in the sense that it'll record not only the settings for a single window but all windows and the entire environment at the point of creating the session.

If we take a look at Figure 16-2, we'll see a sample layout and environment in which we have three files created (foo.txt, bar.txt, and baz.txt), each one loaded in a different window (two windows stacked vertically on top of each other and one long window on the right-hand side). We've disabled line numbers (:set nonumber) in the right window and executed the command :set laststatus=0, which will disable Vim's status bar.

Figure 16-2. *Sample layout/environment at the point of running* :mksession

For us to record this particular setup, we'll have to run the :mksession command. Doing this, you should notice that a Session.vim file has been created inside the same directory Vim was opened from. Much like the .vim file we created when saving a view, the purpose of the Session.vim file is to accurately record everything about our current layout and environment.

If we decided that we wanted to modify the session, either now or at a later date (in this case, you would have to load the session to edit it again; see the next section to find out how to load sessions), you'd have to use a slightly modified version of the previous command, as follows:

```
:mksession!
```

You'll notice the extra exclamation mark (!) at the end of the command, which is a convention that indicates that the command will modify its subject (this is a convention also used by some programming languages, such as Ruby). In this instance, the subject to be modified is the Session.vim file.

The generated Session.vim file is quite long (~1337 lines for me, but this will vary for you, depending on the plug-ins you have installed or any custom key bindings or custom configuration), so I won't repeat it all here. Suffice it to say, however, that the content is similar to the custom View.vim file that we saw in the previous section. To ensure it keeps all details accurate, the file will attempt to copy all settings and details from your .vimrc configuration, along with any local settings you applied at the time of recording the session.

■ **Note** For full details of what specific options can be saved, please refer to the Vim help manual :h sessionoptions.

Loading a Session

Restoring your recorded session works exactly the same way as how you would restore a view file (by using the :source command). The reason we are able to use the same command is because, in both cases, we're dealing with VimL files. Both the view and session files are .vim files containing VimL code that sets Vim's environment/layout configuration. The following is an example that tells Vim to source (i.e., load) the path to a specific session file:

:source path/to/session.vim

■ **Note** To *start* Vim with a particular session (rather than having to use :source within Vim), use the –S flag: vim –S path/to/session.vim.

Removing Sessions

If you decide that you no longer need a session for a particular project, simply delete the Session.vim file. Vim will have no other way to restore session information if there isn't a Session.vim file for it to source from.

Creating a Custom Session.vim

If you've taken a sneak peek at the Session.vim file that Vim automatically generates for you after running the :mksession command, you will have noticed that the file can be quite long and detailed (obviously, because Vim doesn't know what your environment will be like in future, it's doing its job as best it can and recording every conceivable detail).

But what happens if you're not fussy about Vim restoring your environment in the *exact* same state as when you last worked on a particular project? What if you just want to be able to control a small subset of environment settings and manipulate some buffers into an easier layout?

I stated in the previous section that the Session.vim file is just VimL code, and Vim provides us with the :source command, which allows us to load any .vim file, so there is nothing stopping us from creating our own custom file that contains only the code we really need. So let's do exactly that!

I currently have a "session-test" folder on my Desktop. Inside that folder, I've created the file CustomSession.vim, and I've added the following content into it:

```
cd ~/Desktop/session-test
args *.txt
edit foo.txt
sp bar.txt
vert sb baz.txt
```

Let's quickly cover what commands have been added into this CustomSession.vim file. You should already know and be comfortable with all of them, but let's break them down, so you have complete clarity:

- cd ~/Desktop/session-test: Tell Vim to change the working directory to our project directory.

- args *.txt: Let Vim have access to a specific set of files within its argument list.

- edit foo.txt: Edit the foo.txt file (up until this point we've used the :e command, but the :edit command is the long form version, and so I felt it would make the sample code clearer in this context).

- sp bar.txt: Create a horizontal split window that contains the bar.txt file.

- vert sb baz.txt: Create a vertical split window that contains the baz.txt file.

Figure 16-3 (following) demonstrates the result of this custom session.

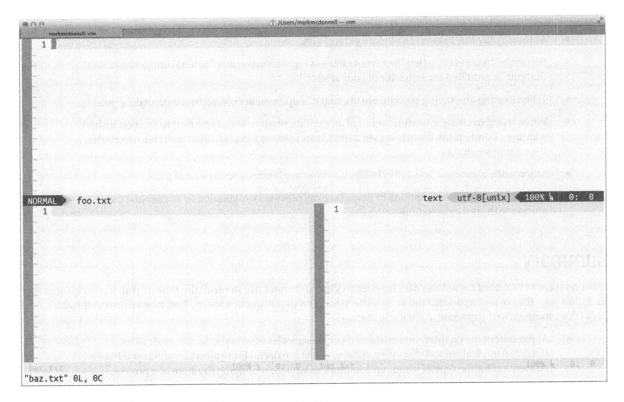

Figure 16-3. *Sample layout generated by a custom session file*

Issues

The Vim documentation indicates that there are some issues you should be aware of when utilizing views and sessions. The first item of concern is something I hinted at in the previous section ("Creating a Custom Session.vim"), but I want to elaborate on this here.

Because sessions are a snapshot of a moment in time, it means that Vim records things that you might not expect to have changed, such as key bindings for your own custom mappings or those of plug-ins that have since changed. Even current mappings will be overridden with older versions (or they may be removed completely). This could be very confusing, if you forget that this side effect is possible.

In a similar vein, if you use a plug-in manager (such as Pathogen, which I'll be covering in Chapter 17), you could run into minor issues, owing to the fact that a Vim session is a snapshot, because Vim records the current "runtimepath" that Pathogen manipulates. You can avoid this issue by telling Vim to not record global options, as follows:

```
set sessionoptions-=options
```

If you're a user of folds in your Vim workflow, you may notice that folds can become confused when you load a view that modifies fold settings.

Plug-ins

There are other areas of sessions that you might feel are lacking, and many plug-ins exist to work around these different issues. Tim Pope, Vim plug-in author extraordinaire, offers one such plug-in called obsession.vim (https://github.com/tpope/vim-obsession), which aims to resolve some small annoyances of the default implementation. Below is a list of some of its features, although I suggest you check out the repository, if you're interested investigating this plug-in further.

- Automatically run :mksession before exiting Vim.

- Re-invoke :mksession when the layout changes (again, saving you from having to remember that you've modified the behavior of your session).

- When loading an existing session, ensure that it is updated according to the preceding points.

- When trying to create a session on top of an existing session, simply allow it to happen without warning. (I don't think there was ever a time I ran :mksession and *didn't* want it to overwrite the current session.)

- Automatically create a Session.vim file, if a directory is provided instead of a file.

- Default to not capturing options or maps (see my previous explanations), as they just mess around with your expectations.

Summary

Sessions seem to be one of those love/hate features in Vim. You either use them all the time or you don't use them at all. Either way, they're an important feature to understand and to pull out of your toolbox when the time is right. Let's take a moment to recap some of what you learned.

- At the start of the chapter, we considered some examples of why you would want to use Vim's session feature and discovered that sessions are useful for projects in which you have a convention for the type of layout and settings, as well for managing the state of a project.

- You learned that there are fundamentally two parts to sessions: a "view" and the "session" itself. A view holds the state for a single window and is useful for simpler requirements, whereas a session can manage multiple views as well as the entire environment for the current Vim workspace.

- You learned how to create views, including the "unnamed" view and numbered views, as well as custom views that are saved to a custom `.vim` file. We also looked at how to load views.

- We took a glimpse inside a custom view file, to see what its contents were and to understand how it works its magic and is able to restore the changes.

- After that, you learned how to create sessions, using both the `:mksession` and `:mksession!` commands (the latter allows users to overwrite an existing session file), and how to load them via the `:source` command, as well as the `-S` flag from outside Vim. We then looked at how to delete sessions and how to create our own custom session file.

- Last, we reviewed some minor concerns about the use of sessions and how they were designed to be a snapshot in time, thereby causing confusion (e.g., overridden or deleted mappings), if not properly understood. We finally took a look at one of many plug-ins that attempts to improve the use of sessions.

CHAPTER 17

∎ ∎ ∎

Plug-ins

Here we are, finally, at the section that new Vim users are usually most excited about: plug-ins! So why is this such an interesting part of the Vim experience? Well, this is where the fun part happens. You get to enhance Vim with all sorts of additional functionality. If you can imagine it, chances are someone has written a Vim plug-in for it. For some users, plug-ins are as much a part of their fundamental Vim experience as choosing a color scheme for your editor.

But on the practical side of the fence, plug-ins offer us the facility to extend an already very powerful text editor with features it was never designed to handle. Throughout this chapter, I'll first make sure you properly understand the plug-in architecture and how to install plug-ins correctly, and then I'll move on to reviewing a wide range of plug-ins (all of which I personally use).

Following is a list of the plug-ins we'll be looking at, but it's important to realize that I won't be covering every single feature that each plug-in offers; otherwise, this book would get a whole lot longer. I may not even cover aspects of the plug-in that some other people might feel is a higher priority. That's OK, I'm giving you a taste of what features are available to you as a Vim user, and if one of these plug-ins peaks your interest, then go ahead and follow the relevant links to the plug-in, to find out more from its documentation.

- Ack/Ag (Silver Searcher)
- Commentary
- CtrlP
- NERDTree
- Surround
- EndWise
- Tabular
- Syntastic
- SuperTab
- Gist
- Fugative
- Dispatch

Proceeding from these "popular" plug-ins is a set of lesser known plug-ins that I don't use as often during my general day-to-day work but still offer some powerful functionality that really comes in handy when the right situation arises.

- BufOnly.vim

- scratch.vim

- Camel Case Motion

- vim-choosewin

- vim-bookmarks

- targets.vim

- wildfire.vim

- ZoomWin

How Do Plug-ins Work?

Yes, Vim's functionality can be extended through the use of plug-ins, but what are plug-ins really? They're code, written in Vim's built-in language, VimL (also known as "VimScript"). We've used incidental pieces of VimL code throughout the book so far and also discussed what it is, way back in Chapter 2. To recap,

> *VimL is the building block behind writing plug-ins and allowing other forms of customization in Vim. I don't go into detail on this topic, as it would require a book unto itself. If you are interested in learning more, a good online resource is available at http://learnvimscriptthehardway.stevelosh.com/.*

—Me! *Pro Vim*, Chapter 2

Before we can understand how plug-ins are installed, we have to look at what a standard Vim directory looks like. By this, I mean, what is the default folder structure within the .vim directory when working with a fresh installation. The following tree visualizes this directory for us:

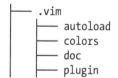

```
├── .vim
│   ├── autoload
│   ├── colors
│   ├── doc
│   ├── plugin
```

What can trip up new Vim users is that there are two types of plug-ins: single and multi (that's not an official name for them, that's just how I describe them). To clarify the former, some plug-ins consist of only a *single* plug-in file. If you want to use one of these types of plug-ins, all you have to do is to place them inside your plugin directory. To clarify the latter, some plug-ins are made up of multiple files/folders, and in such instances, you'll have to manually copy each file into the relevant corresponding folder within your .vim directory.

Let's digress for a moment and consider a sample plug-in, such as NERDTree. (This is a popular plug-in that aims to reintroduce a more traditional navigation functionality back into Vim. I'll review NERDTree later in this chapter.) NERDTree is a multi-file plug-in that has the following tree structure:

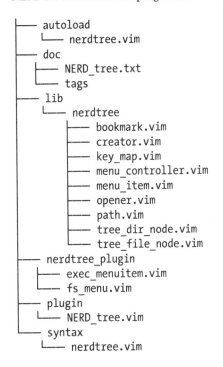

```
├── autoload
│   └── nerdtree.vim
├── doc
│   ├── NERD_tree.txt
│   └── tags
├── lib
│   └── nerdtree
│       ├── bookmark.vim
│       ├── creator.vim
│       ├── key_map.vim
│       ├── menu_controller.vim
│       ├── menu_item.vim
│       ├── opener.vim
│       ├── path.vim
│       ├── tree_dir_node.vim
│       └── tree_file_node.vim
├── nerdtree_plugin
│   ├── exec_menuitem.vim
│   └── fs_menu.vim
├── plugin
│   └── NERD_tree.vim
└── syntax
    └── nerdtree.vim
```

Note that NERDTree introduces its own set of folders/files (e.g., `nerdtree_plugin`), which are referenced internally by the plug-in's VimL code, but the standard set of Vim-specific folders are all there: `autoload`, `doc`, `plugin`.

Vimball

Vim provides a feature called Vimball, which allows plug-in authors to simplify how they bundle up their plug-in code so that it becomes a single `.vba` (Vimball Archive) file.

Vimball is also aimed at making life simpler for *users*; effectively making it easier to install a plug-in, by providing them with a simple set of commands to access the vba file and to split it into its component parts (i.e., plug-in file, doc files, autoload file, etc.).

■ **Note**   For full details on Vimball, please refer to the Vim manual `:h vimball`, which covers topics such as loading, creation, and removal.

The easiest way to install a vba is to open it within Vim, using a two-step process. The first step is passing the vba file to Vim as an argument, as follows:

```
vim MyVimballArchive.vba
```

Once the file is open, the second step is performed from within Vim by executing the following command:

```
:source %
```

> **Note** The % is known as a "wildcard," and essentially it refers to the buffer currently open inside Vim.

Once you run the `:source` command, Vim will extract specific data from within the vba file, then create the required files for the plug-in to work and place them inside the relevant folders: doc, autoload, plugin.

Pathogen: A Plug-in Manager

Sadly, not all plug-ins were created equal. If a plug-in is provided as a vba, then, OK, things aren't so bad, but most plug-ins aren't. The easiest way to install plug-ins for Vim (if you don't want to have to do things manually) is to use a plug-in manager. There are many, but the one I would recommend is Pathogen (https://github.com/tpope/vim-pathogen).

Pathogen makes the process of installing plug-ins easier by allowing you just to take a plug-in and bundle it into a single folder and stick that folder inside a custom folder called ~/.vim/bundle (e.g., ~/.vim/bundle/my_awesome_plugin).

When Vim starts up, Pathogen will kick into action and ensures Vim's runtimepath is modified appropriately, so it knows to look inside the bundle folder for your bundled plug-ins.

Installation

If you've followed my instructions from earlier chapters and cloned the ProVim repository, you'll already have Pathogen set up. If you haven't, then to install Pathogen, you'll have to run through the following steps. The first step is to ensure the autoload and bundle folders have been created.

```
mkdir -p ~/.vim/autoload ~/.vim/bundle;
```

Next, we want to download the Pathogen script into Vim's autoload folder.

```
curl -LSso ~/.vim/autoload/pathogen.vim https://raw.github.com/tpope/vim-pathogen/master/autoload/
pathogen.vim
```

> **Note** If you're using Windows, you will want to make sure to change all occurrences of ~/.vim to ~\vimfiles.

You will now have to update your .vimrc configuration file to include the following snippet of code, to enable Pathogen when Vim starts:

```
execute pathogen#infect()
syntax on
filetype plugin indent on
```

> ■ **Note** There are a few different plug-in managers available for Vim. Another popular option is Vundle (`https://github.com/gmarik/Vundle.vim`), which effectively gives you more granular control over how plug-ins are installed and the order they're loaded, greater flexibility when updating plug-ins, as well as the ability to search plug-ins, although I personally prefer the simplicity of Pathogen.

Vimball Support

Pathogen is also fully capable of handling Vimball Archive files, although it does require a couple of extra steps. If you've read our previous section on Vimball, you'll understand how to manually install them by using the `:source` command. When using Pathogen, it's a similar process.

First, we create a new folder for our plug-in (you can call it whatever you like, but I went with the very catchy MyVBA).

```
mkdir ~/.vim/bundle/MyVBA
```

Second, open Vim and edit the `.vba` file.

```
:e ~/path/to/my.vba
```

Finally, tell Vim to access the Vimball, but instead of using the `:source` command, you'll use the `:UseVimball` command, which tells Vim to place the files inside of the specified location (in this example, `~/.vim/bundle/MyVBA`).

```
:UseVimball ~/.vim/bundle/MyVBA
```

If you didn't use this technique (i.e., you used `:source` to load the vba instead), you'd have to go back and manually find, then copy, each of the plug-in files (`docs`, `autoloader`, `plugin`, etc.) into a new folder inside your `~/.vim/bundle` directory.

> ■ **Note** You don't have to use Pathogen with a Vimball Archive. If you just `:source` the vba, it'll still work as normal with Vim. Pathogen doesn't interfere with preexisting plug-in files and directories. Most users who employ Pathogen prefer to keep all their plug-ins together (which is why the preceding technique comes in handy).

Writing Plug-ins

Writing plug-ins is outside the scope of this book. VimL (the VimScript language) isn't the most enjoyable language to use and can deviate significantly with specific idioms from other shell script languages, such as Bash/Zsh, and also other programming languages.

But there are some options available to you, if you wish to write a plug-in for Vim but don't want to write it in VimL. The first is to use a programming language you're more familiar with (for example, Ruby or Python).

As long as you're using a Vim version greater than 6.0 (which I like to think you are, considering it was released way back on September 26, 2001), you have the opportunity to tap into Vim's internal APIs from other general-purpose programming languages.

Alternatively, you can utilize a language such as TimL (`https://github.com/tpope/timl`), which compiles down to VimL. TimL is a Lisp (`http://en.wikipedia.org/wiki/Lisp_(programming_language)`) dialect, which compiles down to raw VimL.

■ **Note** Lisp is a powerfully succinct dialect that lends itself very well to functional programming and composability. It also makes writing Vim plug-ins a lot more enjoyable and easier to construct than the standard VimL, so TimL is worth investigating.

Generating Help Tags

Some plug-ins don't automatically generate help documentation. If this is the case for a plug-in you're using, and you would like to manually generate help files, you have two options:

- Add call `pathogen#helptags()` to your `.vimrc` file, which will automatically generate help files for any plug-in you install.

- Manually generate them, using native Vim command `:helptags /path/to/plugin/doc`.

Exploring Useful Plug-ins

As mentioned at the start of this chapter, we'll be reviewing a wide range of *practical* plug-ins (some popular and well-known, others not so). What I have listed below isn't the ultimate truth with regard to plug-ins; I don't think there is such a thing, as the Vim world moves pretty quickly, meaning that by the time you read this book, there could be a thousand more plug-ins released into the wild, helping Vim users solve even more complex problems. So let's begin and see what we have to play with . . .

Ack/Ag (Silver Searcher)

> *ack is a tool like grep, optimized for programmers*

> —http://beyondgrep.com/

As the preceding quote indicates, ack (`https://github.com/mileszs/ack.vim`) is actually a command-line tool that has been designed to be faster (and have better features) than the standard grep Unix command you may be used to. We saw how grep (well, `vimgrep`, but effectively the same thing) works, back in Chapter 11, but to recap, grep (and by association ack) is a tool for searching files for a particular pattern. The pattern can be a simple collection of words (e.g., "this is a pattern," which would find a match only if those words appeared exactly like that in a file), or it can be a complex pattern using regular expressions.

The speed enhancement of ack over grep is probably one of the main reasons you'll want to use it (forgetting for a moment the extra options available to ack for filtering content). When measured against a small subset of files, you'll probably not notice much difference, but when the size of your collection grows, you'll find that ack is a marked improvement.

To run ack, you'll need to be in COMMAND-LINE mode. The following command demonstrates the syntax structure of the ack. Like `vimgrep`, ack utilizes Vim's quick-fix window and all the same commands for navigating results within the quick-fix window (see Table 17-1 for a quick reference).

```
:Ack [options] {pattern} [{directories}]
```

Table 17-1. *List of Operators Within Quick-Fix "Search Results" Window*

Operator	Explanation
o	Opens a file (same as \<CR>)
go	Previews a file (opens a buffer, but the quick-fix window maintains focus)
t	Opens in a new tab
T	Opens in a new tab silently (keeps focus away from the new tab)
h	Opens in a horizontal split
H	Opens in a horizontal split silently (keeps focus away from the split)
v	Opens in a vertical split
gv	Opens in a vertical split silently (keeps focus away from the split)
q	Closes the quick-fix window

As an example, I have my Sinderella open source project open in Vim (I have no buffers open, so I'm staring at a blank screen), and I would like to find any instance of the = character. So let's try the following command, to see if it returns what we expect (see Figure 17-1). You'll notice that I wrap my pattern in string delimiters. This is because, when using complex patterns such as a regular expression, you'll notice that the space will require you to group characters related to the pattern, so that they are separate from the other aspects of the command. We don't need the delimiters for such a simple example, but I've grown into the habit of using the delimiters, as, most of the time, I'm using a complex pattern.

```
:Ack '='
```

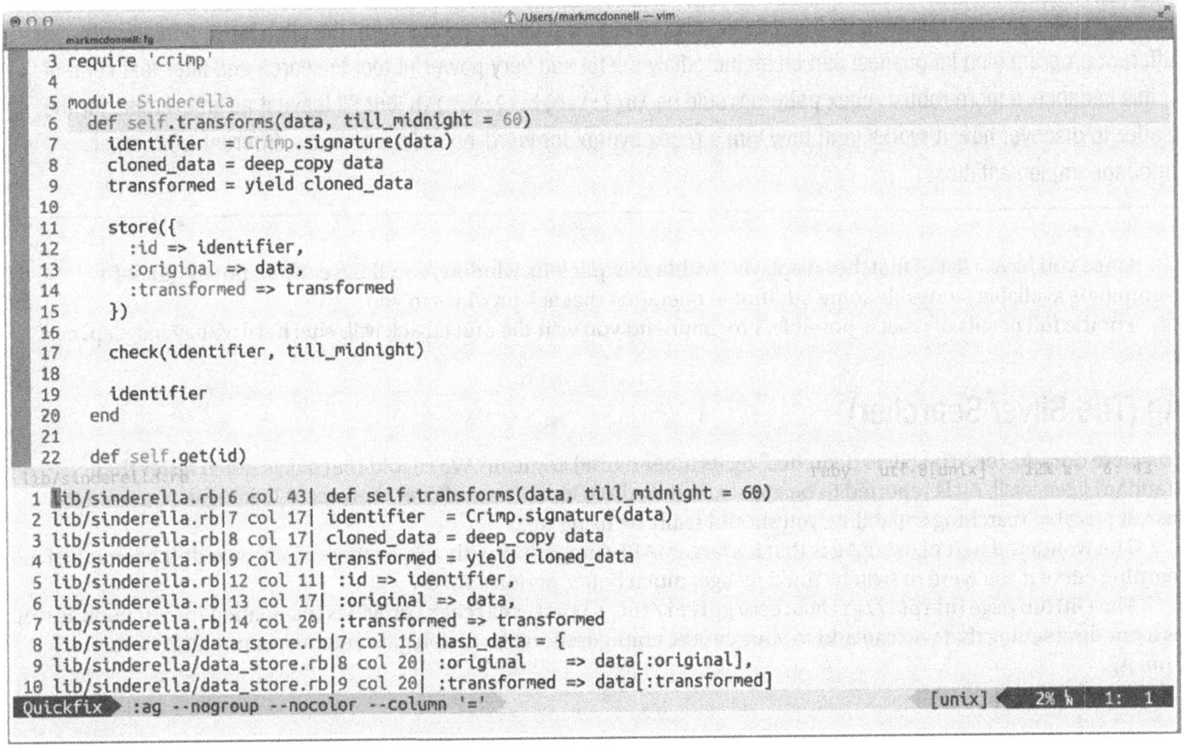

Figure 17-1. *Result of running :Ack '='*

As we can see from Figure 17-1, the pattern has found some matches, but they aren't quite what we expected. The results include files where an = is followed by a > character. I want to ignore => and find only matches that are an = character. So how can we achieve this?

■ **Note** You'll remember that I had no buffers open at the time of running the ack command, but in Figure 17-1, you can clearly see a buffer with some content inside. This is the first result in the list that Vim has automatically opened for us. To prevent this, you can use the :Ack! variation of the command.

This particular problem is where we move from a simple pattern to a complex pattern and have to utilize regular expressions (regexes) to find the matches we're interested in. Now, we won't be covering regexes, as I'm afraid they are way outside the scope of this book, but, luckily for us, the pattern we need can be explained relatively easily. If you want to learn how to write regexes, I can highly recommend www.regular-expressions.info.

With regular expressions, there are many ways to find a match for what you're looking for. As an example, it is possible to write a very simple pattern that doesn't cater to all possible scenarios, or you can write a complex pattern for a simple match that is very defensive and adaptable. The pattern you write will depend on your knowledge of regexes.

Following is one form of regex pattern that is very simple and solves the problem, although it's not very flexible and won't find matches that we would expect it to match (see the following note for more details):

```
:Ack \s=\s
```

■ **Note** The pattern will happily match x = y but not multiple spaces, such as x = y or even x=y, so this is where having an intimate understanding of the regex syntax (and how it differs across Vi/m, the shell environment, and different programming languages) can be an incredibly useful and very powerful tool to search and filter text content. In this instance, a more robust regex pattern would be \b(?:\s*)?=(?:\s*)\b, but I'll leave it as an exercise for the reader to discover how it works (and how Vim's regex syntax for word-boundaries \b are different from other language implementations).

Once you have a list of matches displayed within the quick-fix window, you'll have the standard quick-fix commands available alongside some additional operators that ack provides to you.

For the full details of what is possible, I recommend you visit the official ack web site: http://beyondgrep.com.

Ag (The Silver Searcher)

So where does Ag (or "The Silver Searcher," by its other name) come in? We're told that ack is much faster than standard grep, well, Ag is reported to be approximately three to five times faster than ack! Meaning, if you want the fastest possible searching capability, you should really be using Ag.

The wonderful part of using Ag is that it's largely API-compatible with ack, so there really wouldn't be much of a learning curve if you were to switch. You'd just get much better performance!

The GitHub page (https://github.com/ggreer/the_silver_searcher) provides installation instructions as well as a one-line setting that you can add to your .vimrc configuration file, to delegate your ack command (from Vim) onto Ag.

Commentary

The commentary.vim plug-in (https://github.com/tpope/vim-commentary) manages to be both incredibly useful *and* simple. Its prime focus is to let you comment and uncomment content (that's it). So, as you can imagine, this breakdown is going to be rather short.

If you were short on time, I would say all you have to know is the following command: \\\, which acts as a toggle, so it both comments and uncomments a line or VISUAL selection. There are some other commands available, but I don't use them, as \\\ is sufficient for nearly all my commenting needs. But for reference, take a look at the other commands listed in Table 17-2.

Table 17-2. *List of Alternative Commands for commentary.vim Plug-in*

Command	Explanation
gcc	Comments out a line (takes a count)
gc	(VISUAL mode) Comments out a selection
gc	(NORMAL mode) Comments out a motion (e.g., text object)
gcu	Uncomments an adjacent set of commented lines

CtrlP

CtrlP (http://kien.github.io/ctrlp.vim/) is an extremely useful and powerful fuzzy searching plug-in. In other words, it lets you type part of a file name and returns a dynamic list of results as you type (also known as "fuzzy matching"). Once you have a list of results, you can open one or more of the listed files. This is much easier than having to manually navigate a file directory tree (especially when dealing with an unfamiliar project or code base). There are also many additional options and features that make this an absolutely essential tool to have.

Basic Usage

To initialize CtrlP, you will need to execute the following command :CtrlP.

> ■ **Note**   There is a shortcut key mapping provided, which, as you may have guessed, is <C-p>, but also, in my own configuration files, I've mapped the :CtrlP command to <Leader>t, as I find that an easier key to access.

It may take a moment for you to see anything the first time you run :CtrlP. This is because the plug-in is indexing (and caching) all files recursively downstream from the current directory.

When it's done (which won't take long, even on the first run), you'll see a list of files appear (Figure 17-2). As you type, the list gets filtered further and further. Once you see the file you're after in the list, you can use the arrow keys to move the cursor to the relevant file, then press the <CR> key to have the file you want opened within Vim.

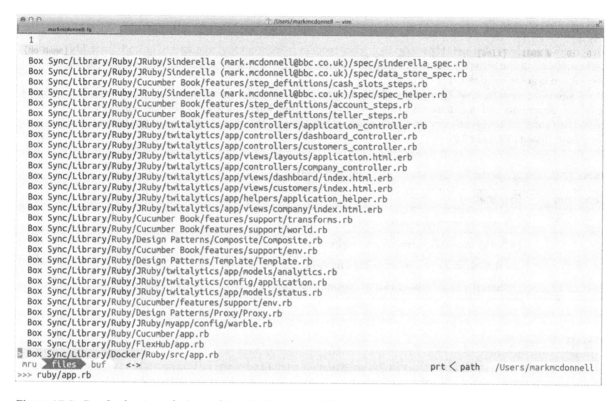

Figure 17-2. *Result of typing ruby/app.rb into CtrlP command-line interface*

Opening Multiple Files

Although CtrlP is very efficient at returning results quickly as you type, it can be quite useful to open multiple files at the same time (whether it be in the current window or a horizontal/vertical split). I use this feature when I'm searching for a group of files that have the same containing folder or namespace.

To use this feature, first start to filter the results and then, when ready, use your arrow keys to navigate the results list and press <C-z> on each file you want to open. (You'll notice that a plus sign appears next to the selected files; see Figure 17-3.) From here, you'll have to run one of the following commands (to determine how the selected files should be opened):

- <C-o>: Opens files in vertical split windows

- <C-x>: Opens files in horizontal split windows

```
  1
+>  Box Sync/Library/Ruby/JRuby/Sinderella (mark.mcdonnell@bbc.co.uk)/spec/sinderella_spec.rb
+>  Box Sync/Library/Ruby/JRuby/Sinderella (mark.mcdonnell@bbc.co.uk)/spec/data_store_spec.rb
    Box Sync/Library/Ruby/Cucumber Book/features/step_definitions/cash_slots_steps.rb
    Box Sync/Library/Ruby/JRuby/Sinderella (mark.mcdonnell@bbc.co.uk)/spec/spec_helper.rb
    Box Sync/Library/Ruby/Cucumber Book/features/step_definitions/account_steps.rb
    Box Sync/Library/Ruby/Cucumber Book/features/step_definitions/teller_steps.rb
    Box Sync/Library/Ruby/JRuby/twitalytics/app/controllers/application_controller.rb
    Box Sync/Library/Ruby/JRuby/twitalytics/app/controllers/dashboard_controller.rb
    Box Sync/Library/Ruby/JRuby/twitalytics/app/controllers/customers_controller.rb
    Box Sync/Library/Ruby/JRuby/twitalytics/app/views/layouts/application.html.erb
    Box Sync/Library/Ruby/JRuby/twitalytics/app/controllers/company_controller.rb
    Box Sync/Library/Ruby/JRuby/twitalytics/app/views/dashboard/index.html.erb
    Box Sync/Library/Ruby/JRuby/twitalytics/app/views/customers/index.html.erb
    Box Sync/Library/Ruby/JRuby/twitalytics/app/helpers/application_helper.rb
    Box Sync/Library/Ruby/JRuby/twitalytics/app/views/company/index.html.erb
    Box Sync/Library/Ruby/Cucumber Book/features/support/transforms.rb
    Box Sync/Library/Ruby/Cucumber Book/features/support/world.rb
+>  Box Sync/Library/Ruby/Design Patterns/Composite/Composite.rb
    Box Sync/Library/Ruby/Cucumber Book/features/support/env.rb
    Box Sync/Library/Ruby/Design Patterns/Template/Template.rb
    Box Sync/Library/Ruby/JRuby/twitalytics/app/models/analytics.rb
    Box Sync/Library/Ruby/JRuby/twitalytics/config/application.rb
    Box Sync/Library/Ruby/JRuby/twitalytics/app/models/status.rb
    Box Sync/Library/Ruby/Cucumber/features/support/env.rb
+>  Box Sync/Library/Ruby/Design Patterns/Proxy/Proxy.rb
    Box Sync/Library/Ruby/JRuby/myapp/config/warble.rb
    Box Sync/Library/Ruby/Cucumber/app.rb
+>  Box Sync/Library/Ruby/FlexHub/app.rb
+>  Box Sync/Library/Docker/Ruby/src/app.rb
  mru   files   buf    <6>                              prt < path   /Users/markmcdonnell
>>> ruby/app.rb
```

Figure 17-3. Selecting multiple files to open (notice the +> indicator)

Refreshing the List of Files

If you have added new files since the last time you used CtrlP, you may find that those new files aren't appearing within your list of files the next time you run a CtrlP search. This is simply because CtrlP caches the initial list of files within your project (to help improve performance).

The solution to this problem is simply to refresh the cache CtrlP holds by pressing the <F5> key, allowing the plug-in to re-index your project.

Pasting from Clipboard

There is one important aspect of CtrlP that you should be aware of, and it exposes a fundamental issue that could affect you in many different ways. I'll demonstrate this by way of a real-world example that affected me personally.

It started with the vim-bookmarks plug-in (the issue I encountered isn't caused by that plug-in, as such, but it did help to highlight the problem area). The issue I had was that Vim would crash when I tried to carry out a fuzzy search for a specific file. I was debugging some code, and the path to the source file was printed on my screen; so I copied it to my clipboard with the expectation that I'd initialize CtrlP, paste in the file path, and then press <CR> to open the file. This is where Vim would throw up lots of errors, and ultimately, I'd have to restart Vim.

This would only happen when pasting (C-v) the file's path into CtrlP. This bug didn't occur when typing the path to the file *manually*, as you typically do with CtrlP.

What transpired was, when pasting from the clipboard directly into CtrlP's command prompt, Vim would emulate the paste action of a user actually typing the pasted content manually . . . *but in NORMAL mode!*

Maybe you can see where things are going to go wrong, but maybe you can't; so let me continue and clarify. The vim-bookmarks plug-in has a custom key binding for the characters ma, meaning that when in NORMAL mode, if you execute the command ma, this will trigger a vim-bookmarks action to occur.

Now look at the file path I was pasting into CtrlP from my clipboard.

```
path/to/js/folder/council_map.js
```

So, each character from the file path was being executed in NORMAL mode, meaning that when searching for the file ni_council_map.js, the ma characters (from the word map in the file name) would cause vim-bookmarks to force open a Vim quick-fix window. Once the quick-fix window was open, CtrlP would continue to enter the remainder of the file name, which was p.js (notice that p.js is now being executed as a command inside the quick-fix window), thus causing an E21: Cannot make changes, 'modifiable' is off error to be displayed, as Vim was attempting to paste—the p from p.js—inside the quick-fix window. Following that, the dot character . was entered (i.e., repeated the last action), which caused the error to occur yet again.

Basically, a cluster of issues arose, which made it difficult to narrow where the bug was originating. But when the problem is broken down into its component parts, we can see exactly what and why this happens, and we can look to resolve the issue.

The author of vim-bookmarks helped point me in the right direction by suggesting I use CtrlP's paste feature (<C-\>), which displays a menu asking you where you want to paste from.

```
Insert: c[w]ord/c[f]ile/[s]earch/[v]isual/[c]lipboard/[r]egister?
```

In this case, I would want to choose c (as that's the clipboard option). This would then take the file path from my clipboard in a safe manner and return a search result list based on that file.

The reason I mention this issue is because (a) it's really confusing when you stumble across it for the first time, and (b) it has changed the way I use CtrlP. I now always use the <C-\> "paste from" feature, as I don't expect myself to be able to memorize every single key binding that all my plug-ins implement.

■ **Note** I could have remapped the ma command to \ma (like so: nmap <Leader>a <Plug>ShowAllBookmarks), but I didn't like that, as it only resolved that single mapping conflict. So, I opted for the workaround provided by the built-in CtrlP feature.

Modify Default Opening Behavior

Although we can use <C-o> or <C-x> to open multiple selected files in either vertical or horizontal split windows, it can be difficult to remember which command does what. (Does <C-o> open in a horizontal split or is it the other way around?) By modifying CtrlP's default behavior when we press <C-o>, we'll be presented with a list of options that include the following items:

- tab
- vertical
- horizontal
- hidden
- clear

Most of these options should be self-explanatory (the files are opened either in multiple tabs, vertical or horizontal splits, or as hidden buffers), with possibly the exception of the last option, clear. This simply means that if you press c (for clear), the selected list of files will become deselected.

To see what this looks like, please refer to Figure 17-4. So how do we enable this particular feature? We have to add the following setting to our .vimrc configuration file: let g:ctrlp_arg_map = 1.

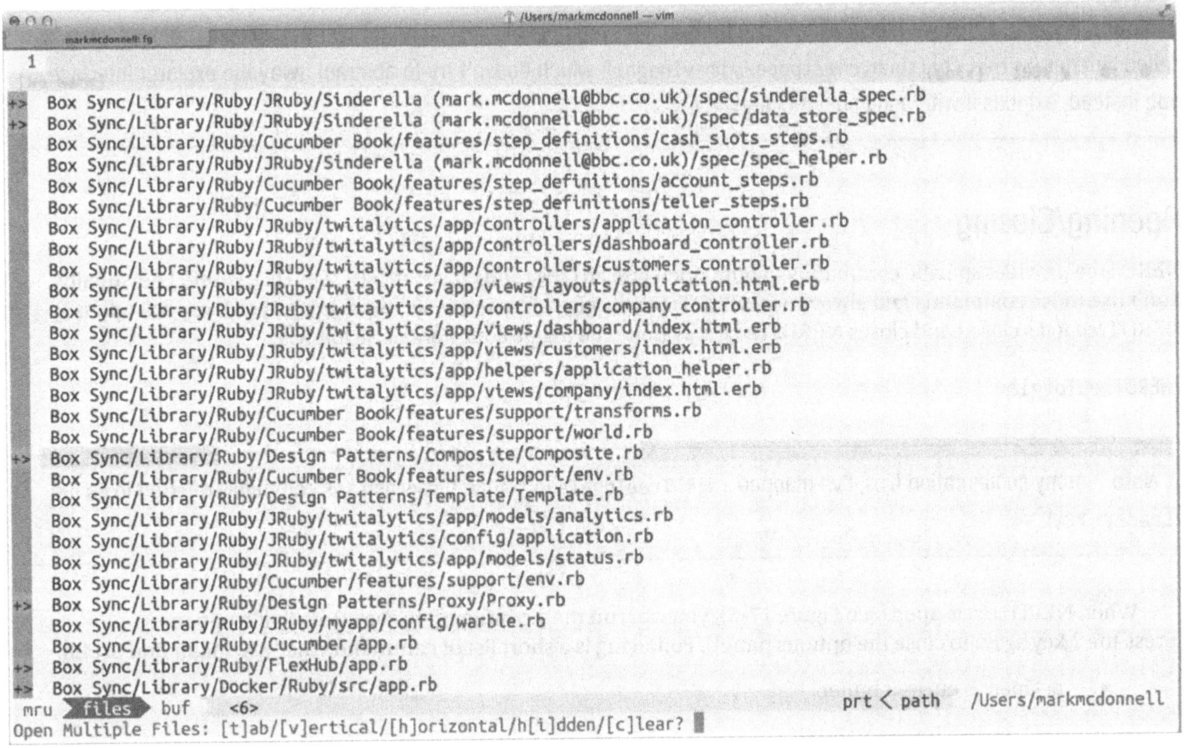

Figure 17-4. *Result of pressing <C-o> after modifying default behavior*

Creating Directories and Files

CtrlP has a less utilized feature, which allows users to dynamically create a file and directory structure (similar to the Unix mkdir command's –p flag). Start by typing a path that you know doesn't exist (add an optional file name to the end of the path) and execute <C-y>, which will ask you how you would like the resulting file to be displayed, as follows:

```
Create a New File: [t]ab/[v]ertical/[h]orizontal/[r]eplace?
```

NERDTree

NERDTree (https://github.com/scrooloose/nerdtree) is a file system explorer similar to something you would find in another text/code editor or operating system (such as the Finder application on the Macintosh OS or Windows Explorer for Windows-based operating systems).

Vim already provides a built-in file explorer called netrw. (I'll be covering this native feature in Chapter 22; but if you're in a hurry, see :h :Explore.) NERDTree is an evolution of netrw that adds some additional useful features (some of which I'll cover in this section), as well as simplifying certain features that also exist within netrw. (For example, creating bookmarks and adding/deleting/moving/renaming files is made much easier with NERDTree, compared to the native Vim file explorer.)

■ **Note** If you're already a heavy user of the built-in file system explorer, you might want to consider another plug-in called Vinegar (https://github.com/tpope/vim-vinegar), which doesn't try to abstract away the explorer interface, but, instead, extends it with additional functionality.

Opening/Closing

NERDTree provides specific commands to both open (:NERDTree) and close (:NERDTreeClose) itself. I personally don't use those commands and always use NERDTree's toggle command instead, which, as you'd expect, opens NERDTree if it's closed and closes NERDTree if it's open. The toggle command is as follows:

:NERDTreeToggle

■ **Note** In my configuration files, I've mapped :NERDTreeToggle to \' (the backslash \ is commonly referred to as the <Leader> key).

When NERDTree is open (see Figure 17-5), you can run the ? command to see all available options (press the ? key again to close the options panel). Following is a short list of commands that you might find useful:

- o: Open in current buffer.
- i: Open in a horizontal split.
- s: Open in a vertical split.
- t: Open in a new tab.
- I: Show hidden files (i.e., dot files).
- C: Change the tree root to the selected directory.

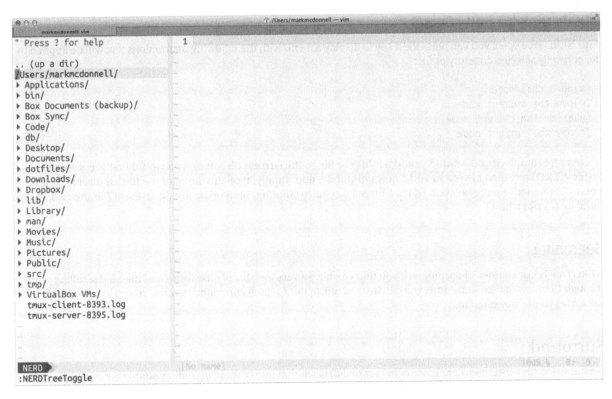

Figure 17-5. *NERDTree, opened from my $HOME directory*

That last option is useful when you have a very large project that you've already started Vim from (meaning the root of that project is your current working directory in Vim), yet you only have to access files located inside a lower-level subdirectory. If you navigate to that directory and press C the next time you open NERDTree, its root directory will be that selected directory, instead of the actual root of the project.

There are many other options available, some of which I'll be covering in the following subsections, but please do refer back to the ? help panel to see the full list of options and features (especially if you're upgrading to a newer version of NERDTree).

Bookmarks

Bookmarks work exactly as you would expect them to. You find a directory that is nested in a deep hierarchy and is otherwise difficult to locate normally, and you tag it with a bookmark, so it's easier to access in future. Your bookmarks are then stored in a .NERDTreeBookmarks file in your $HOME directory, so that they are remembered the next time Vim starts.

To add a bookmark, first move the cursor over the directory you're interested in and then run the following command (remember to change the name accordingly for your new bookmark):

```
:Bookmark {my_bookmark_name}
```

Next time you open NERDTree, you can press the B key to show a list of available bookmarks. Use your arrow keys to navigate to the bookmark you want and then press <CR> to have NERDTree open up the relevant directory.

Modifying Files and Folders

With NERDTree open, you can press the m key to display a menu with the following instructions that will be applied to the currently selected directory or file:

```
> (a)dd a childnode
  (m)ove the current node
  (d)elete the current node
  (c)opy the current node
```

As an example, if you wanted to add a folder or file to the current directory, you would first press m while inside NERDTree, then press a to add a new childnode, and, finally, type the name of the file (or directory) and press <CR> to activate the creation (if it's a directory you're creating, remember to add an extra / at the end, to indicate it's not a file).

Searching

NERDTree is just another Vim window. If you find you have a very long list of directories and files and scrolling through them could take some time, you can instead utilize the / search command to move your cursor to a match for the folder you're interested in.

Surround

Surround (https://github.com/tpope/vim-surround) is another one of those incredibly simple but useful plug-ins. Its primary focus is to let you add or delete surrounding punctuation to either a text object or a selection. If I had to pick one of my most tedious editing tasks (whether it be prose or code), it would have to be wrapping something in quotes or parentheses!

The list of commands the plug-in provides is relatively small, the most of important of which are included in the following list:

- cs: Change surrounding

- ds: Delete surrounding

- ys: Add punctuation

- S: Add punctuation around manual VISUAL selection

Change Surrounding . . .

If you have punctuation around a specific piece of content and you want to swap it to something else, use the cs command. Consider the following content as a sample document we would like to modify:

```
"This is my content wrapped in double quotes"
```

Running the command cs"' will replace the surrounding " with '.

Delete Surrounding...

If you have punctuation around a specific piece of content and you want to swap it for something else, use the ds command. Consider the following content as a sample document we would like to modify:

```
"This is my content wrapped in double quotes"
```

Running the command ds" will remove the surrounding ".

Add (Text Object) Surrounding...

The surround plug-in allows you to add punctuation by way of a Vim text object. Imagine that we have the following content:

```
This is my first sentence. This is my second sentence.
```

If I wanted the first sentence to be wrapped in double quotes, I would run the following command (while my cursor was placed somewhere inside the first sentence): ysis".

Add (Manually) Surrounding...

The surround plug-in allows you to add punctuation by manually selecting a piece of content (this allows us to make very controlled modifications). Imagine that we have the following content:

```
This is my first sentence.
This is my second sentence.
```

If I wanted the first word from both sentences (This) to be wrapped in double quotes, I would run the following command (in this instance, I would move my cursor to the start of the first line and use VISUAL-BLOCK mode to select both words): S".

Right-Side or Left-Side Punctuation?

You might not realize this, but there is a difference between selecting a left curly bracket and a right curly bracket (and the same is true for parentheses and square brackets). The difference is in whether the plug-in will wrap your content directly or if the punctuation will have a space between the content and the punctuation. Following is an example of the difference (imagine that your cursor is at the start of the line):

```
this is my sentence
```

If we ran the following command: ysiw], the result of that command would be

```
[this] is my sentence
```

If, on the other hand, I had used the command ysiw[, the result of that command would be

```
[ this ] is my sentence
```

EndWise

EndWise (https://github.com/tpope/vim-endwise) is a simple plug-in for Ruby developers and is completely automated (there are no commands required to be run by you). What the plug-in will do is automatically add a corresponding end keyword to the specific Ruby construct being created at the time.

For example, if you were to start writing, into a Ruby-formatted file in Vim, the following content:

```
if some_value
```

then if you pressed <CR>, you would see that Vim inserts a closing end keyword automatically for you, so that the resulting content looks like

```
if some_value
end
```

It'll do this for all Ruby constructs that require the end keyword.

Tabular

The Tabular plug-in (https://github.com/godlygeek/tabular) plug-in is something I use fairly regularly to clean up the format of my code. But it can be used to format any piece of content that has a particular pattern to it. As an example, this plug-in makes it incredibly easier to convert the following code:

```
var someThing = "foo";
var someOtherThing = "bar";
var blah = "baz";
```

into

```
var someThing       = "foo";
var someOtherThing  = "bar";
var blah            = "baz";
```

The plug-in provides a Tabularize command, which takes a regular expression to help it find a match to what you want to have aligned correctly. In the preceding example, to get the result we want, we'd execute the following command:

```
:Tabularize /=
```

By default, the command runs against the entire file, but it can also be executed against a range or a VISUAL selection. I would also highly recommend reading through the documentation provided with the Tabular plug-in, as it's very informative and has some good examples you could learn from. To access the plug-in documentation, run :h tabular.

Syntastic

The Syntastic (https://github.com/scrooloose/syntastic) plug-in is a code syntax-checking plug-in (also known as a "sanity check," for those of us deep in the trenches of code warfare). It highlights errors in your code and loads a list of the errors within a location list window for you to review. This is an incredibly useful tool, because it can help avoid broken code and committing code to a repository, only to then have to go back and add additional commits to fix any formatting issues that you missed.

Supported Languages

Syntastic has support for many different language syntax checkers. To see if the file you are editing has a syntax checker the plug-in can access and use to validate your code, you'll have to run the following command while the file of the type you're checking is open within Vim (see Figure 17-6):

```
:SyntasticInfo
```

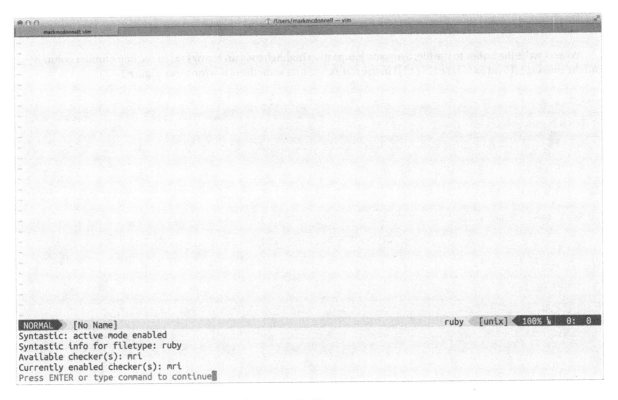

Figure 17-6. *Result of running* `:SyntasticInfo` *on a Ruby file*

■ **Note**   You can cheat a little bit here and use `setf {language}` to indicate that the current buffer is of the file type you're checking against. For example, I opened Vim, and in the empty buffer, I ran the command `:setf ruby` and then ran `:SyntasticInfo`.

Example

Now imagine that I create a file with the following content (this file is broken, because I have two blocks that both use a do keyword, and in both instances, that keyword isn't allowed there):

```
class Blah do
  def something do
    #
  end
end
```

When I write the buffer to the file, Syntastic jumps in to highlight, via an arrow (>>) in the line number column and the message ([Syntax: line:2 (1)]) in the status bar, that something is wrong (see Figure 17-7).

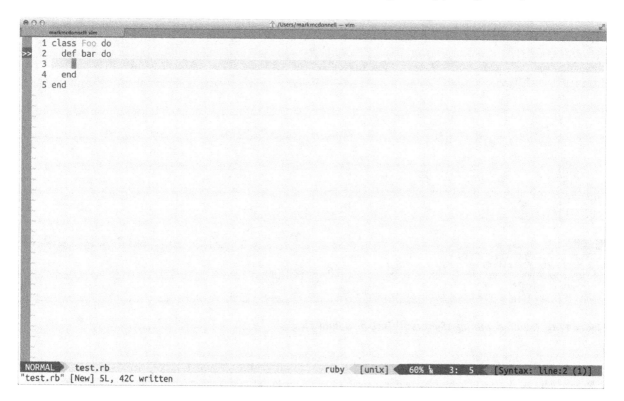

Figure 17-7. *Syntastic indicating an error in both status and line number area*

If I were to run the command :Errors, this would open Vim's location list window (:lopen), and we would see a brief description of the relevant error, giving me an opportunity to fix it (see Figure 17-8).

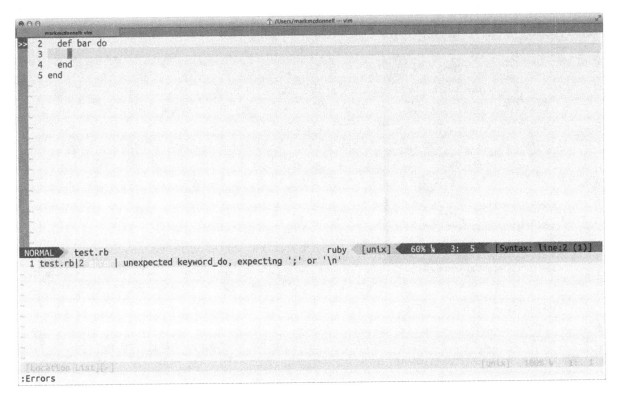

Figure 17-8. *List of errors reported by Syntastic and accessed via* `:Errors`

■ **Note** You have to run `:Errors` first, before opening the location list window, because it avoids conflicts with other plug-ins. I'm OK with this; but you can also add the following line to your `.vimrc` configuration file to have the location list updated automatically: `let g:syntastic_always_populate_loc_list = 1`.

SuperTab

The SuperTab plug-in (`https://github.com/ervandew/supertab`) is great for helping you speed up development. Anytime you want to auto-complete a piece of code, you can just press the `<Tab>` key, and the plug-in will offer you a drop-down list of options to choose from (see Figure 17-9).

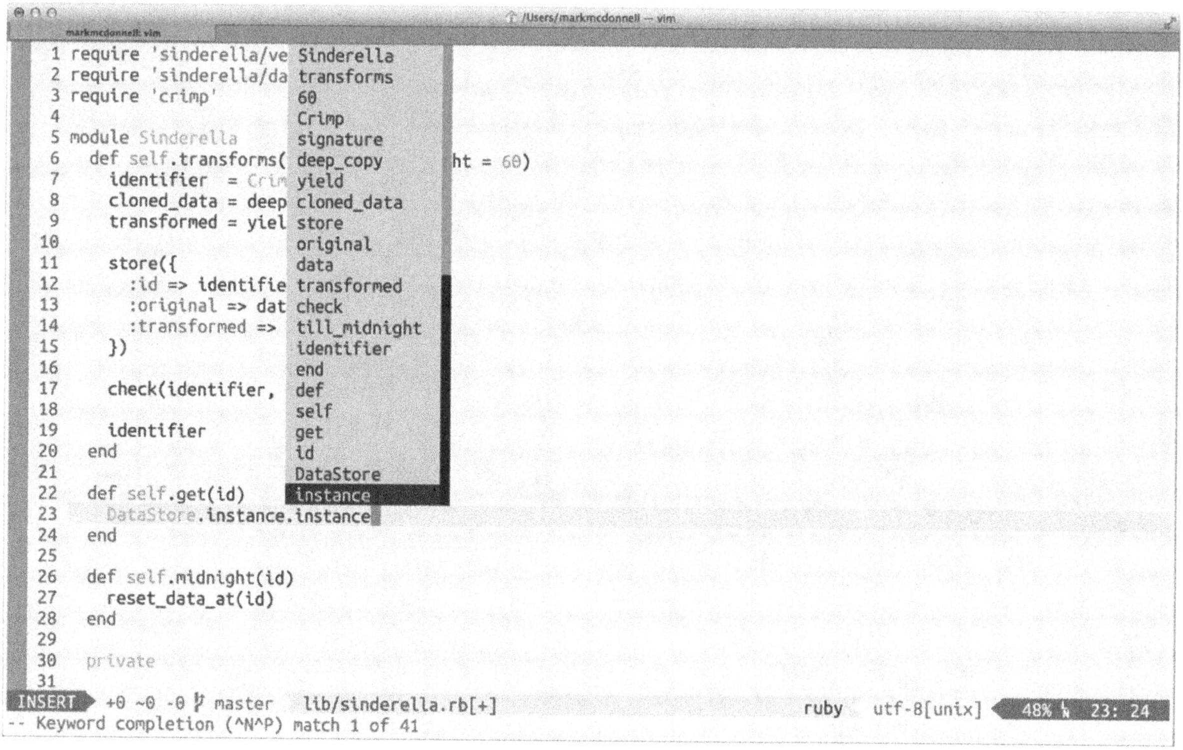

Figure 17-9. *Example of SuperTab's menu options*

Each time you press the <Tab> key, the cursor will move down through the available options until it reaches the end, then it goes back to not selecting any listed option.

Alternatively, you can move up and down the list, using your arrow keys. Either way, you'll have to pick the item you want by pressing the <CR> key (or by pressing the <Esc> key while an option is highlighted).

Gist

The Gist plug-in (https://github.com/vim-scripts/Gist.vim) is a useful tool for letting you quickly knock out a public or private gist on GitHub straight from your current file. It's also quite powerful, in the sense that you can also view all your public, private, and starred gists directly from Vim, and from there, you are able to retrieve, edit, and fork them.

Installation of this plug-in requires the WebAPI plug-in (https://github.com/mattn/webapi-vim), so make sure you have that installed first. Following are some additional settings that you will need to include inside your ~/.vimrc configuration file:

```
let g:github_user = $GITHUB_USER
let g:github_token = $GITHUB_TOKEN
let g:gist_detect_filetype = 1
let g:gist_open_browser_after_post = 1
```

Looking at the preceding configuration settings, you'll notice that I'm passing in two environment variables ($GITHUB_USER and $GITHUB_TOKEN). These two variables hold my username and security token (so the plug-in can gain access to my Gist account).

The gist_detect_filetype option lets the plug-in try to figure out what type of file is being edited (meaning, when pushed up to GitHub's gist system, the file will have the correct syntax highlighting used), whereas the other option, gist_open_browser_after_post, will cause the browser to automatically open the gist on GitHub. Without this option, I would have had to double-click or copy/paste the URL into my browser. But as I nearly always want to view the gist, I decided to have this be the default behavior.

There are many options available, but I've personally found the following list to be the most useful (see :h Gist for more details):

- :Gist: Creates a public gist (this is the default behavior)

- :Gist -p: Creates a private gist

- :Gist -m: Creates a gist out of all open buffers

- :Gist -l: Lists all your public gists (If you press <CR> on any listed gists, that gist will be retrieved and loaded in a split window.)

■ **Note** After pulling down a gist and editing it, write the buffer (:w) to trigger an update to the gist on GitHub.

Fugative

Fugative (https://github.com/tpope/vim-fugitive) is a powerful Git plug-in aimed at removing the need for using the Git command-line tool, by providing corresponding commands within Vim itself.

Personally, I prefer to use the command line for handling my Git requirements (especially when dealing with more complex commands, such as interactive rebasing), so I find myself using only a select subset of the Fugative commands provided.

■ **Note** It's worth mentioning (if not already implied) that using this plug-in does require knowledge of the Git Version Control System. If you would like to learn more, please visit http://git-scm.com/.

The following commands are what I use the majority of the time when within Vim, but do refer back to the GitHub repository, to find links to screen casts and other documentation details:

- :Gstatus: git status

  - -: (within the split pane) toggle for git add

  - P: (within the split pane) git add --patch

- :Gcommit: git commit

- :Gread: git checkout -- filename

- :Gmove: git mv

- :Gblame: git blame

Dispatch

Dispatch (`https://github.com/tpope/vim-dispatch`) is a plug-in focused on wrapping around Vim's built-in `make` command. This plug-in is primarily designed to make working with `Makefiles` easier. But that isn't of much interest to me, as I don't use `Make` for my build scripts. (If you're interested, I use both Rake, provided by the Ruby programming language, and a JavaScript-based build tool called Grunt - `http://gruntjs.com/`). But what is interesting about this plug-in, however, is that it provides a `:Dispatch!` command, and that I find much more useful.

The `:Dispatch!` command creates a new headless process that will run the command you specified, while allowing you to continue working within Vim. This is better than Vim's built-in `:!` command (which also executes any command you specify), as that command, unfortunately, suspends Vim temporarily while the command is running.

Imagine that you have a long-running process (e.g., a test suite that takes a few minutes to complete). It can be frustrating having to sit and wait for it to complete, if you use the `:!` command to execute your test suite via the command line. The `:Dispatch!` command, on the other hand, allows us to run that process and continue working inside Vim.

If at any point we wish to see the current status of the process, we can open Vim's quick-fix window by running the `:Copen` command. Wait a few moments longer and re-execute the `:Copen` command, and you'll see that the content of the quick-fix window has been updated to reflect the latest `stdout`.

Others . . .

The following plug-ins aren't as well-known as the ones I've just covered, but this doesn't mean they aren't worth your time to investigate. Popularity isn't necessarily a sign of quality and/or usefulness.

BufOnly.vim

Through the course of a typical development day, you'll find you have lots of buffers open. This is an unfortunate side effect caused by the ease with which you can jump around a large project directory. We rarely stop to look around and clean up our environment.

At the end of the day, I usually find that I want to close all my buffers, with the exception of the one that I'll continue working on the next day. Other times, perhaps after lunch, I just might think it would then be a good time to clean up after myself and get my list of buffers down to only the essential ones I need for the remaining tasks I have to do, because jumping around and ignoring lots of unnecessary buffers, especially those I know I definitely won't need, is just a waste of mental effort.

The BufOnly plug-in (`https://github.com/vim-scripts/BufOnly.vim`) is useful for solving this specific problem. Once installed, you'll have one of the two following commands available:

- `:BufOnly`: Unload all buffers except the current one.

- `:BufOnly {n}`: Unload all buffers except the specified one (where `{n}` is the number of the buffer you want to keep).

scratch.vim

The scratch.vim (`https://github.com/duff/vim-scratch`) plug-in makes it very easy to create a new disposable scratch buffer. We looked at scratch buffers way back in Chapter 3 (I recommend you go back there, if you're unsure of what a scratch buffer is).

To convert a buffer into a scratch buffer requires a few different settings to be applied. But instead of us having to manually manipulate the buffer so that it replicates a scratch buffer, with this plug-in, we can run one of the following commands to ease this tedious requirement:

- `:Scratch`: Create a new scratch buffer.

- `:Sscratch`: Open the scratch buffer in a new split window.

The buffers created are just an automated version of the process you would normally take to manually create a scratch buffer, and they work in exactly the same way (i.e., they are completely disposable).

Camel Case Motion

Being a programmer introduces issues with using the standard motion operators, such as w, e, and b. An example of this is using motions to try to move across CamelCase words. Imagine that we had the following content (and the cursor was at the beginning of the first line):

```
function testThisObjectDoesSomething() {
    // code
}
```

If I wanted to change the Object to Thing, I would have a hard time doing this using the standard e motion, because pressing e twice would move the cursor to the end of the function identifier (e.g., the cursor would be placed on the last parenthesis on the first line). But I'm able to distinguish more clearly that testThisObjectDoesSomething is a collection of words, rather than just a single word (like the standard motions do).

This is where the Camel Case Motion plug-in (https://github.com/vim-scripts/camelcasemotion) comes in handy. By installing the plug-in and then adding the following configuration to your .vimrc file, you'll be able to avoid this type of programmer problem, by remapping the standard motion operators with a set of enhanced variations provided by the plug-in:

```
map <silent> w <Plug>CamelCaseMotion_w
map <silent> b <Plug>CamelCaseMotion_b
map <silent> e <Plug>CamelCaseMotion_e
sunmap w
sunmap b
sunmap e
```

In the preceding configuration, we copy the w, b, and e motions to the capitalized versions W, B, and E. Next, we overwrite the original motions with our new, enhanced versions.

Now, if we were to run the e motion, we would find that the cursor stops at the end of each word (even those that are part of a larger CamelCased word). In the preceding sample content, we would find that the following stop points are hit:

```
- function
- function test
- function testThis
- function testThisObject
- function testThisObjectDoes
- function testThisObjectDoesSomething
- function testThisObjectDoesSomething()
- function testThisObjectDoesSomething() {
```

vim-choosewin

If you're a heavy user of split windows in Vim, you'll find the ChooseWin plug-in (https://github.com/t9md/vim-choosewin) indispensable. It provides a similar feature to tmux's display-panes command. For those of you who are unfamiliar with tmux (and, in particular, that feature), the command will display over each window a number for you to press in order for the relevant number key to switch focus to the corresponding window.

Vim doesn't mimic tmux's behavior exactly. First, instead of displaying a number in the middle of the screen, Vim will display a letter from the alphabet at the bottom of each Vim window. Second, the letters stay visible until you choose a window to move focus onto. I find this to be much more user-friendly than tmux's implementation, which forces you to pick a window within a very short time frame.

Once the plug-in is installed, you will be able to trigger its functionality, by running the :ChooseWin command. When you press the relevant letter, the cursor will switch focus to that window (see Figure 17-10). If you want to cancel this action, press <Esc>.

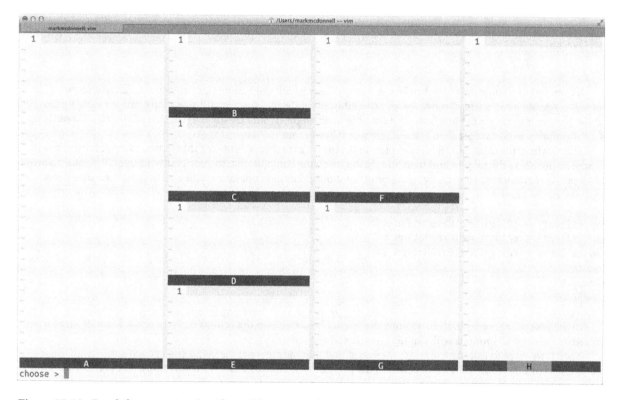

Figure 17-10. *Result from running the :ChooseWin command*

■ **Note**   I've alias'ed the :ChooseWin command to <Leader>ws (\ws), which makes it much quicker and easier to access this feature.

---

vim-bookmarks

The vim-bookmarks plug-in (https://github.com/MattesGroeger/vim-bookmarks) makes it even easier to deal with Vim's marks feature (I covered marks in Chapter 15). Once installed, you will see a flag icon appear beside any marks that have been added to a file (see Figure 17-11).

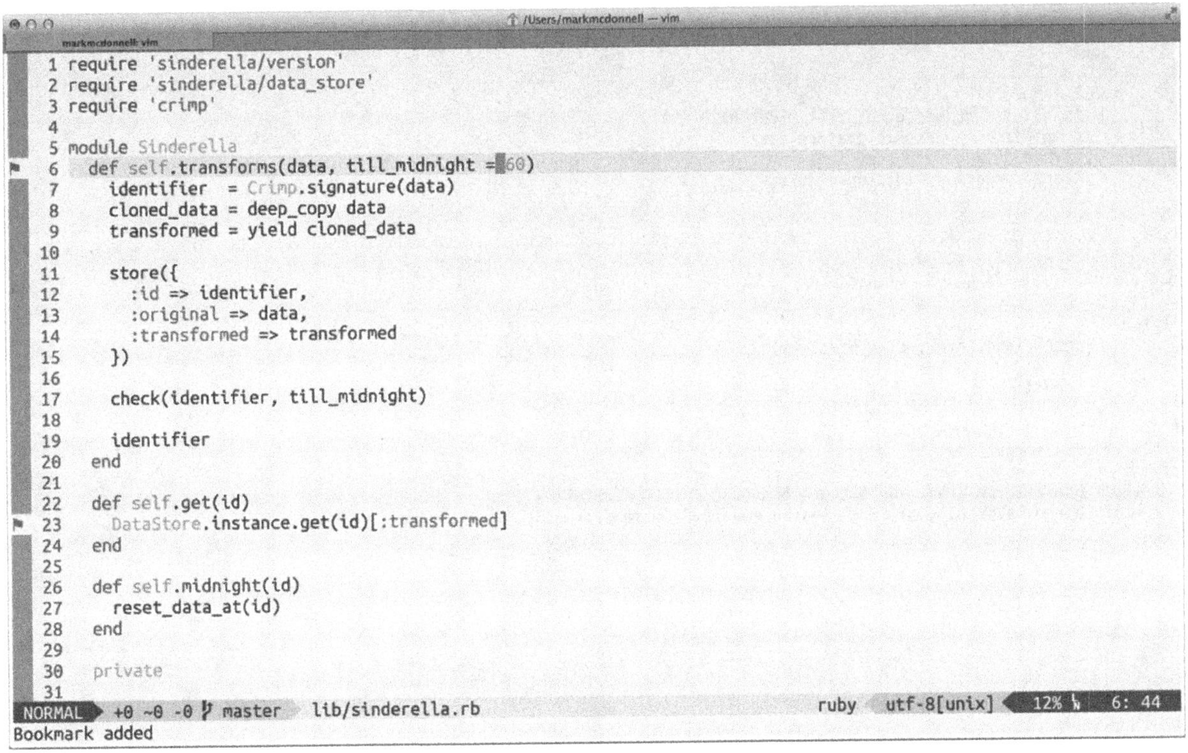

```
  1 require 'sinderella/version'
  2 require 'sinderella/data_store'
  3 require 'crimp'
  4
  5 module Sinderella
  6   def self.transforms(data, till_midnight = 60)
  7     identifier  = Crimp.signature(data)
  8     cloned_data = deep_copy data
  9     transformed = yield cloned_data
 10
 11     store({
 12       :id => identifier,
 13       :original => data,
 14       :transformed => transformed
 15     })
 16
 17     check(identifier, till_midnight)
 18
 19     identifier
 20   end
 21
 22   def self.get(id)
 23     DataStore.instance.get(id)[:transformed]
 24   end
 25
 26   def self.midnight(id)
 27     reset_data_at(id)
 28   end
 29
 30   private
 31
NORMAL  +0 ~0 -0 ⎇ master   lib/sinderella.rb                      ruby  utf-8[unix]   12%    6: 44
Bookmark added
```

Figure 17-11. *Blue flags are indicators of Vim marks provided by the plug-in*

To toggle a mark for a specific line, run the following command: mm. This will add a mark, if one doesn't exist, or remove the mark, if it does.

■ **Note** Any marks added via this plug-in are automatically set to be global marks.

To see all marks recorded by the plug-in (these will be displayed inside a quick-fix window; see Figure 17-12), run the ma command.

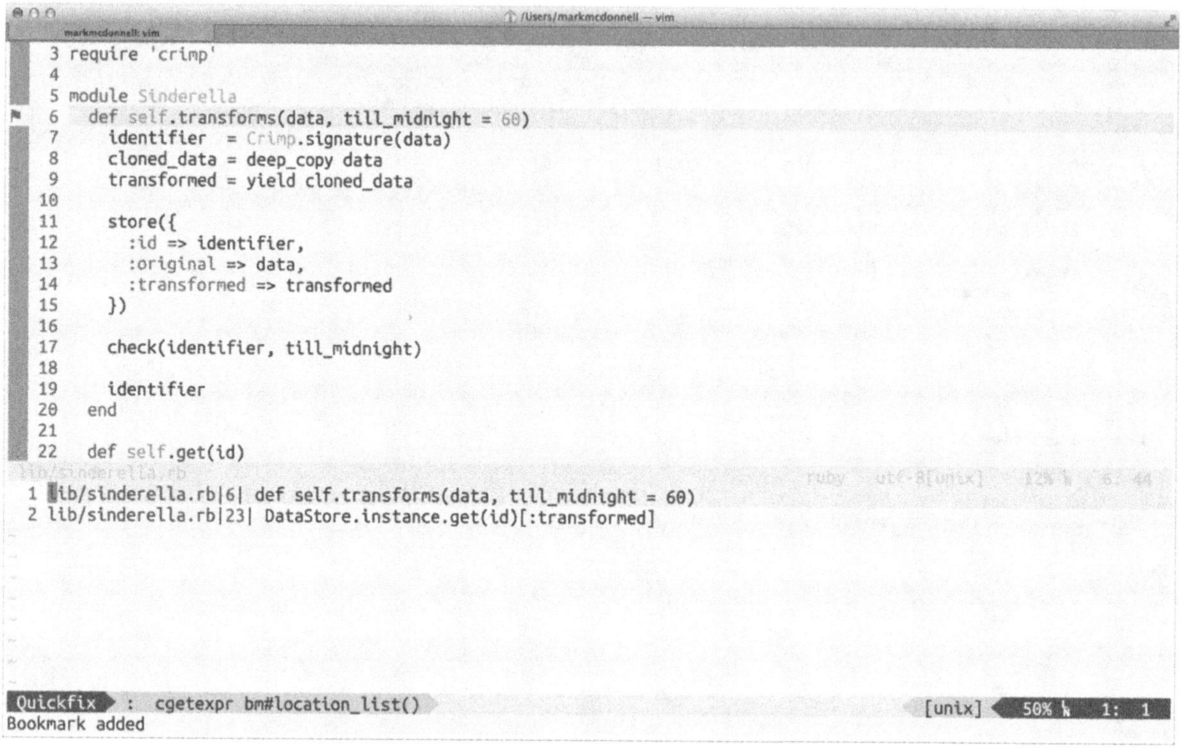

Figure 17-12. *Result of executing the ma command to display all available marks*

To remove all the marks for the current buffer, then run the mc command, and to remove ALL marks, run the mx command.

The vim-bookmarks plug-in has many more options and configuration settings, so it's worth reviewing the GitHub repository for the full details.

targets.vim

The targets.vim plug-in (https://github.com/wellle/targets.vim) extends Vim's built-in text objects construct and makes them even more powerful, by allowing you to have much more granular control (such as being able to expand the range of a text object, using motions). To begin with, let's imagine that we have the following content, and our cursor is currently placed within the first set of parentheses (i.e., (example)):

```
This is (example) text (with many parentheses).
```

If you wanted to edit the content inside the first set of parentheses, the standard Vim text object command ci(works fine (and continues to work fine, as this plug-in *extends* the text objects but doesn't modify any existing commands).

But if we wanted to change the content within the *following* parentheses, we would run into a problem without help from the plug-in. First we'd have to move our cursor inside of the next set of parentheses, and *then* we could execute the ci(command.

That can be a bit tedious, and so with the targets.vim plug-in installed, we would instead run the cin(command, which breaks down to "(c)hange (i)nside (n)ext set of parentheses."

This plug-in also allows us to expand our text object's reach. Imagine that you have the following content (and your cursor is currently placed inside of the second/inner set of brackets):

```
This is a line [with a few [brackets]]
```

If you wanted to change the content of the inner brackets, you could run the standard Vim text object command ci[, and it would work exactly as expected. But if you wanted to edit the entire content of the outer brackets, you would first have to move your cursor to somewhere outside the inner brackets (but still within the outer brackets). Running the preceding command would then work as you want it to. But that's a lot of extra work. It would be nice if I could indicate N levels to expand the change to, and this is where the plug-in motion enhancement comes into play.

What we can do instead is utilize a motion that indicates the number of objects outward that we want the command to affect. In this instance, we would be able to keep the cursor within the inner brackets and run the following extended text object command: c2i[.

This plug-in offers many useful additions, so please refer to the GitHub repository for the complete details.

wildfire.vim

The wildfire.vim plug-in (https://github.com/gcmt/wildfire.vim) works much like a real wildfire; it expands and engulfs things around it! Imagine that you have the following content (and your cursor is currently placed inside the second/inner set of brackets), as follows:

```
This is a line [with a few [brackets]]
```

If you press <CR>, we'll instantly select the content of the next text object the plug-in can find. (In this case, we select the content of the second/inner brackets.).

If we press <CR> again, the selection expands to the next text object, which, in our example, would be the content of the outer brackets.

If we press <CR> one last time, the selection moves to the next text object, which is the entire line.

This is a simple plug-in that has a similar focus to the targets.vim plug-in we looked at in the previous section, but it is still very useful when used in the right circumstances.

ZoomWin

The ZoomWin plug-in (https://github.com/vim-scripts/ZoomWin) provides a key binding that forces your currently focused window to be "zoomed," meaning the window will become full-screen, and any other split windows will be hidden. The reason this feature is useful is because it provides us with more screen space to see what we're working on when we have lots of split windows open.

I don't use this feature very often, because Vim already provides functionality that lets you reduce and increase the size of windows (e.g., <C-w>_, <C-w>|, <C-w>=), and I end up using that functionality more. But there are occasions on which I have so many split windows that I'm not able to properly enlarge a window as much as I would like (see Figure 17-13, for example, in which there is—to be honest—an unreasonable number of split windows, and using the standard Vim commands for controlling the size of an individual window doesn't help to view the contents of any one of those windows).

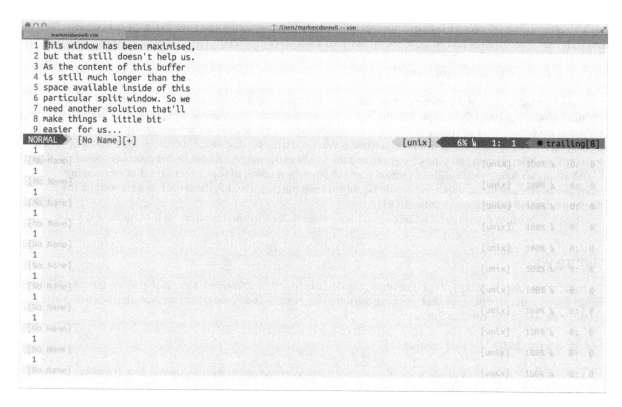

Figure 17-13. `<C-w>_` doesn't help users get much screen real estate

To trigger ZoomWin, we execute the `<C-w>o` key binding, which will cause the current window to become full-screen. To reverse this change, and to bring back the original layout of windows, we can run the `<C-w>o` command again.

At the time of writing, the current release of this plug-in has a performance issue, which means that the process of full-screening a window can be quite slow. (I've seen it take anywhere from approximately 7 to 20 seconds, depending on the number of windows.) Luckily, this problem is fixed in an upcoming release of the plug-in.

The only issue is that the new release is not yet mirrored onto either the `https://github.com/vim-scripts/` or `http://www.vim.org/scripts/` repositories, meaning you'll have to compile it from the source, using its Vimball, which can be downloaded here: `http://www.drchip.org/astronaut/vim/index.html#ZOOMWIN`.

■ **Note** We covered Vimball earlier in this chapter under "How Do Plug-ins Work?"; refer back to that section, if you need to recap how to install Vimball files.

Summary

This has been quite a journey, and as you're now aware, Vim's core functionality (although itself very powerful) is enhanced greatly through the use of plug-ins. Overall, it's an indication of the power of Vim that we can extend the features provided in such a fluent way to allow the user to do even more than just edit text-based content. Let's take a moment to recap some of the highlights.

- We looked at what a plug-in really is, its architecture, and how to manually install plug-ins.

- You discovered that there are two types of plug-ins: one that is made up of a single file and another constructed of multiple files. When installing a plug-in manually, it is your responsibility to ensure that those files are placed in the correct location.

- I covered what a Vimball archive is as well as its purpose (which is to ease plug-in development for the author and the installation of the plug-in for the user) and how to install a vba.

- I discussed plug-in managers, such as Pathogen and Vundle (and there are many more). Depending on your needs, I suggested using Pathogen and covered how to set up and install it.

- We then delved into a collection of popular (and less popular) plug-ins and some of their more interesting features (all of which are practical in real-world situations).

CHAPTER 18

■ ■ ■

Diffing

Regardless of whether you're working with a Version Control System (such as Git/SVN/Mercurial) or not, being able to compare different versions of the same file can be very useful in the right circumstances.

For example, if you're working in a programming environment, you'll likely encounter an issue known as a "merge conflict," when teaming with other programmers. This is when you have a repository of code, and you've forked the project to add feature A, while another team has forked the project to add feature B, and both features require modifying the same file (or set of files). The other team has managed to get their changes merged into the project ahead of you, and so before you can merge your work, you have to pull in the latest copy of the project, resulting in a possible merge conflict, as the same file(s) has (have) been modified in different ways. Vim's built-in diffing feature provides a way to resolve these conflicts.

But maybe you're not a programmer, but a book author, or you're paid to write articles for print/online magazines. If so, you may have to demonstrate to your publisher what specific changes were made to one of your draft submissions. Either way, Vim's facility to analyze diffs and export them in a different format, to demonstrate changes, is a nice utility to have.

In this chapter, I'm going to focus on demonstrating diffing content using a two-way diff and move on to resolving a merge conflict within a Git (Version Control System) repository using a three-way diff. This will give you a good indication of the capabilities and/or limitations of using Vim as a diffing tool, compared to other available options (either free or paid for).

Two-Way Diff

To begin with, let's consider that we have two files, foo.txt and foo-v2.txt. The history of the files goes something like this: we created foo.txt and then made a copy of the file. We then renamed the copy foo-v2.txt and made some additional amendments. Now, consider that we must compare these two files, to see how they differ. There are a few ways we can achieve this.

1. Open Vim, then open the individual buffers in split windows and run :diffthis inside each window (or :windo diffthis).

2. Open Vim, edit foo.txt and then execute :diffsplit foo-v2.txt (you can also use a :vert diffsplit).

3. Outside of Vim, you can run vimdiff foo.txt foo-v2.txt (you can specify up to four files to diff at once).

Any differences between the files being compared will be highlighted, along with the relevant line number. In Figure 18-1 (following) we can see that any differences in the text are highlighted in red. For example, on line 1 of foo.txt, you'll see that the word *foo* should be highlighted in red, while the corresponding change of the word to *bar* in foo-v2.txt is also highlighted in red.

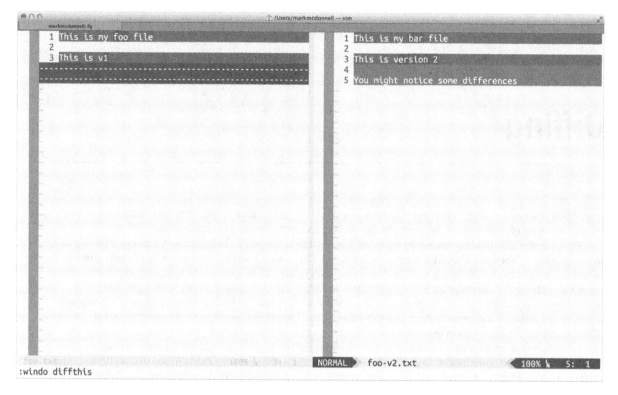

Figure 18-1. *A two-way diff of the files* foo.txt *and* foo-v2.txt

We can also see that lines 4 and 5 in foo.txt are highlighted in green, and within the foo.txt file, they show as dashed lines, to indicate that they didn't exist before. The background of any line in which a change has occurred is highlighted in blue (the red highlight indicates the *specific* change).

If the files you are comparing are quite large (i.e., have more lines of content than you have space to fit into your viewport), you should also note that while scrolling through the files, Vim will keep the line positioning synchronized, to make it easier to see where changes are occurring.

To turn off the diff tool, you'll have to run the :diffoff command. If you're doing a simple two-way diff (like we are here), then running the command in a single window will disable it from the other; otherwise, you'll have to either use the ! variation :diffoff! or you can use :windo diffoff, which will apply the command across all open windows.

■ **Note** Using the −o flag with the vimdiff command will make Vim use horizontal splits rather than vertical splits. To permanently set this option, you'll have to update the value of the diffopt configuration setting (see :h diffopt for more details).

Moving Between Changes

In our simplified example, there are only three changes, so moving between them is relatively quick and easy. But if your diff files are quite large, navigating between each change can be made easier by the use of some key bindings.

-]c: Move to next change
- [c: Move to previous change

diffget and diffput

You may decide that you like the look of some of the changes in the foo-v2.txt file and that you want to incorporate them into foo.txt. To do this, you can use one of the following conflict commands (see Table 18-1).

Table 18-1. *List of Commands for Getting or Putting a Change*

Command	Explanation
:diffget	Gets change (in a three-way diff, it requires a buffer identifier)
:diffput	Puts change (in a three-way diff, it requires a buffer identifier)
do	Gets change (works only for a two-way diff)
dp	Puts change (works only for a two-way diff)

The full syntax structure for the COMMAND-LINE command(s) is:

```
[range]diff{get|put} [buffer_identifier]
```

As you can see, the command can take an optional range, which, in this context, is the number of lines you want to get (or put) from the other file.

■ **Note**   You may be wondering why the command do (diff obtain) is called that and not something more obvious, like dg (for "diff get")? Well, the reason is that there was already a dg (digraph) command (see :h dg).

Simple Example

Let's say we want line 1 from foo.txt to be the same as foo-v2.txt. If our cursor is on line 1 of foo.txt, then we can run either the do command (to *obtain* the same line from foo-v2.txt) or :diffget (with no range or buffer identifier), to achieve the same result. Doing this, we'll see that Vim no longer highlights line 1. (It has intelligently realized that the content is now the same across both files.)

Let's undo the last change we just made, using the u command. You'll notice that the foo.txt is back to its original state, but Vim has failed to update the highlighting, so let's quickly run :diffupdate to fix that. (For more information on this trick, see the section "Diff Highlighting Breaks After Making a Change?").

Specifying a Range

Now that our files are back to how they were to begin with, let's look at getting the lines 3 to 5 from foo-v2.txt into foo.txt, which is slightly more complicated when using :diffget (compared to using :diffput), because foo.txt doesn't have five lines for us to move content into. If our cursor were inside foo-v2.txt and we ran the command :3,5 diffput, it would work fine. But if we tried to use the :diffget command with the same range (like so: :3,5 diffget), it wouldn't work, because Vim recognizes that foo.txt doesn't have five lines of content.

The solution to this problem is to provide the range as 3,$, which indicates that we're starting from line 3, and we'll keep going until the end of the file. When used with :diffget (i.e., :3,$ diffget), Vim will start pulling from foo-v2.txt at line 3 and keep going until the end of the file (which, as we know, has more lines than foo.txt), but it won't complain when pulling that diff into foo.txt, because we've not explicitly specified a line number that doesn't exist.

Diff Highlighting Breaks After Making a Change?

When you make a change to one of the files being diff'ed, you will run the risk of Vim not being able to keep the highlighting for the changes up to date. (This occurs mainly if you're making small changes within a line or more complex changes to the content.)

To resolve this issue, Vim provides a :diffupdate command, which you can run to refresh all window viewports and update the diff highlighting accordingly.

The :diffget and :diffput commands work in either a two-way diff or a three-way diff, but the key binding commands do and dp only work with a two-way diff. The reason behind this is quite obvious when we think about it. Because the do and dp commands aren't able to accept any extra arguments, if there were more than two buffers being used while diffing, how would Vim know which buffer to get content from or put content into? That's why in a three-way diff, we're unable to use these shorthand key bindings.

■ **Note** Vim displays dashed lines where lines have appeared in the alternative file. If you do not care to have that difference indicated, you can disable it by removing the "filler" value from the diffopt configuration setting (see :h diffopt for more details).

Diff to HTML

A nice addition to the diffing functionality is the ability to convert your diff into HTML, although the reason for doing this might not be clear if you're a heavy VCS (Version Control System) user, as you'll likely only generate a diff/patch of your file on the command line and then send that to your colleagues to apply to their own fork of the file.

But what about a less technical user, such as a book publisher? It's unlikely they'll know what to do with a diff/patch file, so if you want to provide them with an insight into what you've changed in your latest file update, you'll have to give them something easier to open. This is where the idea of converting your diff into HTML comes in, because you can send a single HTML file that can be opened right there in their web browser.

Luckily for us, Vim has a built-in command that covers this exact requirement. Simply run the command :TOhtml to have Vim open a split window that contains the HTML representation of your diff (see Figure 18-2).

Figure 18-2. *Example of running: TOhtml on my simple sample two-way diff*

OK, if you're a web developer, you may cry yourself to sleep looking at the HTML that has been generated by Vim, but, thankfully, that's not really a concern. The benefit of this approach is to have a super-easy and efficient way to share a visual diff of your files in a format that is easily openable.

Three-Way Diff (Resolving Git Merge Conflicts)

To finish up this chapter, I want to cover one other important aspect of using Vim as a diff tool, which is resolving conflicts when merging code into a VCS (Version Control System) such as Git. In this section, I'm going to create a merge conflict so you can see (a) how conflicts occur and (b) how you can resolve them. We'll also see in the examples I provide how sometimes a conflict can only really be resolved *manually*.

OK, to begin with, let's take a top-level look at the steps we'll be taking to create a merge conflict example for us to work with. (This will require you to have Git installed and some understanding of Git concepts. If you're unfamiliar with Git, you're free to modify my example to suit your VCS of choice, or, alternatively, you can learn more about Git by visiting www.git-scm.com.)

1.   We'll create a new Git-based repository.

2.   We'll create a file with multiple lines of content.

3.   We'll create a new branch and make a change to our file.

4.   We'll jump back to our master branch and make a change.

5.   We'll jump back to our newly created branch and merge master.

6.   This is where a merge conflict will arise.

We'll move quickly through the Git repository and branch setup of the preceding steps, so that we can focus on the Vim portion of this section. You should be able to just copy and paste the following commands to re-create our merge conflict. (If, however, you're still new to the command-line interface, I would suggest manually typing the commands, to help you become more comfortable working in the terminal.)

- `cd ~/ && mkdir test && cd test`
- `echo "Line 1\nLine 2\nLine 3\nLine 4" > foo.txt`
- `git init && git add . && git commit -m "Set-up"`
- `git checkout -b changes`
- `vim foo.txt`
- `:g /$/exe "normal \<C-a>"`
- `:wq`
- `git commit -am "Increment numbers" && git checkout -`
- `vim foo.txt`
- `:%s/Line/Status:/g`
- `:wq`
- `git commit -am "Line > Status: " && git checkout -`
- `git merge master`

OK, there were some concise commands there, but, I hope, none that is unfamiliar to you, as we've only really used either basic CLI and Git commands, in addition to some Vim commands that you've already seen in previous chapters.

The result of running the preceding set of commands should be the following output in your terminal:

```
Auto-merging foo.txt
CONFLICT (content): Merge conflict in foo.txt
Automatic merge failed; fix conflicts and then commit the result.
```

This is exactly what we expected to see. We've made changes in both the "master" and "changes" branches that between them have caused a conflict that Git isn't sure how to automatically resolve for us when trying to merge the master branch into changes.

Specifically, we're trying to merge a line like Status: 1 from the master branch on top of Line 2 in the changes branch, which can't be automatically resolved. Git can't automatically resolve this issue because it knows that we started with Line 1, but in the current changes branch, we increased the number from 1 to 2; yet on master, we kept the number the same and instead changed Line to Status:, so which change should Git keep, and which should it resolve? Should it keep the change from Line to Status: and not the increase of the number, or vice versa?

Git mergetool

We could simply open up the conflicting file, check the conflicts, and manually resolve them, but it can be error-prone, because the context of what you had and what you now have can become confused (not in our simplified example, but if you've been working on many different files and the changes that have been merged aren't your own changes but another person's, knowing what to merge and what to keep could become very confusing).

To promote a clear and focused understanding of the changes that have been made and where conflicts are to be found, Git provides a feature called a "mergetool," which allows us to define our own software to use for resolving conflicts. In our case, we'll be using Vim as our conflict-resolution tool (specifically, Vim's diffing capabilities).

To use Vim to resolve this conflict with the foo.txt file, we'll have to run the command git mergetool -t vimdiff, which by default will display the following output in your terminal:

```
Merging:
foo.txt

Normal merge conflict for 'foo.txt':
  {local}: modified file
  {remote}: modified file

Hit return to start merge resolution tool (vimdiff):
```

■ **Note** You can disable the prompt to press <CR> (and thus speed up the process of opening Vim and start viewing your merge conflict) by executing the following command: git config --global mergetool.prompt false.

If you press <CR>, you'll open up Vim in a three-way diff (see Figure 18-3), and from here, we can start to look at ways to resolve our conflict. Luckily for us, we already know all the commands required to do this, such as :diffget and :diffput. We just have to become acquainted with the three-way diff layout.

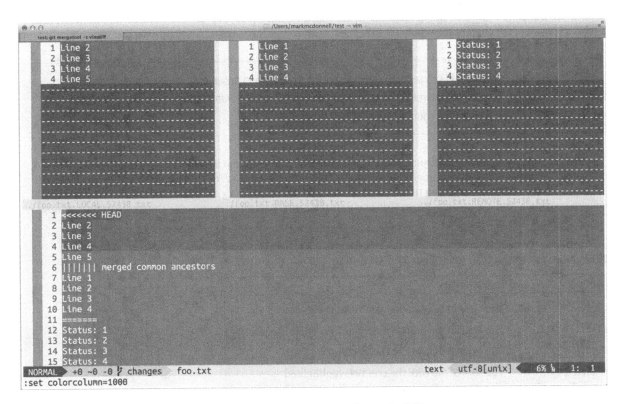

Figure 18-3. *A three-way diff resulting from running* git mergetool -t vimdiff

Once inside Vim, the layout of the viewport is split into four windows across two rows. On the top row, we have three split windows that contain LOCAL, BASE, and REMOTE instances of our conflicted foo.txt file. (They will have specific names, such as foo.txt.BASE.78228.txt.). I'll explain what these files represent shortly. In the bottom row, we have a MERGED window, which holds our source foo.txt file with all the merge conflicts inside it.

As we can see in Figure 18-3, our foo.txt file looks like the following:

```
<<<<<<< HEAD
Line 2
Line 3
Line 4
Line 5
||||||| merged common ancestors
Line 1
Line 2
Line 3
Line 4
=======
Status: 1
Status: 2
Status: 3
Status: 4
>>>>>>> master
```

We can see that the top half is what our content looks like in our current branch (<<<<<<< HEAD), whereas the bottom half indicates what the content looks like in our master branch (>>>>>>> master). The divider between each branch's version of the content is =======

■ **Note**　You'll also notice a ||||||| section, which indicates the common ancestor between the two versions. This can be disabled, if you're not interested in seeing that particular piece of information, by removing the setting merge.conflictstyle diff3 from your .gitconfig file.

In Table 18-2, we can see an explanation of the different windows that are open and what their content indicates. I've also included a number that represents the buffer identifier for that window. This is important to be aware of, because if you're going to use a command such as :*diffget* or :*diffgut*, for a three-way diff, you'll have to provide a "bufspec" value. This value is either the buffer identifier number or the name of the window (e.g., LOCAL, BASE, REMOTE).

Table 18-2. *List of Windows Vim Opens for a Three-Way Diff*

Window	Explanation
LOCAL (2)	The current branch that you're merging *into*
BASE (3)	The state of the branch before any conflicting commits
REMOTE (4)	The branch that you're merging *from*
MERGED (1)	The source file with the conflicts highlighted

To resolve this merge conflict issue, we will want to have our cursor inside of the MERGED window (remember that this particular window holds our source `foo.txt` file with all conflicts indicated by a specific Git notation: `<<<<<<< HEAD` and `>>>>>>> master`) and then execute one of the following commands:

- `:diffget REMOTE`
- `:diffget BASE`
- `:diffget LOCAL`

Our file can have multiple conflicts, so for us to run the `:diffget` command, we'll need our cursor to be placed somewhere inside of a merge conflict block.

Imagine that we have decided to use the master branch's version of the content (this is the content of the REMOTE window). We would run `:diffget REMOTE`, and then Vim would pull the changes into our MERGED window (see Figure 18-4), ready for us to write the buffer and close Vim to resolve the conflict.

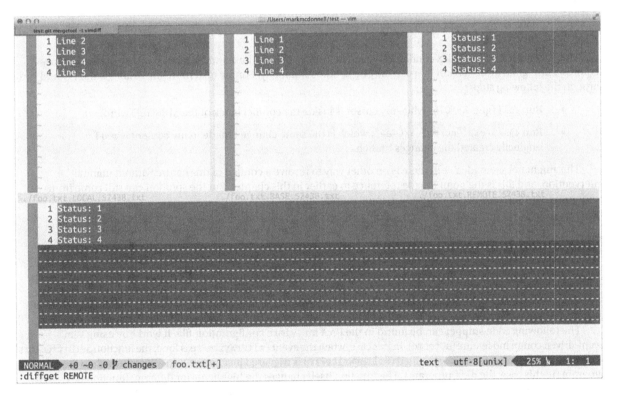

Figure 18-4. *Result of running:* `diffget REMOTE`

■ **Note** You could have resolved this issue in the reverse order, so instead of using `:diffget REMOTE`, you would have moved your cursor inside of the REMOTE window and then used `:diffput MERGED`.

Once you've written the buffer for the MERGED window and then closed all windows to quit Vim, you can run `git status`, to verify that the `foo.txt` file is added to the staging area, ready to be committed. You may also notice that Vim has inadvertently created some additional unstaged files. (These were the files that were inside the LOCAL, BASE, and REMOTE windows during your merge conflict resolution.) These files can be safely removed and are no longer required, once all merge conflicts are resolved.

Complex Conflicts?

To resolve the conflict, I decided that I wanted to merge the upstream changes from master (i.e., the REMOTE window). But what if that wasn't right? Well, in fact, the end result I wanted was a file that looked like the following (a combination of the changes from master and my change in the current branch):

```
Status: 2
Status: 3
Status: 4
Status: 5
```

This is considered a complex conflict and can't be resolved using the standard commands available, because it requires a fine-grain modification that can only be handled manually. For me to achieve the result I want, I would run through the following steps:

- Run `:diffget REMOTE` (while my cursor is inside the conflict block of the MERGED window).

- Run `:g /$/exe "normal \<C-a>"`, which is the same change I made to my content when I originally created the changes branch.

This might not seem ideal, but there is no other way to resolve a conflict of this nature without manual intervention, and this is the point I made reference to earlier in this chapter. But the solution can still come from combining existing commands alongside manual modifications.

Changing the Diff Theme

The default color theme used by Vim's built-in diffing tool is quite ugly (in my humble opinion) and also quite confusing, because there are more colors than there need to be when viewing a diff. When viewing a diff, I prefer to keep things simple and to be able to focus on the problem at hand. To achieve this, I have modified the color scheme to allow for that.

The following code snippet can be found in the ProVim `.vimrc` configuration file. It works by using Vim's event-driven command feature (autocmd). In this case, when the event `FilterWritePre` is fired, the function `SetDiffColors` is executed. The particular event specified (`FilterWritePre`) is triggered just before Vim filters through to the external program (in this case, the `diff` program). The function itself changes the highlights for different functionality, such as changing the color of what is considered a new addition, what has been deleted, which lines have changed, and, finally, what text in the line has specifically changed.

```
fun! SetDiffColors()
  highlight DiffAdd    cterm=bold ctermfg=white ctermbg=DarkGreen
  highlight DiffDelete cterm=bold ctermfg=white ctermbg=DarkGrey
  highlight DiffChange cterm=bold ctermfg=white ctermbg=DarkBlue
  highlight DiffText   cterm=bold ctermfg=white ctermbg=DarkRed
endfun
autocmd FilterWritePre * call SetDiffColors()
```

Summary

This has been an important chapter for covering a topic that seems to cause quite a bit of contention among most Vim users (of all skill levels). As with most things related to Vim, the initial outlook of this feature seems complex and confusing, but, really, the diff'ing capabilities available within Vim are cunningly simple yet still very effective.

For me, just the act of being able to visually lay out a conflict in a multi-window fashion helps to clarify a conflict, compared to just having a linear conflict file. Add to that the fact that Vim is able to highlight different aspects with varying colors, which really does help to differentiate the conflicts that have occurred. Let's now take a moment to recap some of the important points made throughout this chapter.

- We looked at a simple two-way diff (i.e., comparison of two files or two different versions of the same file) using the `:diffthis` command.

- We also looked at some different ways to set up a two-way comparison, using `:diffsplit` and `vimdiff` from the terminal command line.

- Turning off a two-way comparison is as simple as running `:diffoff`; otherwise, if you're diff'ing more than two files, you'll need to use `:diffoff!`.

- The `vimdiff` command can handle up to four unique files to compare between.

- The `diffopt` configuration option allows you to control a few low-level diff settings, such as whether blank lines are highlighted in the diff comparison.

- In long diffs containing lots of conflicts, we can easily navigate through, using the `]c` (next) and `[c` (prev) commands.

- In a simple two-way diff, we can use the `do` (diff obtain) and `dp` (diff put) key bindings to quickly move changes back and forth between each file.

- In all diff variations (e.g., two-way, three-way, etc.), Vim provides the long-form commands `:diffput` and `:diffget` (although, typically, I find myself using `:diffget` the majority of the time).

- We saw that after pulling or putting a change from one file to another, the diff highlighting could mess up, and so to resolve that problem, we run the `:diffupdate` command.

- Being able to view the diff between files and resolve merge conflicts using `vimdiff` is incredibly useful, but being able to provide an easy-to-view visual of the diff conflicts (i.e., viewed as an HTML page in a browser) is made even easier, thanks to the built-in `:TOhtml` command.

- Next, you learned how to resolve a merge conflict within the Git Version Control System, by setting it up to utilize the `vimdiff` tool. Through this, you discovered how Vim's three-way diff works (i.e., LOCAL, BASE, REMOTE, and MERGED windows) and were able to reuse the `:diffget` and `:diffput` commands (alongside some manual edits) to resolve our conflict.

- Finally, you learned how to change the default colors used by Vim when viewing a diff.

CHAPTER 19

Custom Commands and Bindings

Once you feel as though you've mastered all that Vim has to offer, you will eventually decide that you want to optimize your efficiency even further, by abstracting away some of the commands that currently require multiple steps and reducing them to a few keystrokes. These optimizations are both fun and (in practical terms) useful when you become a heavy-duty Vim user.

In this chapter, I'll cover all you need to know about creating your own commands, as well as remapping existing commands into shorter sequences to help improve your Vim efficiency.

There is one minor issue worth considering before running off to create a whole suite of new key mappings for all your favorite commands: what happens when you're forced to use Vim outside of your own custom configuration? This happens more often than you probably realize (admittedly, even more, if you're a programmer). In my day-to-day work life, I might well be doing one, or *all*, of the following (and guess what they all have in common?):

- Helping a colleague (who is also a Vim user)

- Pair programming (remotely via tmux/tmate)

- Remoting onto an external server (AWS EC2 instances)

- Working from inside a virtual machine (Vagrant/Docker)

If you haven't guessed, each of these items requires that I work within an environment that's not strictly my own, and so my custom .vimrc configuration file won't be available. In addition, I might not be working with Vim at all but will be using Vi (which lacks support for many important Vim features). In these instances, knowing the real Vim commands that your mappings are abstracting away is invaluable knowledge.

Since using Vim, I've gone from a mapping maniac to someone who hardly uses custom key bindings at all. (I still keep some of them within my configuration file, but I just don't use them as much, if at all.) What triggered this change was the result of being constantly placed in a position in which I'm working with someone else's Vim setup, not knowing how to do something, because I had memorized only my own mappings for certain commands. I would then go back and look at my custom mappings, only to realize that the default key bindings were actually easier to remember than my own, in the first place.

I now only create my own custom mappings in instances in which the command is something that takes much longer to write and is also a command that I run a lot (for example, :CtrlPBuffer). The :CtrlPBuffer command displays my currently open buffers and allows me to more easily filter and select a buffer (compared to using the native :ls command, which only displays a static list of open buffers). Also, for me to switch the buffer requires an additional command (e.g., :b {N}, where N is the number of the buffer), whereas I can do that as well within the :CtrlPBuffer command. But that's quite tedious to type, especially considering that I use the feature a lot. So I mapped it to <Leader>y (which for me is \y).

Creating Your Own Mappings

With those minor concerns out the way, if you feel the default commands are too verbose (or you just prefer an alternative), you can construct your own command mappings, with a few configuration tweaks.

The process of creating your own mappings is to edit your .vimrc configuration file to include either the map or the noremap commands. I'll explain what these do shortly, but first let's see a quick example.

```
map <Leader>' :NERDTreeToggle<CR>
```

In the preceding example, we map the keystrokes \' to the actual command :NERDTreeToggle (the backslash [\] is the default key referred to as the <Leader> key, although you can reassign it if you wish).

We reviewed the NERDTree plug-in back in Chapter 17, so you should already be familiar with what it does, but just to clarify, for those who have skipped ahead, if I wanted to toggle the file tree view in Vim, I would have to enter the command :NERDTreeToggle, followed by hitting the carriage return key <CR>. Now, you *can* get very quick at typing this, but not as quick as simply pressing the <Leader> key (\) and then the apostrophe key, which conveniently sits right next to the \ key.

Again, the benefit of creating your own mappings is that you can use a shorter sequence of keystrokes, which can make you even more efficient while editing within Vim.

map vs. noremap

As I explained earlier, Vim provides two commands that help you create your own mappings. These are

- map

- noremap

The map command takes two arguments: the first is the new keystroke sequence, and the second is what you're looking to map the first to.

To appreciate the difference between map and noremap, you have to understand another feature that Vim provides, called "recursive mapping." This can be quite a confusing topic to explain, so I'll do so via an example.

- :map j gg: When you press j, it will actually execute gg.

- :map Q j: When you press Q, it will actually execute gg.

Note how Q now maps to gg (although we technically mapped it to j). Well, that's because of recursive mapping. It acts like an inheritance chain, so when you press Q, that maps to j, and j itself is mapped to gg.

To avoid that recursive lookup of commands from happening (let's say we want Q to execute what originally was j's functionality), we would use the noremap (no recursive mapping) command instead, like so:

```
:noremap Q j
```

Mapping Keys in Specific Modes

The mappings we've seen up to this point will work regardless of the mode you're in. If you wanted to map a key only when within a specific Vim mode, you would have to use one of the following mode-specific commands:

- nmap: NORMAL mode

- imap: INSERT mode

- vmap: VISUAL *and* SELECT mode

- • `smap`: SELECT mode

- • `xmap`: VISUAL mode

- • `cmap`: COMMAND-LINE mode

- • `omap`: operator pending mode

■ **Note**   The preceding list is not exhaustive, as I've not included the "no recursive" variations of the commands. For example, the "no recursive" version of a VISUAL mapping would be `vnoremap` not `vmap`.

Let's consider a quick example, whereby we want to map `j`, so that it executes the command `gg`, but only in NORMAL mode. To do that, we would use `:nmap j gg`. Similarly, if we wanted to map `Q` to the `j` command, but only in VISUAL mode, we would use the command `:vmap Q j`.

My Own Mappings

I'm going to list all the custom mappings that I have defined within my own `.vimrc` configuration file, as that will give you an idea of some of the things you might also want to abstract. If you've used the ProVim GitHub repository to set up your current Vim configuration (per my instructions, way back in Chapter 2), you'll already have the custom mappings mentioned in this section.

What is very important to realize is that I no longer use most of these mappings! I hope that this will underscore how when you first start using Vim, you become excited by the power on offer, so you end up creating custom mappings all over the place. But since being put into a position where I don't have access to my own configuration, I have reverted to being more of a Vim purist, so I advocate memorizing the native commands over making custom mappings (except when there are *obvious* advantages over using a custom mapping).

CtrlP

For me, the `<Ctrl>` key is placed in an awkward position on the keyboard. I don't find it as easy to access, compared to the `<Leader>` key. So, although mapping `<Leader>t` to `<C-p>` might seem practically pointless to most people, for me, the following mapping is a great improvement:

```
map <Leader>t <C-p>
```

Earlier in this chapter, I used the following mapping as an example of making an abstraction on top of a standard plug-in command (which I use all the time), which helps to make a massive improvement in the speed of my workflow:

```
map <Leader>y :CtrlPBuffer<CR>
```

NERDTree

I only have one mapping for NERDTree, but, again, it's a command that I execute a lot in my day-to-day activities, so it made sense to alias it.

```
map <Leader>' :NERDTreeToggle<CR>
```

Tabularize

The Tabularize plug-in is definitely one command that is tedious and error-prone to write out by hand, so mapping common patterns is a very practical solution. In this instance, the following patterns are the ones I use the most:

```
map <Leader>e :Tabularize /=<CR>
map <Leader>c :Tabularize /:<CR>
map <Leader>es :Tabularize /=\zs<CR>
map <Leader>cs :Tabularize /:\zs<CR>
```

ChooseWin

I haven't much to say about this mapping. It is one of those mappings that I like to use, although I'm sure some readers would argue that the native plug-in command itself isn't that long or slow to type. (I simply prefer this custom mapping.)

```
map <Leader>ws :ChooseWin<CR>
```

Turn Off Current Search Match Highlights

Funnily enough, I added the following mapping then never used it, and just continued to type the shorthand version of the command :noh. I then did something that most Vim users do . . . I forgot I added it! I rediscovered it by accident and decided to keep it. I whimsically use it every now and then:

```
:nnoremap § :nohlsearch<CR>
```

File System Explorer

There was a time when I wanted to get away from NERDTree and use the native file system explorer (netrw) that comes built into Vim. This mapping made it a little easier to open in the specific format I liked, but to be honest, I don't really use the native explorer as much as NERDTree, because NERDTree has a much nicer API, in my opinion:

```
map <Leader>. :Sexplore<CR>
```

■ **Note**   For more details on netrw, please see :h netrw-contents.

Buffers

I effectively stay away from both of the following buffer mappings, but I've left them in my configuration file, as my fingers still instinctly seek them out. I find, however, that these mappings don't give me any real improvements in speed, so I prefer to use the native commands.

```
" List all open buffers
map <Leader>yt :ls<CR>

" Delete all buffers
map <Leader>yd :bufdo bd<CR>
```

Windows

I actually find the following mappings to be an anti-pattern. By that, I mean the mappings don't offer me anything better than the native commands. My mappings aren't as clear as the native versions, and so I end up trying to remember my own mappings, compared to the native commands (so, in other words, I'd recommend not using these, as it becomes even harder to go without your custom configuration).

```
map <Leader>w- <C-W>- " decrement height
map <Leader>w+ <C-W>+ " increment height
map <Leader>w] <C-W>_ " maximize height
map <Leader>w[ <C-W>= " equalize all windows
```

The following mappings are another set of mappings that I no longer use (sorry!), but the Vim purest in me won out, and, again, I realized that I prefer using the :sp and :vs commands to split my windows, rather than a set of custom mappings that offer me no real improvements in speed.

```
" Make splitting Vim windows easier
map <Leader>; <C-W>s
map <Leader>` <C-W>v
```

Tests

If you're a Ruby developer, the chances are high that you'll use either RSpec (http://rspec.info/) or Cucumber (http://cukes.info/) for implementing tests around your software application (or you'll use both, if you practice "outside-in" testing).

■ **Note**   The practice of "outside-in" testing dictates that you start building a new piece of software by first writing "acceptance tests" (this is the *outside* view of your application). The acceptance test will fail, as you have no code written yet to make it pass. You'll then move inside your application and write unit tests for a specific piece of functionality (this is the *inside* view). Once you have all your unit-level code in place, you'll then be able to complete the cycle by making the relevant acceptance test pass.

The following mappings allow a slightly quicker mechanism for running tests and verifying whether the code I'm working on still passes my suite of tests (whether they be at the unit level—*inner*—or acceptance level—*outer*):

```
" Run currently open RSpec test file
map <Leader>rf :w<CR>:!rspec % --format nested<CR>

" Run current RSpec test
" RSpec can determine the right test to run as long as the cursor is somewhere within the test
map <Leader>rl :w<CR>:exe "!rspec %" . ":" . line(".")<CR>

" Run all RSpec tests
map <Leader>rt :w<CR>:!rspec --format nested<CR>

" Run currently open cucumber feature file
map <Leader>cf :w<CR>:!cucumber %<CR>
```

```
" Run current cucumber scenario
map <Leader>cl :w<CR>:exe "!cucumber %" . ":" . line(".")<CR>

" Run all cucumber feature files
map <Leader>ct :w<CR>:!cucumber<CR>
```

Custom Commands

While creating your own custom mappings is quick and easy, it's also quite simple to create your own custom commands, using Vim's :command feature. The syntax structure of this command looks something like the following:

```
:command [attributes] {name_of_command} {command}
```

Here, we can see that attributes are optional (and we'll see an example of what they look like shortly). The name_of_command is obviously required, because that's the identifier you'll use to execute your custom command. Again, the command itself is mandatory, as this is what will be executed when you call your name_of_command identifier. So, let's see a simple example.

```
:command Foo echo "Bar!"
```

▪ **Note**   It's common practice for custom (user-defined) commands to have their identifier (name_of_command) be "Pascal case." This means that the first letter of each word is an uppercase letter, e.g., FooBarBaz.

In the preceding example, we've defined a new command called Foo, and when we execute :Foo, we'll see that the message "Bar!" is displayed back to us.

That's a simple enough example, so let's extend this further by having the Foo command display a message that we can control at runtime. For example, if we run :Foo baz, I'd expect to see "BAZ!" displayed as a result (i.e., any message we pass in should be made uppercase and have an exclamation point added). The following demonstrates what this would look like in practice:

```
:command! -nargs=1 Foo execute "echo '" . toupper('<args>') . "'"
```

There are a few things worth noting here. The first is that because I had already defined a custom user command called Foo, I couldn't then straightaway (within the same session) define it again, even though it does something slightly different now. To work around this, I had to add an exclamation point (!) onto the end of :command, which tells Vim it's OK to override the currently defined command.

The other new item here is the addition of an [attribute], which in this example looks like –nargs=1 (for more examples, see :h command-nargs). What this does is inform Vim that our custom command takes exactly one argument. We can then reference that argument within our command, using the syntax <args>.

Now, to convert the argument (in this case, baz, which is referenced inside the command as <args>) so that it becomes uppercased, I could've used the substitution command, but I decided against that and opted for using the execute command, which allows us to utilize VimL (see :h execute). In this instance, we use the toupper function, to ensure that the argument is uppercased appropriately.

> ■ **Note** The [attributes] part of the syntax structure covers a set of four categories (argument handling, completion behavior, range handling, special cases). The first you've already seen (-nargs); the rest I don't cover here, but you can access them via the help manual :h command-completion, :h command-range, and :h command-bang. To see all the available VimL functions, visit :h functions.

Practical Example

Ingo Karkat is a well-known Vim user on the Stack Overflow information exchange web site (http://stackoverflow.com/users/813602/ingo-karkat). The custom command discussed in this section was in answer to a question from another user who wanted to be able to automate a common task he found himself carrying out on a regular basis.

The task in question was using vimgrep to search through specific file types in a project using a particular pattern. The format of the search would look like the following:

```
:vimgrep /searchTerm/ **/*.html
:vimgrep /searchTerm/ **/*.scss
```

Ingo's solution was to use :command to construct a new user-defined command that accepted the pattern as an argument and the file type as an argument, thus reducing the amount of typing required and the need to memorize the vimgrep command.

Part of his solution meant having to use a modified version of the attribute we used previously (-nargs). This time, it was defined as –nargs=+, which allows *any number* of arguments (but providing arguments now becomes mandatory).

Let's see the complete solution, which is a custom function called Se (short for "search everywhere"):

```
:command -nargs=+ Se execute 'vimgrep /' . [<f-args>][0] . '/ **/*.' . [<f-args>][1]
```

As discussed, we can see the use of –nargs=+ to allow multiple arguments to be provided, but this solution also utilizes <f-args> to access the supplied arguments (see :h f-args). The <f-args> variable splits the provided arguments at either spaces or tabs and then wraps each argument in quotes. So, if you executed :SomeCommand foo bar, the arguments would be passed in and accessible from <f-args> as "foo", "bar".

Now, how do we extract the individual arguments? Well, Ingo uses a trick of wrapping <f-args> in square brackets [<f-args>], which converts the value into a list and allows us to use Array/List index access to extract the arguments we want. In the preceding solution, [<f-args>][0] extracts the search pattern, and [<f-args>][1] extracts the file type value.

Now that we understand the process and syntax for writing a custom command, we can start to see what a powerful tool we have for constructing our own scripts.

Summary

In this chapter, I have covered how you can manipulate Vim into providing custom key bindings and commands that fit the individual need of the user: you. Let's take a moment to recap some of the things you have learned in this chapter:

- I began with the fair warning (or minor caution) that although creating custom key bindings is fun, the reality is that they can lead you down a false path, whereby you can end up having a hard time working with someone else or on another machine, because you've memorized only your own mappings.

- I clarified my steps for determining whether I should create a custom key binding, and that generally came down to whether the default command is indeed something that I'll mistype or take longer than a few moments to type manually (e.g., :CtrlPBuffer, because of its capitalized letters, is a real pain to type quickly).

- We looked at how you can create your own mapping, and I also discussed how to create mappings for specific modes only (such as INSERT, VISUAL, etc.).

- I also discussed the difference between map and noremap (which is a recursive lookup of commands).

- I went through all my own mappings and gave explanations for their use, and, more important, I explained why I don't use them anymore.

- Finally, I covered an important topic: how to create your own custom commands. I also covered the different mechanisms for providing arguments, and we saw a practical real-world example of its use.

## CHAPTER 20

Terminal Integration

Although there are graphical user interface (GUI) versions of Vim, the original software was designed primarily around running Vim from the terminal environment. You'll typically find that when you become comfortable using Vim, your workflow naturally tends to shift toward working more and more within the terminal environment as well. You'll start to take an interest in more Unix/Linux-based commands (such as navigating through your file system and manipulating files and content), instead of using a separate suite of GUI applications.

This chapter is dedicated to topics and workflows related to the terminal and how Vim can be integrated more tightly with features of the terminal environment.

Suspending Vim

When you're a proficient terminal user, you'll find yourself having to bounce in and out of the terminal environment a lot, to handle different tasks (maybe running your test suite or executing a shell script). If you're working within Vim (and your terminal emulator doesn't offer the ability to spawn new shells via tabs), you'll want to find easier ways to jump between Vim and the terminal. One method is to suspend the Vim process.

Let's be clear, any running application is considered a *process*. So when I say we want to suspend Vim, what I mean is that we want to send the Vim process into a background process, so that it stays running in the state we left it and doesn't close the program.

The command to run to put the Vim process into the background is `<C-z>`, which has to be run from within Vim. Once executed, you'll automatically be taken back to the terminal command-line interface. From there, you can carry out other activities, such as changing directories, creating files, or running shell scripts—whatever else you need to do outside of Vim—all the while keeping Vim active, so that you can quickly switch back to running Vim in the *foreground*, by executing the `fg` command.

Note Depending on what you have to do outside of Vim, there is a better way to execute shell commands while still within Vim. In the following section, we'll review one such solution.

Executing Terminal Commands

As well as being able to suspend Vim (which takes you back to the terminal shell), it would be nice if you could just execute a shell command from within Vim itself. Well, luckily for us, that's possible, using the following COMMAND-LINE command:

```
:! {command}
```

As you can see from the syntax structure preceding, the :! command allows you to pass to it any command that you would typically run from the terminal command-line interface. So, as an example, if you wanted to see what the current working directory was, run the :! pwd command. The result of executing this command is that Vim is pushed into a background process long enough for the command you specified to be run and for you to review the result of the command. Vim will only return to the foreground once you press the <CR> key.

Filtering Content via External Commands

In the previous section, we saw that we could execute shell commands from within Vim, causing Vim to be moved to a background process while the command executed. There are more practical use cases for this feature, mainly, having the ability to manipulate our content via external filters.

Let's consider the tr shell command (man tr). This command translates content from one form to another. A simple example would be converting lowercase characters to uppercase characters.

Now, I realize that converting the case for a set of characters is a feature that is easily performed by Vim, using either the gU or ~ commands, but I normally find that the path to understanding certain concepts begins with an easy example (meaning, let's not make life difficult for ourselves at this early stage; if you can understand this simple example, you'll have all you need to know to explore further).

If we were to make a visual selection of our content, we'd enter COMMAND-LINE mode and then run the following command, which would filter our selected content through the tr command and subsequently convert it into uppercase (the syntax of the tr command is not important, although the following example is simple enough to understand):

```
:'<,'>! tr '[:lower:]' '[:upper:]'
```

▪ **Note**　Filtering content through external shell commands will work with both ranges and visual selections.

Now that we've seen a simple example, let's take this idea of filtering content through external commands a step further. Imagine that we have the following content in our buffer:

```
Xyz  Def  Lmn
Abcd  hijk  opqr
Ef  St  Vw
```

At the moment, it's a bit of a mess; it looks like it's a table matrix of some sort, but the columns are all out of sync. We could manually correct it, or we could use a plug-in (such as Tabular), or we could filter the content through the column Unix command, as follows. (Note: I visually selected the entire buffer.)

```
:'<,'>! column -t
```

The preceding command will manipulate our content so that it now looks as follows:

```
Xyz   Def   Lmn
Abcd  hijk  opqr
Ef    St    Vw
```

Note how the command has nicely formatted our data into a visually more recognizable data structure. From here, we might decide that we want to sort our data by the first column, in ascending order. To do that (again, I've visually selected the content), we'll filter our content through the sort Unix command.

```
:'<,'>! sort -k1
```

I hope that you can start to see the power in being able to filter content through external shell commands, to manipulate data in ways perhaps not possible via Vim's default setup or plug-ins.

Redirect the Shell into Vim

The Unix ecosystem provides many small and focused shell commands, which allow us to string together and compose complex functionality very easily within the confines of the terminal environment, by using the pipe (|) redirection feature.

A basic example of this "composability" can be seen when we want to find a list of files or directories that contain the word foo. We can use the ls command (man ls) to list out all files/directories within the current directory, but that wouldn't narrow down the results to what we were looking for, so we can use the grep command (man grep) to filter the results for us: ls | grep foo.

Because the terminal/shell environment offers so much flexibility and such powerful tools, there are many tasks that we end up running on a day-to-day basis exclusively from the command line. This isn't a book about Unix commands (try www.apress.com/9781484201220, if you're keen on the topic of shell scripting), but you may still have to manipulate certain terminal output within your favorite text editor (which is Vim right?).

Let's consider a very simple example, in which we execute the command ls -la from the terminal shell, which returns the following output to stdout (i.e., my screen, in this instance):

```
total 1840
drwxr-xr-x+  99 markmcdonnell  staff    3366  9 Aug 16:19 .
drwxr-xr-x    6 root           admin     204 25 Oct  2013 ..
drwx------    2 markmcdonnell  staff      68 29 Jan  2014 .Box Sync
-rw-------    1 markmcdonnell  staff       3  7 Feb  2013 .CFUserTextEncoding
-rw-r--r--@   1 markmcdonnell  staff   43012  7 Aug 12:52 .DS_Store
-rwxr-xr-x    1 markmcdonnell  staff      67  1 Feb  2014 .NERDTreeBookmarks
drwx------    2 markmcdonnell  staff      68  8 Aug 15:09 .Trash
-rwxr-xr-x    1 markmcdonnell  staff      58 31 Jul 15:30 .agignore
drwxr-xr-x    8 markmcdonnell  staff     272 27 Feb 16:21 .atom
-rw-------    1 markmcdonnell  staff    1938  7 Feb  2013 .bash_history
-rw-r--r--    1 markmcdonnell  staff       0 19 Jun 09:01 .bashrc
drwxr-xr-x    4 markmcdonnell  staff     136 29 Jun 20:51 .boot2docker
drwx------    2 markmcdonnell  staff      68 26 Jun 07:18 .boxsync
drwxr-xr-x    5 markmcdonnell  staff     170 21 Mar 15:58 .cache
drwxr-xr-x    4 markmcdonnell  staff     136 30 Jun 12:18 .composer
drwxr-xr-x    3 markmcdonnell  staff     102 22 Aug  2013 .config
drwx------    3 markmcdonnell  staff     102  9 Sep  2013 .cups
-rw-r--r--    1 markmcdonnell  staff     574 15 Sep  2013 .dbshell
drwxr-xr-x    3 markmcdonnell  staff     102 29 Jan  2014 .distlib
-rw-r--r--    1 markmcdonnell  staff      55 28 Feb 16:12 .dnc
-rw-------    1 markmcdonnell  staff     101 27 Jun 19:22 .dockercfg
drwxr-xr-x    3 markmcdonnell  staff     102 24 Jan  2014 .docx4all
drwxr-xr-x    3 markmcdonnell  staff     102 24 Jan  2014 .docx4j
drwx------   11 markmcdonnell  staff     374  5 Aug 15:54 .dropbox
drwx------    6 markmcdonnell  staff     204 31 Jul 14:26 .elinks
```

```
drwx------      3 markmcdonnell  staff     102  2 Jun 14:44 .emacs.d
drwx------      9 markmcdonnell  staff     306 14 Mar  2013 .filezilla
drwxr-xr-x      3 markmcdonnell  staff     102 24 Jan  2014 .fop
drwxr-xr-x      5 markmcdonnell  staff     170  6 Jul  2013 .forever
drwxr-xr-x      8 markmcdonnell  staff     272  4 Feb  2014 .gem
-rw-r--r--      1 markmcdonnell  staff     164 22 Apr 16:22 .gemrc_stub
-rw-------      1 markmcdonnell  staff      47 21 Sep  2013 .gist-vim
-rwxr-xr-x      1 markmcdonnell  staff      59  1 Feb  2014 .gitconfig
-rwxr-xr-x      1 markmcdonnell  staff      66  1 Feb  2014 .gitignore_global
-rw-r--r--      1 markmcdonnell  staff    1665 23 Dec  2013 .gitk
-rw-r--r--      1 markmcdonnell  staff     241 14 Mar 14:53 .guard_history
drwxr-xr-x      6 markmcdonnell  staff     204 14 Jan  2014 .heroku
drwxr-xr-x     17 markmcdonnell  staff     578  6 Sep  2013 .ievms
-rw-r--r--      1 markmcdonnell  staff     839 20 Oct  2013 .irb_history
drwxr-xr-x      1 markmcdonnell  staff      55 11 Jun 19:59 .irssi
drwxr-xr-x      3 markmcdonnell  staff     102  4 Aug 10:24 .lein
-rw-------      1 markmcdonnell  staff     432  9 Aug 15:46 .lesshst
drwxr-xr-x      3 markmcdonnell  staff     102 22 Aug  2013 .local
drwxr-xr-x      3 markmcdonnell  staff     102 15 Apr  2013 .m2
-rw-r--r--      1 markmcdonnell  staff       0  4 Sep  2013 .mongorc.js
drwxr-xr-x      7 markmcdonnell  staff     238 25 Jul  2013 .nave
-rw-------      1 markmcdonnell  staff     199 14 Jan  2014 .netrc
drwxr-xr-x      6 markmcdonnell  staff     204 31 Jul 15:24 .node-gyp
drwxr-xr-x    474 markmcdonnell  staff   16116  2 Aug 21:20 .npm
-rw-------      1 markmcdonnell  staff     208 28 Feb 15:57 .npmrc
drwxr-xr-x      5 markmcdonnell  staff     170 10 Jun 12:40 .nvm
-rw-------      1 markmcdonnell  staff      83 21 Mar 12:31 .php_history
drwxr-xr-x      6 markmcdonnell  staff     204  6 Mar  2013 .phpsh
-rw-r--r--      1 markmcdonnell  staff     928  7 Feb  2013 .profile
-rw-r--r--      1 markmcdonnell  staff  169346  1 Aug 14:42 .pry_history
drwxr-xr-x      3 markmcdonnell  staff     102 31 Jan  2014 .psysh
-rw-------      1 markmcdonnell  staff    1024 29 Dec  2013 .rnd
drwxr-xr-x      9 markmcdonnell  staff     306 22 Jan  2014 .rubies
-rw-------      1 markmcdonnell  staff     378 10 Oct  2013 .sqlite_history
drwx------      9 markmcdonnell  staff     306 12 Jun 09:19 .ssh
drwxr-xr-x      6 markmcdonnell  staff     204  4 Mar  2013 .subversion
drwxr-xr-x      1 markmcdonnell  staff      54  1 Feb  2014 .task
-rwxr-xr-x      1 markmcdonnell  staff      56  1 Feb  2014 .taskrc
-rw-r--r--      1 markmcdonnell  staff    2654 14 Jun 16:21 .test.txt.un~
-rwxr-xr-x      1 markmcdonnell  staff      59  1 Feb  2014 .tmux.conf
drwxr-xr-x      4 markmcdonnell  staff     136 20 Sep  2013 .vagrant
drwxr-xr-x     11 markmcdonnell  staff     374  9 Aug 14:06 .vagrant.d
drwxr-xr-x      1 markmcdonnell  staff      53  1 Feb  2014 .vim
-rw-r--r--      1 markmcdonnell  staff      99  9 Aug 16:19 .vim-bookmarks
-rw-------      1 markmcdonnell  staff   33121  9 Aug 16:19 .viminfo
-rwxr-xr-x      1 markmcdonnell  staff      55  1 Feb  2014 .vimrc
drwxr-xr-x      1 markmcdonnell  staff      55  6 Mar 09:38 .vmail
drwxr-xr-x      1 markmcdonnell  staff      57  1 Feb  2014 .weechat
drwx------      3 markmcdonnell  staff     102 21 Jun  2013 .zcompcache
-rw-r--r--      1 markmcdonnell  staff   39440 14 Mar 10:04 .zcompdump
-r--r--r--      1 markmcdonnell  staff   80344 18 Jun  2013 .zcompdump.zwc
```

```
-rw-------    1 markmcdonnell  staff   31522 27 Jun  2013 .zhistory
-rw-r--r--    1 markmcdonnell  staff      17  5 Jun  2013 .zsh-update
-rw-------    1 markmcdonnell  staff  401311  9 Aug 16:19 .zsh_history
-rwxr-xr-x    1 markmcdonnell  staff      55  1 Feb  2014 .zshrc
drwxr-xr-x    2 markmcdonnell  staff      68 28 Apr  2013 Applications
drwxr-xr-x@   4 markmcdonnell  staff     136 19 Jan  2014 Box Documents (backup)
drwx------   20 markmcdonnell  staff     680  4 Jun 09:35 Box Sync
drwxr-xr-x   40 markmcdonnell  staff    1360  6 Aug 13:25 Code
drwx------+  11 markmcdonnell  staff     374  8 Aug 15:09 Desktop
drwx------+   9 markmcdonnell  staff     306  5 Aug 15:54 Documents
drwx------+  11 markmcdonnell  staff     374  8 Aug 15:07 Downloads
drwx------@  13 markmcdonnell  staff     442  5 Aug 15:54 Dropbox
drwx------@  67 markmcdonnell  staff    2278 13 May 18:55 Library
drwx------+   4 markmcdonnell  staff     136  5 Aug 15:54 Movies
drwx------+   6 markmcdonnell  staff     204  5 Aug 15:54 Music
drwx------+   6 markmcdonnell  staff     204  5 Aug 15:54 Pictures
drwxr-xr-x+   4 markmcdonnell  staff     136  5 Aug 15:54 Public
drwx------   17 markmcdonnell  staff     578 21 Jul 15:06 VirtualBox VMs
drwxr-xr-x    6 markmcdonnell  staff     204 17 Jul 09:58 bin
drwxr-xr-x    3 markmcdonnell  staff     102  4 Sep  2013 db
drwxr-xr-x    4 markmcdonnell  staff     136 14 Mar  2013 lib
drwxr-xr-x    4 markmcdonnell  staff     136 14 Mar  2013 man
drwxr-xr-x   15 markmcdonnell  staff     510 21 Jul 13:43 src
```

If I try to pipe that output directly into Vim, using the pipe redirection feature built into the shell (i.e., ls -la | vim), I would see the following error from Vim: Vim: Warning: Input is not from a terminal, and then Vim would promptly crash. The solution to this problem is to add an additional hyphen to the end of the command, like so: ls -la | vim -. This tells Vim to open from stdout.

Once the shell output can be redirected directly into Vim, you are free to manipulate the content in any way you like.

CTags

CTags is a tool that helps to more easily navigate complex projects. The way it works is that you download the command-line program ctags and then execute that command within your project directory, to generate an index of all the files of your project (along with additional options to control the resulting index database file). The generated file is called tags and is placed in the root directory of your project.

Vim has built-in support for CTags, so there isn't anything special you need to do other than run the command that generates a tags file.

What this means is, if you're looking at some code and you see a function being called, but that function is defined in another folder somewhere in your project, you can execute the command <C-]>, which will take you directly to the file that defines that function.

Example

Let's consider an example in which we're working on a PHP application that utilizes the Zend PHP framework (http://framework.zend.com). This particular framework implements a convention of underscores and case sensitivity to map a class name to a particular file in a particular folder structure. If we have a PHP class that has the identifier Foo_Bar_Baz_BaseController, the convention provided by the framework dictates that the file can be found in the following path directory: Foo/Bar/Baz, and there, it will find the physical file BaseController.php.

Now, imagine that we have a file which contains the class, `Foo_Bar_Baz_PageController`, and that class inherits from the `Foo_Bar_Baz_BaseController` class. To do this, we would modify the class to extend from the other, like so:

```
class Foo_Bar_Baz_PageController extends Foo_Bar_Baz_BaseController
```

If I want to now take a look at the base controller file, I could use CtrlP, Ack, or even the long-form `:e` command to locate the base controller file for me to open, but it's easier and quicker (as long as I've generated the relevant CTags file) to move my cursor over the identifier `Foo_Bar_Baz_BaseController` and to simply execute `<C-]>` instead.

In this example, we have a convention that makes knowing where to find files a lot easier. But regardless of that convention, it is still easier to navigate through a large code base with CTags than using any other mechanism. Also, CTags works well in environments that don't have a convention for matching identifiers with a physical location. In these situations, knowing where every possible object is defined might not be possible, and this is where CTags really shines.

Installation

CTags is a separate command-line tool that has to be installed outside of Vim. Installation is easy when using a package manager such as Homebrew.

```
brew install ctags
```

■ **Note** If you're on Linux machines (or if you're using Cygwin on Windows), depending on what package manager your distribution supports (`yum`, `rpm`, `apt`, etc.), you should be able to find the relevant package under the name "exuberant-ctags."

Usage

Once CTags is installed, from your terminal, move inside your project directory and run the following command:

```
ctags -R
```

There are many options for the `ctags` command, but the preceding example is the simplest and most generic. The `-R` flag tells CTags to recursively index files throughout your project.

Depending on the size of your project, the preceding command could take a while to complete. So, I would recommend running it with the `--exclude` flag, to limit the number of files to index, along with the `-V` (verbose) flag, which is useful for debugging purposes. The following is an example:

```
ctags -R -V --exclude=.git --exclude=**/node_modules
```

■ **Note** In the preceding example, we see that the `--exclude` flag can be used multiple times to ensure that specific files are not indexed.

Because I use the CTag command itself so infrequently, I always forget the options, and so I've made life easier for myself by aliasing the preceding command to just `ct`, within my `~/.zshrc` configuration file. My alias is defined as follows:

```
alias ct="ctags -R -V --exclude=.git --exclude=**/node_modules"
```

Tag Stacks

Every time you access a tag (using `<C-]>` to navigate to the relevant indexed file), that tag will be added to a tag "stack." You can view the stack by executing the `:tags` command. Another way to view a specific tag is via tab completion in COMMAND-LINE mode, as follows:

```
:tag [tab-completion]
```

With the preceding command, you'll have to put a space after the word *tag* and then press the `<Tab>` key to see what tags are available (keep pressing `<Tab>` to rotate through the entire tag stack).

If we took the example from earlier in the chapter (opening the `Foo/Bar/Baz/BaseController.php` from within the `Foo/Bar/Baz/PageController.php` file) and wanted to jump back to the previous file (in this case, `PageController.php`), we could obviously use the buffer list, but it is more efficient to use the following command, which jumps up the stack of tag locations recently moved through:

```
<C-t>
```

▪ **Note**   A useful trick is to open an indexed file within a split window, by running the `<C-w>]` command. For a full list of commands, please refer to the Vim help pages (`:h tags`).

Summary

This has been a short but focused chapter, covering a range of terminal-related topics, in the hope of expanding the capabilities of Vim to a much wider set of features and functionality. Let's take a moment now to recap what was covered.

- I discussed application processes and how everything (including Vim) is a process. To push Vim into a background process, the `<C-z>` keystroke is required, and to return Vim to a foreground process, we must run the `fg` command from the terminal command line.

- You learned how to execute shell commands from within Vim, using the `:!` command. This causes Vim to be placed in a background process while the shell command is executing (causing Vim to pause). Vim stays in a background process until we resume it.

- You discovered the power of filtering our content through external commands by manipulating a table matrix of data to be visually more recognizable and then reordering the lines in ascending order. These small and focused commands provide us with a much larger arrangement of flexibility that what Vim has available by default and is exactly why the "Unix philosophy" is so appreciated.

- You then saw how to move in the opposite direction, and instead of filtering content from Vim through external shell commands, this time we piped `stdout` from the terminal directly into Vim, to be manipulated using: `{command} | vim -`.

- Last, we looked at installing and implementing CTags, which is a command-line tool for indexing files and allowing a Vim user to more easily navigate through a large project with a complex architecture by simply executing `<C-]>` when the cursor is placed over a function identifier or class name, etc.

CHAPTER 21

Working with Code

At the beginning of this book, in the introduction, I made a claim that Vim isn't only for programmers, and that it is, in fact, a very serviceable text editor for many users, whether they be system operators, authors, or students. If you work with text, you will find immense value in working with Vim.

Now that that's out of the way, let me clarify (for present purposes): if you're not a programmer, this chapter is going to be a bit of a bore, as it covers techniques and plug-ins related directly to programming. I'll be covering a select few languages, such as Ruby, Clojure, PHP, JavaScript, and Node.

What I will say at this point is that I assume you have experience with the languages being covered, and if you don't, just skip that section, as I won't spend any time on the history of the language or the syntax. These sections are to help experienced developers in the said language get up to speed with how they can use certain Vim plug-ins to improve their workflow.

But before we start diving into specific plug-ins, I want to cover some of the built-in mechanisms Vim provides for making programming (and code in general) a little bit easier to work with.

Auto-indenting

When working with code (regardless of whether you use a language, such as Python, where whitespace is significant), to have an editor that can automatically indent your code is remarkably useful and a great overall time-saver, considering the amount of accumulative hours a programmer will spend indenting his/her code for readability, convention, or even necessity.

For Vim to auto-indent your code, you must enable the relevant setting. This is done by adding the following line to your .vimrc configuration file. What this setting will do is, first, turn on file-type detection (so that Vim will try to figure out what the file is, as it's loaded) and also enable automatic indenting.

```
filetype indent on
```

Note   If you did not install the ProVim configuration files (as covered in Chapter 2), you may not have a .vimrc file in your $HOME directory by default, so you'll have to create one first.

Vim has a set of language files built-in that it can use to identify a particular file. This language file will inform Vim of the conventions generally recognized by that language. If you decide that, in fact, you don't agree with the default settings, you can manipulate them (on a per-language basis) via your .vimrc configuration file.

As an example, Vim will automatically set the number of spaces for an automatic tab indentation to eight. But for most languages, you'll use four spaces, so I prefer to modify my settings to a default value of four, as follows:

```
set shiftwidth=4
```

Then, if I find Vim's built-in language files don't use a tab-size convention that I like, I'll modify only the language that's affected. My personal preference is to set a default of two spaces (per tab) for a few different languages. The languages I would like this setting applied to are shell scripts (such as Bash and Zsh scripts), Ruby, Yaml, and Vim. To accomplish this, you'll find the following in my `.vimrc` configuration file (if you've cloned the ProVim configuration, you'll find these settings already in place):

```
autocmd FileType sh,cucumber,ruby,yaml,zsh,vim setlocal shiftwidth=2 tabstop=2 expandtab
```

This can look quite intense, but the syntax structure of the command is `:autocmd {event_type} {pattern} {cmd}`, so let's break down the preceding real-world sample command into its component parts.

- `autocmd`: This indicates that Vim will automatically carry out some work on the following `{event_type}`.

- `FileType`: This is the `{event_type}`. There are many different event types, but I'd suggest reviewing `:h autocmd-events` for the complete list of available events you can trigger a command from.

- `sh,cucumber,ruby,yaml,zsh,vim`: This is our `{pattern}` that Vim tries to find a match against when the `{event_type}` fires. So, if Vim finds that the `FileType` matches any of the listed types in the `{pattern}`, it'll execute the `{cmd}`.

- `setlocal`: This is part of our `{cmd}` and means the following settings are only applied to the current file/buffer.

- `shiftwidth`: This is part of our `{cmd}`, and you should recognize this setting, as we looked at it earlier. It's the value Vim uses for auto-indenting code.

- `tabstop`: This is part of our `{cmd}` and is the size of a tab in spaces (but a tab that is manually triggered, rather than a tab created from an auto-indent).

- `expandtab`: This is part of our `{cmd}` and will allow Vim to convert a tab into spaces.

■ **Note**   The syntax structure for `autocmd` is actually much more advanced than what I've described. See `:h autocmd`, if you would like to come to grips with the other parts of this command.

Indentation with =

Now that we know how to get Vim to apply automatic indentation of our code while we're editing our content, let's look at how we can trigger this auto-indentation manually, using the = character. Imagine that we have the following JavaScript content (which is obviously not indented at all, and so could do with a little help to get it looking more readable):

```
function foo(){
return {
foo: 'bar',
bar: 'qux'
};
}
```

If this was the only content in the buffer, we could correctly indent the buffer by composing together three different commands, like so: gg=G. What this command breaks down to is

- gg moves the cursor to the start of the line.

- = is the operator we wish to apply to a motion/range.

- G is the motion, so execute = until the end of the buffer.

■ **Note**   If your cursor was already at the top of the buffer, the gg motion could be skipped, meaning you only need to execute =G instead. I added the gg motion as a precautionary step.

The result of executing gg=G is the following nicely indented code:

```
function foo(){
    return {
        foo: 'bar',
        bar: 'qux'
    };
}
```

There are three other variations of the = command. The first allows you to indent a single line, by using a double equation, ==; the second works by applying = to a text object; and the third lets you utilize a motion such as %. You should, I hope, already be familiar with Vim's text objects, since I covered them back in Chapter 5, so you'll probably have already guessed that we can auto-indent a single code block (while inside of it), using the command =i{.

Let's consider another example, but this time we'll apply both the single-line == command and the text object variation, to see how these affect our sample code. Following is our sample content that isn't indented properly, and in this example, you'll notice that we have four functions, foo, bar, baz, and qux, but only foo should be kept "as is" (not correctly indented). This requirement means we can't use the gg=G command from earlier, as this would correctly indent the entire file.

```
function foo(){
// foo
}

function bar(){
// bar
}

function baz(){
// baz
// baz
// baz
// baz
}

function qux(){
// qux
// qux
}
```

Let's use a different = technique to fix each of the functions bar, baz, and qux. For bar, we'll use the single-line technique; for baz, we'll use the text object variation; and for qux, we'll use a motion.

Single-Line Indentation

This is the easiest of the indentation techniques. Move your cursor to the relevant line (in this case 6G) and run the == command.

Text Object Indentation

To fix the baz function's indentation, we need the cursor to be *somewhere* inside of the function block (it doesn't matter where). To make things fair, we'll run the 12G command, which will move the cursor (near enough) to the middle of the function block. From there, we can execute the command =i{.

Motion Indentation

To fix the qux function's indentation, we need the cursor to be on either the opening bracket ({) or the closing bracket (}). As it's just a quick example, we'll show both variations.

Let's start by running the command 16G$, which first moves us to the line with the opening bracket (16G) and then moves us to the opening curly bracket (which is conveniently at the end of the line $). Now that we have our cursor in the right position, we can fix the indentation by using the =% command, which applies the = command to the motion % (you'll remember that % finds a matching bracket).

The other way is a little bit easier but fundamentally the same. First, move the cursor to the closing bracket (in this case, the closing bracket is on the last line of the buffer), using G. Now that we have our cursor in the right position, we can fix the indentation, using the =% command. You'll see that this version required fewer keystrokes, but, ultimately, just take whichever route feels more instinctual to you.

Syntax Formatting

When the filetype option has been enabled (shown earlier), Vim will attempt to auto-detect the file type of any file you open. To do this, Vim tries to find a match of the file extension against a list of built-in syntax files. To see a list of the syntax files that Vim uses, run the following command:

```
:echo glob($VIMRUNTIME . '/syntax/*.vim')
```

By running the preceding command, you should be presented with quite a long list of syntax files (in alphabetical order).

If you currently have a file open, and you would like to know what syntax format Vim has predetermined the file to use, one way of determining this is to run the :set ft? command, which will return filetype={syntax}.

Forcing a Different Syntax Format

Sometimes, Vim doesn't get the syntax detection quite right, which means you'll have to change the predetermined format to one you *actually* want. To understand what I mean by this, let's first see an example.

I write a lot of articles for my web site, www.integralist.co.uk, as well as for other online publishers, and my preference is to use the Markdown format to write these. The file extension for this format is .md, and so Vim's auto-detection interprets this as modula2 rather than Markdown.

There are two ways to fix this: manually each time or by configuration. The former is a simple case of running the following command :setf {syntax}. The latter requires a bit more work within your .vimrc configuration file. To make the change, you'll have to add the following VimL, the function of which I'll clarify afterward:

```
autocmd Bufread,BufNewFile *.md set filetype=markdown
```

So, the first thing we can see is the use of autocmd, followed by a set of events (Bufread and BufNewFile) we require our "action" to affect. In this case, every time we open a new file (and jump back to that buffer within a single session) that has a file extension of .md, we'll execute the command set filetype=markdown, which ensures that the correct syntax file is utilized.

Note   For more information on Markdown and its syntax format, please review
http://en.wikipedia.org/wiki/Markdown.

Although Vim comes with a wide range of syntax files, you may find that it still doesn't support a syntax you wish to use. If this is the case, there is a great GitHub repository (https://github.com/sheerun/vim-polyglot) that provides a lengthy list of additional syntax files.

Ruby

Developing Ruby applications in Vim can be made easier through the use of a few plug-ins that add some simple features that can make a big difference to your editing workflow. Following is a list of Ruby plug-ins I'll be covering:

- https://github.com/tpope/vim-endwise
- https://github.com/vim-ruby/vim-ruby
- https://github.com/tpope/vim-cucumber
- https://github.com/ecomba/vim-ruby-refactoring
- https://github.com/skalnik/vim-vroom

vim-endwise

We'll start with a nice simple plug-in, which is absolutely essential for any Ruby developer and will automatically add an end keyword to any relevant block of code, thus saving you the hassle of having to do it yourself. This plug-in will work with the if, unless, class, do, while, and begin blocks (as well as many more standard Ruby keywords).

If you were to create a new function by typing def foo and then press <CR> to move the cursor down a line to start typing the body of your function, you would be pleasantly surprised to discover that an end keyword had been added automatically, to close off the block for you.

vim-ruby

If you're using a version of Vim greater than 6.0, you'll actually have the files that make up this plug-in built into Vim by default (which is good). But if you're the type of person who enjoys having the newest features (or you're, unfortunately, stuck using a much older version of Vim, which I really hope isn't the case), you'll want to have this plug-in installed.

Some of the features this plug-in provides are syntax highlighting for both Ruby and eRuby syntax files, in addition to auto-indentation and code-completion support. There is also support for compiler plug-ins, which allow your Ruby code to be executed with the appropriate executables.

There isn't much to demonstrate with this plug-in. The only thing I can say is that if you're developing with Ruby in Vim, this plug-in will ensure that your experience is much more pleasant.

vim-cucumber

If you're developing applications using Ruby, then chances are you'll also be using the Cucumber behavior-driven framework, which lets you describe business requirements in plain English. As with the vim-ruby plug-in, this plug-in is now built into the latest version of Vim. But if you prefer to have the cutting-edge release of features (or you're using an older version of Vim), you'll want to have this plug-in installed.

The plug-in provides syntax highlighting and indentation rules for the Gherkin specification files. Gherkin is the language that lets the business describe its requirements, and each step in the specification file maps to a corresponding code file that implements that step's requirement.

The plug-in also provides a small list of custom mappings to help locate the source code for a given step. Each mapping will open the relevant code file for a step but differ in how the code file is opened. (For example, does it replace the current buffer or will it be opened inside a split window? And if it is opened in a split window, should the cursor be placed inside the split or kept where it is in the current buffer?) The following list of commands includes all there are to remember:

- [<C-d> (or]<C-d>): Opens the corresponding step definition in the current buffer

- <C-w>d (or <C-w><C-d>): Opens the corresponding step definition in a new split window and moves the cursor into that split

- [d (or]d): Opens the corresponding step definition in a new split window and moves the cursor into that split

vim-ruby-refactoring

There are many books on the topic of good code design and refactoring existing code to build upon recognized design patterns. This plug-in assists with your refactoring by providing a set of commands (and mappings) that you can use to automate the process.

We'll take a look at some small examples using the commands :RAddParameter, :RExtractConstant, and :RExtractMethod. There are many other commands, but I think these will suffice to give you an idea of what the plug-in can do. For additional examples, please refer to the plug-in documentation.

■ **Note**   There are also methods that help in working with RSpec tests.

:RAddParameter

"Add Parameter" refactoring allows us to inject a dependency into our method (or class constructor). Simply have your cursor positioned somewhere inside the method definition and run the command. You'll be asked to provide a value, which can be anything you like: a comma-separated list or, maybe, an options hash—whatever you need it to be.

Imagine that we have the following code snippet:

```
class Foo
  def initialize
    # code
  end
end
```

If we execute the command :RAddParameter (while our cursor is inside the method definition, we want to refactor), we'll be asked to enter a Parameter name. So, we'll enter the value x, y, z, and this should modify our code to look like the following updated snippet:

```
class Foo
  def initialize(x, y, z)
    # code
  end
end
```

:RExtractConstant

"Extract Constant" refactoring allows us to take back control over unidentified constants, which most of the time will appear as an in-line value. Typically these in-line values are known as being "magic" (i.e., "What does it mean?" or "What does it represent/refer to?").

To demonstrate this refactoring, let's consider that we have the following code snippet, which contains a class with one method. This method simply sums a set of values, but we don't know what those values mean.

```
class Foo
  def sum
    32 + 27
  end
end
```

In this example, we could say that the values are constant values and, therefore, won't change, and so can be made into a constant, with the help of the :RExtractConstant command. The first thing you have to do is to select the value you want to extract. So let's visually select the number 32 from the sample code and then execute :RExtractConstant, whereby you'll be asked to provide a "Constant name:". You can now can enter the name you want your constant to have. We'll enter mark_age, and that will result in the following modification:

```
class Foo
  MARK_AGE = 32
  def sum
    MARK_AGE + 27
  end
end
```

■ **Note** You'll notice that the constant you enter will be converted into uppercase automatically, which is the convention in Ruby.

:RExtractMethod

"Extract Method" refactoring is very useful in making your code clearer and easier to comprehend. If you ever find a piece of code that doesn't make sense, rather than add a code comment to try to explain what it does, extract the code into a separate method whose identifier (i.e., its function/method name) adequately explains the code's purpose.

To demonstrate this refactoring, let's imagine we have the following code snippet, which is a class whose constructor has an ambiguous expression whose purpose or context is unclear:

```
class Foo
  def initialize(x, y, z)
    (x + y) * z
  end
end
```

We can see that it takes in some dependencies and then carries out a calculation using those dependencies, but what is the end result supposed to represent? If we visually select the expression and execute the :RExtractMethod command, we'll be asked to provide a "Method name:". If we enter the value as custom_dimension, the code will be modified, as shown following. Note how the ambiguous code's purpose is now clearly identified within a separate method.

```
class Foo
  def initialize(x, y, z)
    custom_dimension(x, y, z)
  end

  def custom_dimension(x, y, z)
    (x + y) * z
  end
end
```

■ **Note**   Typically, I find this to be one of the most important and consistent refactorings I do on a regular basis.

---

vim-vroom

For the seasoned Ruby developer, writing tests will be high on your priority list, and that requires a quick and efficient way to actually run your tests, to ensure they pass. Yes, you can open up a new terminal tab (or send Vim into a background process), or maybe open a new pane in tmux, but it's much nicer to be able to execute a command within Vim that will handle this for you without having to change context too much or needing to know anything about screen multiplexes such as GNU Screen or tmux.

This is where the vim-vroom plug-in comes into play. Like all good plug-ins, it has a simple focus, which is to run your entire suite of tests, a single test, or the last test that was run. It works with RSpec and Cucumber and other test frameworks and provides a large number of custom configuration settings. It also has a very small set of commands (two to be exact).

- :VroomRunTestFile (mapped to <Leader>r) will run all tests in the current file or the last test file that was run.

- :VroomRunNearestTest (mapped to <Leader>R) will run the nearest test in the current file or the last test that was run.

If you have some additional requirements to ensure that your tests run in the right context, the commands are able to be executed by using :call (see :h call for more info) and will accept a hash parameter that controls how the tests should be run. For example (if using RSpec), you could run the following:

```
:call vroom#RunTestFile({'options':'--drb'})
```

The preceding command would be evaluated into

```
bundle exec rspec --drb {file-to-be-tested}
```

Please refer to the plug-in's documentation for more information on what additional parameters can be passed and for which test framework.

Clojure

Clojure development is a tricky beast in Vim (compared to, say, developing in Emacs), because it's built around the premise of using an REPL (Read Eval Print Loop) to help write code, and this itself provides extremely fast (and useful) feedback during the development process.

The main issue is that there is no built-in REPL or shell (unless you open a new tab in your terminal emulator or put Vim into a background process while you execute code, although that approach isn't very useful either), so you'll need a way to mimic having a REPL environment.

Clojure is a Lisp-based language (if you're unfamiliar with Lisp, just think of it as "the one with all the parentheses"); therefore, having a plug-in that can make writing and reading very terse code easier is also a plus, to my mind.

Let's take a look at the plug-ins we're going to be covering:

- https://github.com/tpope/vim-fireplace/

- https://github.com/tpope/vim-sexp-mappings-for-regular-people

- https://github.com/kien/rainbow_parentheses.vim

The vim-fireplace plug-in is what allows us to mimic an REPL-driven environment and is absolutely essential for Clojure development. The second plug-in provides some nice utility commands for manipulating Lisp-based syntax. The last plug-in helps to make the parentheses much easier to interpret. The preceding plug-ins have been listed in order of importance (and, coincidentally, complexity), but I will be reversing the order for the purposes of explanation.

Rainbow Parentheses

This plug-in is very simple: it color-codes your parentheses, making it easier to visualize the start and stop of an expression in what would otherwise be a very dense or terse piece of Lisp code (see Figure 21-1).

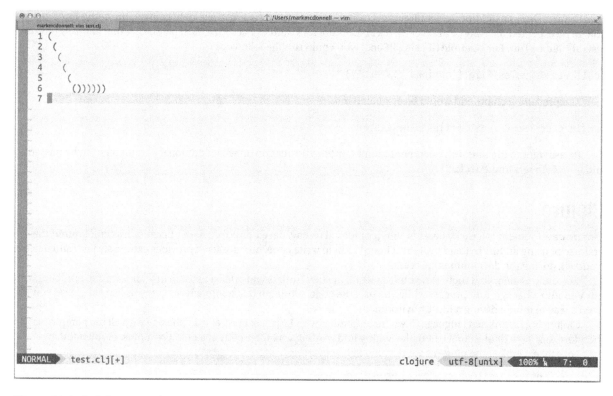

Figure 21-1. *Rainbox parentheses in action*

sexp

The vim-sexp-mappings-for-regular-people plug-in provides new functionality that allows for easier development in Vim for Lisp-based programming languages. It has a few really nice features, such as automatic handling of parentheses syntax and custom mappings for many different types of list manipulation.

■ **Note**   The title for this section doesn't use the full plug-in name, for the sake of readability. To be clear: there is another plug-in called vim-sexp, which is the basis of the vim-sexp-mappings-for-regular-people plug-in (the latter is what we're covering). The reason there is a variation of vim-sexp was to help make the plug-in's mappings more idiomatic to a terminal-based Vim user.

Automatic Parentheses Matching

The first feature of this plug-in is the easiest to explain by way of an example. If you're developing a web application in Clojure, chances are you're using the Ring (http://github.com/ring-clojure/ring) HTTP abstraction library. Ring has a set of tests that look something like the following:

```
(deftest test-app
 (testing "main route"
   (let [response (app (request :get "/"))]
     (is (= (:status response) 200))
     (is (= (:body response) "Hello World"))))

 (testing "not-found route"
   (let [response (app (request :get "/invalid"))]
     (is (= (:status response) 404)))))
```

Without any form of colored parentheses, the preceding chunk of code can be considered quite *dense*, because of the number of parentheses used in the Lisp syntax. Imagine starting to type the preceding code from scratch. It would be very easy to miss a parenthesis from the end of one of those forms. But with this plug-in, that's not possible, as the moment you type an opening parenthesis, the corresponding closing parenthesis is added for you. For this feature alone, it's worth installing the plug-in.

List Manipulation

Using the preceding code snippet again for our example, let's say we want to move the testing form "not-found route" to be above "main route." Typically, you might use the % command to help you select the entire form, and then, rather than use copy and paste to move the form, you'll use the :m{n} command (where {n} is the line number you want to move the selection to).

The problem with that process is that there are quite a few steps to take, compared to using the plug-in for an actual solution, which, if you're interested, is just moving your cursor to the form you want to move and then executing the mapping <f command. Note that it indicates the direction (<) and also the context (f for the form, or e for an element). You can use the same letters, but with a different direction (for example, >f or >e).

An example of using the element mappings (<e and >e) would be if you wanted to swap elements in the form (= (:status response) 404), and by that, I mean if you wanted the (:status response) and 404 elements to swap places so that the form became (= 404 (:status response)). To do that requires that you have your cursor on (or somewhere inside) the relevant element and execute either <e or >e, depending on which element you were moving.

Similarly, although less likely, if you wanted to move a parenthesis, you would have the <(, <), >) and >(mappings. So, if you wanted the form (println (1)) to become ((println 1)),then, although syntactically incorrect, it would be as simple as moving your cursor to the relevant parenthesis and executing <(.

Finally, there are the <I and >I mappings, which move your cursor to the first column inside the nearest form and then enter INSERT mode. For example, if we had the form (print 1) and wanted to change the value printed from 1 to 123, we would use the >I mapping to move the cursor between the 1 and closing parenthesis, ready for you to modify the value appropriately.

■ **Note** The plug-in also provides additional mappings for the surround.vim plug-in, to make deleting and changing outer brackets or parentheses much easier.

Fireplace

Few people seem to notice this, but the name for this plug-in was chosen because it has the letters *repl* already inside it: fi*repl*ace. The main requirement for this plug-in to work is Leiningen (http://leiningen.org). If you're a Clojure developer, this shouldn't be surprising to you, as it's the most popular tool available for managing Clojure projects.

The flow of working with a REPL in Vim is as follows:

- Open Vim in one terminal tab (vim).

- Open a Leiningen REPL in another terminal tab (lein repl).

- Run a command within Vim to connect to the REPL.

- Select Clojure code and run commands that evaluate in the REPL.

When you open the Leiningen REPL tool, you should see the following output within the terminal, and the item of interest is the port number that the REPL is currently opened on (in this example, 55248):

```
nREPL server started on port 55248 on host 127.0.0.1
REPL-y 0.3.0
Clojure 1.5.1
    Docs: (doc function-name-here)
          (find-doc "part-of-name-here")
  Source: (source function-name-here)
 Javadoc: (javadoc java-object-or-class-here)
    Exit: Control+D or (exit) or (quit)
 Results: Stored in vars *1, *2, *3, an exception in *e

user=>
```

There are two very important items we need to get right when using vim-fireplace: the first is to make sure that you open Vim and the Leiningen REPL from the same directory. If either process is in a different directory to the other, the process will fail. The second is to make sure you have a Clojure file open within Vim when trying to connect to the Leiningen REPL. If you don't have a Clojure file open (i.e., you have an empty buffer visible), the relevant command to connect to the Leiningen REPL won't be available (or you could just use :setf clojure on the empty buffer).

■ **Note**   At the time of writing, I opened an issue on the vim-fireplace GitHub repository regarding a problem with having a space in the directory path to the Clojure project I was working on. It seems that the plug-in errs when using a path that has a space and works when the path has no spaces (e.g., ~/Some/Project is fine but ~/Some Other/Project would not work). Until this issue is resolved, I would suggest ensuring that your project paths have no spaces.

Connecting to the Leiningen REPL

To begin with, let's go to Vim and run the :Connect command, which will return the following response for you to reply to:

```
Protocol>
 1. nrepl
Type number and <Enter> or click with mouse (empty cancels):
```

We can see there is only one option available (nrepl), so we'll type in the associated number (which is 1) and then press <CR> to confirm that choice. After doing this, we'll see the following response displayed, awaiting our feedback:

```
:Connect
Protocol> nrepl
Host> localhost
```

In this instance, just press <CR>, to confirm localhost as the value you want to use. After that, you'll see another line added, Port>, which requires us to now type into the command-line bar the port number the Leiningen REPL is connected to (remember that this was 55248) and then press <CR> one final time, to see that Vim has now successfully connected to the Leiningen REPL, as follows:

```
Connected to nrepl://localhost:55248
Scope connection to: ~/path/to/my/Clojure/project
```

■ **Note**   You can contract this command to :Connect nrepl://127.0.0.1:{port}.

Viewing Clojure Documentation

Now imagine that we have opened a Clojure development file that contains the following content: (println 123), and you move your cursor so that it is positioned somewhere over the function println. To see the documentation for this particular function, we would simply press K, and Vim would display the relevant response within the command prompt, as follows:

```
clojure.core/println
([& more])
  Same as print followed by (newline)
Press ENTER or type command to continue
```

There are alternative methods for finding information while within Vim, which is done by using one of the following commands:

- :Source: Displays the source code for the given symbol
- :Doc: Displays the documentation for the given symbol
- :FindDoc: Displays a list of documentation for the given symbol

Source Code

Keeping with the same imaginary file that contains the content (println 123), let's consider that we don't know how the println function was written but would now like to see its source code.

If your mouse was positioned over the `println` symbol, you could execute the command `[d` to display the following output within the command prompt:

```
(defn println
  "Same as print followed by (newline)"
  {:added "1.0"
   :static true}
  [& more]
    (binding [*print-readably* nil]
      (apply prn more)))
Press ENTER or type command to continue
```

Evaluating Expressions

There are a few commands provided by the vim-fireplace plug-in that allow you to evaluate the contents of your buffer in different ways. Let's review each of them individually. But first, let's imagine we're working from the following new buffer

```
(println 1)
(println 2)
(println 3)
```

The first item we want to look at is the `:Eval` command, which takes an optional range. If no range is given, the command will evaluate and display the result of the current expression underneath the cursor. If we provide a range such as `:%Eval`, the entire file will be evaluated, and if we provided a range such as `:1,2Eval`, both lines 1 and 2 would be evaluated, like so:

```
1
2
nil
Press ENTER or type command to continue
```

Sometimes, for simple one-liners, you want to quickly test their output but don't want to write out the code into your buffer first, just to then run a command over it for evaluation to find it doesn't work as intended. It would be nice just to write some code that is immediately evaluated and then thrown away. This is where the `cqp` command comes in. This command opens a one-line REPL for you to work inside. Write your code, then press `<CR>`, and the result of the evaluation is immediately displayed.

Although there are many other commands available with this plug-in (see the GitHub repository for the complete details), I just want to demonstrate one other command, which is `cpp`. This command simply evaluates the current expression under the cursor and displays the result. Most of the time, this is all I need when sifting through code and want to see exactly what it does.

There is a command similar to `cpp`, which is `cqq`, and it does exactly the same thing as `cpp` (i.e., evaluates the current expression), but it will first open a quick-fix window, so that you can make any modifications you require to the expression before it is evaluated. The reason the `cqq` command is quite useful is because, sometimes, you want to introduce a side effect (such as `println`) that allows you to more easily debug the output.

PHP

Although previous day jobs have required me to work with the PHP language, I'm personally not a big fan of it (at least not versions lower than the current latest release, 5.5), but I won't start a discussion about the pros and cons of the language here. Instead, I'll link to some useful plug-ins below and highlight some of their benefits. If you are working on a PHP application, the following plug-ins should make life a little easier.

PIV

The PIV plug-in (`https://github.com/spf13/PIV`) offers some nice features, such as using automatic code folding on all functions within your files, which lets you focus more clearly on the job at hand, as it helps to reduce any visual noise (as the PHP syntax, in my very humble opinion, can cause even the simplest logic to become a bit of an eyesore).

The plug-in also provides an updated set of syntax files to bring Vim up to date with the latest versions of PHP. Along with this is better code completion and better automatic code formatting/indenting rules.

Last, a really useful addition to the Vim experience is having PHP's documentation built into Vim. So, when reviewing a piece of code that someone else has written, and they've used a function you don't recognize (or don't use often enough to remember how it really works), you can move your cursor over the function identifier and press K to have Vim open up the documentation for that specific function, and it doesn't require an Internet connection.

vim-phpqa

The vim-phpqa plug-in (`https://github.com/joonty/vim-phpqa`) integrates very well with a few common PHP utilities, such as PHP Linter (for catching basic syntax errors), PHP Code Sniffer (for enforcing a standard set of coding conventions), Mess Detector (for detecting potential code smells), and Clover (for demonstrating test code coverage). The last two utilities require XML files to control execution rules, which have to be defined within your `.vimrc` file. Please refer to the plug-in's home page for configuration details.

Vdebug

The Vdebug plug-in (`https://github.com/joonty/vdebug`) helps to integrate Vim with a PHP debugger. Vdebug isn't strictly a "PHP only" utility (it started out life that way but has since evolved into a multi-language plug-in). Vdebug now works with PHP, Python, Ruby, NodeJS, and a host of other languages. The reason it can do this is because it relies on external debugging applications implementing the DBGP protocol. In this case, the popular Xdebug for PHP fulfills this interface requirement.

For PHP, the granddaddy of debuggers is Xdebug (`http://xdebug.org`). The Vdebug author recommends that you read the plug-in help guides for specific instructions for setting up the integration with Xdebug. This is because the help files include a very wide range of notes and tips, so it's well worth investigating. To access the help files, run the command `:help Vdebug`.

■ **Note**　Pathogen doesn't always generate help tags when you install a plug-in, but you can trigger it manually by using: `call pathogen#helptags()`.

Node

Considering that Node has been around since 2009, I'm surprised there aren't more plug-ins built around its ecosystem, but as Node is really just JavaScript, perhaps that's why it seems like there hasn't been much progress in that area. That being said, there are two very useful plug-ins for anyone doing Node-based development:

- `https://github.com/moll/vim-node`
- `https://github.com/sidorares/node-vim-debugger`

vim-node

The vim-node plug-in is still fairly young and has high hopes of becoming an essential part of your Vim toolkit for developing Node applications. Its current implementation provides the following features, which are designed to help you quickly navigate your project and external modules:

- Use the `gf` command when your cursor is inside the parentheses of a `require('...')` call, to load the file or module it references.

- Press `[I` while your cursor is positioned on top of a keyword, to have Vim display a list of where else that keyword appears in the file (including linked files and modules).

- The `:Nedit` command allows you to edit any module specified.

- The `:Nopen` command is similar to `:Nedit` but will also set `lcd` to the directory of the specified file/module.

■ **Note**   If a file or module can't be located in your path, the plug-in will attempt to retrieve it from GitHub, which will require an Internet connection (something to be aware of while traveling).

---

node-vim-debugger

The node-vim-debugger plug-in is a step-by-step debugger that greatly enhances the usability and capabilities provided by the standard debugger that Node itself includes. To use the plug-in, you'll first have to install it, using NPM (Node's package manager): `npm install -g vimdebug`.

Once installed, you'll have to add a debugger statement somewhere in your code and run your application using the command `node --debug-brk {your_app.js}`, followed by running `node-vim-inspector` in another tab. (This spawns a new node-vim-inspector agent.) From there, you have one more step, which is to have Vim connect to the agent, and to do that, you'll have to open Vim using `vim -nb`.

When you start Vim this way, you'll find that your application code is automatically opened up, and an arrow in the left column indicates the current position. You can now execute a number of different commands that will cause the debugger to step through your code.

- `<C-c>`: Causes execution to continue

- `<C-i>`: Causes debugger to step inside the next function

- `<C-o>`: Causes debugger to step over the next function

- `<C-n>`: Causes debugger to step to the next operation

- `<C-u>`: Causes debugger to move back up one stack level

- `<C-d>`: Causes debugger to move down one stack level

- `<C-p>`: Sets a new breakpoint

All the while you'll notice (especially if you use tmux to create multiple split terminal screens) that the node-vim-debugger window will update to reflect the current flow of the program, allowing you to gain an insight into what the state the application is in at every step.

Summary

In this chapter, I've covered a wide range of topics. We began by looking at how Vim handles indentation, both automatically and manually, using the = command. You also saw how to configure Vim's indentation rules via the `.vimrc` configuration file. From there, you moved on to learning about Vim's system files and how they determine what the current file format should be.

We finally moved on to reviewing plug-ins for the Ruby and Clojure development environments, and I gave a quick tour through PHP and Node to see what's on offer for those languages. There is no shortage of plug-ins available online for these (and many other) languages, but I hope this chapter has given you a taste for what's out there.

CHAPTER 22

Practical Tips and Tricks

We now have arrived at the final chapter for the Vim half of this book! I hoped you have enjoyed your journey so far and are excited at the prospect of using Vim as your future text editor of choice. What you are soon to discover is that the real fun with Vim starts here, because now that you are more than proficient at using Vim, you can begin to experiment and define your own workflow.

In this chapter, we'll be reviewing different techniques and tips that utilize both features of Vim that you should now be acquainted with, as well as other features that didn't quite fit into the flow of earlier chapters but are important to be aware of nonetheless. Some are fun little tricks, but most are really useful and practical tools and solutions to specific problems. But have no illusions; this is but a *very* small selection of tips and tricks. The beauty of Vim is its ability to surprise; you never stop learning!

Built-in File System Explorer

Most people who use Vim are so used to setting up their environment with plug-ins such as NERDTree and CtrlP to help them navigate their projects that they forget (or, more likely, they just don't realize) that Vim actually has a pretty good built-in file system explorer, called netrw (Figure 22-1). To open it, you have to run the :Explore command.

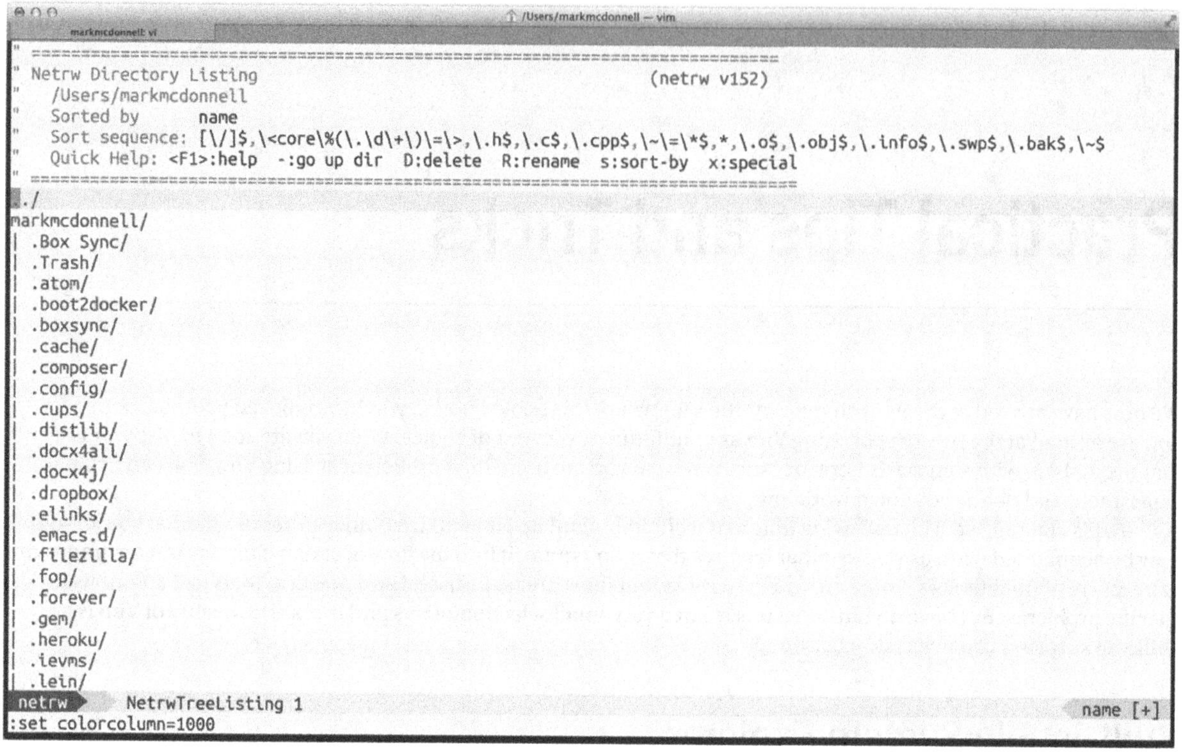

Figure 22-1. *Vim's built-in file system explorer* `netrw`

■ **Note** `netrw` is surprisingly powerful; it has support for editing files across remote machines using either scp or ftp protocols. I'd suggest having a good read through the help files, `:h netrw`, to see what other gems you can discover with this feature.

Navigating

Once you have the explorer open, you can use either the arrow or home keys to navigate the list of directories/files, and when your cursor is on a directory you want to expand, or a file you wish to open, simply press `<CR>`.

■ **Note** The default behavior is to open a file in the current window (which is the split window that was displaying the file explorer).

I personally don't like the default behavior of the file explorer. I much prefer opening the explorer in a horizontal split window, by running the `:Sexplore` command (Figure 22-2). We'll see shortly some additional configuration we can apply to enhance this setup further.

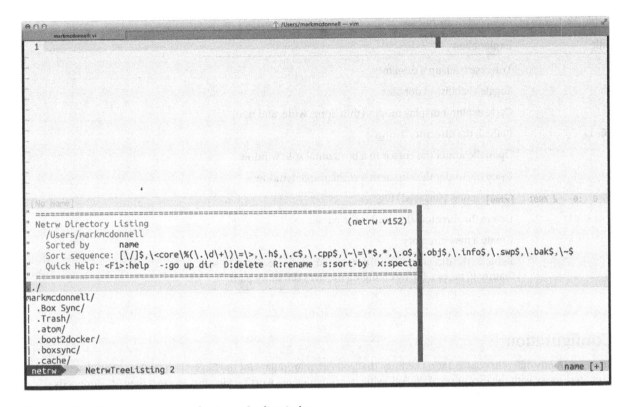

Figure 22-2. *The* netrw, *open in a horizontal split window*

There are a couple of other layout modes available, such as opening the explorer in a vertical split window (similar to NERDTree), using the :Vexplore command. Interestingly, there is the exact same layout using the :Lexplore command, the difference being that the latter command acts like a toggle.

If you were short on screen space (maybe because you had many window splits open), it would be best to open the explorer in a separate tab. To do that, you have to run the :Texplore command.

Default Action for Opening a File

The default action for opening a file (using <CR>) is to open the buffer within the current window. (This would replace the explorer with the file buffer content.) To jump back to the explorer, run the :Rexplore command.

■ **Note** Alternatively, you could simply press either the o or v keys to open the file in either a horizontal or vertical split window. This would leave the explorer window untouched and still visible.

Other Features

Table 22-1 offers a short list of key bindings that you should find helpful in your day-to-day use of the netrw explorer.

Table 22-1. *List of Useful netrw Mappings*

Title	Explanation
-	Traverse back up a directory
gh	Toggle visibility of dot files
i	Cycle explorer display modes (thin, long, wide, and tree)
<C-l>	Refresh the directory listing
o	Open file under the cursor in a horizontal split window
v	Open file under the cursor in a vertical split window
%	Create a new (unsaved) file
D or <Del>	Delete the directory/file under the cursor
d	Create a new directory
R	Rename the directory/file under the cursor. You can use this feature to move a file by changing the file's directory path.

Configuration

There are many different configuration settings that you can manipulate for the file system explorer. You'll never want to change most, with the exception of the following items, which are worth reviewing, to see if they fit your needs better than the default setup.

Faster Browsing

Vim has different caching levels for its file system explorer (slow, medium, and fast). The default is set to medium.

- *Slow*: We don't cache anything. Every time we move inside a directory, Vim will grab its content again.

- *Medium*: Only reuses directory listings when browsing through a remote directory (e.g., :e [protocol]://[user]@hostname/path/), as, otherwise, network conditions could slow down access

- *Fast*: We cache everything. Vim will only re-grab the content of a directory if it hasn't seen it before (you'd need to force a refresh using <C-l>).

If, for example, you wished to change the default to fast, you would run the following command (or add it to our .vimrc file):

```
let g:netrw_fastbrowse=2
```

For all options and details, see the help files, :h netrw_fastbrowse.

Change the Default for Opening Files

The default behavior of opening a file (`<CR>`) is to replace the current explorer window with the content of the file buffer. You do have other key bindings (such as o and v, amongst others) that give you different options for where the buffer gets opened (e.g., a horizontal or vertical split window). But if you have a preference that you end up using all the time, it might make more sense to change the default behavior of `<CR>`, by modifying the configuration option `g:netrw_browse_split`.

For example, if we wanted to change the default so that when we pressed `<CR>` on a file it would open in a new tab, we would run the following command (or add it to our `.vimrc` file):

```
:let g:netrw_browse_split=3
```

For all options and details, see the help files, `:h netrw_browse_split`.

Visual Layout

Vim provides multiple layouts for the explorer. Most people stick with the default setting, but I personally prefer the one that more closely resembles a traditional file system explorer, in which the files are listed in a tree-style format. To change the layout, as I've described, we would need to change the `g:netrw_liststyle` configuration option, by either running the following command or adding it to our `.vimrc` file:

```
let g:netrw_liststyle=3
```

For all options and details, see the help files, `:h netrw_liststyle`.

Hiding Files

The file system explorer by default displays ALL files. (This includes hidden files, also known as dotfiles.) If you wish to change the default behavior of this feature so that it hides multiple types of file formats, you'll have to change the value of the `netrw_list_hide` configuration option.

For example, imagine that we want to hide only `.ruby-version` files. We would have to run the following command (or add it to our `.vimrc` file):

```
let g:netrw_list_hide= '.*\.ruby-version$'
```

Vim's explorer also has a built-in method that lets you use patterns that are defined inside your `.gitignore` file, as well as additional patterns that you would like to define outside of that file.

The following example demonstrates how we can tell the explorer to hide all files that are matched by the content of our `.gitignore` file, as well as any files that match the `.ruby-version` file pattern we saw earlier (we could execute this command directly within Vim or add it to our `.vimrc` file):

```
let g:netrw_list_hide= netrw_gitignore#Hide().'.*\.ruby-version$'
```

For all options and details, see the help files, `:h netrw_list_hide`.

Glob-Based Searching

Back in Chapter 4, we looked at Vim's :edit command, but we skipped one important detail, which is that the command will happily accept a file glob (also referred to as a "wildcard"). Imagine that you have Vim open with the following directory structure:

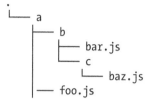

If we were to execute the command :e **/*.js, followed by pressing <Tab> (multiple times), it would result in Vim attempting to cycle through all files that match the globbing pattern we've provided.

In this example, we've said, "match any folder (and any number of subfolders) and any files within those folders that end with the .js extension. We don't mind what the file name is, as we're only really interested in matching specifically JavaScript files."

If we look back at the sample directory structure we have, pressing <Tab> three times will result in the following files being displayed in the command line:

- a/b/bar.js

- a/b/c/baz.js

- a/foo.js

Once we see a file we're interested in, we can press <CR> to open the chosen file within the current Vim window.

Moving Around Code

Earlier in the book, we looked at different motion commands. Specifically, the following group of motions was particularly useful for navigating around code:

- %: Move between parentheses/brackets

- [(: Move to previous available parenthesis

- [): Move to next available parenthesis

- [{: Move to previous available bracket

- [}: Move to next available bracket

With these motions fresh in our mind, let's review some code that demonstrates how best to utilize them. Following is an example of some JavaScript code that demonstrates three nested functions:

```
function foo(){
    function bar(){
        function baz(){
            return {
                a: 1,
                b: 2,
```

```
            c: 3
        };
    }
  }
}
```

Imagine that your cursor is currently placed on the middle line b: 2, and you would like to move to the opening curly bracket ({) of the third line, which, in this case, would be the line containing function baz(){.

You can't use the % motion, because that only matches against a set of parenthesis or brackets on the current line. You also can't use the f or F operators for the same reason. They only work on a line basis, and searching for the bracket using ?{ is more keystrokes than we would like, as that would match all previous brackets, and we'd have to press n more than once to navigate to the specific bracket we wanted to access.

For this example, the most efficient way to navigate to the relevant bracket we want is to use the following [{command, along with a count prefixed to indicate the number of times to execute the command (in this case, we don't want the previous opening bracket but the one before that), like so: 2[{.

Following is a similar example using Clojure code (which is a Lisp dialect, meaning there are more parentheses than you might be used to):

```
(def add1 (fn [y] (+ 1 y)))
```

Let's imagine that our cursor is inside the inner most set of parentheses (+ 1 y) and we would like to move to the opening parenthesis just before the function declaration, which, in this case, is the (fn part of the code. Much like the previous example, none of the standard motions, such as %, F, or ?(would work as efficiently as 2[(, as they require more keystrokes than our proposed solution.

Deleting via Search Patterns

One useful efficiency tip I've discovered (and which really demonstrates the power of composition) is the ability to delete content (starting from the current cursor position) up to another specific character, by passing control to Vim's search facility (e.g., either the ? or / commands). To see this, let's imagine we have the following content:

```
This is my example text. It has many sentences.
It also spans more than one line.
```

Now, imagine that your cursor is currently on the *m* of the word *many* (on the first line), and you want to modify the content so it now reads

```
This is my example text. It has more than one line.
```

How would you think to do this? You could move into VISUAL mode and select the content manually, or you could guess at the number of words and use either the e or w motions, but neither option is ideal. Perhaps you do something clever, such as run a substitution command, as follows:

```
:%s/\vmany.+\n.+(m)/\1/g
```

But for goodness sake, don't ask me how long it took me to write that (with syntax and formatting mistakes and figuring out how best to handle new lines in the content), and therein lies the problem. It works but it's prone to errors and much more complex, whereas the best way to solve this problem is by delegating control to Vim's search functionality: d/m.

In the preceding example, we're saying we want to delete (d) from the current cursor position up to the cursor position before the pattern we found a match for (e.g., with /m, we're trying to find the next m character), which is the most efficient way to handle editing across multiple lines.

Duplicating Lines

Every now and then you'll have a need to duplicate a line, either directly below the line that needs to be duplicated or to some other place in the current buffer. When this problem arises, I've found there are a few different ways you can handle it.

The first is to use the :t. command, which is a combination of t (itself a synonym for "copy"; see :h :t) and the . command (you'll remember from Chapter 5 that this is the "repeat" command). In this instance, :t. would paste the copied content into the following line. You could also specify a line number to copy to. For example, :t5 would copy the current line (or selection) to line 5 of the buffer.

We can also use yyp, which means to yank the current line (yy) and paste (p) it into the following line. We could even add a count to the beginning of that command, if we needed to duplicate the same line multiple times.

■ **Note** You can duplicate a specific line (or range of lines) to another line by using the following command :1t10, which would copy line 1 into line 10.

Moving Lines

Similar to duplicating lines of content is the common requirement to move lines of content. In this instance, we can use the move (:m) command in much the same way as we use the :t command.

If we want to move the current line down by one, we would execute :m+1, whereas if we wanted to move the current line up by one, we would execute :m-2 . . .wait, what? Yes, you read that correctly. Imagine we have the following content:

A
B
C
D

If we wanted line three (C) to be one line up (consequently making the order A, C, B, D), we would have to move the line up by two and not one. That's because the move command actually places the specified line one line *below* the destination. So when our cursor is on line three and we run :m-2, what we're telling Vim is to move the line up by two (which would be line one) and then insert it (thus sticking it on line two).

Increment/Decrement Numerical Values

When dealing with numbers, there are occasions when we need to increase or decrease a numerical value. In this situation, what most people will do is replace the values directly, but, in fact, if your cursor is on top of the relevant number (and you're in NORMAL mode), you can increase or decrease the value, using either one of the following commands:

- <C-a>: Increment number

- <C-x>: Decrement number

Removing Line Breaks

In programming, it's surprising how often (especially while refactoring code) I need to remove a line break and shift some text back up to the current line. What I also find quite remarkable is when long-term Vim users do this type of change manually (e.g., enter INSERT mode and start deleting backwards), when all they have to do is press J instead. For example, imagine that we have the following JavaScript code:

```
var foo = function(){
  bar()
};
```

If you wanted to make this a one-line file, move your cursor to the first line (it doesn't matter what column position it is within the line) and press J twice. You'll end up with the following:

```
var foo = function(){ bar() };
```

That doesn't seem like much of a fuss, especially when you consider that the alternative (even if you use other Vim commands) is still quite a lot of hassle and time-consuming. Let's say our cursor was at the start of the first line. We could achieve the same result in a more verbose fashion using 2GdOi<Backspace><Esc>jI<Backspace><Esc> (I won't bother breaking down that command, because, by now, you should be more than comfortable reading/ interpreting it), but I'm sure you'll agree it's a lot of extra work in comparison!

I hope you can now see how something as simple as removing a couple of line breaks can actually be quite time-consuming. (Imagine making that sort of change with a normal text editor like Notepad or TextEdit?) In fact, I'd contend it would take more time using Vim's standard commands than it would just moving the cursor around with the arrow keys and manually deleting all whitespace until the code was on one line. But that's why the J key is so useful.

Ranges

Some Vim commands allow execution against a specified range. Following are some sample scenarios in which you might make good use of ranges.

Copy and Paste

Imagine you have the following:

```
My first line
My second line
My third line
My fourth line
```

If you wanted to duplicate the first three lines at the end of the file (regardless of cursor position), you could use a range to handle this much more easily than if you were to use standard Vim commands by themselves. But before we look at the final solution, let's first see how we could do this without a range: ggVjjy4ggp.

That's an awful lot of steps. But with a range, this is made much easier, simpler, and, best of all, much more efficient! Our actual solution looks like the following :1,3t4. Let's break this command down into chunks, so that we can understand what we've written.

- :: Begin the command by entering the command prompt.

- 1,3: Specify a range (in this case, lines 1 to 3).

- t: Yank (copy) the lines specified by the range.

- 4: Paste the yanked content after the fourth line.

Deleting

Imagine you have the following content:

```
My first line
My second line
My third line
My fourth line
My fifth line
My sixth line
My seventh line
My eighth line
My ninth line
```

If we wanted to delete the lines 4 through to 7, the manual way to do this would be 4GVjjjd. That's approximately nine keystrokes! Compare that to using a range such as :4,7d, which is much simpler. Another way to do the same thing is to execute :4d 4, which tells Vim to start at line four and then delete four lines (starting with the current line).

Character-Level Edits

Although rare, there are a few occasions when some of the existing motions aren't as granular as we need them to be. I find the h and l motions (which are part of the Vim "home key" range: hjkl) to be really useful when I need very fine control over what I'm changing or deleting.

Imagine that I have the word *dogs* and that my cursor is positioned at the start of the word. I want to change the word from *dogs* to *rugs*. To do this using the standard w and e motions would mean changing the entire word, when, really, I only want to change the first two characters.

If I use the l motion, I can change just the first two characters of the word. For example, this would be the command: c2l. That command will delete the characters do and place me into INSERT mode, so that I can enter the replacement characters ru.

Because my example is so simplistic, I'm sure the preceding motions don't appear to be very useful. But if you have a very long word that requires a level of granular editing not possible via w or e, you'll soon realize how useful the h and l motions can be. Even with this simplistic example, the alternatives are longer and not as efficient as using character-level motions.

Loading External Content

A powerful feature of Vim is the ability to load content from another file by using the "read file" (:r) command. Imagine we have the following content:

```
a
b
c
d
```

If your cursor was on the third line (c) and you wanted to load the content from the file ~/Desktop/foo.txt into your file, running the following command would insert the content of that file on the line after the third:

```
:r ~/Desktop/foo.txt
```

You can also load a file's content into a specific line of your buffer, regardless of where your cursor currently sits, by specifying a range, as follows:

```
:0r ~/Desktop/foo.txt
```

In the preceding example, we use the range of 0 to insert the content at the very top of our buffer.

You may notice a problem when you try to load content from a Rich Text Formatted file (a file with the `.rtf` extension). In this instance, instead of the content you were expecting, it can display lots of weird content within the buffer, as it tries to convert the content into plain text formatting. To work around this issue, we can install the following plug-in: `https://github.com/vim-scripts/textutil.vim`, which can seamlessly convert the content to plain text.

Partial File Writing

If you want to write a specific section of your buffer to another file, you can do so by using the standard "write" command (`:w`) and providing it a range, in addition to the path to the file to write to:

```
:1,10 w ~/Desktop/foo.txt
```

In the preceding example, we're telling Vim to write the lines 1 to 10 from the current buffer to the file `foo.txt`.

You can also append lines to an existing file (instead of creating a new file or overwriting an existing file), by using the standard Unix redirection operator `>>`, like so:

```
:1,10 w >> ~/Desktop/foo.txt
```

Pasting from Within INSERT Mode

Back in Chapter 13, I ever so briefly touched upon a command without really explaining its primary function. The command I'm referring to is `<C-r>`, which, when executed in INSERT mode, will allow us to specify a register to pull content from.

Imagine that we have a buffer open with the content `Here is my content` and a numbered register (let's say the zero numbered register) with the word *funky* stored inside it. If I were already in INSERT mode and I wanted the content to read `Here is my funky content`, instead of manually typing the word *funky*, I could pull that content from the zero indexed register, using the `<C-r>0` command, without first having to exit INSERT mode.

Pasting Without Affecting the Register

When we looked at Vim's register feature way back in Chapter 6, we discovered that deleting content within the buffer could cause both the unnamed and numbered registers to update to hold that content, and this can cause us a slight workflow problem.

Now this might sound like I'm making a mountain out of a molehill, but I've seen enough people get tripped up by the scenario I'm about to describe that I feel it's worth looking at in more detail.

Imagine that you have yanked some text from your buffer, and you intend to replace some other content elsewhere in your buffer with this yanked text. When yanking content, it'll end up in three separate registers:

1. `""`: The unnamed register

2. `"0`: The numbered register

3. `"*`: The clipboard register

At this point, you'll go off and find the content you want to replace, and you might think to delete it first and then just run the paste (p) command, as you believe the previously yanked content to be stored in the "* register.

The problem we've just hit is that deleting content as we have in the sample scenario will replace the unnamed register and the clipboard register with the deleted content. So, when we paste from the clipboard, we don't get the expected result.

The simplest solution to this problem is not to delete the content but, rather, just directly replace the content by visually selecting it first and *then* pasting! That way, you can paste *over the top* of the content without affecting the clipboard register.

An alternative approach would be to change or delete the content into a specific named register ("ad1, which equates to "choose the "a named register and delete the current letter") and so avoids the clipboard register being accidentally updated.

Another alternative is just to delete as normal and remember to paste from the numbered register. (I personally hate this method, as I can never seem to remember what numbered register holds the content I want.)

Moving Between Found Items

When you use the f command, you specify the character you want it to locate on that specific line your cursor is currently on. If the character you're looking for appears multiple times on a single line, you can use the ; and , commands to move forward and backward between these multiple matches.

■ **Note**   You can also move a set number of characters when you specify a range. For example, 2f! will move the cursor to the second instance of an exclamation point on the current line.

Sorting

One feature of Vim I find myself neglecting a lot is its :sort command, which provides the ability to do basic alphanumerical sorting of content. Imagine that we have the following unsorted content:

```
5
3
1
7
2
```

Running the :sort command would sort our content, like so:

```
1
2
3
5
7
```

I personally find this feature most useful when working with CSS, because I like to keep my CSS properties in alphabetical order (to make it easier to find the setting I'm after). Imagine that we have the following CSS content:

```
h4 {
  font-size: 11px;
  margin: 15px;
  background: red;
}
```

If you select the content inside the brackets (using the vi{ command) and then run the :sort command, the result will be alphabetically sorted properties.

```
h4 {
  background: red;
  font-size: 11px;
  margin: 15px;
}
```

NORMAL Mode Commands in the Command Prompt

Vim provides us the ability to execute NORMAL mode commands directly from Vim's COMMAND-LINE mode. This is an incredibly powerful feature when used in the right situation, and if we were to consider writing our own Vim plug-in, it would allow us to automate certain tasks that would otherwise be impossible to achieve. We saw this used briefly in an earlier chapter alongside the global command (:g), but it's such a powerful feature that I wanted to revisit it again here. Let's imagine that we have the following content:

```
foo
bar
baz
```

If we wanted to add an exclamation point to the end of each line, the simplest way to do this would be to run the following command:

```
%normal A!
```

This tells Vim that our command should be applied to the entire buffer (%) and that we want to run commands as if we were in NORMAL mode and typing the keys ourselves. So, we tell Vim we want to append to the end of the line (A) with an exclamation point (!).

Repeat NORMAL Commands

Another example of using the :normal feature is to manually make a change and then repeat it over a visually selected range. So, again, imagine that we have the following content:

```
foo
bar
baz
```

If your cursor was placed on the first line, and you executed the command A!, we would see an exclamation point (!) placed at the end of that line. If we now wanted to duplicate that change over the other two lines, we could run the following command, which first selects the entire line we're interested in affecting, then selects an extra line down (Vj), and then triggers the repeat command via the COMMAND-LINE mode (:normal .), so that it affects the specified selection

```
Vj:normal .
```

Time-Based Undo

Vim can apply the concept of time when considering changes we want to undo (or redo). It does this via the :earlier and :later commands. On a basic level, these commands work on a state basis, meaning if you make three changes to a buffer and then run :earlier 2, Vim will revert two changes back, so only the first change is still applied.

For example, imagine you have the following content:

```
This is my content
```

If your cursor is at the start of the buffer and you execute the x command three times, the buffer will resemble the following state:

```
s is my content
```

If I execute :earlier 2, the buffer will then resemble the following state:

```
his is my content
```

Similarly, if at this point I decide to execute :later 2, the buffer will resemble the following state:

```
s is my content
```

These commands will also work on the basis of time, as long as we add the appropriate suffix to the count. For example:

- :earlier 5d (days)
- :earlier 1h (hours)
- :later 10m (minutes)
- :later 5s (seconds)
- :later 2f (file states; i.e., go back two buffer writes)

■ **Note** The time-based commands (d, h, m, s, f) are dependent on how long you've kept your session open.

Simultaneous Scrolling

It can sometimes be useful to scroll two (or more) separate windows at the same time, so that they move together line by line. Imagine that you're quickly scanning two different versions of the same file to see where they differ . . .

■ **Note**   I admit this isn't the best example, as that's exactly what `:vimdiff` is for. But, hey, let's just roll with this for now.

. . . In each window, you'll have to run the following command (you could use the `windo` command to make things easier, if you have lots of windows open):

```
:set scrollbind
```

This will cause Vim to keep the scrolling of these windows in sync with each other. To toggle the feature off, you would have to run the following command in each of the windows (or in only one of the windows, if you only had two split windows). Again, you can use the `windo` command to make this easier.

```
:set noscrollbind
```

■ **Note**   You may prefer to use `scb`, which is a shortcut for `scrollbind`.

Spell-Checking

Another useful feature of Vim, which shouldn't be surprising, as Vim is still ultimately considered a text editor, is the ability to spell-check.

■ **Note**   Vim provides a spell-checker only; meaning, it doesn't validate your grammar.

To turn on Vim's spell-checking feature, run the following command:

```
:setlocal spell spelllang=en_gb
```

The preceding command uses `:setlocal` to apply the `spell` command only to the current buffer. If you want to turn on spell-checking for all open buffers, swap it for `:set`. Also, feel free to change the language to something more appropriate to your native language (e.g., `en_us`).

To turn off spell-checking, run the following command:

```
:setlocal nospell
```

Spelling Mistake Indicators

When using Vim's spell-checking feature, you should note that Vim will highlight certain words in different colors (Figure 22-3). The colors depend on your theme and other color-based configuration settings (see `:h highlight-groups` for more information on how to change your Vim's color settings).

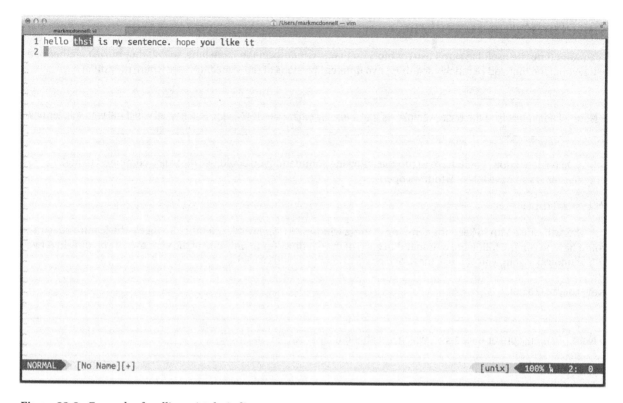

Figure 22-3. *Example of spelling mistake indicators*

With my own configuration, incorrectly spelled words are set to be highlighted with a red background and white text, and words that aren't properly capitalized are highlighted with a white background and red text.

The reason I chose those particular colors was that I wanted incorrectly spelled words (a very big concern when writing) to be bold and red, so that I couldn't miss them, whereas words that weren't correctly capitalized were something I wanted to be alerted to but wasn't as concerned with as misspelled words, so I reversed the colors.

In my .vimrc configuration (you'll have this also, if you're using the ProVim .vimrc configuration file), I configure the highlighting colors so that no matter what color scheme is being loaded, the custom colors I've set are guaranteed.

```
fun! SetSpellingColors()
  highlight SpellBad cterm=bold ctermfg=white ctermbg=red
  highlight SpellCap cterm=bold ctermfg=red ctermbg=white
endfun

autocmd BufWinEnter * call SetSpellingColors()
autocmd BufNewFile * call SetSpellingColors()
autocmd BufRead * call SetSpellingColors()
autocmd InsertEnter * call SetSpellingColors()
autocmd InsertLeave * call SetSpellingColors()
```

Spelling Suggestions

Vim also has a nice feature that suggests an alternative word for *any* word you highlight. (It doesn't matter if the word is misspelled.). For example, execute the z= command while your cursor is on top of the incorrectly spelled word tihs to have Vim suggest a list of alternative words (see Figure 22-4).

```
● ○ ○                        ⬆ /Users/markmcdonnell — vim
         markmcdonnell vi
Change "thsi" to:
 1 "This"
 2 "Thai"
 3 "Thais"
 4 "Thus"
 5 "These"
 6 "Those"
 7 "Three"
 8 "Thee"
 9 "Thigh"
10 "Phis"
11 "His"
12 "Tass"
13 "Thad"
14 "Than"
15 "That"
16 "Them"
17 "Then"
18 "Thin"
19 "Thom"
20 "Thud"
21 "Thug"
22 "Toss"
23 "Ohs"
24 "Psi"
25 "T's"
26 "Thy"
27 "Thaw"
28 "The"
29 "Theo"
30 "They"
31 "Thor"
Type number and <Enter> or click with mouse (empty cancels): █
```

Figure 22-4. *Vim spelling suggestions*

As you'll see, Vim displays a list of numerically ordered alternatives for you to choose from. You can then type the number of the word you want to use (or just press <CR> with a blank value to cancel the action).

Auto-complete Spelling Suggestions

If you enter INSERT mode and move your cursor anywhere inside the misspelled word, you can use the following command to trigger an auto-complete drop-down list, offering alternatives "as you type":

<C-x>s

Searching for Spelling Mistakes

Vim makes it easy to navigate through a long document filled with misspellings by providing the two following commands:

-]s: Move to the next misspelled word
- [s: Move to the previous misspelled word

Repeating Spelling Corrections

If you're like me, chances are you've made the same mistake over and over throughout your file. If that's the case, once you've used z= to fix a typo, you can then use the following command to repeat that same fix to the rest of the file automatically:

:spellr

. . . and the Rest?

Vim's spell-checking feature has many additional options and settings, so I would strongly recommend viewing the following help files for all the details:

:h spell

Renaming Multiple Files Inside Vim

In Chapter 11, we discussed a few different ways that we could efficiently execute "search and replace" functionality across multiple buffers. We initially used Vim's built-in bufdo command and then looked at a more efficient shell-based solution using the Unix sed command.

In this section, I want to take a look at how we can rename multiple files within Vim, not because it's a good idea, but as a mechanism to demonstrate some other features of Vim that you might not have seen yet. It also helps us to visualize how we can combine different types of Vim commands to create very powerful results.

This section is broken down in subsections, as it's quite a lengthy process to describe what's going on. I hope I'll be able to keep your focus long enough to explain the solution in its entirety.

■ **Note**   There is a rename command, which simplifies exactly this problem we're trying to solve. You can install this command on all major operating systems. For example, on Mac OS X, use brew install rename.

Expressions Inside a Substitution

Before we get started, I think it might be wise if I explain a command that will become *part* of the solution to our bigger problem. Let's imagine that we have a buffer that consists of ten empty lines, and we execute the following:

:let counter=0 | 4,7 g/^/let counter=counter+1 | s/^/\=counter/

What the preceding command will do is insert the numbers 1, 2, 3, and 4 onto lines 4, 5, 6, and 7 (one number per line; so, line 4 will have the number 1, line 5 will have the number 2, and so forth).

You have already seen most of what makes this command work (e.g., you learned about both the global and substitution commands back in Chapter 11), but what you might not be familiar with is the ability to pipe values through to multiple commands within COMMAND-LINE mode.

Let's break down the preceding command to see what's happening. (I would recommend testing the command within a buffer that has ten empty lines, as I described previously, so that you can properly understand the result of executing this command when reading through the explanation.)

- First, we define a counter variable that holds the value zero (let counter=0).

- Next, we pipe (i.e., pass) counter through to the following command, using the pipe character (|).

- We apply a search pattern to lines four to seven of our ten-line buffer. In this example, I've used a pattern that is guaranteed to match (i.e., we use the pattern /^/, which translates to "if this line has a start position, then there is a match"). We then update the counter value for each line.

- We pipe the result of the previous command through to the following command, again using the pipe character (|).

- At this point, we pass the substitute command four different values for counter (s/^/\=counter/), while also using the expression register to execute counter and, subsequently, return the value of the counter at that point for the substitution.

The two important points to take away from the breakdown is that, first, we can construct complex programs by piping the results of each program through to the next and, second, we can use the expression register within the substitution command to produce more dynamic modifications.

Sample Process

Let's consider a sample project that has three files, A.txt, B.txt, and C.txt, which we want to rename so that each file matches the following criteria:

- Is lowercase (e.g., A becomes a)

- Includes the current date (e.g., A.txt becomes a-2014-Aug-27.txt)

Most of the setup will be carried out inside of Vim, whereas renaming the files will be handled by the shell. We'll use the mv command, like so:

```
mv Original.txt New.txt
```

The solution involves us taking a line such as A.txt and converting it into mv A.txt a-2014-Aug-27.txt. To make it easier to understand, let's quickly break down the job into tasks, so that we know what we need to do.

- Load the list of files within Vim.

- Modify each file listed, so it uses the shell's mv command.

- Execute the content of the buffer as a shell script.

The entire solution is shown in the following list, after which I'll break down the individual parts, so that you can properly understand what's happening. (I'm sure that third step is looking mighty scary right about now!)

- :r! ls

- ggdd

- :%s/\v(\w)(\.txt)/mv & \L\1-\2/ | %s/\.txt$/\=strftime("%Y-%b-%d") . ".txt"/

- :w !sh

In the first step, we're utilizing the read (:r) command with the filter command (!) to pass the remaining arguments (ls) through to the shell (which, in this case, returns a list of files from the current directory).

When we read in the result of the ls command, the content is placed on the line *under* our cursor (so, in an empty buffer, the content will be placed on line 2). This means line 1 is effectively empty; we don't *need* to remove that empty line, but my OCD is kicking in, and I would like to see that empty line disappear, so I execute ggdd to handle that.

Some of you might be thinking, "Why not specify a range?" Yes, we could've done that (e.g., :0 r! ls) and had the content placed into the buffer, starting from line 1, but that would mean we would have an empty line at the end of the file instead, and my OCD would kick in again, so I decided to go with the more readable version and didn't bother to specify a range.

The third step is the real "meat and potatoes" of the work. This is what converts our list of file names into a fully constructed mv command. This step is itself a combination of two separate steps. You can see where the split is by looking for the pipe (|), which separates the two halves.

First Half . . .

In the first half, we execute a substitution command, which, you may remember from Chapter 11, has a basic form that looks like: s/{pattern}/{replacement}/. We provide the entire buffer for the range and use the "very magic" (\v) mode at the start of the substitution pattern, so that we don't have to escape the regular expression capturing parentheses (ultimately avoiding making this command any more complicated than it may already appear).

The pattern we search for is the file name, and we make sure we capture the file name and its extension as two separate entities.

Because we want to execute this file as a shell script, we need our list of files to look like a list of mv shell commands, so our replacement pattern does exactly that (mv & \L\1-\2), by writing out mv, followed by the entire result of the search pattern matched (&). This means that the & for the first line equates to A.txt and to B.txt for the second line, and so on.

So, at this point, we have constructed (for the first line) something that looks like mv A.txt, and now we have to finish the command, so that it has a name that represents the new file name, which has to look something like a-2014-Aug-27.txt.

The construction of the date is done in the second half (I'll come back to that). The converting of the file name to lowercase is where we bring in the use of a feature known as "pattern atoms" (see :h pattern-atoms for a list of all the available atoms).

The specific atom we've used in this example is \L, which effectively converts whatever follows it into lowercase. Remember: When writing our search pattern, we captured the file name and the extension as two separate entities; therefore, to access those within our replace pattern, we use the format \n (where n is the number of the capture group). This means that to lowercase the file name, we use \L\1.

The final part of this "first half" is to write out (as part of the replacement text) -\2, which equates to a hyphen followed by the content of the second capture group. In this case, \2 is the file extension (.txt).

This means that executing the code :%s/\v(\w)(\.txt)/mv & \L\1-\2/ has converted the following buffer content:

```
A.txt
B.txt
C.txt
```

into

```
mv A.txt a-.txt
mv B.txt b-.txt
mv C.txt c-.txt
```

As you can see, we're *almost* there, but not quite, because we don't have the dynamically generated date in place. This is where we move on to the second half of the solution.

Second Half . . .

Now, we could have executed the second half of this overall solution as a separate *step*, but I wanted to demonstrate how to use the pipe (|) operator, which allows us to construct complex commands from multiple smaller commands.

Let's just quickly refresh ourselves on what the second half of our solution looks like.

```
%s/\.txt$/\=strftime("%Y-%b-%d") . ".txt"/
```

We can see that we're again using the substitution command against the entire buffer (`%s/{pattern}/{replacement}/`), in which the pattern we're searching for is the file extension (`\.txt$`) at the end of the file.

Remember: At the moment, each line looks like this: `mv A.txt a-.txt`, so we can't just search for the pattern ".txt," as that would match in two places within one line, so we use the dollar anchor (`$`) to indicate that the `.txt` we're interested in is the one that is found at the end of the line.

For the replacement, we want to keep the `.txt` extension, but we have to prefix it with the current date, so that the replacement should look something like `2014-Aug-27.txt`. This is achieved by using the expression register (as we saw earlier in this chapter) `\={stuff} . ".txt"`, where `{stuff}` is replaced by some dynamic function call (in this case, to VimL's `strftime` function). The period (dot) character between `{stuff}` and `".txt"` is VimL's way of concatenating two different expressions.

This leaves us with the call to `strftime("%Y-%b-%d")`, which is what generates the current date for us. At this point, if you had your list of files read into Vim and you executed the full command `:%s/\v(\w)(\.txt)/mv & \L\1-\2/ | %s/\.txt$/\=strftime("%Y-%b-%d") . ".txt"/`, then you would see the buffer modified as we've described, ready to be executed within the shell.

Executing the Buffer As a Shell Script

Now that we have a buffer resembling a shell script, we want to pass that buffer over to the shell, to execute and, subsequently, cause the relevant files to be renamed as we need them to be.

As we can see, this is fairly straightforward to achieve by writing the buffer *not to a file location* but directly to the shell standard input (`:w !sh`).

■ **Note** An alternative way to execute the buffer as a shell script is to use `:% !sh`, which sends the entire buffer through to the shell. The benefit of this option is that you can also provide a range, instead of the entire buffer, and execute only the range.

Folder-Specific Custom Configuration

The `.vimrc` configuration file is the foundation of most Vim users. It allows us to tweak and modify how Vim works to a very granular level, and all from a centralized location that can be sync'ed easily with online services so as to allow for simple sharing of identical configuration across multiple machines.

But sometimes, we require Vim to work in a different way, depending on the project we're working on. For example, my Vim theme is dark, but while I was working on this book, I was required to use a light theme to help the images you see to stand out more, compared to the dark theme I like to use while I'm working. Now, I could have manually changed the theme, using the command `:colorscheme {some_light_theme}`, but it would have become quite annoying to change the theme manually every time I needed to switch when writing this book. So, instead, I decided to automate the process by loading a separate configuration file whenever I was inside my "ProVim" folder.

To do this, I needed a new configuration file, so I created one titled .vim.custom. (There was no real convention there, I just needed something that wasn't .vimrc.) I placed this file inside the directory ~/Projects/ProVim. The content of the file was simply :colorscheme Tomorrow (which is a light theme, and if you're using the ProVim configuration files, you'll already have this).

I then added the following VimL to my .vimrc file:

```
if filereadable(".vim.custom")
  source .vim.custom
endif
```

When Vim loads, it will check to see if the file .vim.custom is accessible, and if so, it'll source it. If you have very simple needs, perhaps this solution will work OK for you, but it is flawed. If I open Vim from within a subdirectory (such as ~/Projects/ProVim/Chapter22), the .vim.custom file won't be accessible, because it's located in the parent (ProVim) directory.

I've seen different types of workarounds to this issue, but they all suffer from the same problem of being unable to determine what the root directory is. There are many plug-ins available that attempt to resolve this issue in one way or another, and which one you choose can sometimes come down to what's the simplest to implement.

I personally use https://github.com/thinca/vim-localrc, which only requires me to add a .local.vimrc file, and the plug-in will intelligently figure out how to load it. The plug-in also works with multiple config files within different subdirectories and loads each of them sequentially. The following diagram illustrates this (files are loaded as indicated by their number):

```
Projects
└── ProVim
      ├── .local.vimrc (1)
      ├── Foo.txt
      └── Chapter1
            ├── .local.vimrc (2)
            ├── Bar.txt
            └── Version2
                  └── .local.vimrc (3)
                  └── Baz.txt
```

Summary

This chapter has covered a wide variety of topics with the aim of giving you a better idea of the different ways you can use familiar Vim features and uncover some really useful functionality (most of which I've stumbled across from simply reading the Vim manuals). Let's recap some of the items we've seen in this chapter.

- Vim's built-in file system explorer netrw (accessible via :Explore and :Sexplore, among other command variations) covers a lot of the functionality provided by the popular NERDTree plug-in.

- We went back and looked in more detail at how Vim can handle glob-based searches of files to edit (e.g. :e **/*.txt).

- We looked at Vim's built-in mappings for navigating "blocks" (i.e., %, [(, [), [{ and [}).

- Editing and deleting content is made easier by filtering through Vim's search command (e.g., d/{pattern}).

- I covered some smaller details of how to duplicate and move lines (simple tasks, but I wanted to briefly elaborate some of their nuances).

- You learned how to increment and decrement numerical values, using the mappings `<C-a>` and `<C-x>`.

- I demonstrated how a seemingly simple command such as `J` can be used to solve what would otherwise be a problem requiring a more complex solution.

- We looked at a couple of examples that demonstrate how ranges can make certain tasks (such as copy/paste and deleting) much easier and more efficient.

- I then moved on to explaining the benefits of potentially very granular edits, using character-level motions (e.g., changing the next two characters on the right of the cursor `c2l`).

- We took a look at how to read in external content, using the `:read` command, and how to write a partial selection of your buffer by specifying a range to your `:w` command. We also saw how you can *append* content using the `>>` operator.

- We saw how to paste content directly from a register while inside INSERT mode, in addition to how to paste content without affecting the current state of the register.

- Moving between search matches (using `/` and `?`) is made much easier with the motions `;` and `,`.

- Vim has a built-in sorting program (`:sort`) that makes certain tasks (such as working with CSS properties and keeping them in order) a lot easier, by automating what would otherwise be a manual process.

- Vim also has a powerful feature within COMMAND-LINE/Ex mode that allows us to utilize NORMAL mode commands as if they were being typed by the user.

- You discovered that Vim has a very rich conceptual understanding of time and provides a few different commands for helping to navigate through prior (and future) changes made to content (using `:earlier` and `:later`).

- You learned how to bind one (or more) split windows, to keep the scrolling of those files in sync. (This is a setting used by Vim when carrying out a diff analysis.)

- We dove into Vim spell-checking capabilities, and I demonstrated how you can change your `.vimrc` configuration file to ensure a consistent color highlighting experience when using Vim's spell-checker.

- I demonstrated a complex example of renaming multiple files that utilized a few different concepts, such as reading in content from the terminal shell and piping together multiple commands that include pattern atoms for manipulating matches and loading dynamic data into the replacement patterns, using Vim's expression register.

- Finally, you learned how to control Vim's settings and configurations on a folder-by-folder basis, first in a simplified form, and later with the help of a small plug-in.

CHAPTER 23

Terminal Multiplexer

The terminal emulators we use on a day-to-day basis do their job admirably. Having direct access to the shell environment is a fundamental way of life for most software engineers, as it gives us a sense of power and efficiency that cannot be matched by GUI-based applications and mouse interactions.

But even a reasonably modern terminal application can fall short in many areas (such as the Terminal.app on Mac OS X). As an example, imagine your terminal window is busy with a long-running process, and you want to interact with another part of your application or project (but you want to keep an eye on the current process, so that you know when it's finished). One way you could do this is to create a new terminal tab and simply switch back and forth. This isn't a very elegant solution or efficient, but it would work.

But some terminal emulators don't let you create tabs, so if you're one of those unfortunate souls, you'll have a worse option ahead of you, which is to use your mouse to reduce the size of your terminal and then open a new instance of your terminal application and resize that new instance so you can see both terminal windows at once (that is, if you even *have* a GUI; if you don't, then . . . well, you're *almost* out of luck).

Imagine a similar (but much more typical) example: you're a software engineer and you're writing new (or modifying existing) tests for your application. Ideally, you want to be able to make changes to your tests and application code while getting immediate feedback as to whether any of those changes have broken your test suite. You want a fast feedback loop. This is where being able to split your terminal window becomes a very useful tool.

But just being able to split a window into one or more screens isn't the only problem that has to be solved. Software engineers open many different types of files during a typical workday, and sometimes, you may find yourself in a situation in which the files you have open would be easier to read and modify if they were placed in a different layout that just wasn't possible using a standard terminal emulator.

In Figure 23-1, we can see we're not just splitting a terminal window into equal-sized chunks. We have window C, which spans the full width of the screen, while windows D, E, and F are a third of the overall screen, and windows A, B, G, and H split 50% of the available screen dimensions.

```
-------------------------------------
|   A        |    B       |
-------------------------------------
|            C            |
-------------------------------------
|  D   |   E   |   F      |
-------------------------------------
|   G        |   H        |
-------------------------------------
```

Figure 23-1. *Example of a complex layout of terminal windows*

We also want to be able to manipulate these windows very easily, through shorthand key bindings, and change their dimensions (and even change the layout of the windows, so that they are rearranged into a different format, to fit with the work we do later on in the day).

Humans are also creatures of habit, meaning that there will be a particular layout of windows that we find works best for us 90% of the time, and, so, being able to automate the creation of a particular layout is another feature that would be useful.

Finally, a tool that has the capability to allow me to share my screen seamlessly, so that I can pair program with another individual and have him/her take over the typing on my machine, is incredibly useful when you're a remote worker.

Having complete control over our terminal environment—how it looks and behaves—is a very powerful idea, and one that is possible through the use of an application called tmux. In the next section, I'll explain a little about what tmux is and means, as well as how to install and configure it.

■ **Note**   Some readers may have heard of a recent terminal emulator called iTerm2 (`http://iterm2.com` [for Mac OS X only]), which allows you to make split windows (among other features) but suffers from much less ubiquity than my tool of choice: tmux. For example, if I'm on a remote Linux server, I can quickly download and install tmux and be up and running. I can't do that with a program that is limited to a single operating system. As with Vim, ubiquity is the key.

---

tmux

tmux is short for [*t*]*erminal* [*mu*]*ltiple*[*x*]*er*. A multiplexer is simply a fancy way of describing an application that lets you easily manage multiple terminal windows within one screen.

tmux runs a server/client architecture, meaning that when you start the application, it will fire up a single server, and every tmux instance you create on your machine will ultimately connect to that single tmux server. The benefit of this design is that while your machine is running, you can *detach* a tmux "session" (i.e., close tmux but keep the details of that session open, as it'll be stored on the tmux server running in a background process), so you can then *reattach* to the session at another time.

■ **Note**   Visit `http://tmux.sourceforge.net/` for frequently asked questions and helpful information (such as documentation, IRC, and mailing list details), as well as to download binaries of the software.

---

tmux provides a lot of powerful features (most of which were described indirectly via the introduction of this chapter), which I've summarized into a few categories following:

- Ability to connect to existing local and remote sessions

- Advanced window and pane management

- Ability to move windows between different sessions

- Scripted automation

The usefulness of tmux truly reveals itself once you start utilizing it on a day-to-day basis and incorporating it firmly into your workflow. By the time we're finished, you should have a much better understanding of the power and flexibility tmux provides and will wonder how you ever managed without it.

Terminology

Let's take a brief detour to consider the terminology we'll be using to describe tmux's functionality. This will help to understand different tmux concepts as we move through the following chapters.

Prefix Command

The purpose of a multiplexer is to help you load multiple programs within a single window. Because you are effectively loading a program *within* a program (e.g., loading Vim inside a tmux window), tmux must avoid command conflicts with the subprograms being loaded. To do this, it introduces the concept of a prefix command, which helps to differentiate tmux commands from other programs you use.

▪ **Note**   The default prefix for tmux commands is <C-b>.

Let's take a look at a quick example, to clarify what the prefix command does and why. I appreciate that we have yet to even open tmux, but the concept of a prefix key is fundamental to using tmux in the first place, and so I'm hoping you'll indulge me for just a moment longer, while I attempt to explain it.

Imagine we have tmux running, and for those who have never seen tmux before, you'll likely not notice much difference in your terminal's appearance (other than a bar at the foot of your screen, but I'll come back to this and describe what the bar is and what it means later), because visually, tmux should act as a container *around* your terminal.

Now, let's say we want to open a text file within Vim (e.g., vim ~/foo.txt) and modify the content by deleting a specific selection. Chances are you would open the file in Vim, find the content you want to delete, select it, and execute the d command. The problem with this process is that tmux assigns its own functionality to the d key (a command for detaching from a session; again, if this doesn't make sense, don't worry too much for now, as I'll cover sessions in due time). This is a perfect example of why tmux commands have a prefix: to avoid conflicts with other programs loaded within a tmux screen.

Due to tmux commands having a prefix, we can safely use Vim (or any other program) and not have to worry that executing a command within our subprograms will cause a side effect in tmux. In the previous scenario, we would detach from our tmux session using the command <C-b>d (where <C-b> is the prefix, followed by the d to indicate we wish to *detach* from the session).

Throughout the rest of the book, I'll refer to the prefix key <C-b> as just <P> (for [P]*refix*). This means the structure of all tmux commands in this book will take the form <P>{key-binding|:command-prompt}. In the preceding example, in which we detached from the tmux session using the key binding <C-b>d, we would represent this using <P>d (see the following note regarding the "command prompt").

▪ **Note**   tmux provides a "command prompt" (similar in ways to Vim's COMMAND-LINE/Ex modes), which you can access by using <P>:, followed by a command. For example, <P>:{command}.

The reason for shortening the prefix command in the following chapters is, first, to make the commands shorter and easier to read, but more important, I'll be showing you how you can change the prefix key to be any key combination you like. So if you end up using this book as a reference, and you happen to have changed the prefix to be something else (let's say <C-a>), it would be easier to mentally replace <C-b> with your own prefix.

Help?

Unfortunately, if you need help with tmux commands, you don't have as rich a support feature as Vim's built-in `:help` documentation, but there are still a few options available to you, which are useful to know about.

Command and Key Binding References

tmux provides a quick reference list of all available key bindings, which you can access either via a key binding or the command-line prompt (or even from outside tmux itself).

To access the key binding reference via a key binding, you would use `<P>?`. To access this reference via the command prompt, you would use `<P>:list-keys`. Finally, you can also access this list from *outside* of tmux, using `tmux list-keys` (allowing you to utilize this information in some form of scripted automation, which I'll cover in more detail in Chapter 28).

The `list-keys` command will only display a list of available tmux key bindings. This does not include all commands that are executable within the tmux command prompt. For that list, you would use `<P>:list-commands` (or `tmux list-commands`, if you're outside of tmux); there is no key binding variation.

If you would like to see some extra information regarding each of the tmux sessions you have open, the following command will display this information for you: `<P>:info` (or `tmux info`, if you're outside of tmux).

Manual

Although the Internet has lots of useful information about how to do certain things in tmux, ultimately, the best resource of documentation is the official manual, which is linked to from the tmux web site and is directly accessible at `www.openbsd.org/cgi-bin/man.cgi/OpenBSD-current/man1/tmux.1`.

Alternatively, and more usefully, you can access this documentation via your terminal, using the command `man tmux` (which also makes it much easier to filter and search through).

Message Feedback

One annoyance with tmux is when you execute a command incorrectly. What you'll notice happen is that tmux *tries* to be helpful by displaying a message telling you the correct format of the command it thinks you were trying to execute. But, unfortunately, that message only displays for a fraction of a second and then disappears, not leaving you enough time to see what the requirements of the command actually are.

Luckily, tmux provides a key binding that shows us the complete list of messages tmux has passed to us during our current session (the list of messages is displayed in ascending order, so the oldest messages are at the top, and the most recent at the bottom): `<P>~`. (You can also access this feature via the command prompt `<P>:show-messages`.)

Installation and Configuration

I mentioned earlier that one of the benefits of using tmux over other solutions is its ubiquity across different platforms. Installing tmux is remarkably simple for such a powerful and distributed piece of software, as we can see in the following options.

Mac

To install tmux on Mac OS X, the simplest option is to use the popular Homebrew package manager (`http://brew.sh/`):

```
brew install tmux
```

Linux

If you're working from a Linux machine, then use your package manager of choice (e.g. Apt, Yum etc). For example, if you're using Apt then you would run the following command:

```
sudo apt-get install tmux
```

> ■ **Note** At the time of writing, the majority of package managers only have version 1.8 available. If you wish to install a more recent version of tmux then you'll need to modify your package manager to point to another registry where tmux can be acquired. As an example, for Apt you would first execute `add-apt-repository ppa:pi-rho/dev` followed by `apt-get update` and finally executing the install command `apt-get install tmux`

Windows

If you're on a Windows machine, you can install tmux as a Cygwin package.

> ■ **Note** If Cygwin is already installed, you'll have to rerun `setup.exe` and make sure to select the tmux package.

Configuring tmux

tmux can be configured to work however you require it to. You can change the way it looks, the key bindings it uses, and many different additional optional settings. This configuration is primarily handled by a `.tmux.conf` file, usually placed within your $HOME directory (e.g., ~/ but can be moved using a symlink).

If you used the ProVim repository from the start of the book (we cloned it as part of our terminal/Vim setup), you'll find a `.tmux.conf` file already created and populated with useful default settings. When we come to opening tmux for the first time, you should see something similar to Figure 23-2.

Figure 23-2. *Expected tmux view, if using the ProVim configuration file*

If you haven't used the configuration file from that project, let's take a look at it now, so that you can understand what we're using (and what I'll assume you have in place as well). After, I'll break down what each set of settings does, so that you can decide if you would like to use/keep them or not.

■ **Note** It may actually be better to skip this section until you've reached the end of the book. That way, you'll have more experience with the features of tmux to make a judgment about what settings you want to keep within your own configuration. There is no harm, however, in reading through this now, if you're interested!

```
unbind C-b
set -g prefix C-Space

bind-key L last-window

bind-key -r h select-pane -L
bind-key -r j select-pane -D
bind-key -r k select-pane -U
bind-key -r l select-pane -R
```

```
bind-key Up     select-pane -U
bind-key Down   select-pane -D
bind-key Left   select-pane -L
bind-key Right  select-pane -R

bind-key v split-window -h
bind-key s split-window -v

bind-key r source-file ~/.tmux.conf

bind-key -n C-k clear-history

bind-key < resize-pane -L 5
bind-key > resize-pane -R 5
bind-key + resize-pane -U 5
bind-key - resize-pane -D 5
bind-key = select-layout even-vertical
bind-key | select-layout even-horizontal

set -g default-terminal "screen-256color"

set-window-option -g utf8 on
set -g status on
set -g status-utf8 on

set-option -g status-keys vi

setw -g mode-keys vi

set -sg escape-time 0

set-option -g allow-rename off

set-option -g default-shell /bin/zsh

set -g base-index 1

set -g history-limit 30000

set-option -g renumber-windows on

set -g status-right '#[fg=colour234,bg=white,nobold,nounderscore,noitalics] ◀#[fg=colour250,
bg=colour234] %a #[fg=colour247,bg=colour234] ◁#[fg=colour247,bg=colour234] %b %d ◁ %R #[fg=colour252,
bg=colour234,nobold,nounderscore,noitalics]#[fg=red,bg=colour234] ◀#[fg=white,bg=red] #H'
set -g status-bg white
set -g status-justify 'left'
set -g pane-border-fg white
set -g pane-active-border-fg red
set -g message-bg red
set -g message-fg white
setw -g window-status-separator '  '
setw -g window-status-current-format '#[fg=colour231,bg=colour31,bold] #I ▷ #W #[fg=colour31,
bg=white,nobold,nounderscore,noitalics]▶'
```

> ■ **Note** In the preceding code snippet you'll notice some some symbols that we use to help improve the design of our tmux status bar, such as ◀ and ▷. If you were to look at the .tmux.conf file on GitHub (https://github.com/ Integralist/ProVim/blob/master/.tmux.conf) you'll likely see a different symbol. This is because the display of the icon will depend on whether you have UTF-8 enabled and the relevant font installed. The font you need is Ubuntu Mono derivative Powerline.ttf and you can download this font from the ProVim GitHub configuration.

Change the Default Prefix

In the following code snippet, we're changing the default prefix command to <C-Space>. This is an important setting that I personally find makes a positive difference in my use of tmux.

I typically find that on a laptop (and certain external keyboards), the default prefix of <C-b> is too awkward to use on a day-to-day basis. I've tried many variations, such as <C-a>, and even just `, as my prefix key, but none of them was as comfortable as <C-Space>. (This also means, as I'm a heavy Vim user, that my little finger is conveniently placed on the <Ctrl> key ready for a <C-w> command to be fired off.)

```
unbind C-b
set -g prefix C-Space
```

As you can see, we're first unbinding the default prefix <C-b>, then we're resetting the prefix globally (-g) to <C-Space>.

Quick Access to Last Window

If you find yourself jumping around different tmux windows a lot, you'll realize the benefit of a simple binding, such as the following code snippet demonstrates, which lets you quickly jump back to the last window you were just in (saving you from having to remember the identifier number of the window).

I'll cover what "windows" and "panes" mean in the context of tmux (and how they work), in the following chapters, so don't worry too much about them now. If it helps, just think of windows as equivalent to Vim tabs, and panes as equivalent to Vim split windows.

```
bind-key L last-window
```

Vim Style Movements

The following code snippet allows me to use similar bindings to Vim's home row keys when moving to and from different panes. I actually don't use these bindings that much, as I prefer to use the arrow keys (see the following section).

```
bind-key -r h select-pane -L
bind-key -r j select-pane -D
bind-key -r k select-pane -U
bind-key -r l select-pane -R
```

Again, we're using tmux's bind-key function to create the custom binding of <P>{h|j|k|l}, and those bindings end up running tmux's select-pane function, with its corresponding flag to indicate the direction of the pane to be selected.

The -r flag tells tmux that the command is allowed to be recursive. This simply means that when the prefix command is hit, and the user then presses one of the keys h, j, k, or l, he/she can press one of those keys *again*, to cause the action to be triggered one more time.

■ **Note** The amount of times you can press on a custom key binding that has been set to "recursive" depends on the repeat-time configuration (default value is 500ms). See the tmux manual for more information.

In other words, if I had three tmux panes (with my focus being on the pane farthest left of the screen), and I wanted to move to the one farthest right, then I could execute <P>ll (thus moving two panes to the right), and this would be more efficient than executing <P>l<P>l.

Arrow Movements

The following bindings I use a lot! I find these much more useful and efficient than executing the relevant select-pane commands within tmux's command prompt (that would become hideously tedious).

```
bind-key Up    select-pane -U
bind-key Down  select-pane -D
bind-key Left  select-pane -L
bind-key Right select-pane -R
```

Simpler Pane Creation

I don't use the following key bindings any more. I used to use them a lot, but I found myself getting caught out when working from a tmux configuration that wasn't my own (e.g., remote server work or pair programming with a colleague), and so I decided it was just easier to memorize the default <P>" and <P>% command (we'll see these bindings again in later chapters).

```
bind-key v split-window -h
bind-key s split-window -v
```

Source .tmux.conf

I don't use the following binding very often, but it is handy to have included in your configuration, as it makes it very quick and easy to reload your .tmux.conf file, if you've made a change to it.

```
bind-key r source-file ~/.tmux.conf
```

Clear Pane History

I would say that I've probably used this feature once in my entire tmux career! I've included it here simply for the sake of completeness (as you may find the need for it that I never did). The binding does exactly what you might expect: the current pane has its command history removed.

```
bind-key -n C-k clear-history
```

Easier Pane Management

Being able to easily resize panes (you'll notice we use the `resize-pane` function and pass through a default of five columns/rows) and balance out my layouts (I'll explain this in a moment) are essential tools for my day-to-day workflow.

```
bind-key < resize-pane -L 5
bind-key > resize-pane -R 5
bind-key + resize-pane -U 5
bind-key - resize-pane -D 5
bind-key = select-layout even-vertical
bind-key | select-layout even-horizontal
```

The last two bindings use tmux's `even-vertical` and `even-horizontal` layout feature, to help balance the many panes you might have open, so that they have equal distribution (i.e., each pane is made the same size).

For example, take a look at Figure 23-3, which demonstrates what a typical tmux session might look like (many different sized panes open), then take a look at Figure 23-4, to see what the `even-vertical` command does to that layout. Finally, take a look at Figure 23-5, to see what the `even-horizontal` command does to the layout.

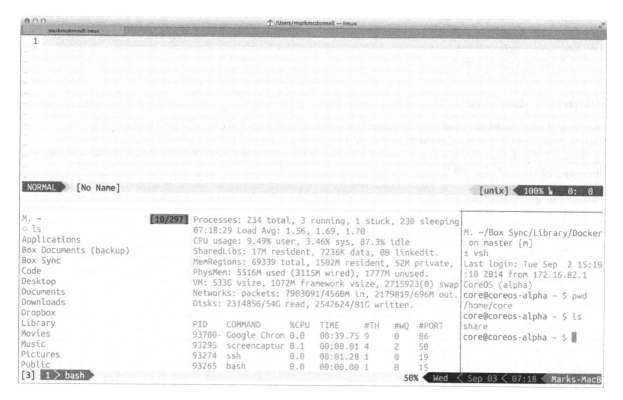

Figure 23-3. *A typical tmux session, with multiple panes open*

As you can see from Figure 23-3, we have multiple panes open (again, I'll cover how to create panes soon enough in another chapter), which utilize a different process in each pane.

The top pane has Vim open, and the bottom left pane is displaying the result of running the ls command, while the bottom middle pane is displaying the result of running the top command (and so it isn't static content but updates regularly, as you would expect). The last pane is an SSH session into a CoreOS Linux box I have built on my laptop (made available by the use of Vagrant, which is a tool for allowing quick and easy creation of reproducible development environments—www.vagrantup.com/).

In Figure 23-4, we can see the result of the key binding <P>=, which actually triggers tmux's select-layout function, and we pass it the value of even-vertical. You should also notice that the result is panes that are vertically stacked evenly on top of each other (as even-vertical suggests).

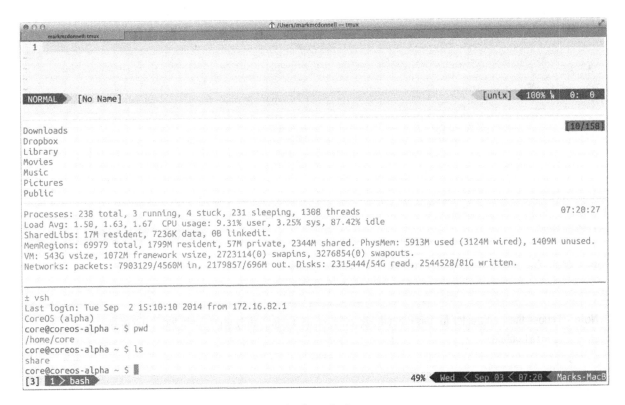

Figure 23-4. *The same tmux session with even-vertical applied*

■ **Note** I chose the = character for this custom key binding, as it adequately represents the result of the even-vertical option.

In Figure 23-5, we can see the result of the key binding <P>|, which actually triggers tmux's select-layout function, and we pass it the value of even-horizontal. You should also notice that the result is panes that are horizontally stacked evenly next to each other (as even-horizontal suggests).

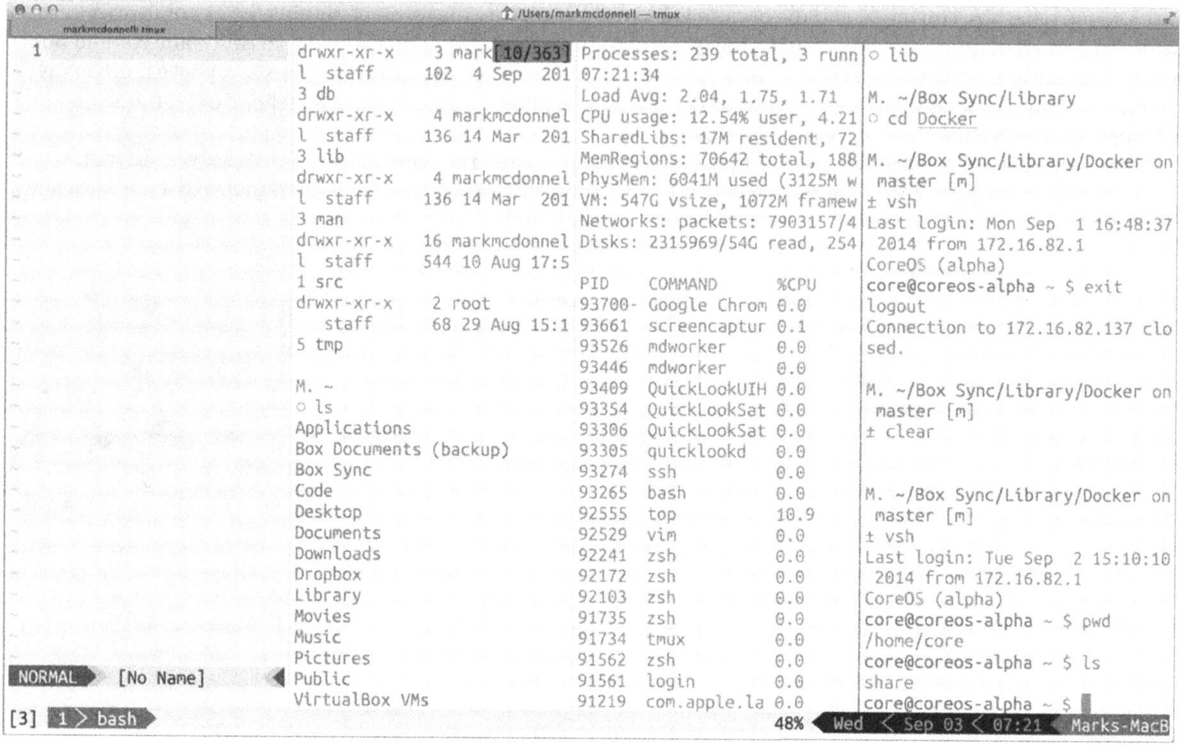

Figure 23-5. *The same tmux session with even-horizontal applied*

■ **Note** I chose the | character for this custom key binding, as it adequately represents the result of the even-horizontal option.

Color Correction

To ensure that tmux uses the correct color profile, we can inform tmux what the color support is for our terminal emulator application, by changing the value of the default-terminal option to be a derivative of "screen," in this case, that our terminal supports 256 colors.

Although I have this setting in place, it's strictly not needed, as the default value for the TERM environment variable will ensure that tmux loads the right color profile (but only certain versions of Mac OS X have 256-color support, so you may have to tweak this value to suit your OS requirements).

```
set -g default-terminal "screen-256color"
```

Enable utf8

In the opening chapters of this book, we used special fonts for configuring our Vim status bar. We use these same fonts to control the look of our tmux status bar (see the "Change the Status Bar Appearing" section, following), and because of this, if we don't enable utf8 support in tmux, those characters won't display properly in the tmux status bar.

```
set-window-option -g utf8 on
set -g status on
set -g status-utf8 on
```

Command Prompt Movements

The `status-key` option lets us modify how we move our cursor around while typing within the tmux command prompt (e.g., the command prompt is accessed using `<P>:`), meaning, if we set the value to `vi`, we can utilize some basic Vi motions.

If we enter the command prompt and type some text (or, more appropriately, some tmux commands), we can press `<Esc>` and then use some basic Vi style motions, such as `w`, `e`, and `b`, to move around, and `i`, to start typing again.

```
set-option -g status-keys vi
```

Cancel Immediately

I like to set the `escape-time` setting to zero, so that anytime I press `<Esc>`, that action is triggered immediately. If I don't have this setting, tmux will wait a fraction of a second to make sure that `<Esc>` isn't being executed as part of a sequence of commands.

```
set -sg escape-time 0
```

Prevent Program Window Renaming Trigger

tmux tries to be helpful by renaming the window tab to represent the process that is currently running. I don't like that behavior, as I prefer to manually rename my window tabs (I'll cover how to do this in an upcoming chapter).

As an example, if I were in a normal directory, the window tab would be renamed to `Zsh`, to represent that I'm in a shell environment. If I were to start up a Pry session (Pry is a Ruby `CLI REPL` tool), because I use JRuby (a Java implementation of the Ruby programming language), then the underlying process would be Java, and so my window tab would be renamed `java`.

After disabling this setting, if I manually rename my window tab to `Foo`, then no matter what I do or open in that window, the window tab will continue using the same name that I gave to it.

```
set-option -g allow-rename off
```

Change the Default Shell

This is a setting I don't necessarily need to have, but I like to be explicit and keep it in. The default value is determined by the `SHELL` environment variable, which for me (and you, if you followed the terminal setup from the beginning of this book) is set to `/bin/zsh` anyway and means that for all new windows you open in tmux, it will use that shell as its default.

```
set-option -g default-shell /bin/zsh
```

Human Numbering

All tmux windows (by default) are indexed from zero, which I find highly irritating, as there is no reason for it to be that way. This setting fixes this problem, by forcing tmux to index windows by starting from the number one.

```
set -g base-index 1
```

Increase Scroll-back

When scrolling tmux's screen buffer (don't worry if you don't understand what that means right now, as I'll cover it in the next chapter), we can't keep scrolling forever. There is a limit of 2000 buffer lines that tmux will store in its history. Certain processes can easily produce output that exceeds this limit, meaning we will find ourselves scrolling through a large stack trace error, and we'll stop halfway through the output, as we can't scroll back any further in the buffer's history. To resolve this issue, we can increase this limit, using the `history-limit` option.

```
set -g history-limit 30000
```

Automatic Window Renumbering

You'll see in an upcoming chapter how to create new windows, and in doing so, you'll notice that tmux automatically numbers each window (starting from the `base-index`). If we had three windows open, then the windows would be numbered 1, 2, and 3 (with the assumption that the `base-index` option was set to 1).

If we removed the second window, the default result would be two remaining windows, numbered 1 and 3. But with the `renumber-windows` option turned on, this would mean tmux could automatically renumber the windows to 1 and 2.

```
set-option -g renumber-windows on
```

Change the Status Bar Appearing

It seems the first thing most tmux users want to do is to configure the appearance of their tmux status bar. It is the source of a lot of information, and so I can appreciate that users are passionate about getting it to look perfect for their needs.

In Figure 23-6, we can see what the tmux status bar will look like when using the `.tmux.conf` provided by the ProVim configuration. Let's take a moment to review the different parts of the status bar that we've styled.

Figure 23-6. *The tmux status bar redesigned by our `.tmux.conf` configuration*

- `[test]`: This is the name of the tmux session.

- `1 > zsh`: This indicates there is one window running a Zsh shell.

- `83%`: This is my battery percentage.

- `Wed < Sep 03 < 17:54`: This is the current date and time.

- `Marks-MacB`: This is the name of my computer.

Following is the relevant code inside the `.tmux.conf` file that creates this status bar:

```
set -g status-right '#[fg=colour234,bg=white,nobold,nounderscore,noitalics] ◀#[fg=colour250,bg=colour234]
%a #[fg=colour247,bg=colour234] ◁#[fg=colour247,bg=colour234] %b %d ◁ %R #[fg=colour252,bg=colour234,
nobold,nounderscore,noitalics] ◀#[fg=red,bg=colour234]
≤ #[fg=white,bg=red] #H'
set -g status-bg white
set -g status-justify 'left'
set -g pane-border-fg white
set -g pane-active-border-fg red
set -g message-bg red
set -g message-fg white
setw -g window-status-separator '  '
setw -g window-status-current-format '#[fg=colour231,bg=colour31,bold] #I ▷ #W #[fg=colour31,
bg=white,nobold,nounderscore,noitalics]▶'
```

■ **Note**   The battery percentage you see in Figure 23-6 is a custom setting that I've not included within the ProVim setup, because it requires an external script that has been untested on Linux/Windows. For more details, visit https://github.com/richo/battery/.

Summary

So, this introduction to tmux has been quite fast-paced. I hope you're now even more excited to reach the upcoming chapters and discover more about how to use tmux. With your custom configuration in place, you can move on to learning some of the more practical uses of tmux. Let's quickly recap some of the things we've seen so far.

- We began by considering some of the failures of standard terminal emulators and how tmux can help solve those issues.

- I explained the meaning behind the name *tmux* and what the architecture pattern is (i.e., a server/client model), including the ability to attach, detach, and reattach to preexisting sessions.

- Next, I covered the tmux terminology (such as the prefix command), so you have a clear language to help you understand the upcoming chapters.

- I also briefly covered the different ways you can get help with tmux.

- Last, we looked at installing and configuring tmux, followed by a breakdown of the ProVim tmux configuration file.

CHAPTER 24

■ ■ ■

Fundamentals

In the previous chapter, we became acquainted with the concept of tmux and what this program could offer us in the way of resolving some standard terminal emulator annoyances. In this chapter, we're going to start using tmux and investigate some of its different constructs and terminology, such as the following:

- Sessions
- Buffers
- Panes
- Windows

By the end of this chapter, you'll know enough about tmux to be a confident user and start integrating it into your workflow. There will still be much more to learn (and after this chapter, we'll start to investigate tmux's other features), but for now, consider what you learn here to be an essential and solid foundation upon which we'll be building.

Sessions

tmux is designed around the idea of a "client-server" model (this introduces three new terminologies: client, server, and session), and this means that when we start tmux (from our terminal application), we're effectively using the tmux *client*. The client will attempt to create a new *session* on the tmux *server*, and if a server doesn't exist, one will be started up in a background process to which our client can connect.

Within a session, we can do anything we could do normally within the terminal environment. The only difference is that, now, all our activity is recorded within a tmux session.

Let's consider a quick example that demonstrates why sessions are so useful. We start work in the morning by opening a new tmux session. In this session, we'll be working on our company's latest project, "X." But after lunch, we realize that although we're not quite finished with what we needed to get done, we have to jump onto an older project, "A," so we can fix some critical bug. In this scenario, we currently have quite a few tmux "windows" and "panes" open (I'll explain these features later on in this chapter, but for now, consider them similar to tabs and split windows in Vim parlance). It would be nice if we could keep our entire working environment in place, so that we can move on to this other project, and then when done with "A," we can come back and reinstate the entire "X" environment exactly as we left it.

This type of scenario occurs more often than you probably realize, and although there are ways to work around it without the use of tmux, they're not as elegant (as you'll see). The reason we have this power to detach and attach sessions at our leisure is because of tmux's client-server model, which means that while our computer is running, the tmux server will stay alive (thus keeping open all the different sessions we've created).

Creating a Session

To create a new tmux session, we run the `tmux` command from our terminal application. Doing this will create and connect to a new session that is automatically named by tmux (unless you provide a name; see Figure 24-1).

Figure 24-1. *Example of a new tmux session (automatically numbered)*

■ **Note**   tmux sessions are named numerically by default. So if you run `tmux`, it will create a session whose identifier is 0. If you were to run the `tmux` command again in another terminal, the next session would be identified as session 1 (and so forth).

To help distinguish between different sessions you have running, you can give them a descriptive name. To do this, you can run the following command:

```
tmux new -s my_session
```

In the preceding example, we use the `-s` flag to indicate that we want to give the session we're about to create the name "my_session." When you start a new session, you are automatically connected to it, but you can start new sessions and not connect, by adding the -d flag, which indicates a "detached" state, as follows:

```
tmux new -s my_session -d
```

Listing Sessions

When you have multiple sessions open, it can be hard to remember them all, so tmux provides a complete list of every session you have created. To view the session list (Figure 24-2), you can run one of the following commands:

- `tmux ls` (from outside tmux)

- `<P>:list-sessions` (from inside a current tmux session)

Figure 24-2. *Example of listing current sessions (inside tmux)*

When using the latter command, the list will be displayed within the current tmux pane. To close the list, simply press `<CR>`.

Selecting a Session

If you have multiple sessions open and you want to jump around the different sessions currently available, tmux makes this very easy, by providing not only commands that can be executed via the command prompt but also custom key bindings. (Admittedly, I personally don't have much need for this type of feature, but, hey, it's interesting nonetheless, I think).

The following command will list all available sessions and allow you to use the arrow keys to navigate the list and select the session you wish to move to, by pressing `<CR>` when your cursor is placed on the relevant session you want to open (see Figure 24-3 for the output):

`:choose-session`

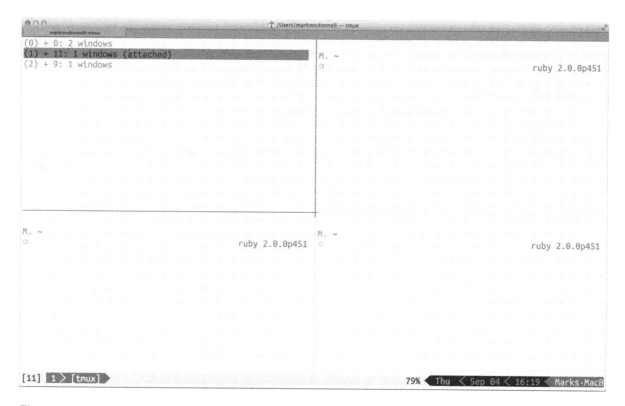

Figure 24-3. *Example of running* `:choose-session` *inside a single pane*

■ **Note**   The current session is automatically highlighted.

The following key bindings will also allow you to move through all sessions sequentially:

- `<P>(`: Move to next session
- `<P>)`: Move to previous session

Renaming Sessions

Most of the time, when I create a new session, I'm being lazy (and/or forgetful), and I won't specify a name for my session. When I come back to look at what sessions I have open (so I know what session I want to go back to), it can be tricky to determine what session holds what project, if they're all just numerically identified.

In such instances, it can be helpful to rename your sessions, so that they become more descriptive of what they hold. This can be done while inside of tmux, using the `<P>$` command. Doing so will drop you into tmux's command prompt, allowing you to enter a new name.

> ■ **Note** You can access this feature from the command prompt by using `<P>` and then typing `:rename-session -t {current_id} {new_id}`. You can also access this feature (as with other command prompt-based commands) from outside tmux, using `tmux rename-session -t {current_id} {new_id}`.

Closing vs. Detaching

Because tmux uses a client-server model, we can close our client but still keep the session open and running. There are a couple of commands that are easily mixed up (a command to detach from the session and another for actually closing the session). They may be similar, but they do have subtle but very important differences that you need to be aware of.

- If you have multiple panes open, executing `exit` or `<C-d>` within the terminal shell (for that pane) will cause the pane to be closed. (If you have multiple panes open, then the remaining panes will stay open until you run the same command within those panes).

- If you only have one pane open within a window, executing `exit` or `<C-d>` within the terminal shell (for that pane) will cause the pane/window to be closed. If you have only one window, the entire session will be closed. (If you have multiple windows open, only that window will be closed).

- Executing `<P>d` from any pane or window will cause the tmux client to detach from the current session.

Application Bootstrap

tmux also allows us to create a new session and have it start up automatically inside a program of our choosing. The following command demonstrates how we can start a new session that automatically opens Vim:

```
tmux new -s my_session vim
```

> ■ **Note** This only works with a single application. This means you can't specify multiple programs to be opened, without using more advanced automation commands (which we'll see in Chapter 28) as tmux doesn't know how to handle multiple programs. For example, if there were two programs specified — `tmux new vim top` — then tmux won't know how to load both of them (`vim` and `top`).

Buffers

When you establish a tmux session, you're presented with a *viewport* to the standard terminal screen. Effectively, it doesn't look like much has changed (if it weren't for the tmux status bar now appearing at the bottom of the screen). This viewport is referred to as a *buffer* (specifically an "output buffer"). What this means is that any information presented to you is actually farmed off to `stdout`, which, in this case, is your terminal screen.

Scrolling the Buffer

Because this is just a viewport, if there was too much information to display and it didn't fit in your current screen, it would appear "off screen," and you would have to scroll back up the screen to see the content you missed. For us to scroll the buffer so that we can see the additional content that didn't fit our screen, we have to execute a command that puts us into tmux's "copy mode," as follows:

```
<P>[
```

■ **Note**   Just to reiterate, as all key binding commands can also be accessed via the command prompt, so copy mode can be accessed by executing <P>:, followed by typing copy-mode.

You'll know when you're in copy mode by the fact of tmux displaying a counter in the top right of the screen (Figure 24-4). This counter will look something like [0/28441] (it'll change depending on context).

Figure 24-4. *tmux in copy mode, indicated by top-right scroll position*

To explain what the counter represents, let's consider the preceding example. In the example, I ran the command tree, to display the tree structure of all files and folders within my $HOME directory. This means there is lots of content that is impossible to fit onto a single screen, and so it appears outside the screen viewport. When I entered into copy mode, it displays the counter [0/28441], which tells us that there are currently 28441 buffer lines that have scrolled off the screen. The first number (0 in this case) is the current offscreen line.

That might not make much sense, so let's demonstrate what I mean by that explanation. At the moment, while in copy mode, I'm at the bottom of the visible buffer. There are 28441 lines of the buffer currently offscreen. If I use the up arrow key to move up the buffer, the first number will stay set to 0, until I reach the top of the viewport. Once my cursor moves one line *beyond* the viewport, you'll see that the number zero changes to 1, and then for every line after that I go upward, it increases, until I reach the top of the buffer itself, where the number will stop at 28441 (as I've reached the top of the offscreen buffer content).

Navigating Copy Mode

You can navigate the copy mode by using both arrow keys, as well as the standard Vim key bindings `hjkl`. If you want to jump directly to a specific offscreen line, use the following command: `:{line_number}`. So if you wanted to jump to the 50th line outside the viewport, you would execute `:50`.

■ **Note**   This command doesn't require the prefix, so it's not `<P>:50` but, literally, consists of pressing `:`, followed by the line number (while in copy mode).

You can also use familiar Vim bindings such as gg and G to move to the top and bottom, respectively, of the buffer content. The tmux copy mode also provides both a forward and backward search facility similar to Vim, as follows:

- `/{search_phrase}` = search *forward* through the buffer
- `?{search_phrase}` = search *backward* through the buffer

To exit copy mode you can press either one of the following keys:

- `<CR>`
- `q`

Panes

In tmux, the "panes" feature works in a similar way to how split windows work within Vim. It effectively splits the current viewport into subsections. Each split of the screen is referred to as its own *pane* and contains a new shell instance for us to work from.

When tmux connects to a session, you will note that you begin with a single window (and, thus, a single pane inside that window). The window is also referred to as the *viewport*.

To split the window into separate panes, you'll need to decide whether you want to split it into either a horizontal or vertical pane. To split the viewport into two panes that sit horizontally to each other, you would execute one of the following commands:

- `<P>:split-window -h`
- `<P>%`

To split the viewport into two panes that sit vertically to each other, you would execute one of the following commands:

- `<P>:split-window -v`
- `<P>"`

■ **Note**   Remember to check the ProVim `.tmux.conf` file, as you'll find some custom key bindings that replace `<P>%` and `<P>"` with `<P>v` and `<P>s`, which feels more at home for Vim users (although I personally prefer to use the default bindings).

Differences Between Vim and tmux

Unfortunately, the definition of *vertical* and *horizontal* is slightly different between Vim and tmux (nothing is ever easy).

To clarify: In Vim, if you want windows to be placed next to each other horizontally, you would say you want to create a vertical split (e.g., it splits the screen using a vertical bar), but in tmux, you would say you want to split the screen horizontally (e.g., place the panes next to each other horizontally).

Both semantics make sense, but as I learned Vim before tmux, I'm more used to Vim's logic. Because of this, my tmux alias' are focused on Vim's way of thinking about splitting the screen viewport.

```
bind-key v split-window -h
bind-key s split-window -v
```

Closing

As I mentioned earlier, to close a pane, you just have to run the command `<C-d>` or type `exit`; but these only work when any programs in the pane are closed, and we're back in the terminal shell. What happens, though, if we have to force-close a pane? I have had this problem quite a few times when running certain applications that have hit a fatal error and can't use either `<C-c>` or `<C-d>` to stop them.

In those instances, running the `<P>x` command will act as a "force quit." It'll display a message (within the command prompt) asking if we would like to "`kill-pane {pane_number}? (y/n),`" to which the response would be y, for *yes*.

Navigating

tmux makes splitting the current window viewport into multiple panes very easy and inexpensive, but it does offer a few different ways to navigate your pane layout. There is a simple sequential command that effectively rotates you through each pane in a sequence (e.g., moving in one direction), until you reach the pane you want to work inside. Using the `<P>o` command does this.

There is also a command prompt variation that allows you to move in any direction. The following list demonstrates moving left, right, up, and down:

- `<P>:select-pane -L`
- `<P>:select-pane -R`
- `<P>:select-pane -U`
- `<P>:select-pane -D`

The command prompt version of a command can be quite tedious to execute, so it's best to create a set of custom key bindings to help make this task a little quicker and easier. As mentioned in the previous chapter, if you have the ProVim configuration setup, you'll already have a `.tmux.conf` configuration file that includes the following custom bindings:

```
# Vim style
bind-key -r h select-pane -L
bind-key -r j select-pane -D
bind-key -r k select-pane -U
bind-key -r l select-pane -R

# Arrow keys
bind-key Up    select-pane -U
bind-key Down  select-pane -D
bind-key Left  select-pane -L
bind-key Right select-pane -R
```

We can also jump straight to any pane we want to focus on by running the <P>q command. When executed, this command will display a numeric value on top of each pane. While the numbers are visible, you will be able to specify the pane you want to move your cursor inside of, by simply typing the relevant number.

■ **Note**   The numeric identifiers for each pane only appear for a brief moment, and jumping to a pane only works while they are visible. So, act quickly and press the number of the pane you want to jump to while the identifiers are on screen.

The <P>q command is again a key binding built into tmux that simply executes the command prompt variation :display-panes (see Figure 24-5). So, if you're looking to do some kind of scripted automation of tmux (which I'll cover in a later chapter), being aware of the command prompt versions can be useful.

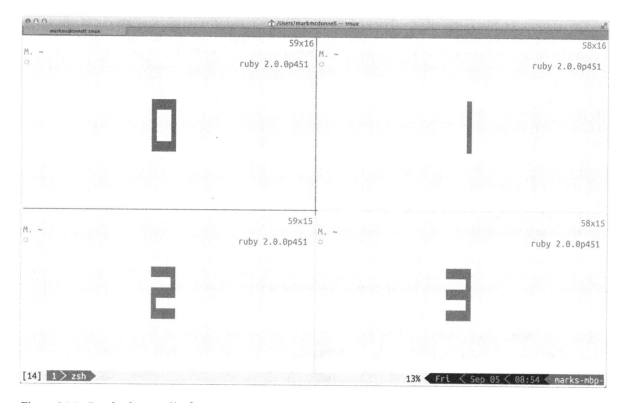

Figure 24-5. *Result of tmux* `:display-panes` *command (before confirming selection)*

Resizing

To resize a pane in tmux, you'll need the `:resize-pane` command. The following is an example of its syntax structure:

```
<P>:resize-pane -t {pane_id} -D {amount}
```

In the preceding example, we're telling tmux to target (`-t`) the pane we want to resize (replace `{pane_id}` with a numeric id value), and then we tell it what direction (`-d`) to resize and what amount to resize by (replace `{amount}` with a numeric value).

For all details of this command, see the documentation, but for the majority of users, the following flags/options are what they need to know:

- `-U`: Resize window upward.

- `-D`: Resize window downward.

- `-L`: Resize window to the left.

- `-R`: Resize window to the right.

There is also a slightly simpler form, in which you can leave off the target, and tmux will assume you want to resize the current pane, as follows:

```
<P>:resizep -D {amount}
```

As we saw in the previous chapter, if you're using the ProVim setup, you'll already have a `.tmux.conf` file containing a set of custom key bindings that make it easier to resize the *current* pane, as shown following:

- `bind-key < resize-pane -L 5`
- `bind-key > resize-pane -R 5`
- `bind-key + resize-pane -U 5`
- `bind-key - resize-pane -D 5`

Balancing

When creating a new split pane, tmux will try to keep them evenly balanced (i.e., of equal size), but after a while, you can find they shift out of balance. This can happen by chance but more often when you manually resize your panes to give more focus on a particular file.

For example, if you're doing test-driven development, you'll likely have two panes open: one holding your code under test, and the other displaying the results of your tests. Chances are, you want your test-results pane to be quite small and take up less space than the other pane holding the code being tested. To do this, you'll end up manually resizing the panes.

If you want to evenly distribute the space of yours panes (i.e., have them use an equal amount of space), use one of the following commands:

- `<P>:select-layout even-horizontal`
- `<P>:select-layout even-vertical`

■ **Note** We saw the effect of these commands in the previous chapter, so please refer back to Figures 23-4 and 23-5.

Windows

In tmux, windows work in a similar way to how "tabs" work within Vim. Goodness knows it would be nice if there were some consistent naming for these features across programs, but alas, it was not to be. Regardless, to create a new window, run the `<P>c` command (or `:new-window`, if you're using the command prompt).

You'll notice when creating a new window that tmux will automatically name it after the process that's running. For example, it will name the window `zsh`, as that binary is the default terminal shell running.

At any point, if you have to rename the current window, you can do this very simply, using the `<P>,` command. At this point, tmux will ask you to enter a new name for the window. If you're using the command prompt, the following example demonstrates the syntax structure:

`:rename-window -t {window_id|window_name} {new_name}`

Summary

In this chapter, we've covered the majority of the fundamental concepts that tmux is composed of. Let's take a quick look at what was covered so far.

- We discussed how tmux sessions work, such as how to create/list/select/rename and attach/detach a session, as well as what benefits they provide.

- We then moved on to the concept of buffers and the screen viewport. I explained how overflowing content is displayed outside of the viewport and is still available within the current buffer, as well as how we can navigate the buffer, using tmux's copy mode.

- After that, we looked at how panes work and at their relationship to tmux windows, how we can create/manipulate and navigate panes, and how we can trigger a window or entire session to be closed, by removing all available panes.

- Finally, we covered the concept of tmux windows and how to create and rename them.

CHAPTER 25

Modifications

Using tmux "out of the box" is useful enough as it is, but most of the time, we'll want to make our lives a little easier, by adding some additional customizations (such as we did in Chapter 23, when we added custom configuration to our .tmux.conf file).

The modifications we'll be making this chapter aren't all strictly tmux configurations. For example, the following section contains modifications aimed at workarounds for reducing complexity and duplication through the use of shell alias' and functions. Other sections are aimed at further modifications to the .tmux.conf file itself.

The number of modifications you make will be down to what it is you're trying to simplify for yourself. For myself, I find I only require a small number of modifications that revolve around minor abstractions and fixing issues that I've stumbled across while using tmux.

Abstractions

There is a vast amount of tmux specific commands (each with varying options), which can be difficult to memorize. I find that the easiest way to resolve that particular problem is to abstract away the commands for something more palatable.

For example, I would find myself constantly having to look up the documentation for how to create named sessions, or attach to an existing session. No matter how often I would run those commands, I could not commit them to memory.

I decided that the simplest solution was to abstract the relevant commands that I found myself having the most difficulty with into some simple wrapper functions. These functions would be added into my .zshrc shell configuration file.

Note   If you're using the ProVim configuration setup, you'll already have the following modifications in your .zshrc.

Most of the abstractions that I've created use standard shell functions; for others, I use a shell alias. Either way, you're free to use them or to modify them to suit your own needs, or even remove them completely and use the plain vanilla tmux commands, if you find this easier than working with abstractions.

Creating New Sessions

The first abstraction I made was to the command I probably use the most: creating a new "named" tmux session (as seen in the following code snippet):

```
function tmuxnew() {
  tmux new -s $1
}
```

Now this isn't necessarily a difficult command to remember, but if we're going to be abstracting other tmux commands, there is no harm in keeping things consistent. To execute this command, all I have to do is type tmuxnew {my_session_name} (you can shorten the name, if you prefer, to tn or tnew; whatever works for you) into my terminal shell, and if I forget to provide a name, the command will fail to run and remind me that I've not specified a session name.

But this in itself can be a bit long-winded, because we have to think up a unique name for each session we create. It would be better if we could create a new session that was named after the project directory in which we are currently residing. That's what the following alias does for us. We simply run tat, and it'll pick up the name of the current folder and use that, as in the following:

```
alias tat="tmux new-session -As $(basename $PWD | tr . -)"
```

The way it works is by utilizing the –A flag for the new-session command. The –A flag makes new-session behave like attach-session, if the specified session name already exists. From there, instead of hard-coding in a session name (which wouldn't be very useful), we use the shell's $() command substitution feature, which evaluates the commands specified within the parentheses before the main/containing command is run. The returned value from the subshell commands is what is used for the session name.

To get the folder name, we use the basename command and pass it the current working directory name ($PWD). So if $PWD returned /Users/markmcdonnell, the basename for that path would be markmcdonnell.

Finally, we pipe (|) the folder name through to the translate (tr) command, which converts any dots (.) into hyphens, to ensure the session name is valid. This avoids issues wherein the folder name is x.y.z, by converting it into a valid name, such as x-y-z, before passing it to the new-session command.

■ **Note**   This technique was pioneered by http://robots.thoughtbot.com/.

Attaching to Sessions

As you can probably imagine, there are similar abstractions that we can make at this point, such as the following code snippet, which indicates that I want to connect to a specific named session:

```
function tmuxopen() {
  tmux attach -t $1
}
```

Typically, I'll execute tmux ls to get a list of open sessions, and then once I have that list of sessions and I know what session names I have already, I can run tmuxopen {my_session_name} to reattach to the specified session.

Destroying Sessions

When I want to kill a specific session completely, I use the following function:

```
function tmuxkill() {
  tmux kill-session -t $1
}
```

For me, to use this function, I have to know the name of the session I want to kill, so I'll execute tmux ls first, to get a list of open sessions, and then once I have that list of sessions, I'll know which sessions I have already. Then I can run tmuxkill {my_session_name} to destroy the specified session. But what happens when we want to destroy *all* our tmux sessions?

■ **Note**   In the following example, I will demonstrate a manual solution to the problem of destroying multiple tmux sessions at once, by using a collection of Unix commands. There is a simpler solution using tmux's built-in command tmux kill-server. The reasoning behind showing readers a more manual process is to encourage you to become more comfortable working from the command line and to take advantage of tools that can help you resolve issues for which there are no built-in commands.

OK, so we could execute the tmuxkill function multiple times, but that's just slow and very tedious. Instead, we can use some Unix wizardry to help make killing all our tmux sessions much easier:

```
alias tmuxkillall="tmux ls | cut -d : -f 1 | xargs -I {} tmux kill-session -t {}"
```

This might seem long and confusing, but with a little background information on the individual commands, it can start to make a little more sense. I'm not going to get into the nitty-gritty of how each of the commands works, as this isn't a book about Unix, but I will try and break it down as simply as I can.

A top-level view of the alias shows us that we have three commands in place (tmux ls, cut, and xargs), and each command is separated by a pipe (|), which means the result from the previous command is passed through to the next command.

The tmux ls command displays into stdout (i.e., the terminal screen) a list of open tmux sessions that looks something like the following output, which highlights that I have three separate sessions running on my machine (one called my_session, another called work, and the last called side project):

```
my_session: 1 windows (created Thur Aug 28 17:01:34 2014) [118x32]
work: 4 windows (created Fri Aug 29 09:59:12 2014) [118x32]
side project: 2 windows (created Mon Aug 25 08:29:05 2014) [118x32]
```

From this output, we can see that the part we need is before the colon (:), as that is the session name. For us to be able to parse the session name from the output, we have to use the cut command. We tell the command to use the colon as a "field" delimiter (-d :), which means it'll split each line of output into chunks, using the colon as its indicator of where to make a split. Then we tell the command to return us the first chunk or field (-f 1).

Now that we have the session name, we pass that through to xargs to handle. We first tell xargs to hold the value we're passing to it, so we can reference it using the syntax {} (we do this via the -I {} flag). We then tell xargs what command we want it to execute (in this case, tmux kill-session -t {}), and where we typically would use the session name, we place a {}.

Because we've used the cut command (which processes multiple lines of data), each listed tmux session will be processed and parsed for its session name and passed to xargs to handle triggering the kill-session command.

Extending the Message Display Time

By default, tmux sets the length of time a message is displayed onscreen to 750 milliseconds. This is a remarkably short amount of time for you to decipher the message that's being highlighted to you by tmux. Typically, I'll misuse a tmux function, whereupon tmux will notify me of the correct syntax (or the error), by utilizing its own display-message command.

Inevitably, I always miss what the message said (or didn't get enough time to read the entire message, or the commands correct options), and so I have to resort to executing <P>~ to display all messages that have recently been sent, just so I can get a longer glimpse at the message I missed.

Instead of opening a list of old messages, a better solution is to extend the display message time, using the display-time command. Let's extend to two seconds the message display time for all currently open windows (using the -g flag), by adding the following setting to our .tmux.conf file:

```
set-option -g display-time 2000
```

Repeatable Keys

When creating your own key bindings, tmux provides an additional flag (-r), which lets you control how the key is repeated. In Chapter 23, I demonstrated a basic usage of the bind-key command's -r flag, but in this section, I want to cover another example of how it is useful. Specifically, I would like to demonstrate how this flag can help to improve tmux's ability to switch panes.

To begin, let's imagine we have two panes open horizontally next to each other. The left pane has a text document open in Vim (NORMAL mode), and the right pane (the currently focused pane) is a terminal shell. Now imagine we want to move to the left pane (which has Vim open) and then start moving the cursor to the right (while within Vim).

To do this, you would first execute <P><Left-Arrow> to move the cursor into the left tmux pane, and then once inside the left pane (and subsequently within Vim), you would press <Right-Arrow> to start navigating through the Vim buffer.

What you would typically find is that the cursor would not move to the right of the buffer (inside of Vim); instead, the cursor would move back to the right tmux pane. But why? The cause of this is to do with the use of tmux's default configuration and the -r flag when defining our custom key bindings.

A naive workaround to this problem would be to simply wait a fraction of a second before we pressed the <Right-Arrow> key. But a better solution is to prevent the problem altogether, by re-creating the default bindings ourselves to not use the -r flag, as shown in the following code sample (this is already part of the ProVim .tmux.conf file):

```
bind-key Up    select-pane -U
bind-key Down  select-pane -D
bind-key Left  select-pane -L
bind-key Right select-pane -R
```

The -r flag indicates that the key binding can be "repeated." What this means in a practical sense is that when you execute the key binding, you can press another tmux binding key without having to include the prefix. This helps to chain lots of tmux commands together more efficiently.

Hence, when you execute the <P><Left-Arrow> (to move to the pane holding Vim), followed by <Right-Arrow> (which you'd expect to move the cursor within Vim to the right), it, in fact, moves the cursor back over to the right pane, as if you had pressed <P><Right-Arrow>.

Restoring Broken Commands

Along with adding your own abstractions and working around subtle nuisances in how tmux interacts with other programs, you may also notice some problems with your terminal shell environment.

For me, one of the biggest annoyances was that my bck-i-search command (which allows us to search iteratively back through our previous command history) stopped working while within tmux.

The reason for some of this was owing to my rebinding <C-r> to dynamically source the .tmux.conf file, whereas other machines I would be working on would have all kinds of different custom settings that could cause conflicts.

I found the easiest solution was to add the following snippets, which helped resolve these issues by redefining the key bindings to do exactly what I expected them to:

```
bindkey '^R' history-incremental-search-backward
bindkey '^A' beginning-of-line
bindkey '^E' end-of-line
```

Summary

This was a relatively short chapter, but I trust you found the topics covered interesting and helpful in resolving some practical concerns when using tmux in your day-to-day workflow. Let's have a quick recap.

- We started by looking at some abstractions for creating and attaching to new sessions and automating the session naming process by utilizing some basic Unix commands to parse out the current folder name.

- Similarly, we looked at how we can kill individual sessions and, again using some basic Unix scripting, kill all open tmux sessions.

- We looked at how best to resolve an issue of the short amount of time a message is displayed onscreen, using the display-time command.

- We moved on to resolving an issue with the default tmux configuration, whereby interacting with Vim was made problematic, due to the bind-key and its -r repeat flag.

- Finally, we looked at resolving issues with standard terminal commands that break once executed in the terminal, within a tmux session.

CHAPTER 26

Copy and Paste

One of the most arduous tasks within tmux is the need to be able to copy and paste content from a buffer. The problem isn't so much copying content from our buffer (although that isn't the simplest of tasks, as we'll see in the first few sections of this chapter), but more so that there is no native capability to paste content that has been copied from a tmux buffer into other external programs.

In this chapter, we'll look at how copy and paste works in general (for all platforms) and then review some workarounds for the issue of copying content from tmux into another program for both Mac and Linux.

Note Some of the solutions provided in this chapter are dependent on the use of tmux 1.8+.

Copy Mode

In tmux, all content is placed inside a buffer, and if there is not enough screen space to hold all of the buffer content, it will effectively be scrolled "off screen." So for us to be able to go back and view the offscreen buffer content, we first have to get tmux into "copy mode."

I briefly covered copy mode in Chapter 24, but just to quickly recap: to enter copy mode, either execute the key binding <P>[or the command <P>:copy-mode, which routes through tmux's command prompt.

Once you're inside copy mode, you can navigate around, using the arrow keys and quit copy mode, by pressing either q or <Enter> when you're done.

Note The Linux keys to quit copy mode are <Esc> and q but not <Enter>.

For us to begin making a selection of text, we'll have to press <Space>, and this will result in the text being highlighted as we start navigating around with the arrow keys. To copy our selection, we have to press <Enter> for the selection to be placed into tmux's "paste buffer" (space in memory).

Note The Linux key for selection is <C-Space>, and the key to copy the selection to the paste buffer is <Esc-w> (or, more accurately, whatever your "modifier" key is set to on your keyboard: <M-w>).

Paste Buffer

Once you have content in the paste buffer, you can then paste it into any other tmux buffer you have open, which includes buffers that are open within a completely different tmux session (see Figure 26-1)!

Figure 26-1. *Example of tmux's paste buffer*

The paste buffer keeps a history of all copied content, so you can copy multiple items and then keep track of them within the paste buffer. To list the current items stored within the paste buffer, you can either execute the key binding <P># or the command <P>:list-buffers, which routes through tmux's command prompt.

Each item in the paste buffer is numbered, so you can easily identify the order in which items were added (newest items are placed at the top). To close the list-buffers screen, either press q or <Enter> (or q and <Esc>, if you're a Linux user). If you would instead like to see the full content of the latest buffer, there is a shortcut command that does that and is run via the command prompt <P>:show-buffer.

The show-buffer screen is only a temporary visual aid. The content is not taken out of the paste buffer, and it is not placed inside your current buffer. If you would like to paste the latest item within the paste buffer into your current buffer, you can use the <P>] key binding or the command <P>:paste-buffer, which routes through tmux's command prompt.

You can also capture the current pane in its entirety, using the command <P>:capture-pane, and from there, you can even save the latest paste buffer directly into a file, if you want, using the command <P>:save-buffer ~/Desktop/foo.txt. (See Figure 26-2.)

```
● ● ●                                                ⬜ foo.txt — Edited
-rw-r--r--   1 markmcdonnell  staff   39440 14 Mar 10:04 .zcompdump
-r--r--r--   1 markmcdonnell  staff   80344 18 Jun  2013 .zcompdump.zwc
-rw-------   1 markmcdonnell  staff   31522 27 Jun  2013 .zhistory
-rw-r--r--   1 markmcdonnell  staff      17  5 Jun  2013 .zsh-update
-rw-------   1 markmcdonnell  staff  437963 10 Sep 18:39 .zsh_history
lrwxr-xr-x   1 markmcdonnell  staff      55  1 Feb  2014 .zshrc -> /Users/markmcdonnell/Dropbox/dotfiles/.
zshrc
drwxr-xr-x   3 markmcdonnell  staff     102 27 Aug 09:24 Applications
drwxr-xr-x  22 markmcdonnell  staff     748  5 Sep 11:03 Code
drwx------+  12 markmcdonnell  staff     408 10 Sep 18:27 Desktop
drwx------+   9 markmcdonnell  staff     306  9 Sep 14:25 Documents
drwx------+  14 markmcdonnell  staff     476  9 Sep 14:25 Downloads
drwx------@  13 markmcdonnell  staff     442  9 Sep 14:25 Dropbox
drwx------@  67 markmcdonnell  staff    2278 13 May 18:55 Library
drwx------+   4 markmcdonnell  staff     136  9 Sep 14:25 Movies
drwx------+   6 markmcdonnell  staff     204  9 Sep 14:25 Music
drwx------+   6 markmcdonnell  staff     204  9 Sep 14:25 Pictures
drwxr-xr-x+   4 markmcdonnell  staff     136  9 Sep 14:25 Public
drwx------  20 markmcdonnell  staff     680  3 Sep 09:55 VirtualBox VMs
drwxr-xr-x   6 markmcdonnell  staff     204 17 Jul 09:58 bin
drwxr-xr-x   3 markmcdonnell  staff     102  4 Sep  2013 db
drwxr-xr-x   4 markmcdonnell  staff     136 14 Mar  2013 lib
drwxr-xr-x   4 markmcdonnell  staff     136 14 Mar  2013 man
drwxr-xr-x  16 markmcdonnell  staff     544 10 Aug 17:51 src
drwxr-xr-x   2 root           staff      68 29 Aug 15:15 tmp
-rw-r--r--   1 markmcdonnell  staff      60  9 Sep 14:44 tmux-client-8393.log
-rw-r--r--   1 markmcdonnell  staff   30253  9 Sep 14:44 tmux-server-8395.log

M. ~
○                                                                          ruby 2.0.0p451
```

Figure 26-2. *Output from capturing a pane and saving it to a file*

If you have lots of items within your paste buffer and you need a specific item to paste into your current buffer, you can select the item you require by executing either the key binding <P>= or the command <P>:choose-buffer, which routes through tmux's command prompt. For example, you could open Vim within your current buffer and enter INSERT mode, then run <P>=, to begin navigating the list of items within the paste buffer, and then select one to have its content pasted directly into Vim.

■ **Note**   If you're using the .tmux.conf configuration provided in Chapter 23, then be aware that the default tmux command <P>= (which maps to <P>:choose-buffer) has been overridden. So you'll either want to remove the custom key binding the configuration file assigns to <P>=, or use the long form <P>:choose-buffer.

Pasting Between Programs

The problem that confuses most tmux users is the inability to paste what has been copied from the tmux paste buffer into a different program (because the paste buffer is not the same thing as the operating system's clipboard). We'll take a look at how to resolve this in both the Mac and Linux operating systems.

Plug-in Solution

Before I jump into the manual process, there is a more automated solution, involving installing a tmux plug-in called tmux-yank (https://github.com/tmux-plugins/tmux-yank), which works for both Mac AND Linux operating systems and is very simple to install by either following the manual installation steps or using a tmux plug-in manager (https://github.com/tmux-plugins/tpm).

Mac OS X

If you're using Mac OS X as your development environment, the solution involves the installation of a program called reattach-to-user-namespace and a modification to your .tmux.conf file.

The tmux program running on Mac OS X has issues accessing the namespace it originates from, meaning tmux requires an additional program to reattach it to that namespace. This is a bug that Apple fixed for the popular multiplexer Screen (www.gnu.org/software/screen/), but the patch isn't possible to apply to tmux, owing to private undocumented functions being utilized by Apple. This means we have to implement our solution.

First, to install the reattach-to-user-namespace program, you can either manually compile it, by following instructions from its online repository here: https://github.com/ChrisJohnsen/tmux-MacOSX-pasteboard, or you can take the easier route and install it using the Homebrew package manager, which can be downloaded by following the current instructions found at http://brew.sh/.

```
brew install reattach-to-user-namespace
```

The following code snippet demonstrates the changes we have to make to our .tmux.conf file to configure tmux correctly:

```
set -g default-command "reattach-to-user-namespace -l '/bin/zsh'"
bind-key -t vi-copy 'v' begin-selection
bind-key -t vi-copy 'y' copy-pipe "reattach-to-user-namespace pbcopy"
```

Effectively, we've instructed tmux to use the wrapper program (reattach-to-user-namespace) as the default command that should be run when a new tmux window is created. The specified program then wraps around the Zsh shell.

The other two key bindings will make tmux more like Vim (i.e., more familiar and easier to work with), by implementing similar key bindings for making a selection and yanking content from the buffer. Once you have this modification, you will be able to enter copy mode and simply hit v to begin making a selection of the buffer and then, when ready to copy, press y to yank.

■ **Note** For a complete breakdown of why the access to system clipboard is broken on Mac OS X, and to understand how the solution works (including implementation details of the reattach-to-user-namespace program), I highly recommend having a read through the GitHub repo https://github.com/ChrisJohnsen/tmux-MacOSX-pasteboard, which covers all of this in painstaking detail.

Linux

If you're using Linux, you'll have to make sure you have xclip installed first. Depending on your distribution, the installation can be done using either a yum install xclip or apt-get install xclip, so pick what's relevant to you.

Once xclip is installed, you should simply have to add the following changes to your .tmux.conf file:

```
bind-key -t vi-copy 'v' begin-selection
bind-key -t vi-copy 'y' copy-pipe "xclip"
```

■ **Note** Depending on your distribution, the bindings may have to be modified to suit. For example, we can also use an alternative method of `tmux save-buffer - | xclip -i -sel clipboard` to copy content, and `tmux set-buffer \"$(xclip -o -sel clipboard)\"; tmux paste-buffer` to paste.

Working from a VM

If you're running Linux within a virtual machine (VM) from the Mac operating system (using VirtualBox, VMWare, or some other virtualization software, in addition to something such as Vagrant to manage the setup/tear-down of VMs), you'll find that the preceding solution doesn't work. This is because you're running a GUI-less version of Linux that has no concept of a system clipboard.

The clipboard programs you can install on Linux are typically developed to work using a system known as X-Windows. So even if you install something like `xclip` on your Linux VM, you'll still have issues getting the preceding tmux configurations to send tmux selections to the `xclip` program (as a terminal-only version of Linux inside a VM won't have the required X-Windows dependencies).

If you're using Vagrant to start and manage your VMs, then the solution to this problem is quite simple. First, you'll have to install and run the software XQuartz (http://xquartz.macosforge.org/, which is a Mac OS equivalent of the X-Windows system). Second, you'll have to modify your `Vagrantfile` to include the following option, so that when you start up your VM, Vagrant can forward the XQuartz program onto the VM to use (meaning `xclip` will start working):

```
config.ssh.forward_x11 = true
```

Finally, you'll want to modify the `.tmux.conf` setting, so it looks like the following snippet:

```
bind-key -t vi-copy 'v' begin-selection
bind-key -t vi-copy 'y' copy-pipe "xclip -selection clipboard"
```

Summary

Let's take a moment to summarize some of things you've learned over the course of this chapter.

- We discussed the fundamental issue of copying and pasting with tmux across different programs, along with some complexity with the commands required to select and copy specific portions of tmux's screen buffer.

- We first took a look at tmux's copy mode and what its purpose is (which is to allow us to scroll back through content that wasn't possible to fix in the screen's viewport). You also learned the different commands and key bindings that help us navigate through copy mode (and the variations between Mac and Linux).

- Then we moved on to reviewing tmux's paste buffer, how content is stored in the paste buffer, and how you might retrieve content, using specific key bindings or more granular control with commands such as `:choose-buffer`. (You also discovered how to copy an entire pane's content using the `:capture-pane` command.)

- Finally, we looked at a quick solution for ensuring we're able to properly copy and paste from tmux into different unrelated programs, as well as how to make the process easier, by utilizing some key bindings that make tmux behave more like Vim.

CHAPTER 27

Pane/Window Management

Being able to efficiently manage your tmux windows and panes is a skill that usually is acquired over a long period of time, as you find yourself becoming more comfortable with this powerful screen-management tool.

In this chapter, I'm going to review some key binding shortcuts and offer up some tips that will, I hope, help you become much more proficient in your daily workflow. We'll begin by looking at how we can better manage tmux panes and then look at some of the tmux window features available.

Pane Management

Much like when using Vim, you'll find that a common process is creating lots of windows (as well as creating multiple panes within those windows) for handling the different aspects of individual tasks. The number of windows and panes you open is dependent on the type of work you do and the user in general, but regardless of background, the following tips will help you keep control.

Moving Between Two Commonly Used Panes

Imagine that you have four panes open in a grid format (i.e., two panes in one row and two panes below in a second row), as the following diagram indicates:

```
---------------------
|  A   |   B   |
---------------------
|  C   |   D   |
---------------------
```

If your cursor were currently focused inside the A pane, and you wanted to get to the D pane, the quickest route to doing so would be to use the display-panes command (or the key binding <P>q).

But this is always a mental hurdle to jump over when you're trying to work quickly and are bouncing back and forth between specific panes, i.e., moving back and forth between the panes A and D.

In these scenarios, I personally find the last-pane command (or, more specifically, the key binding <P>;) to be a much more efficient way of moving back and forth between two commonly used panes.

Full-Screen Current Pane

This is one of the most useful features of tmux panes, because it helps to keep other content hidden. The typical use case I have for this is when I have two panes open, one running Vim and the other my terminal shell that's watching some code files for changes and then displaying the results of my code's suite of unit tests.

In this scenario, I'll usually move my cursor's focus into the pane containing Vim and run <P>z (or the long form command, <P>:resize-pane -Z) to cause the pane to fill the window (subsequently hiding the other pane I have open), so I can work primarily on my code.

From there, I'll continue working as normal, and if there is ever a point at which I have to refer to my terminal to check my test suite output, I simply move into the other pane, which triggers the full-screen mode to stop (or I would execute the same <P>z key binding again to revert back).

Break a Pane Out into a Separate Window

Sometimes, a pane can start to contain so much content or process output that you wish you had more room for it. In most cases, you can use the previous tip of going full-screen with <P>z, but depending on the context, you might be more comfortable just moving the content to a new window.

Luckily for us, tmux has a built-in command that handles that exact issue; it's the break-pane command, and it has a nice key binding shortcut <P>!

Convert a Window into a Pane (Within Another Window)

In the previous example, we broke a pane out of a window, so it became its own self-contained window. In this section, we want to do the reverse behavior, which can be achieved using tmux's join-pane command, like so:

```
<P>:join-pane -s {source_window} -t {target_window}
```

In the preceding example, we tell tmux to join the source window into the target window. This will remove the source window as a separate window and convert it into a new pane within the target window.

Rotate Panes Within Current Window

When you have multiple panes open, it can be useful to rotate them, so that you have one pane aligned next to another relevant pane (maybe to make some comparisons of data easier).

In Figure 27-1 (following), we can see that we have four panes open. In the top left, we're running htop (http://hisham.hm/htop/); in the top right pane, we're running vtop (http://parall.ax/vtop); within the bottom right pane, we're running the standard/ubiquitous top command; and within the bottom left pane, we have an empty terminal pane not running anything.

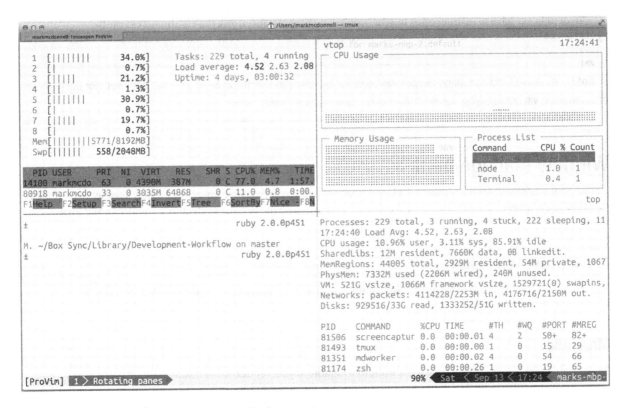

Figure 27-1. *Example of some processes running in separate panes*

If we decided that we wanted to have the bottom-right pane (top) placed in the top-left position (so that it was placed to the left of the top-right pane currently holding the vtop process), we would run either the <P>} key binding (to rotate the pane clockwise) or the <P>{ key binding (to rotate the pane counterclockwise).

In this example, it wouldn't matter which pane we currently were focused on. We would just execute the relevant command until the panes were positioned exactly how we needed them to be.

Changing Pane Layouts

There are built-in algorithms that tmux uses to provide a different layout when triggering the <P><Space> key binding. This binding can be executed multiple times and will cause the layout of the panes to change, whereby you can stop whenever you find a layout that suits your current working environment.

Synchronizing Pane Input

Imagine that you have a group of panes open, and for each pane, you are SSH'ed into a different remote server (for which you're tailing some system log file). If you wanted to execute the same set of commands for each of the processes running on each of the servers, then instead of doing this manually (i.e., executing the command in the current pane and moving to the next pane and repeat), we can automate this slightly.

To do this, we have to instruct tmux to synchronize each open pane, using the command `<P>:setw synchronize-panes`, so that any input entered into any one of the panes will be replicated across all of them.

■ **Note**   By default, the command toggles the behavior, but you can specify an `on` or `off` status as well (for the purpose of automation via shell scripts), for example, `:setw synchronize-panes off`.

Window Management

Unlike panes, windows aren't as much of a large management concern. There are also a limited number of use cases for handling windows. Once created, you'll either want to navigate them, close them, move them, or swap them around. Let's take a look at each of these suggestions.

Navigating Windows

There are a couple of ways to navigate through windows: manually (using key bindings) and via a visual list. Let's review both of these options . . .

Manually

To navigate manually, you again have a few options available to you: sequential or indirect. When navigating sequentially, we can use the key bindings `<P>n` (to move to the next window) or `<P>p` (to move to the previous window). When navigating indirectly, we can use the key binding `<P>{n}`, whereby you'll replace {n} with the numerical index of the window.

Visual List

We can have tmux display a list of the available windows for us and then use our arrow keys to navigate the list. We display the list, using the `<P>w` key binding or via the `choose-window` command (see Figure 27-2 for an example).

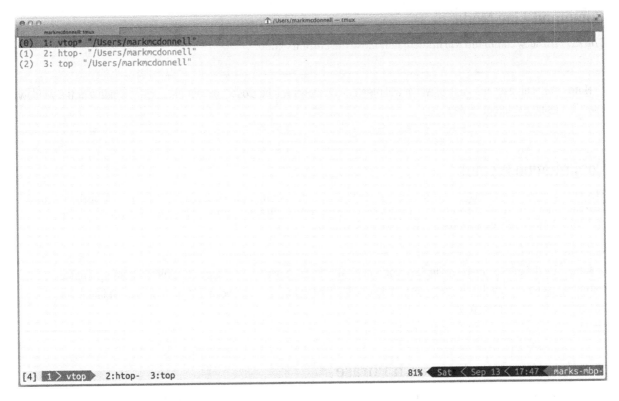

Figure 27-2. *Output of the* `choose-window` *command*

When you have used your arrow keys to highlight the window you wish to access, simply press `<CR>` to jump to the relevant window.

Closing Windows

There are three ways to close a window, as follows:

1. Immediate key binding

2. Command-line prompt

3. Confirmation prompt key binding

Immediate

Most of the time, I'll use the `<C-d>` key binding, which sends an EOF (http://en.wikipedia.org/wiki/End-of-file) signal to the terminal process, causing it to instantly terminate.

Command-Line Mode

The kill-window command will immediately close the current window.

Note You can pass the -a flag, which will mean *all* windows will be closed, except the current window or the window specified using the target -t flag.

Confirmation Prompt

The <P>& key binding is an abstraction around the kill-window command. It utilizes tmux's confirm-before feature (see the following Note) to ensure that a message is displayed within the command-line prompt, asking you to confirm whether you are sure you want to close the window.

Note By default, the confirm-before command will display a generic message constructed from the original command being executed. This message can be modified using the confirm-before's -p flag. You can find more information in the tmux manual.

Finding Windows by Search Phrase

If you want to find a window by either its identifier (i.e., the name you gave the window) or by its contents, the <P>f key binding might be what you're after. You can also use the find-window command itself.

Moving and Switching Windows Within the Current Session

Thanks to tmux's client-server architecture, we have the extraordinary power to move a window not only between a single session but also between completely different sessions, using the move-window command. Let's see a simple example first, in which we move the window into another position within the current session.

Imagine that we have three windows open (indexed 1, 2, and 3), and we want to move window 1 to the end of the list. To do this would require running the following command:

```
<P>:move-window -t 4
```

You can see in the preceding example that we specify an index that isn't already taken and is higher than any defined (in this case, 4). This works by using the target (-t) flag to specify what index we want to move the window to.

Similarly, we can swap two windows. Using the same example as previously (three windows, indexed 1, 2, and 3), imagine that we wanted to swap windows 1 and 3. To do this, we would run the following command:

```
<P>:swap-window -s 1 -t 3
```

In the preceding example, we've used the swap-window command, along with the source flag (-s), indicating the window we want to swap and the target flag (-t) to indicate the alternate window it should be swapped with.

Moving Windows Between Different Sessions

It can be useful to reduce a complicated multi-window group of sessions down to a single session. In order to do this, you would have to decide what windows from each session you wanted to keep and somehow move them into another session that was to act as your consolidated session.

To achieve this result, we could use the `<P>.` key binding (or the long-form `move-window -t {session:window_id}` command). When you run `<P>`, tmux will ask you to choose a window. This means you will have to enter the name of the session you want to move the window into.

You can also specify a specific window index that you want it to move to. For example, `foo:2` would move the window to the `foo` session and position the window into index 2. If you were to specify a numeric session identifier that wasn't recognized, the window would be moved to that index within the current session.

We don't even have to be in a specific session to be able to move a window into another session. In the following example, we use the "source" flag (`-s`) to indicate that we want the index 1 window within the `foo` session to be moved into the `bar` session.

```
tmux move-window -s foo:1 -t bar
```

> **Note**   If the current window has the same name as the session you're moving it into, the move will fail, as tmux will get confused and think you're trying to move the window back into itself.

Sharing Windows Between Sessions

You may find that, rather than moving a window to another session, you wish you could just share it. This is possible by using tmux's `link-window` command. Imagine that we have two tmux sessions, `foo` and `bar`, both having one window each. The `foo` session's window is named `fwin`, and the `bar` session's window is named `bwin`.

If we were currently inside the `foo` session, and we decided that we wanted to share the `fwin` window with the `bar` session, we would simply have to execute the command as follows: `<P>:link-window -t bar:2`.

Note, in the preceding command, that we don't specify a source. This is because we're inside the `foo` session. If we were not, we would have used the `-s` flag to identify the source session/window.

Now, any changes that are made to the `fwin` window, whether it be inside the `foo` session or the `bar` session, will be reflected in the other session. But be careful, as closing the window in one session will close it in any other session it is shared with.

> **Note**   Sometimes when sharing a window, you might hit upon a conflict, whereby the destination session already has a window with the same identifier. To resolve this problem, you can choose to "kill" the window in the destination session, by adding the -k flag to the command.

Summary

You've learned some important shortcuts in this chapter. These techniques can not only make you more proficient with multitasking across many different sessions but also give you more tools to extend the automation side of your tmux working environment. Let's quickly recap what was covered.

We started by looking at some of the different techniques for manipulating and managing tmux panes, such as how to move back and forth between two common panes, converting the current pane into full-screen mode to allow us to take advantage of the extra space, converting a window into a pane and changing the layout of panes within a single window, and synchronizing the input for multiple panes.

Finally, we began to review the options available for manipulating and managing tmux windows. This included considering multiple ways to navigate through windows, using key bindings or a more traditional visual list; closing windows, using either key bindings, command-line prompt, or an extra abstraction layer that incorporates the confirm-before command; filtering a list of windows, using a search pattern; and moving windows between either the current session or even external sessions, as well as how to share windows between multiple sessions.

■ ■ ■

## CHAPTER 28

Scripting and Automation

In this chapter, we'll review some different built-in tmux commands that allow us to control to a very granular level how existing tmux sessions look and function, as well as modifying the boot-up process to open multiple sessions and to construct complex environment layouts within those sessions.

We'll also be taking a look at three variations of this process. The first will demonstrate both simple and advanced ways to instruct tmux what to open and how.

The second example will demonstrate how to run shell commands without triggering a new window to be generated, whereas the third example will return to a similar concept, as shown in the first example, but this time, utilizing a very popular open source alternative called tmuxinator.

Finally, I'll make mention of some additional tmux programs related to restoring and attaching existing processes.

Example 1: Automation

Following, we'll first examine a basic example, to give you an idea of how we can automate tmux to construct a specific layout. After that, we'll look at a slightly more complex example, to help demonstrate how we can chain together different tmux commands to give us total control of the layout and content of a tmux session.

Simple Example

To get us started with our simple demonstration of how to construct layouts programmatically, let's first put together a set of basic requirements.

1. Instruct tmux to connect to the last active session.

2. Access the first window open within that session.

3. Open Vim (*and* drop us into Vim's INSERT mode).

The command we need to actually fulfill these requirements is very simple and looks like the following:

```
tmux send-keys -t 1 "vim" "C-m" "i" "programmatic content here"
```

In the preceding example, we're executing the send-keys command from outside tmux, to indicate that this could well be dropped into an automated shell script, but it's fine to execute this via the tmux command prompt. The send-keys command requires us to specify a target (-t), and all the arguments that follow the target are "keys" to be sent to that target and executed sequentially.

So, in this case, we tell it to connect to pane one, but pane one of what? How does tmux know what session to connect to? In this instance, it uses the last active session we were connected to. Next, we pass the string "vim", followed by the string "C-m", which triggers Vim to open (this is effectively another way of describing the <Enter> key).

Finally, we execute "i" (which, if that key were pressed when Vim was open, would drop us into INSERT mode), followed by "programmatic content here", which, if you're playing along at home, you'll notice is entered into the current Vim buffer for us.

Targeting Specific Sessions

As we saw previously, we can target a pane in the latest session and control it with any command we wish to send to it. But we can also specify a *specific* session we want to target, as follows:

```
tmux send-keys -t foo:2 "vim" "C-m"
```

In the preceding example, we're telling tmux to open Vim and to specifically target (-t) the foo session and the second pane within that session (:2).

Advanced

Now that we've seen some basic sample usage, let's use some more tmux commands and string them together to build up a complex automated layout.

What we want to do in this example is automate the creation of a new session. In this session, we want two windows. The first window should show us the result of the top command. The second window should have Vim open and entered into INSERT mode. Let's consider what this automation looks like.

```
tmux new -s foo -d "top" && \
tmux split-window -t foo:1 && \
tmux break-pane && \
tmux send-keys "vim" "C-m" "i"
```

In the preceding example, we're executing a long list of commands (using the logical && operator to run them sequentially) across multiple lines (by using the backslash character, \), but we could very well place this command inside of a single line of a shell script and execute it that way. Let's now break down the preceding command, so that we can better understand what it's doing.

- tmux new -s foo -d "top": We create a new session named foo and detach it (e.g., we don't jump into tmux; we stay at the terminal, and we tell tmux to run the top command inside the first window of that detached session).

- tmux split-window -t foo:1: We tell tmux to split the first window inside the foo session. (This creates two panes in the first window: the first pane holds the results of our top command, and the second pane is empty and holds our cursor's focus.)

- tmux break-pane: In the previous command, we targeted the foo session, so we won't have to tell tmux to target it again when we execute the break-pane command. Now, we tell tmux to break the current pane into its own window (this means the empty pane we created earlier is now its own window).

- tmux send-keys "vim" "C-m" "i": tmux's current focus is the new window we just made via the break-pane command, and so from here, we tell tmux to open up Vim and enter INSERT mode (we saw this in our earlier "simple" example).

Example 2: Shell Commands

tmux provides a feature called `run-shell` that (as the name suggests) lets you run shell commands within tmux, but crucially, it doesn't create a new window for the results to be displayed in. Instead, the results are displayed temporarily within "copy mode" of the current (or specified) buffer.

Let's see the syntax structure of the command, and then we'll take a quick look at an example of how we can use it.

```
<P>:run-shell [-b] [-t {pane_id}] "{shell_command}"
```

In the preceding syntax structure, we can see that the tmux command accepts a -b flag, which allows us to run the shell command as a background process. This is useful because, if it's a long-running process, we don't want to be blocked by it. We can also instruct tmux to display the result of the command within a target pane of our choice, using the -t flag. Finally, we have the command itself we want to execute.

Note   The -b and -t flags are optional. If you don't specify a target pane, the current pane is used.

Once you run this command, the result of the shell command is displayed within tmux in copy mode, allowing you to scroll through the buffer. The `run-shell` command can be useful in situations in which we want to bind multiple commands to a single key binding. For example:

```
bind-key e select-pane -L \; run-shell "ls -la && ls ~/Desktop"
```

In the preceding example, we bind multiple tmux commands to the e key (we've bound the `select-pane` and `run-shell` commands), and that single key binding (when executed) will attempt to select the next pane to its left and then run the `ls -la && ls ~/Desktop` command, displaying the results within that pane's copy mode.

This command can also be useful for automating tmux via external scripts. For example, if you have an existing session open with two windows, you could script tmux at some point in time to execute a shell command to target the results into one of the panes within that session.

Conditional Key Bindings

There is a powerful and dynamic feature in tmux that lets you test your environment and bind a different set of commands to a custom key binding, depending on the result of your test.

As an example, the following code snippet uses tmux's `if-shell` command to first check if the folder Dropbox exists. If the value returned from the test is greater than zero, that means the folder exists, and we'll see the message "Folder exists" displayed. Otherwise, if the folder doesn't exist, we'll see the message "Folder does not exist."

```
bind-key u if-shell "test $(ls | grep Dropbox | wc -l) -gt 0" "display-message 'Folder does not
exist'" "display-message 'Folder exists'"
```

What this ultimately means is that you can cater your tmux key bindings to suit the environment it is running in. For example, in Chapter 26, we looked at binding a different command, based on whether you were running on a Linux platform. We could have used the `if-shell` function to dynamically bind the value, depending on whether the `xclip` function was available or not. (I didn't do that, as there was other functionality that was specific to Linux that required modification.)

Example 3: tmuxinator

Remember our first example where we wrote a script to automate the construction of different layouts for us? Well, there is a Ruby-based project called tmuxinator (https://github.com/tmuxinator/tmuxinator) that simplifies the script-writing process, by allowing us to trade our shell script for a YAML configuration file.

You can install tmuxinator by using the following command: `gem install tmuxinator`. To create a new project is as simple as running the following command:

```
tmuxinator new {project}
```

After running the preceding command, you should notice that a `.tmuxinator` folder has been created in your user's `$HOME` directory, and inside that folder will be a YAML file named after your project.

For example, if the command you executed was `tmuxinator new foobar`, you should see the following folder structure within the directory in which you ran that command:

```
.
├── .tmuxinator
│   └── foobar.yaml
│
```

The content of the YAML file will look something like the following (these are the default settings, which you'll want to change to suit your own project requirements):

```
name: foobar
root: ~/your_directory
windows:
  - editor:
      layout: main-vertical
      panes:
        - vim
        - guard
  - server: bundle exec rails s
  - logs: tail -f log/development.log
```

In the preceding YAML file, you'll see that the `windows` key defines different windows you want to have open when you run the project. You can see that, by default, if you specify a window key, the value is a command that tmux can run. In the preceding example, we have a `server` window that tells tmux to run the `bundle exec rails s` command (which starts up a web server for a Ruby on Rails–based project), and the `logs` window runs the `tail -f log/development.log` command, which displays information from a specific log file on our file system.

The `editor` window is a little bit more interesting, as it gives us more control over the layout of our `editor` window. In the preceding example, we can see we've defined a `layout` we want to use (in this case, `main-vertical`), along with a set of panes we want the window to contain, and what commands to run within those panes (in this case, execute the `vim` and `guard` commands).

Now, whenever we want to run our project, we use the following command:

```
tmuxinator start {project_name}
```

Depending on your requirements and experience writing your own provisioning shell scripts, you might find tmuxinator is a welcome addition to your toolset and that the configuration format works better for you than rolling your own tmux-focused shell scripts.

Restoration

There are two areas of tmux that have (up until recently) been problematic and have gone unresolved, but we'll take a look at some potential workarounds that could be the first steps toward finally finding a resolution. They are:

1. Attaching an existing process to a new tmux session

2. Restoring state upon a system restart

Attaching Processes

The first issue is one that can (at the time of writing) only be resolved for the Linux environment by installing a binary called Reptyr (https://github.com/nelhage/reptyr), using your package manager of choice. For example, either `yum install reptyr` or `apt-get install reptyr` should do the trick.

The reason this solution is Linux-only is because Mac OS X and other Unix environments don't support the `ptrace` shell command (among other required Linux-based system architecture). Although this restriction might not be such a big deal if you mainly use a Mac for GUI-based work and a virtual machine (e.g., tools such as VirtualBox and VMWare alongside Vagrant and Docker) for your development environment.

The usage process itself is pretty simple.

- First you make your process a background process (i.e. `<C-z>`).

- Disown the process from its parent (e.g., `disown {process_name}`).

- Start your multiplexer (e.g., `tmux`).

- Attach process (e.g., `reptyr $(pgrep {process_name})` or `reptyr {pid}`).

■ **Note** Reptyr can work with other multiplexers (e.g., `screen`).

Restoring State

The problem of restoring state, when your operating system restarts, is a tricky one, because there is only so much that can be done to record the data you were working with and the state it was in at the point of shutting down.

Luckily, there is a tmux plug-in called tmux-resurrect (https://github.com/tmux-plugins/tmux-resurrect), which solves this exact problem and will go to great lengths to restore all of the following items:

- All sessions, windows, panes, and their relevant order

- The current working directory for each tmux pane

- Exact pane layouts within tmux windows

- Active and alternative sessions

- Active and alternative windows for each session

- The tmux windows that have focus

- The active pane for each tmux window

- Programs running within a tmux pane

- Restoration of Vim sessions (this is optional)

> ■ **Note**   The author of the tmux-resurrect plug-in also provides a tmux plug-in manager
> (`https://github.com/tmux-plugins/tpm`), which makes installing tmux add-ons and plug-ins much easier.

Summary

In this chapter, I've covered some very important and fundamental functionality of tmux, which allows us to control the way tmux works and, if used in the right situations, can help to automate the entire process of bootstrapping your working environment. Let's take a moment to review what you've learned.

- First, I demonstrated how to programmatically control tmux, using the `send-keys`, `split-window` and `break-pane` commands (including how to target specific sessions).

- We then saw how to execute shell commands and review the results within the current pane. (You now know that we can also direct the output of any shell command into any tmux pane of our choosing, by using the `-t` flag.) You also learned how to conditionally bind a key command, based on some dynamic equation.

- We also examined the popular tmuxinator Ruby program, which helps to automate complex layouts via a simple YAML configuration file.

- Finally, we reviewed some potential workarounds to traditionally complex problems related to restoring state within tmux (caused by a system restart) and also how to attach an already running process to a tmux session.

CHAPTER 29

■ ■ ■

Pair Programming

When using tmux, we sometimes forget how powerful the client/server model that it implements is. For example, we all know that because of the client/server model, we can create multiple sessions on a single server and then at any point, we can jump between sessions, as we are able to connect to any session on the tmux server that we have running in the background.

But who's to say that the server has to be running on *our* machine! This is where this chapter steps in, to help demonstrate how you can utilize tmux to benefit users who are pair programming.

If you've not heard the term before, *pair programming* is the process of two developers sitting around a single computer and working together to solve the problem they've been presented with. The process takes the form of one developer typing code, while the other developer helps keep the thought process flowing (e.g., they aren't just sitting around twiddling their thumbs, waiting to jump on the keyboard). After a few hours, the pair will swap positions, allowing the other person to take a different mindset and approach to the problem they are solving.

As you can imagine, this is typically done in a single location (i.e., both developers are in the same room, sitting at the same computer), but what happens if you have to pair program with a colleague who works remotely? Well, this is where using tmux can help, but before I dive into the details of how this works, I would like first to present you with a one-line solution . . .

■ **Note**   I'm making the assumption that the person you're pairing with is also a Vim and tmux user.

The Simple Route

I would argue that the easiest way to pair program with a colleague is by using the free service http://tmate.io/, which allows you to install their software tmate onto your computer and thus share your computer with a remote colleague.

To install the software, please refer to the web site for instructions (tmate is available for both Mac OS X and Linux distributions). Once installed, you can execute the single command tmate, which first utilizes a modified version of tmux (so you'll notice that it will pick up your local .tmux.conf configuration file), and once started, will display an ssh command for you to provide to your colleague, allowing him/her access to your computer. The ssh command will look something like the following: ssh abcd1X0frvh1egxSysQYa1GIz@am.tmate.io.

Once your colleague has connected to the session, you'll see a small message at the foot of the tmate program, indicating that a user has joined the session: Your mate has joined the session (212.58.231.91).

From here, you can do most things you can do using standard tmux (although there are *some* commands that won't work, such as moving a window). It's important to remember that the user who has connected to the tmate session now has complete control over your computer, and so that user could effectively rm -rf / and wipe your computer clean (or install any kind of software when you weren't looking), so take care to whom you give the ssh command.

I would almost always recommend this as your go-to solution, as it's super-simple to set up, compared to doing things manually yourself (which we'll see in the next section).

The Custom Route

There are multiple ways to pair program using tmux. In the preceding section, we used a simple predefined route that automates some of what we will be looking at within this section. For example, we could open ssh access on our own computer, which would allow another user to connect directly to our machine. Alternatively, we could install tmux on a remote server and have both users connect to that single server, and, again, from there, we would have a few different options available to us.

Each option presents different pros and cons, and I'll aim to demonstrate each one, so that you can choose for yourself which is the most appropriate. I want to state upfront that I don't have the luxury of a dedicated server, and I'm far too cheap to spend even a few pennies spinning up some Amazon EC2 instances (although they are very cheap). So, instead of having a real server, I'll use Vagrant (www.vagrantup.com) to set up these examples and use it to mimic different user logins.

■ **Note** Vagrant is a tool for making the creation of virtual machines quick and easy. I'll cover it in more detail in the next chapter, but for now, I'll cover just enough to carry out the examples.

Vagrant Setup

To get started with Vagrant, first download it from www.vagrantup.com and install it. Vagrant has a hard dependency on a virtualization program, such as VirtualBox, which can be downloaded from www.virtualbox.org. Once you have both installed, you're ready for the next step.

Vagrant is a command line–based tool, and it works by reading configuration settings from a file called a Vagrantfile. The following code snippet shows the content of the Vagrantfile required to bring up an instance of a Linux Ubuntu instance:

```
VAGRANTFILE_API_VERSION = "2"

Vagrant.configure(VAGRANTFILE_API_VERSION) do |config|
  config.vm.box = "ubuntu/trusty64"
end
```

You'll probably have noticed that the configuration is written using Ruby programming and that it's also quite a small file (there are many configuration settings available, but for our purposes, this is all we need).

To bring up our Linux Ubuntu instance, we simply run the following command vagrant up, (you'll need to run this command from the same location as your Vagrantfile) which will then send a stream of output to our terminal screen, informing us that Vagrant is spinning up a new Ubuntu instance for us. Once the instance is successfully brought up, you can log in to the VM (virtual machine) by running the command vagrant ssh.

■ **Note** Vagrant works with multiple virtualization programs. The main two are VirtualBox and VMWare. If you have more than one of them installed (and VirtualBox is not the default), the vagrant up command will require an additional flag that indicates the provider to use, for example, --provider=virtualbox or --provider=vmware_fusion.

Share Session via Single-User Account

In the following steps, we'll be creating a single user on our VM (if you're applying this to a real-world situation, this would be a case of you creating a new user on a remote server), which means two individual users can then log in to the VM, using this new single/shared account. Once the first user is logged in, he or she will create a new tmux session.

- Log in to the VM:

    vagrant ssh

- Switch to root user (so you can add new users):

    su

- Create new user foo:

    adduser foo

- Close connection to the VM:

    exit

- Reconnect to the VM using the new foo user:

    ssh -i $(vagrant ssh-config | grep IdentityFile | awk '{print $2}') -l foo -p 2222 -o
    UserKnownHostsFile=/dev/null -o StrictHostKeyChecking=no 127.0.0.1

- Create a new session called pairing:

    tmux new-session -s pairing

■ **Note**   The ssh command to access the VM using the new foo user is quite intense. This is because the default user for the vagrant ssh command is root. You can work around this by modifying the Vagrantfile to include config.ssh.username = "foo" and then running the command vagrant reload to cause the change to take effect. Since you already added the foo user inside the VM, this means you could now use vagrant ssh instead.

Now, in another terminal window, run the following commands, which effectively is us simulating another user on a different computer logging in to the same machine the previous user has logged in to. (If you were trying to apply this to a real-world situation, this would be one in which two users log in to a machine using the same account, and because they're using the same account, they will see the same tmux session.)

- This is the same command as above; we're logging into the VM:

    ssh -i $(vagrant ssh-config | grep IdentityFile | awk '{print $2}') -l foo -p 2222 -o
    UserKnownHostsFile=/dev/null -o StrictHostKeyChecking=no 127.0.0.1

- This command isn't necessary; it simply proves the session is available for us to connect to:

    tmux ls

- Attach to the relevant tmux session:

    tmux attach -t pairing

The downside of this approach is that although two separate users are now able to pair program together using a single tmux session, the users are intrinsically linked; meaning if one user creates a new window, the other user will automatically be focused on that new window (i.e., you can't have one user work independently within his/her own window, although we'll solve this problem in the next section!).

Individual User Control

To solve the problem of two users (logged in under a single shared account) not being able to independently work in a single tmux session is oddly quite simple to achieve. The solution is in how the second user connects to the existing tmux session created by the first user.

When the first user logs into the VM (as the foo user), he/she will create a new tmux session with the following command:

```
tmux new-session -s firstuser
```

When the second user logs in to the VM (again, as the foo user), he/she will create a new session as well, but the difference is that that user will target the other user's session, using the –t flag, like so:

```
tmux new-session -t firstuser -s seconduser
```

Once this is done, both users will be able to see the same windows, but any new windows created occur independently of each user, so one user doesn't automatically get thrown into the new window.

Share Session with Multiple Users

If you would prefer to have users log in to a machine using their own logins but still share a tmux session so they can pair program, the solution is to modify where tmux stores its socket information and assign group access to the new location. We just need to make sure that the individual users are added to the group, so they can access the socket information and thus share the session information.

▪ **Note**   You won't be able to work independently inside the tmux session, if using the socket technique (see the next section for a workaround).

The following steps must be carried out before the two users log in to the server. (This is because their user accounts are added to a new group. If you're applying this to a real-world situation, you might not have to create the two user accounts, as they might already exist, and so you'd just need to make sure the user accounts are added to the relevant group.)

- Log into the VM:

    ```
    vagrant ssh
    ```

- Switch to root user (so you can add new users and groups):

  su

- Create a new foo user:

  adduser foo

- Create a new bar user:

  adduser bar

- Create a new baz group:

  addgroup baz

- Create a directory to hold our socket data:

  mkdir /var/qux

- Apply the baz group to the socket data folder:

  chgrp baz /var/qux

- Change the permissions for the socket data folder, which will ensure that any new files added are accessible to the group:

  chmod g+ws /var/qux

- Add the foo user to the baz group:

  usermod -aG baz foo

- Add the bar user to the baz group:

  usermod -aG baz bar

- Switch to the new foo user:

  su foo

Now, in another terminal window, run the following commands, which effectively is us simulating another user on a different computer logging in to the same machine the previous user has logged in to, but this time, the user is logging in with his/her own bar account (which was created in the preceding steps):

- Log in to the VM:

  vagrant ssh

- Switch to the new bar user:

  su bar

Now, at this point, we have two users logged in to the VM under different user accounts. If the `foo` user were to create a new session using the standard tmux command (i.e., `tmux new-session -s mysession`), the `bar` user would still not be able to see that session, because the session was created using the default socket location.

To work around this issue, we have to use the `-S` (socket-path) flag when creating the session. So, if the `foo` user executes the following command: `tmux -S /var/baz/pairing`, he or she will be dropped into a new session, in which the data is stored in a file called `pairing`.

Now, the `bar` user can connect to that session, by using the following command: `tmux -S /var/baz/pairing attach`.

Remotely Accessing a Local VM

Finally, in this section, we'll review some additional features of Vagrant that *can* let us utilize the Vagrant setup and pair program remotely, using Vagrant's sharing functionality (which allows you to share your VM), and will also let us have independent control over tmux windows. The Holy Grail!

For what I'm about to propose to work, the person who is going to share his/her VM has to sign up for a free account with Vagrant (visit `https://vagrantcloud.com`). Once that person has an account, we'll be able to proceed, by having the person sharing the VM log in to their Vagrant Cloud account via the command line, by executing the `vagrant login` command.

Once logged in, the same user will share his/her VM by executing the command `vagrant share --ssh`, which will ask the user to enter a password, to secure the connection. After this is done, Vagrant will display a sample command that you can provide (along with the password) to the user you wish to pair program with. The command will look something like the following:

```
vagrant connect --ssh {dynamically_generated_name}
```

The user who shared his/her VM will have to open a new terminal shell and execute the following commands:

- `vagrant ssh`: Log in to the VM.

- `adduser foo`: Create a new shared user.

- `su foo`: Switch to that user.

- `tmux new-session -s foosession`: Create a new session.

When the other user you shared the link with has connected to the shared VM, he or she will have to run the following commands:

- `su foo`: Switch to the new shared user.

- `tmux new-session -t groupedsession -s mysession`: Create a new session but specify the `foosession` as their target session.

Summary

This has been quite a technically intensive chapter, although it has covered lots of fundamental aspects, to get tmux to bend to your specific requirements. We've used a few different features of Vagrant to help us mimic the situation in which you would ultimately be connecting to a real server (or opened up SSH access on your own machine).

We also demonstrated how Vagrant's built-in VM sharing functionality can help us to work locally on our own machine and to share it with a remote user, while still taking advantage of tmux pair programming with independent control over tmux windows (which is both incredibly powerful and useful).

But if all of that seems like hard work, remember that the third-party tool `http://tmate.io` can take care of all of that hard work for you (with the exception of the independent window access).

CHAPTER 30

Workflow Management

Software engineering and web development in particular have changed quite significantly over the past few years. We now have tools at our disposal that would seem almost magical in the past. In this chapter, I am going to demonstrate some of these programs alongside tmux and Vim, to show you how you can get a more realistic and accurate development environment. I'll also be demonstrating use of the programs Reptyr and tmux-resurrect, so you can see how they fit into your typical workflow.

But before we get into the details of "how," let's consider the "why." What problems are these tools trying to solve? Well, to answer that, we have to know a bit of the history that got us to where we are today. The *traditional* (and massively simplified) web development process would have taken steps that resembled something like the following:

- Open your editor of choice and write code.

- Upload code to your web server.

- Check your application to see if everything worked.

For large organizations, this type of development was fraught with danger and potential downtime to the services they offered their customers, and so this process evolved to include defensive mechanisms, such as writing tests for your code, to ensure fewer bugs made their way into the production environment. The process continued to evolve until we had a set of accepted "best practices," such as, for example, TDD (Test-Driven Development), which was the principle of writing tests first, *before* writing any code, so as to ensure more focused, efficient, and cleaner code.

But all these defensive programming techniques were unable to resolve, arguably, the most fundamental issue that you've likely heard uttered a few times in your career: "but it works on my machine." Effectively, this statement would be uttered by a programmer in the moment of confusion when, after all the tests and checks had passed, and we were "all systems go," we would proceed to upload the application to the server and watch as certain aspects of the software failed to work as intended.

The reason for this is that we weren't developing our applications in an environment that accurately represented the live server environment. How can you ever know for sure whether your application will work, if you're developing it on a Mac- or Windows-based operating system, and yet its destination is a Linux server whose architecture is sufficiently different to cause even simple errors, such as "case sensitivity."

Because of this issue, tools such as Vagrant (http://vagrantup.com) stepped in to try and resolve the problem, by providing software engineers a common ground to work from. With a tool such as Vagrant, you can replicate your live server environment, by creating a new virtual machine that runs the same operating system and software packages, as well as utilizing the same provisioning scripts as would your live server. At this point, I would recommend visiting the web site and downloading/installing the version of Vagrant that is most relevant to your operating system.

Example Repository

To make things easier, and to save on having to type it all out yourself, you can download a fully working development environment that includes all the topics, techniques, and software that I'm about to describe to you. You should be able to run the following Git command to download the project:

```
git clone https://github.com/Integralist/Linux-and-Docker-Development-Environment.git
```

Once inside the cloned directory, you should notice a file called Vagrantfile. This file is what Vagrant uses to configure the development environment. As long as you have Vagrant installed, you can run the vagrant up command from your terminal, to create the environment. (When you run the command, make sure you are inside the directory that contains the Vagrantfile.) This will cause VirtualBox to trigger a new instance of the development environment, which, in this case, is a Ubuntu-based Linux server, to be started.

■ **Note**   This is a book about Vim and tmux, so I won't be explaining how the code in the Vagrantfile or the provisioning script works (although both are heavily commented, so you should be able to get by).

What we should end up with is an Ubuntu instance that has Vim, tmux, and Git installed, along with the Reptyr program. We should also have Docker (www.docker.com) installed and a container created that runs our application (in this example, it's a "Hello World" Ruby application). Docker is a solution for building modular and distributed applications.

Reptyr

The Reptyr program allows you to attach to your tmux session processes that are already running (or, in fact, any terminal multiplexer, such as screen). This can be really useful in situations in which you have some long-running process that is already running by the time you come to log on to the server. Instead of having to stop and start the process (and subsequently losing any important information it may have gathered), you can open tmux and reattach the process so it's now running inside tmux.

The way it works is complicated. If you're really interested in the implementation details, I recommend that you read the documentation on the GitHub repository at https://github.com/nelhage/reptyr.

To see an example of how this works, we must log in to the VM (virtual machine) that Vagrant has brought up for us. To do this, you'll run the command vagrant ssh, and from that point, you'll be able to complete the remaining steps, which are as follows (i.e., execute each step as a separate command):

- top
- <C-z>
- bg
- disown top
- tmux
- reptyr $(pgrep top)

If you have followed the preceding steps, you should have a tmux session open, and the top program (which was originally started *before* you created the tmux session) has been successfully moved inside tmux.

Let's now go through each of the preceding steps one by one, to clarify what we've done. First, we started a new instance of the top program, which displays information about running processes on our VM. Next, we suspended the top program by running the command <C-z>. (This temporarily suspends the process from running but keeps it alive, so we can resume it later.)

We then ran the bg command to convert the last process (top, in this case) into a background process. The reason we do that is so the next step can be taken, which is to run the disown top command (the disown command disassociates the specified process with its parent process). The reason for disowning the process is to allow us to re-associate it with the tmux process.

Next, we start a new tmux session, and within tmux, we run the command reptyr $(pgrep top), which passes the result of the pgrep top command (the result being the process id for the top program) into the Reptyr program, causing the top program to be placed into our tmux session.

tmux-resurrect

The tmux-resurrect plug-in gives you the ability to restore the state of tmux, even after a system restart. It does this by recording all your data at the point of executing a specific tmux key binding and restoring the data when running a specific tmux key binding.

Although this plug-in can be extremely useful, you might be wondering why I don't install it by default as part of my "Linux and Docker Development Environment" GitHub repository? The reason for this decision is that the plug-in has limited use in a disposable workflow environment (i.e., one with no persistent storage).

What I mean by that is, if I was using tmux (and this plug-in) directly on the host machine (i.e., on my Mac OS), it would be useful, because when I shut down my Mac at the end of a workday and then start it up again in the morning, I have a persistent storage drive, which means I'll be able to restore my tmux sessions.

But when you're working from a virtual environment, you don't have persistent storage in the same way, and so when you shut down a VM and restart it, the entire operating system is rebuilt from scratch. But this isn't to say this isn't a useful plug-in to have installed on your main host machine (as I don't just use tmux from within a VM; I use it all the time on my Mac OS).

Installation

To install the plug-in, you'll have to first download the repository, using the following command (we download the code into ~/tmux/plugins/resurrect):

```
git clone https://github.com/tmux-plugins/tmux-resurrect ~/tmux/plugins/resurrect
```

Once we have the plug-in downloaded, we can tell tmux to load it, by adding the following command into the .tmux.conf file:

```
run-shell ~/tmux/plugins/resurrect/resurrect.tmux
```

If tmux is already running, I suggest you source the .tmux.conf file, by executing the source-file ~/.tmux.conf command.

■ **Note** There are many additional settings that you can enable, such as restoring Vim sessions (e.g., set -g @resurrect-strategy-vim 'session'). I recommend reading the plug-in documentation for the full details.

Sample Usage

Using the plug-in is very easy. Once you have tmux open and in a state that you want to record, execute the key binding `<P><C-s>`, to store the current layout and contents.

Once you restart the machine (you can mimic this by executing the tmux command `<P>:kill-server`) and open tmux afresh, you'll notice that the state is lost. To resume the previous state, simply execute the key binding `<P><C-r>`, and after a brief moment, you should see your earlier layout.

Summary

We've finally arrived to the end of the last chapter. I've hoped you've enjoyed yourself. Everything that you've learned from this book is merely the beginning.

The true joy of using tools such as Vim and tmux is that there is so much more to learn and to utilize. As you become more and more confident with the tooling, you'll discover new ways to take advantage of them.

I would enjoy very much hearing your feedback, so feel free to open discussions and comments on the ProVim GitHub repository (`https://github.com/Integralist/ProVim`). But for now, let's take a moment to look back on what we have seen in this final chapter.

- At the start of the chapter, I briefly discussed the evolution of a traditional development process and how certain practices were put in place to ensure consistency between development and production environments. (This is where such tools as VirtualBox and Vagrant were introduced.)

- We moved on to downloading an example repository that with a single command (i.e., `vagrant up`) would be able to re-create a complete Linux environment, with development tools installed and ready to use, thereby demonstrating the power of having a virtual workspace that is completely deposable and configurable to match a live production environment.

- From there, we took a look at the Reptyr program and how it is useful for attaching existing processes to another process (in this case, tmux), so that we don't have to worry about losing any state we may have accumulated before running tmux.

- We also looked at the tmux-resurrect plug-in, which demonstrates how tmux's layout and content (even down to individual panes and Vim context) can be persisted through a system restart. Powerful tooling, indeed.

Index

■ **Z**

Get the eBook for only $10!

Now you can take the weightless companion with you anywhere, anytime. Your purchase of this book entitles you to 3 electronic versions for only $10.

This Apress title will prove so indispensible that you'll want to carry it with you everywhere, which is why we are offering the eBook in **3 formats** for only $10 if you have already purchased the print book.

Convenient and fully searchable, the PDF version enables you to easily find and copy code—or perform examples by quickly toggling between instructions and applications. The MOBI format is ideal for your Kindle, while the ePUB can be utilized on a variety of mobile devices.

Go to www.apress.com/promo/tendollars to purchase your companion eBook.